MS-DOS®
Developer's Guide

MS-DOS®
Developer's Guide

John Angermeyer
Kevin Jaeger

Howard W. Sams & Co.
A Division of Macmillan, Inc.
4300 West 62nd Street, Indianapolis, IN 46268 USA

International Standard Book Number: 0-672-22409-7
Library of Congress Catalog Card Number: 86-60031

Edited by: *Katherine Stuart Ewing*
Illustrated by: *Wm. D. Basham and Ralph E. Lund*
Designed by: *T. R. Emrick*
Cover Art: *Kevin Caddell*

Printed in the United States of America

Trademark Acknowledgments

All terms mentioned in this book that are known to be trademarks or service marks
are listed below. In addition, terms suspected of being trademarks or service marks
have been appropriately capitalized. Howard W. Sams & Co., Inc., cannot attest to the
accuracy of this information. Use of a term in this book should not be regarded as
affecting the validity of any trademark or service mark.

COMPAQ is a registered trademark of COMPAQ Computer Corporation.
CompuPro is a trademark of Vyasin Corporation.
Concurrent CP/M-86, Concurrent PC-DOS, and CP/M are registered trademarks and
Concurrent DOS 286 is a trademark of Digital Research, Inc.
IBM is a registered trademark of International Business Machines, Inc.
Intel is a trademark of Intel Corporation.
Lattice is a registered trademark of Lattice, Inc.
Microsoft, MS and Xenix are trademarks and MS-DOS is a registered trademark of
Microsoft Corporation
National Semiconductor is a registered trademark of National Semiconductor, Inc.
Novell and Netware are registered trademarks of Novell, Inc.
Seattle Computers is a trademark of Seattle Computer Products, Inc.
Ungermann-Bass is a registered trademark of Ungermann-Bass, Inc.
UNIX is a trademark of AT&T Bell Laboratories.
UCSD is a registered trademark of The Regents of University of California.
UCSD-p System is a registered trademark of Pecan Software Systems, Inc.

This book is dedicated to my parents, to Daniel and Jeanette, and to all my friends.

John Angermeyer

To my wife Janis and daughter Branwyn, for reasons that they know best, to Eric and my parents, and to Alan Perlis and John Zornig of Yale University.

Kevin Jaeger

Summary Contents

Contents

Contents

Contents

PART III   RECOVERY

Contents

PART V   PRODUCTS

Contents

Preface

He felt like somebody had taken the lid off life and let him look
at the works.

Dashiell Hammett, *The Maltese Falcon*

In one sense, this book is about the technical aspects of programming in
a particular manner within a specific environment. In another sense,
this book is about discovery and the process of discovery.

Too often we accept the circumstances that we see before us as absolute limits on our world. This is especially true of devices of great complexity such as computers. What we have worked to accomplish in this
book is the removal of some of those limits and, more importantly, to
give you, the reader, the confidence to go on to lift the barriers even further.

Some of the topics we have addressed are

- the fictitious conflict between structured programming and the
  use of assembly language

- effectively using those elusive, poorly documented, "advanced"
  assembly language features, such as macros and conditional
  assembly

- getting the best of two worlds by combining high-level languages
  with assembly language for easy programming and readability
  without sacrificing speed and compactness

- customizing your system to take advantage of that old peripheral
  from your previous system or that new gadget you like but
  nobody supports

- writing your own "magic" functions like SuperKey and Sidekick through the use of memory resident programs

- accessing the power of the 8087 and 80287 math coprocessors without the expense or limitations of high-level languages or manufacturer specific libraries

- recovering valuable data after the program crashes

- rescuing erased files that you thought were gone forever

Each of these topics addresses an area that is usually left to experts, but with the aid of this book, you can become the expert. This is no empty promise, for once you know how to learn about your system, you can continue to uncover new mysteries.

The collection of discussions in this book is organized in a manner similar to a compendium of articles. Each discussion is presented in its own chapter and may be read and referenced independently of the other chapters. Each chapter covers a topic that relates directly to program development within the MS-DOS environment. Because of the informative nature of this book and the way it is organized, it can also be read from beginning to end, thus yielding a greater confidence in your programming endeavors.

Although we assume that readers have some familiarity with the MS-DOS operating system, with the 8086 family of microprocessors, and with assembly language programming, this book, with its reference style, is appropriate for computer users with a variety of programming experience.

Part 1, *Coding and Programming*, is divided into four chapters. The first two chapters comprise our discussion of structured programming in the MS-DOS environment, with special emphasis on assembly language. These chapters deal with coding, design, and organization of assembly language programs. Chapter 3 discusses memory management techniques with emphasis on the principles of memory-resident programs. Chapter 4, wherein we discuss some of the special techniques needed for programs that run under tight timing constraints, is devoted to real-time programming.

Part 2, *Devices*, is devoted to devices in general and in particular. Chapter 5 explains the mechanics of creating device drivers under MS-DOS, whereas Chapters 6 and 7 explore some of the more esoteric devices: the 8087 and 80287 math coprocessors and Local Area Networks (LANs).

Part 3, *Recovery*, presents magnetic media formatting and recovery-related subjects. Chapter 8 provides an in-depth description of how floppy disks are formatted under MS-DOS and shows how you can recover damaged or erased files. Chapter 9 deals with techniques for recovering data lost in memory.

Part 4, *Compatibility*, consists of Chapter 10, which discusses compatibility of the different MS-DOS versions, machine implementations, and other operating systems. Included are programming considerations and cautions related to function calls, interrupts, error codes, and disk formats.

Part 5, *Products*, comprises Chapter 11, which deals with high-level languages and how they are used in conjunction with assembly language. Included is information on methods by which MS-DOS functions and interrupts may be accessed from high-level languages.

In addition to Chapter 11, Appendix D has been included to provide information about new product versions that were released after this book was written. The information in this appendix affects the information presented throughout the book.

This book is by no means a complete presentation of application development, nor do we necessarily have the "right" way to program. Rather, we have tried to introduce some of the more immediate topics of programming that can be readily applied to actual problems. Should you decide to pursue the study of these topics, check the numerous references that can be found in some of the more specialized technical works. These references provide all the detail you desire, and some of them are listed in the bibliography at the end of this book.

Acknowledgments

The authors would like to thank Kim House and Robert Lafore for their many helpful comments, criticisms, and suggestions during the editing of our manuscript. Their valuable input helped in the fine tuning of this book. We would also like to thank Larry Skene for his valuable information about IBM PC DOS.

Special thanks are also due to Alan Stacy for his valuable knowledge, research, and writings on networking environments for MS-DOS systems.

We would also like to thank ComputerHouse of San Rafael, California, for answering our many questions and providing MS-DOS for our CompuPro system.

CODING AND PROGRAMMING

Part I

Structured Programming 1: Tools for Structured Coding

Chapter 1

When hackers gather 'round their electronic campfires to discuss the mysteries of structured programming, comments are likely to center on a small set of language constructs like the IF-THEN-ELSE statement. A devotee of Pascal or C may lecture on the structured benefits of a higher level programming language versus those of assembly language. Heated arguments about the use of GOTO may possibly ensue. For all that, they are not telling the complete story. Such discussion is really focused only on structured coding. As you will soon learn, structured programming is possible in any language. Even some assembly languages support all those nifty high-level control structures. One of them is Microsoft's Macro Assembler for MS-DOS, affectionately known as MASM.

The Need for Shorthand Statements

Before beginning our presentation of high-level control structures in assembly language, we first look at some of the advantages of higher level languages. At the most basic level, anything that can be done in a higher level language also can be done in assembly. Everything ends up at the assembly language level anyway. What then is gained from the use of a high-level language? Terseness! The ability to express a programming idea in a form that is readily understood by the coder or reader. Consider that each assembly language statement more or less corresponds to one machine instruction. On the other hand, a single higher level statement may expand to tens or even hundreds of machine code instructions. (For anyone who doubts the hundreds, check a FORTRAN subroutine call with embedded argument calculations.)

Table 1-1 shows the same fragment coded in both FORTRAN and 8086 assembly language. This fragment computes the sum of 1...NUM for a given NUM:

Table 1-1. FORTRAN versus Assembly Language

FORTRAN		Assembly Language
SUM = 0		mov sum,0
DO 100 I = 1, NUM		mov ax,1
100 SUM = SUM + I loop:	cmp	ax,num
		jg loop_end
		add sum,ax
		inc ax
		jmp loop
	loop_end:	

No doubt the assembly language routine could be further optimized to reduce either the amount of object code produced or the execution time. But no matter how you look at it, it is easier to write the routine in FORTRAN than in assembly. To code the assembly language routine, many more decisions need to be made. Because of the extra work involved in assembly, coding mistakes are more likely. I may know for a fact that the FORTRAN routine will run perfectly, but I may still harbor doubts about the assembly routine. Why do these doubts exist? Because each line of the FORTRAN routine is an entire thought, whereas the assembly language routine requires many lines to complete the same thought.

In short, using higher level constructs results in easier coding and more reliable code. These constructs make coding less complicated, which allows the programmer to concentrate on the logic of the program while assuming that the actual implementation is correct. Programmers would like to have faith in their work. Tools that support this faith make for better programmers.

Introduction to Macros

Assembly language coding thus would be greatly enhanced if there were a way to create a shorthand for commonly used statements. MASM provides this with the *macro* facility. With macros, programmers define blocks of assembly statements, then with individual references direct MASM to include the respective blocks in the assembled program. Here are the two steps required to create and use a macro:

Step 1, defining the macro:

```
;; Define     "Function Request" as DOS_CALL
dos_call      macro
              int 21h             ; call MS-DOS to perform function
              endm
```

Step 2, using the macro:

```
dos_call                                    the macro "call"
```

What appears in the listing:

```
    dos_call                                the macro "call"
+   int 21h ; call MS-DOS to perform function
```

When the program is assembled, the statement "dos_call" is replaced by the statement "int 21h", including the comment. The listing file contains the line "dos_call" as a reference, but the object file contains only the code for "int 21h." This operation is known as *macro substitution* or *macro expansion*.

When processed by the assembler, the macro reference is replaced by the code that the macro represents. The macro does not generate a CALL instruction to the macro code, although macro references are sometimes referred to that way.

As with everything in programming, macros have to follow strict formulas. The form for defining macros is

```
mname       MACRO      argument_list
              .
              .                          <body of the macro code>
              .
            ENDM
```

The name of the macro is defined as *mname*, and *argument_list* is a list of arguments, separated by commas. The argument list may be blank if the macro contains no arguments (as in our example *dos_call)*.

This was a simple demonstration. If that were all that a macro could perform, it would be a sorry creature indeed. Luckily, macros may be *tailored* using the arguments section. The next macro shows an example of this tailoring.

7

```
;; Define "Print Character" as PRINT_CHR
print_chr macro    char
          mov ah,05
          mov dl,&char
          dos_call
          endm
```

Now, when we use this macro

```
          print_chr 'A'                              the macro "call"
```

the following appears in our listing file:

```
          print_chr 'A'                              the macro "call"
+         mov ah,05
+         mov dl,'A'
+         int 21h ; call MS-DOS to perform function
```

The "&char" in the macro has been replaced with the " 'A' " in the macro call. (Yes, we refer to using macros as *calls*. It's okay as long as you remember that no CALL instruction is involved.) The " + " that appears at the beginning of the line is MASM's way of informing the programmer that the code is the result of a macro expansion. Note too that the macro *print_chr* contains a reference to the previously defined macro *dos_call,* which was expanded into the "int 21h" statement that *dos_call* represents. MASM continues to evaluate macro calls to any level to which they are nested until the symbol table storage area of MASM overflows. Nesting is another way of saying that macros may call macros that call macros and so on.

The name "char" in the *print_chr* macro is called a *dummy argument.* Whenever the dummy argument "char" appears in this macro, "char" is replaced with the value that was used in the call to the macro. In the *print_chr* example, replacing "char" means that any place in the macro that "char" appears, it was replaced with the character "A."

Note that any name chosen for a dummy argument is used exclusively for that argument in the macro. Thus if you were to choose a dummy argument with the name "AX," you would not be able to refer to the "AX" register in that macro!

The same warning about naming dummy arguments applies to naming the macro itself. Should you choose to define a macro with the name "add," you would find that all references to the opcode ADD in the program would generate an expansion of the macro *add.* You can even redefine MASM directives if you wish. It is therefore very important not to create a conflict of names.

The "&" in front of "char" in the *print_chr* macro is used to append the value of "char" to the string "mov dl,." The "&" is not needed to evaluate the dummy argument, which happens anyway, but to tell MASM that "char" is a dummy argument, not just part of the larger string "mov dl,char." The "&" operator is especially important when dummy arguments are contained in larger strings, as this next example demonstrates.

```
The Macro Definition   The Macro Expansion
example macro arg               example Y
    mov dl,arg         +        mov dl,Y       correct
    mov dl,&arg        +        mov dl,Y       correct
    mov dl,argZ        +        mov dl,argZ
    mov dl,&argZ       +        mov dl,argZ
    mov dl,arg&Z       +        mov dl,YZ      correct
    mov dl,Xarg        +        mov dl,Xarg
    mov dl,X&arg       +        mov dl,XY      correct
    mov dl,XargZ       +        mov dl,XargZ
    mov dl,X&argZ      +        mov dl,XargZ
    mov dl,Xarg&Z      +        mov dl,XargZ
    mov dl,X&arg&Z     +        mov dl,XYZ     correct
    endm
```

Strictly speaking, the "&" is not required in the *print_chr* macro. MASM was able to detect that "char" is a dummy argument because "char" stands alone following a comma. However, it is a good habit to use "&" even when not required because it highlights the dummy argument when you read the macro and makes clear to MASM just what is intended.

LOCAL Labels

So far, the macros we have used have been confined to generating simple assembly instructions. However, let's assume that we want to design a macro to choose between the smaller of two numbers and to place that result into another location. A macro to accomplish this might look something like this:

```
min        MACRO    result,first,second
           mov      &result,&first
           cmp      &first,&second
           jl       order_ok
           mov      &result,&second
order_ok:
           ENDM
```

When we invoke *min*, it produces the proper code, but we have a problem: Even though the macro evaluates perfectly, it can only be used once. Because the label "order_ok" can only be defined once in a program, when the macro is used in two places MASM complains that **Symbol is multi-defined.**

We can make a small change in the macro to allow us to specify a label parameter in addition to the others:

```
min        MACRO    result,first,second,order_ok
           mov      &result,&first
           cmp      &first,&second
           jl       &order_ok
           mov      &result,&second
order_ok&:
           ENDM
```

When we invoke the new *min,* as shown below, we can specify what name is to be used for the jump label. Now *min* can be reused again when needed, but we still have to think of a new name for the jump label each time. However, the actual name is quite unimportant to us because the label is private to the *min* function.

```
           min      ax,bx,cx,jmp1    the macro "call"
+          mov      ax,bx
+          cmp      bx,cx
+          jl       jmp1
+          mov      ax,cx
+    jmp1:
```

There's a better way to create a new name each time *min* is called. MASM provides the LOCAL directive for just this purpose. When MASM encounters LOCAL, a unique label is automatically generated for that name. To put it another way, it's as if the LOCAL parameter was included in the MACRO parameter list, but MASM filled in the actual argument. A word of caution. LOCAL statements must be placed directly after the MACRO definition line! After the LOCAL directive is included the new *min* macro appears as this:

```
min        MACRO    result,first,second
           LOCAL    order_ok
           mov      &result,&first
           cmp      &first,&second
           jl       order_ok
           mov      &result,&second
order_ok:
           ENDM
```

When we invoke *min* this time, the expanded listing appears as given below. The value of "order_ok" has been replaced by "??0000."

Every time we call it, "order_ok" is replaced by a new value generated by MASM.

```
            min     ax,bx,cx            1st "call"
    +       min     ax,bx
    +       cmp     bx,cx
    +       jl      ??0000
    +       mov     ax,cx
    +   ??0000:
            min     ax,bx,cx            2nd "call"
    +       mov     ax,bx
    +       cmp     bx,cx
    +       jl      ??0001
    +       mov     ax,cx
    +   ??0001:
```

Of course, it is still possible to encounter a label conflict if you decide to use labels that begin with "??." If you avoid using labels beginning with "??," you can call the *min* macro as many times as you like.

The use of local labels is not restricted to jump addresses alone. Local labels can also be used with data, as the following macros demonstrate. In this case the macros are used to insert text strings into the data segment and simultaneously create a reference to the string in the code segment. By comparing the source code with the macro expansion in Listing 1-1, you can see how much clearer using macros is.

Listing 1-1 also contains a few other useful macros to ease the task of writing .EXE programs. Once you define these macros, you never again need to worry about getting the syntax of .EXE programs correct!

Listing 1-1.   Hello World Program

```
; ***********************************************************
;
; M A C R O   D E F I N I T I O N   S E C T I O N
;
; ***********************************************************
doscall MACRO
        int     21h                 ; call MS-DOS function
        ENDM
initstk MACRO
stk_seg segment stack
        db      32 dup ('stack   ')
stk_seg ends
        ENDM
initprg MACRO   segment
        assume  ds:segment
start:                              ; main entry point
        mov     ax,segment
        mov     ds,ax               ; set up data segment
        mov     es,ax               ; set up extra segment
        ENDM
```

Listing 1-1. cont.

```
finis   MACRO
        mov     ax,04C00h             ; terminate process
        doscall
        ENDM
dis_str MACRO   string                ; display a string
        mov     dx,offset string
        mov     ah,09h
        doscall
        ENDM
type_s  MACRO   string                ; define and display string
        LOCAL   saddr
cod_seg ends                          ; stop code segment
dat_seg segment                       ; change to data segment
saddr   db      string,'$'            ; define string in data segment
dat_seg ends                          ; stop data segment
cod_seg segment                       ; return to code segment
        dis_str saddr                 ; display string
        ENDM
; *************************************************************
;
; P R O G R A M   S E C T I O N
;
; *************************************************************
        initstk                       ; set up stack
cod_seg segment                       ; define code segment
main    proc    far                   ; main (and only) procedure
        assume  cs:cod_seg
        initprg dat_seg               ; initialize data segment
        type_s  'Hello world!'        ; say "hi" to the folks at home
        finis                         ; terminate program
main    endp
cod_seg ends
        end     start                 ; define starting address
```

You can enter the program exactly as it appears, assemble and run it, and it displays the words "Hello world!" Not very impressive in itself, but if the macros used are stored in a library file, writing .EXE programs becomes much easier. Let's look at the expanded program listing, shown in Listing 1-2.

Listing 1-2.   Macro Expansion for Hello World Program

```
;    *********************************************************
;
;    P R O G R A M   S E C T I O N
;
;    *********************************************************
          initstk                     ; set up stack
+   stk_seg segment stack
+           db      32 dup ('stack   ')
+   stk_seg ends
    cod_seg segment                   ; define code segment
```

Listing 1-2. cont.

```
        main    proc    far ; main (and only) procedure
                assume cs:cod_seg
                initprg dat_seg                  ; initialize data segment
+       mov     ax,dat_seg
+       mov     ds,ax                            ; set up data segment
+       mov     es,ax                            ; set up extra segment
                type_s 'Hello world!' ; say "hi" to the folks at home
+       cod_seg ends                             ; stop code segment
+       dat_seg segment                          ; change to data segment
+       ??0000  db      'Hello world!','$'       ; define string in ...
+       dat_seg ends                             ; stop data segment
+       cod_seg segment                          ; return to code segment
+               mov     dx,offset ??0000
+               mov     ah,09h
+               int     21h                      ; call ms-dos function
                finis                            ; terminate program
+               mov     ax,04C00h                ; terminate process
+               int     21h                      ; call ms-dos function
main    endp
cod_seg ends
        end     start                            ; define starting address
```

The first point to notice is that the use of the "LOCAL saddr" in the *type_s* macro worked fine as a label for the data statement. When using labels with data, remember not to use the ":." Next, notice how the macro expansion uses the reserved word "segment" in the macro *initprg*. No problem! Remember that the dummy argument names in the argument list override any other MASM definitions.

Note that a number of lines weren't included in the listing file. For one example, *initstk* did not show the expansion of the "dup" statement. The statement was assembled, but MASM suppressed the complete expansion. Also, the statement "assume ds:data_seg" is missing from *initprg*.

Both of these exceptions occur because of the way MASM processes macros. The default condition suppresses listing source lines that do not generate code. The "assume" statement is a MASM directive and generates no code of its own, therefore it is not listed. On the other hand, the "ends" segment end directives are listed and produce no code either. There are still mysteries in MASM for all of us to ponder.

Please don't take the code presented as a model for good programming. Although the idea of using macros for the prelude and postscript of .EXE programs is a good one, it is poor practice to embed the names of important symbols in the macros themselves. If the name of the data segment were other than "dat_seg," unnecessary confusion would be created within the program. Either *type_s* should be passed the name "dat_seg" as an argument, or *initprg* should always assume that the data segment is "dat_seg."

Macro Listing Directives

If you wish to see the complete listing of a macro, place the MASM directive .LALL in the assembly file. You can do this now, generate a .LST file, and compare it with the original listing in our example. You see that the "assume ds:data_seg" is now shown. To change the listing mode back, use the .XALL directive. This restores MASM to the default mode. If you wish to suppress all macro expansions, use the .SALL directive.

Macro Libraries

The term "macro library" is actually something of a misnomer. Macro libraries are not really libraries at all in the sense that Microsoft LINK or Microsoft LIB would understand. Macros must be included at compile time, because they are directives for MASM and MASM only. LINK or LIB do not know what to do with them. Instead, macro libraries are really *include* files. They can be defined in a separate file, called MYLIB .MAC or STANDARD.MLB or whatever (you can choose any valid file name you like) and included in the assembly by placing an *include* directive in the source file, such as:

```
INCLUDE    A:MYLIB.MAC
```

The rules regarding the file name and drive specification are the same as for the rest of the system. Within the listing file, lines obtained from an include file begin with a *C*, just as macro expansion lines begin with a +. Source lines from the include file begin with a "C," just as macro expansion lines began with a " + ." Of course, if you have a large library and don't want to clutter your .LST file with macro definitions, turn off listing with the .XLIST directive before the include, then turn the listing back on with .LIST after the include.

The use of macro libraries provides justification for the next macro directive introduced. Although you very rarely define a macro in a program and then want to "undefine" it (you would just delete it!), you quite commonly may include a macro library for the purpose of using just a few of the defined macros. The rest of those macro definitions take up valuable storage space in the MASM symbol table and macro storage area. The way to recover this space is with the PURGE directive. PURGE allows you to remove definitions for specified macros. To remove the macros defined in our previous example, we would issue the directive:

```
PURGE      doscall,initstk,initprg,finis,dis_str,type_s
```

This frees all the space occupied by the macro definitions and leaves us with a clean slate.

Macro Repeat Directives—REPT

Another macro facility provided by MASM is the ability to loop through a block of macro code. Three loop varieties are provided, each with specific uses.

For our first example, let's assume that we wish to create an area in the data segment for handling files. We use the file handle method of accessing files, and because we may want to use more than one file, we write our routine to give unique names to each block.

```
file_head        MACRO     fnum
file_hand_&fnum       dw    ?           ; file handle
file_nmax_&fnum       db    49          ; maximum size of file name
file_nlen_&fnum       db    ?           ; actual length of file name
file_name_&fnum       db    50 dup (?); file name buffer
            ENDM
```

Why didn't we use the LOCAL directive for "fnum?" Because the labels are not local to the macro itself. They must be accessed from other parts of the program to set the file name, access the file handle, etc. This macro could still be improved. What if we want to use two files at once, say, in a file to file copy program? We would need to call *file_head* twice:

```
file_head     1         ; 1st file block
file_head     2         ; 2nd file block
```

Instead, we can write *file_head* to define as many blocks as we need, using the REPT directive. The macros appear in Listing 1-3.

Listing 1-3.   Define File Access Block

```
fcnt        =         0         ; initialize and define symbol
file_head2  MACRO     fnum
file_hand_&fnum    dw    ?         ; file handle
file_nmax_&fnum    db    49        ; maximum size of file name
file_nlen_&fnum    db    ?         ; actual length of file name
file_name_&fnum    db    50 dup (?); file name buffer
         ENDM
```

Listing 1-3. cont.

```
file_head      MACRO      fnum
               REPT       fnum     ; repeat block "fnum" times
               file_head2    %fcnt; create block #"fcnt"
fcnt           =          fcnt + 1
               ENDM                ; end of repeat block
               ENDM                ; end of file_head macro
```

As the expansion in Listing 1-4 demonstrates, when we call the *file_head* macro, it calls macro *file_head2* twice, each time using a different value of "fnum." Of course, this macro expansion with the default listing status doesn't show the intermediate calls to *file_head2*. However, we can see the effects of the REPT in the two file control blocks that were created. Notice that the REPT directive must be terminated with ENDM, just like the MACRO directive. All repeat blocks must end with ENDM. Another ENDM must also appear at the end of each macro definition.

Listing 1-4. Define File Access Block Macro Expansion

```
               file_head    2
+      file_hand_0    dw    ?            ; file handle
+      file_nmax_0    db    49           ; maximum size of file name
+      file_nlen_0    db    ?            ; actual length of file name
+      file_name_0    db    50 dup (?); file name buffer
+      file_hand_1    dw    ?            ; file handle
+      file_nmax_1    db    49           ; maximum size of file name
+      file_nlen_1    db    ?            ; actual length of file name
+      file_name_1    db    50 dup (?); file name buffer
```

In addition to the REPT directive we also used a counter. Counters are symbols which have a numeric value. They must be defined using the " = " equate operator so that they may be changed. (In MASM, "equ" is used to define static symbols that are never changed, whereas " = " is used to define dynamic symbols that have values which may be changed.) The counter used with the *file_head* macros is "fcnt." The counter "fcnt" is incremented for each pass in *file_head*. But why were the labels in *file_head2*, "file_hand_0," etc., rather than "file_hand_fcnt?" How did the name "fcnt" get replaced with its value? The answer is in the percent sign (%) operator preceding "fcnt" in the call to *file_head2*. The percent sign forces the replacement of a symbol with its numeric value. Because we used the percent sign, we needed two macros. If we had tried to evaluate and substitute *fcnt* in a single macro, as with:

```
            REPT        fnum        ; repeat block "fnum" times
file_hand_&%fcnt    dw    ?         ; file handle
```

the operation would fail, resulting in the symbol:

```
file_hand_fcnt    dw    ?           ; file handle
```

The percent sign operator (%) only operates on macro *arguments* in a macro call! In addition, the symbol's value must be an absolute (non-relocatable) constant.

Another important aspect of our macros is that the counter "fcnt" is initialized outside the macro block. This is because we don't want to reset "fcnt" to zero each time we call *file_head* (which would cause duplicate labels). However, "fcnt" must be initialized somewhere, or the statement:

```
fcnt            =           fcnt + 1
```

would cause the error message **Symbol not defined.**

More about Macro Repeat Directives—IRP and IRPC

MASM supports two other macro repeat directives in addition to the REPT directive. These directives are IRP (indefinite repeat) and IRPC (indefinite repeat character). Neither really repeats indefinitely. Instead, each one repeats as long as arguments remain in the argument list. Listing 1-5 shows a simple repeat macro called *test_mac* that is designed to add items to the data segment.

Listing 1-5.   Simple IRP Repeat Macro and Expansion

```
test_mac    MACRO       args            ; define "test_mac"
            IRP         dummy,<&args>
            db          dummy           ; add item
            ENDM                        ; end of "IRP"
            ENDM                        ; end of "test_mac"

            test_mac    'one'                               1st call
+           db          'one'           ; add item
            test_mac    <'two','three','four'>              2nd "call"
+           db          'two'           ; add item
+           db          'three'         ; add item
+           db          'four'          ; add item
```

On each pass through the repeat block, the next value in the argument list is used for the value of "dummy." By using the IRP directive we were able to use one macro call to do the work of three. On the second call to *test_mac,* the IRP block repeated the "db" once for each of the three strings in the argument list.

We've also introduced two special symbols for macros, the angle bracket (< and >) operators. The *test_mac* expects only one argument, but we want to send it a list of arguments. The angle brackets accomplish this by making the text inside of them into a single literal. So " 'two','three','four' " becomes one argument rather than three. However, MASM does not send the angle brackets to the receiving macro. Inside *test_mac,* "args" has the value " 'two','three','four', " not "<'two','three','four'>". This is why additional angle brackets were added in the IRP directive.

This reasoning does not apply to strings! The quotes that enclose strings are not stripped, and adding an extra layer really confuses things. If we use the define byte statement as

```
              db        'dummy'              ; add item
```

MASM evaluates the line as

```
    +         db        'dummy'              ; add item
```

which would give us quite a few dummies but not what we want. We could force the use of the actual argument through

```
              db        '&dummy'             ; add item
```

but MASM would be trying to evaluate

```
    +         db        ''one''              ; add item
```

This causes a special error known as **Text area read past end.** This error also occurs if you accidentally create an endless recursive macro call. Essentially, MASM runs out of places to store all the symbols in use. Beware! This error message repeats endlessly until you abort MASM through <**CONTROL-C**>.

Macro Summary

From what we've learned, we see that macros use a type of programming shorthand so that once we've defined a block of code, we may include it repeatedly through a simple macro call. We've seen that macros are defined with a MACRO statement that gives the macro its name, and optionally provides for macro arguments. The macro definition is then ended with an ENDM statement. After the definition has been completed, the macro call is made using the macro's name, followed by any parameters the macro requires.

You've also seen how MASM can generate unique labels using the LOCAL directive and how repeat directives are used. Your knowledge of repeat directives and some of their uses is expanded in the next section.

The Microsoft *Programmer's Reference Manual for the MS-DOS Operating System* contains macro definitions for each of the system calls. In addition, it also contains some general macros for common tasks, such as moving a string.

This manual is a good place to study the use of macros and gain some additional experience in structuring macros. Table 1-2 summarizes the macro directives that MASM uses. Table 1-3 lists the special macro operators. Table 1-4 summarizes macro listing directives. You will find these tables useful.

Table 1-2.   Macro Directives

Directive			Explanation
mname MACRO parameter_list			MACRO DEFINITION Signals the start of a *macro* definition block; *parameter_list* defines the dummy arguments to be used within the block.
ENDM			END MACRO Signals the end of a MACRO definition or of a REPT, IRP, or IRPC repeat block. *Required!*
EXITM			EXIT MACRO Exits a macro expansion when encountered. Used most often with conditional assembly.
LOCAL	symbol_list		LOCAL SYMBOL Defines the symbols in *symbol_list* as unique symbols to the assembler. Expanded into ??xxxx where xxxx is a hexadecimal number.
PURGE	macro_list		PURGE MACRO DEFINITION Deletes the definitions of the macros listed in *macro_list*.

Table 1-2. cont.

Directive		Explanation
REPT	expression	**REPEAT** Repeats the block of instructions between REPT and ENDM *expression* number of times.
IRP	dummy, <parameter__list>	**INDEFINITE REPEAT** Repeats the block of instructions between IRP and ENDM for each value in the *parameter__list*, replacing *dummy* with the value of the parameter on each expansion.
IRPC	dummy,string	**INDEFINITE REPEAT CHARACTER** Repeats the block of instructions between IRPC and ENDM for each character in the *string*, replacing *dummy* with the character on each expansion.

Table 1-3. Special Symbols for Macros

Symbol	Explanation
&argument	Concatenates dummy arguments or symbols with text. Especially required to substitute dummy arguments within quoted strings.
;; comment text	Indicates a macro comment. These comments are never listed in the macro definition.
!char	Indicates that the next character is a literal. Used to include &, %, etc. in macro expansions where these symbols would otherwise be interpreted as special.
%symbol	Used to convert a symbol or optionally an expression to a number in the current radix.
<text>	The angle brackets (< and >) are used to define the text between them as a literal. Everything within the brackets may be passed as a single argument to a macro.

Table 1-4. Listing Directives for Macros

Directive	Explanation
.XALL	List source and object code for macro expansions, except source lines that do not generate code. .XALL is the default condition.
.LALL	List all lines for macro expansions, except comments preceded by two semicolons (;;).
.SALL	List none of the code produced by macro expansion.
.LIST	List source lines. Reverses .XLIST but does not change the state of macro listing as determined by .XALL, .LALL, or .SALL.
.XLIST	Suppress all listing. Overrides all other directives.

We're halfway to our structured control macros now. To complete the job of creating macros for structured control, we need to control just when and what is assembled into the program. That is the topic of the next section.

Conditional Assembly

When writing assembly language programs, it would be nice to be able to optionally include certain sections of code. When using macros, it also would be nice to be able to choose different code depending on the arguments passed to the macro. MASM provides these capabilities through the use of conditional assembly.

What are some of the cases where conditional assembly can work for you? Assume that you are writing a rather large program, and like most large programs, it has some bugs. You decide to place some debugging statements in the program to let you know what is happening. However, once it seems to be running right, you want to remove them so that the program executes more smoothly. Of course, because the program probably contains still more bugs, back go the debugging statements. Adding and deleting statements can get rather tedious. Conditional assembly can be used to solve this problem. Listing 1-6 shows the effect of a switch called "DEBUG" on the statements in a conditional assembly block. A good deal of the program has been edited and the .SALL switch used to suppress some of the *type_s* macro expansion. Our interest is only with those lines related to conditional assembly.

Listing 1-6.   DEBUG Statements Conditional Assembly—FALSE

Part A—Source Listing

```
FALSE   EQU     0
TRUE    EQU     0FFFFh
DEBUG   EQU     FALSE
...
type_s  ''hello world!''
IF      DEBUG                                   Begin Conditional Block
type_s 'Hi - I made it to this point in the program'
ENDIF                                           End Conditional Block
...
```

Part B—MASM Listing

```
type_s 'hello world!'
+       mov     dx,offset ??0000
```

Listing 1-6. cont.

```
+                mov      ah,09h
+                int      21h                ; call ms-dos function
         ENDIF
```

This example was assembled with the value of the "DEBUG" switch set to FALSE. As a result, all that appears of the conditional block in the MASM listing is the ENDIF statement after the *type_s* expansion. That is how MASM indicates that there was a conditional block there but that it wasn't assembled. When the value of the DEBUG switch is changed to TRUE, MASM produces a different program, as shown in Listing 1-7.

Listing 1-7.   DEBUG Statements Conditional Assembly—TRUE

MASM Listing

```
         DEBUG    EQU      TRUE
  . . .
         type_s   ''hello world!''
+                 mov      dx,offset ??0001
+                 mov      ah,09h
+                 int      21h                ; call ms-dos function
         IF       DEBUG
         type_s   'Hi - I made it to this point in the program'
+                 mov      dx,offset ??0002
+                 mov      ah,09h
+                 int      21h                ; call ms-dos function
         ENDIF
```

This time, the debugging statements are included. MASM also includes in the listing the line that caused the statements to be assembled. If you would like to see all conditional assembly directives in the listing file, whether or not they evaluate TRUE or FALSE, use the .LFCOND (list false conditions) directive. You can later suppress the listing of FALSE conditions with the .SFCOND (suppress false conditions [listing]) directive. Basically, a conditional assembly block begins with some type of IF statement (see Table 1-5 for a complete listing) and terminates with an ENDIF statement.

A common use of TRUE/FALSE switches in conditional assembly occurs in systems programming (programming the operating system of a computer). If you have a copy of the source assembly for your computer,

Table 1-5.   Conditional Assembly Directives

Directive		Explanation
IF	expression	IF TRUE If *expression* evaluates to a nonzero number, the statements in the conditional block are assembled.
IFE	expression	IF FALSE If *expression* evaluates to 0, the statements in the conditional block are assembled.
ELSE		ELSE If the conditional assembly directive evaluates FALSE (does not assemble the conditional block), the alternative statements in the ELSE block are assembled. Terminates the IFxxxx block but must be followed by ENDIF. Only valid after an IFxxxx statement.
ENDIF		END of IF BLOCK Terminates an IFxxxx block or ELSE block.
IF1,IF2		IF MASM PASS 1, IF MASM PASS 2 Assembles the conditional block if the MASM assembler is in the pass indicated. See text for the relationship of IF1 and IF2 to IFDEF and IFNDEF.
IFDEF IFNDEF	symbol symbol	IF symbol DEFINED IF symbol NOT DEFINED Evaluates whether *symbol* is defined or declared external. IFNDEF is the opposite of IFDEF. See text for relationship to assembler passes.
IFB IFNB	<argument> <argument>	IF argument BLANK IF argument NOT BLANK Evaluates whether the *argument* is blank. Used with macro arguments to see whether an argument has been provided. IFNB is the opposite of IFB. The angle brackets are required.
IFIDN IFDIF	<str1>,<str2> <str1>,<str2>	IF *str1* IDENTICAL TO *str2* IF *str1* DIFFERENT FROM *str2* Evaluates whether string *str1* is identical to string *str2*. IFDIF is the opposite of IFIDN. The angle brackets are required.

take a quick look at it. You most likely find that conditional assembly has been used extensively. Conditional assembly allows the designer to write one operating system, and through the use of conditional assembly "switches," configure the system to a particular set of equipment. These switches, like the DEBUG switch in our example, can cause the proper system to be generated (proper configuration to be made) for a given type, number, or configuration of memory, boards, peripherals, drivers, and so forth.

For the purposes of the MASM assembler, any expression that evaluates to zero, or has a value of zero, is considered to be FALSE. A non-zero expression is considered TRUE. The value FFFF (hexadecimal) is commonly used for the symbol TRUE. This allows TRUE to be used in any bit operation. For example, the bitwise AND of 0001 and 1000 is 0000 so that although both are true, the AND of them would be false. Remember that MASM uses the same operators for both logical and bit operations.

Relational Operators

In addition to using symbols with preassigned values or arithmetic expressions, MASM supports relational operators, which may be used to control conditional assembly statements. Relational operators are those that express the relationship between two values. *Less than, greater than, equal to,* and *not equal to* are all examples of relational operators.

These operators allow such things as range checking and special actions and in fact support what amounts to a programming language. Through the use of relational operators, you can create quite complex program structures that automatically adjust themselves to a particular environment (for example, sizing a data area to fit a reserved area of memory). However, when using relational operators, MASM doesn't always do the expected thing.

If you are used to working with signed integers, you may think of 0FFFFh and –1 as the same value. With some exceptions, MASM also uses the values interchangeably. Although earlier versions of MASM had some problems dealing with negative numbers, the newer versions (1.2 and later) do know that –1 is equal to 0FFFFh. However, when comparing the magnitude of two numbers, MASM treats them differently. A simple test illustrates:

True	FFFF	dw	1 gt −1	Obvious
False	0000	dw	1 gt 0FFFFh	65535, not −1
True	FFFF	dw	−1 ge 0FFFFh	−1 = −1
False	0000	dw	−1 gt 0FFFFh	−1 not gt −1

What is demonstrated here is that MASM considers 0FFFFh to be a positive number, 65535 to be exact, except when it is being compared with –1 at which time 0FFFFh is treated as –1. Confusing as this is, forewarned is forearmed.

The full list of relational operators in MASM appears in Table 1-6. An example use of these operators is contained in the structured coding macros appearing at the end of this chapter.

Table 1-6. Relational and Logical Operators for Conditional Assembly

Operator	Explanation
EQ exp1 EQ exp2	TRUE if exp1 equals exp2
NE exp1 NE exp2	TRUE if exp1 not equal to exp2
LT exp1 LT exp2	TRUE if exp1 is less than exp2
LE exp1 LE exp2	TRUE if exp1 is less than or equals exp2
GT exp1 GT exp2	TRUE if exp1 is greater than exp2
GE exp1 GE exp2	TRUE if exp1 is greater than or equals exp2
NOT NOT exp	TRUE if exp FALSE, otherwise FALSE
AND exp1 AND exp2	TRUE only if both exp1 and exp2 are TRUE
OR exp1 OR exp2	TRUE if either exp1 or exp2 are TRUE
XOR exp1 XOR exp2	TRUE if exp1 equals logical NOT of exp2
FALSE 0000 hex	IF TRUE, any zero expression is FALSE
TRUE FFFF hex	IF TRUE, any nonzero expression is TRUE

Listing directives for conditional assembly appear in Table 1-7.

Table 1-7. Listing Directives for Conditional Assembly

Directive	Explanation
.LFCOND	List conditional assemblies that evaluate to FALSE condition.
.SFCOND	Suppress listing of conditional assemblies that evaluate to FALSE condition. .SFCOND is the default setting.
.TFCOND	Toggles the listing of FALSE conditional assembly as determined by the MASM /X switch. Operates independently of the .LFCOND and .SFCOND switches.
.LIST	List source lines. Reverses .XLIST but does not change the state of conditional assembly listing as determined by .LFCOND, .SFCOND, or .TFCOND.
.XLIST	Suppress all listing. Overrides all other directives.

Conditional Assembly Summary

From a quick overview of conditional assembly, we see how it is possible to control what code is included in the assembled program. So far, we have investigated the use of conditional assembly to ease the task of including optional code. But we have only scratched the surface. Only one of the ten possible forms of conditional operators was used in our examples. What of the rest of these operators? They are intended primarily for use with macros. To that topic, we now turn.

Conditional Assembly and Macros

Although conditional assembly is frequently used with explicitly defined switches, when it is combined with the MASM macro facility, conditional assembly's greatest potential is realized. There are a number of features of conditional assembly that are intended specifically for operation with the macro facility. Let's lay some groundwork to explain the possibilities of these features.

Macros may be classified in two groups. First, there are those macros designed to create a definite structure depending upon some input, where the structure is well defined and the input is of an expected class. The *file_head* macro, designed to insert a file definition block, is an example of this classification of macro.

The second class of macro is intended to generate a structure that is dependent on information that is unavailable to programmers or that they consider trivial and desire to ignore. These macros often must be able to process many classes of arguments and must determine the argument's class. At other times, these macros may maintain private data or counters in order to release the programmer from bookkeeping chores. The structured control macros contained in the last part of this chapter are prime examples of the latter. Of course, some overlap usually exists between these classes of macros.

To explain further, in one type of macro, the programmer uses the macro facility to avoid some typing or other drudge work. In the other type, the programmer uses the macro facility as a kind of higher level structure, depending on the assembler to supply the missing information. The programmer intentionally hides the details of implementation for the purpose of simplifying the programming job.

One example of a higher level macro is using macros to simplify the use of assembler mnemonics. Although most of the 8086 processor's instructions may be used with either register or memory operands, quite a number do not allow immediate operands. The PUSH instruction is one example, although the 186/188 and 286 do allow pushing immediate data onto the stack.

It is quite simple to design a *pushi* (push immediate) macro that transfers the desired argument to a register and pushes the register. However, if a macro were to be used to implement a more general push operation, it is not only desirable that the macro be able to push immediate data, but it is also desirable that the macro be able to decide whether such an operation is even required. In other words, the programmer would use a general *pseudo-opcode* that would apply to all cases. The pseudo-opcode would actually be a macro that would evaluate the operands and generate either a standard or extended instruction as required.

The first step in being able to write such a general purpose macro is to be able to determine just what the macro operands are. MASM provides a number of special purpose operators to accomplish this task.

Determining Operand Types

In the 8086/8088 environment there are four basic types of operands. These are register, immediate, memory, and addresses. For those that are data oriented, a number of subtypes are possible. Registers include the special cases of the accumulator (general register A) and the segment registers. All three data types may be subclassified as either 8-bit or 16-bit data. Addresses may be either near (offset only) or far (offset and segment).

How do we go about distinguishing among all these types? We use the MASM operators .TYPE and TYPE. Table 1-8 shows the results of using these operators with various classes of operands.

Table 1-8.   .TYPE and TYPE MASM Operators

Rules for .TYPE and TYPE

Operator	Result	
.TYPE Bits 5 and 7	8x	Defined external
	2x	Defined local
	0x	Invalid reference
.TYPE Bits 0 through 2	x0	Absolute mode
	x1	Program related
	x2	Data related
TYPE used with data variable	01	Byte variable
	02	Word variable
	04	Double word variable
	08	Quad word variable
	10	Ten-byte variable
	xx	Structure of size xx
TYPE used with program label	FFFF	Near program label
	FFFE	Far program label

.TYPE and TYPE Examples

Variable Type	.TYPE	Definition	TYPE	Definition
Immediate	20	Defined local	0	Invalid
Register	20	Defined local	0	Invalid
Data label	22	Defined local	x	Number of bytes
Near label	21	Defined local	FFFF	Near label
Far label	21	Defined local	FFFE	Far label
MASM op-code	00	Invalid	0	Invalid
Nonsense	00	Invalid	0	Invalid

Some further examples may be constructed. Although .TYPE recognizes the names of the various registers, it does not recognize a register construct such as [BX] or ARRAY[BX][SI]. Single character constants, such as A, are recognized as locally defined variables by the .TYPE operator.

Nothing recognizes a forward reference during the first pass of the assembler. IFDEF returns a **not defined** result, .TYPE returns an **invalid,** and TYPE returns a zero length. Only one rule may be applied to forward references: Avoid them if at all possible.

Phase Errors and Other MASM Eccentricities

An important warning is associated with the use of MASM operators. MASM is a two pass assembler that assigns values to symbols on the first pass, then evaluates the symbols on the second pass. Program labels and data labels are symbols. Their values are determined during the first pass, then used during the second pass to generate the code.

Consider the following chain of events. If a forward reference occurs, MASM does not recognize the label on the first pass and is not able to determine its type. Attempting to reference this symbol produces the error message **Symbol is not defined.** MASM encounters this error when processing the first pass but suppresses it and continues the assembly. MASM is able to cover up by assuming the type of the symbol from the context in which the symbol appears. If this guess is wrong, MASM may end up producing the message **Phase error between passes,** or MASM may shorten the instruction and place NOP instructions after it as place holders.

There are two ways that phase errors may be avoided during normal use of MASM. In the majority of cases, MASM is able to determine the operand type from the context. Programmers rarely jump to locations in the data segment and don't usually add program addresses. For those special cases where MASM makes a wrong guess, the programmer may set the assembler straight by using the PTR (pointer) override operator. With PTR the programmer may explicitly specify the type of a forward reference so that MASM does not guess incorrectly.

However, by attempting to produce multipurpose instructions with macros, we greatly increase the chance of guessing wrong in these cases. If our multipurpose instruction is intended to be able to process any operand class, exact meaning becomes more difficult to determine from context. In addition, although the use of PTR may aid in some of these cases (as we shall see in the *push_op* macro), its use defeats the purpose of using macros to relieve the programmer of burdensome detail.

By examining how a wrong guess produces a phase error we may more easily avoid its occurrence. Because phase errors are the result of certain symbols (such as labels) changing value between passes, it is important that macros produce the same amount of code on each pass. This preserves the values of those labels located after the macro and is also why MASM pads shortened instructions with NOP instructions. Program labels generated by the macros must also remain constant from pass one to pass two.

String Matching—an Example

Unfortunately, the .TYPE operator's readiness to recognize immediate operands as well as registers, etc., greatly reduces its usefulness in detecting the type of a macro operand. Because it is especially useful to know whether an argument to a macro is a register, we must construct a method for determining this. Knowing whether the argument is a register usually is useful only when combined with the implicit assumption that if it's not a register and not a defined memory reference, the argument is assumed to be an immediate data reference.

    A common use of conditional assembly with the IRP or IRPC directives is matching. The purpose in these cases is to see whether a macro argument is a member of some set. In this case, string matching is used to solve the problem of determining whether an argument is a register. Because all that the .TYPE operator can determine is that registers are both locally defined and absolute, a string matching macro is used to explicitly check for a register name. The *?reg* macro shown in Listing 1-8 accomplishes this function.

Listing 1-8. Register Name Match *?reg* Macro

```
FALSE    equ     0
TRUE     equ     0FFFFh
;; **** ?REG--Test to see whether an argument is a register
;;
?reg     MACRO   arg
?isr8 =          FALSE
?isr16 =         FALSE
         irp     reg,<ax,bx,cx,dx,bp,sp,si,di,cs,ds,es,ss>
         ifidn   <&&reg>,<&arg>
         ?isr16  =       TRUE
         exitm
         endif
         endm
;; If match, stop here
         if      (?isr16)
         exitm
         endif
;; If not match yet, try the rest
         irp     reg,<ah,bh,ch,dh,al,bl,cl,dl>
```

Listing 1-8. cont.

```
        ifidn   <&&reg>,<&arg>
        ?isr8   =       TRUE
        exitm
        endif
        endm
;; If match, stop here
        if      (?isr8)
        exitm
        endif
;; If not match yet, try uppercase
        irp     reg,<AX,BX,CX,DX,BP,SP,SI,DI,CS,DS,ES,SS>
        ifidn   <&&reg>,<&arg>
        ?isr16  =       TRUE
        exitm
        endif
        endm
;; If match, stop here
        if      (?isr16)
        exitm
        endif
;; If not match yet, try the rest
        irp     reg,<AH,BH,CH,DH,AL,BL,CL,DL>
        ifidn   <&&reg>,<&arg>
        ?isr8   =       TRUE
        exitm
        endif
        endm
        ENDM
```

The heart of this macro, as with any matching macro, is the three
lines:

```
        irp     reg,<ax,bx,cx,dx,bp,sp,si,di,cs,ds,es,ss>
        ifidn   <&&reg>,<&arg1>
        ?isr16  =       TRUE
```

These lines may be interpreted as performing the following function:

> For *reg* equals *ax* to *ss* do . . .
> If *reg* equals the argument *arg* . . .
> The argument is a register!

There are two interesting things to note about this register name
matching macro. One, it is necessary to explicitly check for the register
name in both lower- and uppercase. The IFIDN conditional assembly directive compares strings for an exact match. Even with the extra effort,
the *?reg* macro is not foolproof. It does not match a register name that
has one uppercase character and one lowercase character ("aL," for example).

Second, two separate checks are performed: one for 16-bit registers and one for 8-bit registers. In the current implementation, separate checks doesn't gain us anything, but it will be used in the next example.

The *?reg* macro has two additional syntax elements. One is the EXITM exit macro directive. This directive is used to stop processing of the *?reg* macro when a match is found.

Less obvious is the use of the double ampersand in the IFIDN statement. According to the Microsoft MASM manual, the user must "supply as many ampersands as there are levels of nesting." This rather laconic pronouncement doesn't do justice to the complexity of the problem. The "levels of nesting" doesn't apply to how many blocks deep the reference occurs but rather to how many blocks deep the definition occurs. Thus "arg1" gets away with only one "&," whereas "reg," which is defined in a nested block, requires the double ampersand, "&&." Microsoft does not state whether there is a limit to the allowed number of nesting levels or the number of ampersands that may be required. In cases where multiple ampersands seem indicated, the extra effort of trying a few examples to ensure proper operation is worth it.

The demonstration of the *?reg* macro in Listing 1-9 shows that this macro functions as expected. Do note that the register "bP,", which MASM would recognize, is rejected by *?reg*. This could be construed as a coercive argument for consistency in typing.

Listing 1-9. Test of the *?reg* Register Name Match Macro

```
        ?reg    ax      ; is "AX" a register?
FFFF    dw      ?isr16                          TRUE
        ?reg    CS      ; is "CS" a register?
FFFF    dw      ?isr16                          TRUE
        ?reg    zork    ; is "ZORK" a register?
0000    dw      ?isr16                          FALSE
0000    dw      ?isr8                           FALSE
        ?reg    01234h  ; is "1234" a register?
0000    dw      ?isr16                          FALSE
0000    dw      ?isr8                           FALSE
        ?reg    bP      ; is "BP" a register?
0000    dw      ?isr16                          FALSE—case change
0000    dw      ?isr8                           FALSE
```

Parsing Macro Arguments

With a macro that can recognize register names, you can now implement a general PUSH macro, which we'll call *push_op* (push operand). (Note: We considered the name *pusha* [push all], but PUSHA is a defined opcode in the Intel 186, 188, and 286 chips. Its use as a macro could restrict upward compatibility. Of course, you can always implement the PUSHA instruction via a *pusha* macro for 8086 or 8088 processors and be ahead of the game.)

As mentioned previously, it is necessary to make some assumptions about the operand type in those cases where it is not defined and not a register. In the *push_op* macro, we assume that unknown operands are immediate data references. *Push_op* references the macro *?reg*, and *?reg* must be included in the program for *push_op* to function. See Listing 1-10 for the *push_op* macro.

Listing 1-10. *Push_op* **Generalized PUSH Macro**

```
;; **** push_op Generalized Push Operand Macro
;; If the operand is defined, it may be one of:
;;      register
;;      data reference
;;
;; If the operand is NOT defined, it is assumed to
;; be an immediate reference.
push_op          macro     arg
         .SALL
         ifdef   &arg                  ;; operand is defined ...
          ?argtyp = .type &arg         ;; ... then get type
          if      ((?argtyp and 3) eq 2)  ;; operand is DATA
           ?argsiz = ((type &arg) + 1)/2 ;; ... get size in words
           ?argoff = 0                 ;; ... set offset to 0
           rept ?argsiz                ;; ... repeat each word
            ?argadd = word ptr &arg + ?argoff   ;; get type ptr
         .XALL
         push    ?argadd               ;; ... push memory direct
         .SALL
            ?argoff = ?argoff + 2      ;; ... next word of data
           endm
          endif
          if      ((?argtyp and 3) eq 1)  ;; operand is PROGRAM
           push_imof      &arg         ;; ... push label offset
          endif
          ife     (?argtyp and 3)      ;; operand is ABSOLUTE
           ?reg &arg
            if     (?isr16)            ;; operand is REGISTER 16
         .XALL
         push    &arg                  ;; ... push direct
         .SALL
            else
             if    (?isr8)             ;; operand is REGISTER 8
             irpc chr1,&arg1
         .XALL
         push    &&chr1&&x             ;; save short register
         .SALL
             exitm
             endm
             else                      ;; assume immediate
         push_im &arg                  ;; ... push immediate
```

Listing 1-10. cont.

```
    endif
   endif
  endif
 else                              ;; ... push immediate
 push_im &arg
 endif
 endm
```

Push_op makes use of the *?reg* macro's ability to distinguish between 16-bit and 8-bit registers. Because the PUSH instruction does not accept an 8-bit register, the IRPC macro directive is used to obtain the first character of the register name. *Push_op* then appends an "x" to form the name of the 16-bit register, which PUSH accepts. Note that the use of double ampersands is required again in this statement and that they are required on both sides of the dummy argument as string concatenation occurs at each end.

For those cases that are assumed to be immediate data, the *push_im* macro is called. This macro is more complicated than absolutely necessary, because it assumes that no registers are available for use in transferring the immediate data to the stack. Instead, the macro uses the base pointer (BP) to address the stack. After saving the BP and AX on the stack, *push_im* slides the immediate data under the AX contents, swapping it with the contents of the old BP. After restoring the BP contents to its previous location in the BP, the macro retrieves the contents of the AX by popping them off the stack. The *push_im* macro is shown in Listing 1-11.

Listing 1-11. *Push_im* Immediate Data PUSH Macro

```
;; **** push_im Immediate Data Push Macro
push_im        macro    arg
      .XALL
      push     bp                 ;; save base pointer
      mov      bp,sp              ;; move stack pointer to BP
      push     ax                 ;; save accumulator
      mov      ax,&arg            ;; get immediate data
      xchg     [bp],ax            ;; swap old BP and imm. data
      mov      bp,ax              ;; restore old BP from AX
      pop      ax                 ;; restore accumulator
      .SALL
      endm
```

This rather convoluted operation also may be adapted to swapping items on the stack. However, playing with the stack can be dangerous. If your computer supports interrupts, this operation should only be done with interrupts disabled so that the integrity of the stack is preserved.

For those cases that attempt to push program locations on the stack, we assume that the programmer desires to save the actual offset of the label. Thus, the *push_imof* macro was created to push the offset of the label as immediate data. It differs from the *push_im* macro solely in its use of the instruction

```
mov     ax,offset &arg
```

as opposed to the simple move that appears in *push_im*. See Listing 1-12 for the *push_imof* macro.

Listing 1-12. *Push_imof* **Offset of Immediate Data**
PUSH Macro

```
;; **** push_imof Offset of Immediate Data Push Macro
push_imof macro          arg
        .XALL
        push    bp               ;; save base pointer
        mov     bp,sp            ;; move stack pointer to BP
        push    ax               ;; save accumulator
        mov     ax,offset &arg   ;; get offset of immediate data
        xchg    [bp],ax          ;; swap old BP and imm. data
        mov     bp,ax            ;; restore old BP from AX
        pop     ax               ;; restore accumulator
        .SALL
        endm
```

The last discrete case that *push_op* recognizes is an attempt to push memory data onto the stack directly. Here the difficulty lies in the fact that the stack only accepts 16-bit data. By using the PTR override directive, you can convince MASM to save the desired data one word at a time. *Push_op* contains a loop that repeats the operation for each word of the data element being saved, incrementing the address by two on each pass. Thus double word, quad word, ten byte, and structured variables may be saved onto the stack.

Finally, note that the *push_op* macro still does not process any references that contain complex addressing (such as 2[BP], etc.) If it proves necessary, you can implement such checks by using the IRPC macro directive to check the argument for brackets, base plus index addressing, and base plus offset addressing.

The final test of the *push_op* macro appears in Listing 1-13, which shows the code that results from a few example calls of the *push_op* macro.

**Listing 1-13.   Example Expansion of *Push_op* Generalized
PUSH Macro**

```
dat_seg segment
datq    dq      4040414142424343h
dat_seg ends
        .
        .
        .
start:
        push_op ax                          general register save
+               push    ax
        push_op cs                          segment register save
+               push    cs
        push_op al                          short register save ...
+               push    ax...               becomes general reg.
        push_op 01234h                      word constant save
+               push    bp
+               mov     bp,sp
+               push    ax
+               mov     ax,01234h
+               xchg    [bp],ax
+               mov     bp,ax
+               pop     ax
        push_op 'A'                         byte constant save
+               push    bp
+               mov     bp,sp
+               push    ax
+               mov     ax,'A'
+               xchg    [bp],ax
+               mov     bp,ax
+               pop     ax
        push_op start                       program label offset save
+               push    bp
+               mov     bp,sp
+               push    ax
+               mov     ax,offset start
+               xchg    [bp],ax
+               mov     bp,ax
+               pop     ax
        push_op datq                        Quad word variable save
+               push    ?argadd             1st word
+               push    ?argadd             2nd word
+               push    ?argadd             3rd word
+               push    ?argadd             4th word
        .
        .
        .
```

This expansion shows everything as expected. The last operation in
the listing, where *push_op* is used on a quad word variable, may not be
clear. Each push has the same argument. What isn't visible from this
trimmed listing is that each line has a relocatable address, 0000 for the

first word, 0002 for the second word, and so forth. Unfortunately, we can't squeeze a 132-column listing into this book, so you'll just have to try it out if you want to check on it.

This example is especially useful because it demonstrates one area where macros are nearly always preferred over subroutines. When dealing with stack manipulations (as in *push_im* and *push_imof*) macros are able to perform the operation without "worrying" about the effects of the CALL instruction on the stack. This is especially important when placing or removing data from the stack because a subroutine cannot alter the top of the stack and return without causing major problems.

A Few Warnings about Conditional Assembly and Macros in MASM

When using macros, we tend to forget that macros generate in-line code and not calls to routines. Although this has the advantages of generating fast code and frees us from some restrictions in using the stack, production of in-line code results in larger code. As a designer, your responsibility is to judge when a macro, with its quick execution, is called for and when a subroutine, with its space-saving ability and greater structure, is called for. Generally, use macros when the code is small, time critical, or you need to configure the routine to the individual circumstance. Use subroutines when the code is larger, is of a general nature that can be reused, or, so that it can be verified easily, is convenient to have in one place.

Another confusing issue with macros relates to the use of symbols. You remember that symbols are defined through the use of the "equ" or "=" operators. These symbols are then evaluated by MASM and replaced by their values. It sometimes happens that we programmers forget that macro arguments are not symbols and vice versa. According to the MASM manual, macro arguments are replaced by the actual parameters using one-for-one text substitution. Macro arguments may be created by one macro, and using the text substitution ability, passed as a complete text string to another macro. This is not possible with symbols. Indeed, symbols may only be assigned text values using the "equ" operator, which does not allow them to be modified. The "=" operator only allows symbols to be given numeric values or TYPE attributes. An example of this limitation, and of one way to overcome it, appears in our presentation of structured control statements that follows.

Structured Control Statements in Assembly Language

Now that we have all of the tools necessary to build our structured control statements, let's do it. The most common and useful control statements are shown in Table 1-9.

Table 1-9.   Structured Control Statements

Statement	Structure
IF-THEN	IF <condition> (execute if condition TRUE) ENDIF

IF-THEN-ELSE	IF <condition>
	  (execute if condition TRUE)
	ELSE
	  (execute if condition FALSE)
	ENDIF

DO-WHILE	WHILE <condition> (execute if condition TRUE) END__WHILE
REPEAT-UNTIL	REPEAT (execute if condition FALSE) UNTIL <condition>

FOR-DO	FOR <var> = <begin> to <end>
	  (execute for each integer value of *var* between *begin*
	  and *end*, inclusive, incrementing or decrementing *var*
	  by one each loop)
	END__FOR

CASE-OF-<var>	CASE <var> OF
	  <case A>:
	  (execute if *var* = A)
	  <case B>:
	  (execute if *var* = B)
	  .....
	  <case N>:
	  (execute if *var* = N)
	  <default>:
	  (execute if no match)
	END__CASE

The statements in Table 1-9 are those that are used most frequently to implement structured control in structured programming. Some languages have an abundance of them, others lack many. It was only recently that FORTRAN gained use of the IF-THEN-ELSE structure in FORTRAN-77. Out-of-the-box assemblers almost never have these structures implemented for coding purposes, even though many support IF-THEN-ELSE for conditional assembly. The reason is simple: Assemblers are supposed to be at a lower level than high-level languages. Because we have decided that these structures can make our programming life easier, we can implement them, using the tools that we've just learned.

There is one structure that we have left out. This is the CASE statement. The structure that we have presented is taken from PASCAL syntax but is nevertheless similar to that used in C and other languages. The problem with the case statement is that you must check the key variable *var* against each case that appears in the list. If the initial statement and the cases are not contained in the same macro, you can't know what the key variable was. Remember that MASM does not allow strings to be used with the "=" symbol assignment operator.

You can create a variation of case statement by listing all the possible cases and their destination labels as arguments to one macro. This pseudo *case* macro is discussed in a following section of this chapter.

The complete listing for the rest of the definitions of our structured control macros appears in Listing 1-14. Note the heavy use of macro comments (;;) to save room in the macro storage areas. These macros generate many symbols. They may be used in any legal order to a theoretical limit of 89 nesting levels. However, MASM runs out of storage long before that limit is reached. No initialization is required. All symbols are self-initializing.

Listing 1-14.   Structured Control Macros

```
PAGE    50,132                     ; set listing to full screen
;; ************************************************************
;;
;; M A C R O    D E F I N I T I O N S
;;
;; ************************************************************
FALSE   EQU     0               ; define "FALSE"
TRUE    EQU     OFFFFh          ; define "TRUE"
;; ** TESTSYM ***************************** SUPPORT MACRO **
;; Test to see whether nesting level has been defined. If not,
;; then set ?SYMDEF to initialize the counter for that level.
;; All processes normally on Pass #1--start counters at 0
;; All symbols must be reset on the beginning of Pass #2
;; Note that "?p2sw ..." symbols stand for "Phase 2 SWitch"
;; Check that nesting level 10 is first level to be reinit.
;; Note: The value of 10 is chosen for the initial level to
;; reserve 2 digits for the nesting level.
;;
testsym         macro   p1,p2
        IF1                         ;; if 1st pass, check for defined
        IFNDEF  &p1&p2
?p2sw&p1&p2     =       TRUE        ;; set pass two, redefine switch
?symdef         =       FALSE       ;; cause counter initialization
```

Listing 1-14. cont.

```
        ELSE
?symdef       =         TRUE      ;; allow counter increment
        ENDIF
        ENDIF
        IF2             ;; if 2nd pass, cause reinitialization
        IF      (?p2sw&p1&p2)   ;; if not reinitialized ...
?p2sw&p1&p2   =         FALSE   ;; clear pass two, redefine switch
        IF      (?p2sw&p1&10)   ;; ... and check level 10 for init
        %out    * ERROR--&p1 nesting level not closed on pass 2 *
        ENDIF
?symdef       =         FALSE   ;; force reinitialize of counter
        ELSE
?symdef       =         TRUE    ;; allow counter increment
        ENDIF
        ENDIF
        endm
;; ** ZEROSYM ***************************** SUPPORT MACRO **
;; Initialize the nesting sequence counter on 1st use.
zerosym       macro   p1,p2
&p1&p2 =      0
        endm
;; ** INCSYM ****************************** SUPPORT MACRO **
;; Increment nesting sequence counter.
incsym macro  p1,p2
&p1&p2 =      &p1&p2 + 1
        endm
;; ** DECSYM ****************************** SUPPORT MACRO **
;; Decrement nesting sequence counter.
decsym macro  p1,p2
&p1&p2 =      &p1&p2 - 1
        endm
;; ** MKJMP2 ****************************** SUPPORT MACRO **
;; Insert actual JMP instruction and destination into code.
mkjmp2 macro  p1,p2,p3
        jmp     &p1&p2&p3
        endm
;; ** MKJMP ******************************* SUPPORT MACRO **
;; Reformat symbols for evaluation for JMP instruction.
mkjmp  macro  p1,p2,p3
??tmp  =      &p3&p2
        mkjmp2  p1,p2,%??tmp
        endm
;; ** MKLBL2 ****************************** SUPPORT MACRO **
;; Insert actual JMP destination label into code.
mklbl2 macro  p1,p2,p3
&p1&p2&p3:
        endm
;; ** MKLBL ******************************* SUPPORT MACRO **
;; Reformat symbols for evaluation of JMP destination label.
mklbl  macro  p1,p2,p3
??tmp  =      &p3&p2
        mklbl2  p1,p2,%??tmp
        endm
;; ** IF ********************** STRUCTURED CONTROL MACRO **
;; Structured IF macro--IF true
```

Listing 1-14. cont.

```
ift     macro   p1
        local   iftrue
        j&p1    iftrue          ;; jump to IF section of code
        IFNDEF  ?if_level       ;; set up new level of nesting
?if_level       =       10
        ELSE
?if_level       =       ?if_level + 1
        ENDIF
        testsym ?if_nest,%?if_level     ;; set up new sequence #
        IF      (?symdef)
        incsym  ?if_nest,%?if_level
        ELSE
        zerosym ?if_nest,%?if_level
        ENDIF
;; Insert jump tp ELSE or IF NOT section into code.
        mkjmp   ?if_,%?if_level,?if_nest
iftrue:
        endm
;; ** IFELSE ********************* STRUCTURED CONTROL MACRO **
;; Structured ELSE macro
ifelse macro
        IFNDEF  ?if_level
; ERROR--IFELSE without opening IFT statement
        EXITM
        ENDIF
        IF (?if_level LT 10)
; ERROR--IFELSE without opening IFT statement
        EXITM
        ENDIF
;; Generate IFELSE code
        incsym  ?if_nest,%?if_level
        mkjmp   ?if_,%?if_level,?if_nest
        decsym  ?if_nest,%?if_level
        mklbl   ?if_,%?if_level,?if_nest
        incsym  ?if_nest,%?if_level
        endm
;; ** IFEND ********************** STRUCTURED CONTROL MACRO **
;; Structured END macro for use with IFT
ifend macro
        IFNDEF  ?if_level
; ERROR--IFEND without opening IFT statement
        EXITM
        ENDIF
        IF (?if_level LT 10)
; ERROR--IFEND without opening IFT statement
        EXITM
        ENDIF
;; Generate IFEND label
        mklbl   ?if_,%?if_level,?if_nest
?if_level       =       ?if_level - 1
        endm
;; ** DOWHILE ******************** STRUCTURED CONTROL MACRO **
;; Structured DO_WHILE macro
dowhile         macro   p1,p2,p3
        local   iftrue
```

Listing 1-14. cont.

```
        IFNDEF  ?do_level           ;; set up new level of nesting
?do_level       =       10
        ELSE
?do_level       =       ?do_level + 1
        ENDIF
;; Set up new sequence number for nesting level
        testsym ?do_nest,%?do_level
        IF      (?symdef)
        incsym  ?do_nest,%?do_level
        ELSE
        zerosym ?do_nest,%?do_level
        ENDIF
;; Insert top-of-loop label for jump
        mklbl   ?do_,%?do_level,?do_nest
;; Insert condition check into code
        cmp     &p1,&p3
;; Jump to DO_WHILE_TRUE section of code
        j&p2    iftrue
;; Step to next label in sequence
        incsym  ?do_nest,%?do_level
;; Insert end-of-loop jump into code
        mkjmp   ?do_,%?do_level,?do_nest
;; Begin the DO_WHILE_TRUE section of code
iftrue:
        endm
;; ** DOEXIT ******************** STRUCTURED CONTROL MACRO **
;; Structured DO_EXIT macro for use with DOWHILE
doexit macro
;; Insert end-of-loop jump in code
        mkjmp   ?do_,%?do_level,?do_nest
        endm
;; ** DOEND ******************** STRUCTURED CONTROL MACRO **
;; Structured DO_END macro for use with DOWHILE
;; DOEND macro generates the code for a structured ENDDO
doend   macro
        IFNDEF  ?do_level
; ERROR--DOEND without opening DOWHILE statement
        EXITM
        ENDIF
        IF (?do_level LT 10)
; ERROR--DOEND without opening DOWHILE statement
        EXITM
        ENDIF
;; Back step to previous label in sequence
        decsym  ?do_nest,%?do_level
;; Generate jump to beginning-of-loop
        mkjmp   ?do_,%?do_level,?do_nest
;; Step to next label in sequence
        incsym  ?do_nest,%?do_level
;; Generate DOEND label
        mklbl   ?do_,%?do_level,?do_nest
?do_level       =       ?do_level - 1
        endm
;; ** REPEAT ******************** STRUCTURED CONTROL MACRO **
;; Structured REPEAT macro
```

Listing 1-14. cont.

```
;; REPEAT generates the code for a structured REPEAT-UNTIL
repeat macro
        IFNDEF  ?rep_level        ;; set up new level of nesting
?rep_level      =       10
        ELSE
?rep_level      =       ?rep_level + 1
        ENDIF
;; Set up new sequence number for nesting level
        testsym ?rep_nest,%?rep_level
        IF      (?symdef)
        incsym  ?rep_nest,%?rep_level
        ELSE
        zerosym ?rep_nest,%?rep_level
        ENDIF
;; Insert top-of-loop label for jump
        mklbl   ?rep_,%?rep_level,?rep_nest
        endm
;; ** UNTIL ********************** STRUCTURED CONTROL MACRO **
;; Structured UNTIL macro for use with REPEAT
until   macro   p1,p2,p3
        local   iftrue
        IFNDEF  ?rep_level
; ERROR--UNTIL without opening REPEAT statement
        EXITM
        ENDIF
        IF (?rep_level LT 10)
; ERROR--UNTIL without opening REPEAT statement
        EXITM
        ENDIF
;; Insert condition check into code
        cmp     &p1,&p3
;; Jump to UNTIL .TRUE. section of code
        j&p2    iftrue
;; Insert beginning-of-loop jump into code
        mkjmp   ?rep_,%?rep_level,?rep_nest
iftrue:
?rep_level      =       ?rep_level - 1
        endm
;; ** FOR *********************** STRUCTURED CONTROL MACRO **
;; Structured FOR macro. Use of this macro as follows:
;;      FOR     counter,begin,end,dir,step
;;
for     macro   p1,p2,p3,p4,p5
        local   first
        local   iftrue
        IFNDEF  ?for_level        ;; set up new level of nesting
?for_level      =       10
        ELSE
?for_level      =       ?for_level + 1
        ENDIF
;; Set up new sequence number for nesting level
        testsym ?for_nest,%?for_level
        IF      (?symdef)
        incsym  ?for_nest,%?for_level
        ELSE
        zerosym ?for_nest,%?for_level
        ENDIF
```

Listing 1-14. cont.

```
;; Insert counter initialization into code--(bypass 1st step)
        mov     &p1,&p2         ; initialize count
        jmp     first           ; begin FOR loop
;; Insert top-of-loop label for jump
        mklbl   ?for_,%?for_level,?for_nest
;; Insert step calculation into code--check for proper step at same
time
        IFIDN   <p4>,<+>
        inc     &p1             ; increment count
        ELSE
        IFIDN   <p4>,<->
        dec     &p1             ; decrement count
        ELSE
; ERROR--improper step specification in FOR statement
        EXITM
        ENDIF
        ENDIF
first:                          ; check for continuation
;; Insert condition check into code
        cmp     &p1,&p3         ; reached end yet?
;; Jump to FOR_TRUE section of code
        IFIDN   <p4>,<+>
        jl      iftrue          ; no--continue FOR loop
        ELSE                    ;; default to "-" step
        jg      iftrue          ; no--continue FOR loop
        ENDIF
;; Step to next label in sequence
        incsym  ?for_nest,%?for_level
;; Insert end-of-loop jump into code
        mkjmp   ?for_,%?for_level,?for_nest
iftrue:
        endm
;; ** FOREND ******************** STRUCTURED CONTROL MACRO **
;; Structured FOR_END macro for use with FOR
;; FOREND generates the code for a structured FOR Loop.
forend macro
        IFNDEF  ?for_level
; ERROR--FOREND without opening FOR statement
        EXITM
        ENDIF
        IF (?for_level LT 10)
; ERROR--FOREND without opening FOR statement
        EXITM
        ENDIF
;; Back step to previous label in sequence
        decsym  ?for_nest,%?for_level
;; Generate jump to beginning of loop
        mkjmp   ?for_,%?for_level,?for_nest
;; Step to next label in sequence
        incsym  ?for_nest,%?for_level
;; Generate FOREND label
        mklbl   ?for_,%?for_level,?for_nest
?for_level      =       ?for_level - 1
        endm
;; ******************************************************************
```

How the Structured Control Macros Work

The complexity of these macros results from the need to support nested control structures. Consider the example illustrated in Figure 1-1. Each IF-THEN-ELSE structure requires three jump statements with three unique labels. Because we cannot use symbols to store the unique labels generated by the LOCAL directive, we must resort to creating our own labels from counters. This provides the direct control required for the task.

For single levels of nesting, a simple counter would suffice. Note how in Figure 1-1, the IF-THEN-ELSE associated with condition *b* uses the labels in the sequence 3,4,5. This would be easy to implement because the labels are used in the same order in both jump instructions and destination labels. However, a simple counter becomes "confused"

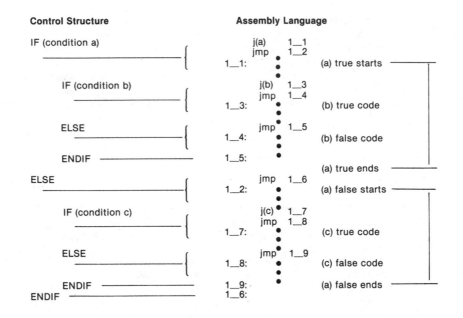

Fig. 1-1.   IF control structure and corresponding assembly language.

as soon as we nest the control structures. A glance at the sequence of labels for all three IF-THEN-ELSE statements shows a distressing lack of order. This problem is overcome by using a separate counter for each nesting level.

Unique labels are ensured by including three pieces of information in each label. First, there is an identifier for the type of structure, such as "?if__," "do__," and "?rep__." The question marks are used to reduce conflicts with user defined symbols or labels. The second piece of information is the nesting level, which is used to distinguish between label number n at one nesting level and label number n at another nesting level. Lastly, the value of the counter is included to provide a unique label for each jump at a particular nesting level.

For comparison, Listing 1-15 shows these unique three part labels as generated by our structured control macros. The first two digits of the number are the nesting level, which starts at 10 so that two digits are always reserved for the nesting level. This prevents level one, counter eleven (1-11) from being confused with level eleven, counter one (11-1).

Listing 1-15. Nested IF-THEN-ELSE Structure

Condensed Source Code

```
        ift     e                       condition (a)
          ift     e                     condition (b)
          ifelse                        "else" for condition (b)
          ifend                         end of condition (b)
        ifelse                          "else" for condition (a)
          ift     e                     condition (c)
          ifelse                        "else" for condition (c)
          ifend                         end of condition (c)
        ifend                           end of condition (a)
```

Expanded Listing

```
        ift     e                       condition (a)
+       je      ??0000
+       jmp     ?if_100
+??0000:
; execute if condition (a) is true
        ift     e                       condition (b)
+       je      ??0001
+       jmp     ?if_110
+??0001:
; execute if condition (b) is true
        ifelse                          "else" for condition (b)
+       jmp     ?if_111
+?if_110:
; execute if condition (b) is not true
        ifend                           end of condition (b)
+?if_111:
        ifelse                          "else" for condition (a)
+       jmp     ?if_101
+?if_100:
; execute if condition (a) is not true
        ift     e                       condition (c)
+       je      ??0002
+       jmp     ?if_112
+??0002:
; execute if condition (c) is true
        ifelse                          "else" for condition (c)
+       jmp     ?if_113
```

Listing 1-15. cont.

```
+?if_112:
; execute if condition (c) is not true
        ifend                               end of condition (c)
+?if_113:
      ifend                                 end of condition (a)
+?if_101:
```

The condensed source corresponds exactly to that presented in Figure 1-1. By taking a close look, you see that the expanded macros created the same structure as the assembly language section in Figure 1-1.

Because of the three part labels, each type of structured control macro has to maintain a set of counters. This set includes a counter symbol to indicate the current nesting level. In order to generalize the task of maintaining these counters, we have created the following macros: *testsym, zerosym, incsym,* and *decsym.* These macros are passed their arguments which they then append to create each counter, consisting of the type identifier ("?if_") and the current nesting level.

Tricks and Warnings

When time comes to create the actual jump instructions or jump destination labels, we use the macros *mkjmp, mkjmp2, mklbl,* and *mklbl2.* The actual labels consist of the type identifier and *numbers.* The only way to evaluate a symbol to its numeric value in MASM is through the percent sign operator (%), which is only valid when applied to an argument of a macro call. We want to evaluate the symbol defined by the two pieces of the counter, such as:

```
mkjmp2 p1,p2,%&p3&p2
```

However, the MASM manual informs us that the ampersand operator (&) may not be used in macro calls. We are thus required to create a temporary variable and use that.

```
??tmp =        &p3&p2
      mkjmp2 p1,p2,%??tmp
```

This brings up an interesting point. The first form, which contains the ampersands in the macro call, does work. Choosing to use a "hidden" feature involves trading off ease of use against future compatibility or even future support. In addition, you must always ask whether an unsupported or illegal feature can be depended on to perform consistently. The resolution of this dilemma is left up to the reader.

The authors used this illegal feature in a program that generates no code but solves the famous "Towers of Hanoi" problem in a recursive manner. In addition to gaining generality, our method of creating counter symbols from their various parts allows creation of new counters as needed. These counters must be initialized before use, or the first attempt to increment or decrement them results in a **Symbol is not defined** error. Using the IFDEF conditional operator, a check is made to see whether initialization is required on each use of a symbol.

Initialization brings up yet another warning associated with MASM. As we have stated, MASM is a two pass assembler that defines symbols on the first pass and uses them on the second. This implies that symbol definitions are preserved from pass one to pass two. Thus, when MASM begins its second pass, all of the counters from pass one are defined already and contain their last value. If the symbols are not reinitialized at the beginning of the second pass, a phase error results because the starting counter values are different.

Now, IFDEF is required to initialize the symbols on the first pass because we have no idea just how many counters we will require, but the use of IFDEF is insufficient for the second pass. We have solved this problem by creating the *?p2sw* ... symbols, which are checked on the second pass to see whether the counters must be reset to their zero values. The name is derived from *Phase 2 SWitch*. This checking process also provides an opportunity to check that the nesting levels are at the outermost level, indicating that the IF-IFEND, DOWHILE-DOEND, etc., are properly paired.

Listing 1-16 contains sample expansions for the structured control macros defined above. As you can see, we have suppressed those portions of the expansion that do not produce code or jump labels. If you want to see these macros' workings in more detail, use the .LALL directive. Use only a short example because many steps are involved in processing these macros. The number of steps also explains why the time required to assemble a program increases. Don't expect fast assemblies with these macros, just fast coding.

Listing 1-16.   Expanded Use of Structured Control Macros

```
;
; START OF CODE
;
       ift      e
+                je      ??0003
+                jmp     ?if_102
```

Listing 1-16. cont.

```
+           ??0003:
 ;  execute if true
            ifelse
+                   jmp         ?if_103
+           ?if_102:
 ;  execute if not true
            ifend
+           ?if_103:
 ;  ------------------------------------------------------
            dowhile ax,[le],bx
+           ?do_100:
+                   cmp         ax,bx
+                   jle         ??0004
+                   jmp         ?do_101
+           ??0004:
 ;  execute while ax [le] bx
            doexit
+                   jmp         ?do_101
 ;  break out of code
            doend
+                   jmp         ?do_100
+           ?do_101:
 ;  ------------------------------------------------------
            repeat
+           ?rep_100:
 ;  execute until condition met
            until   ax,[e],bx
+                   cmp         ax,bx
+                   je          ??0005
+                   jmp         ?rep_100
+           ??0005:
 ;  ------------------------------------------------------
            for     ax,10,20,+
+                   mov         ax,10       ; initialize count
                    jmp         ??0006      ; begin FOR loop
+           ?for_100:
+                   inc         ax          ; increment count
+           ??0006:                         ; check for continuation
+                   cmp         ax,20       ; reached end yet?
+                   jl          ??0007      ; no-continue FOR loop
+                   jmp         ?for_101
+           ??0007:
 ;  execute for ax = 10 to 20 by 2's
            forend
+                   jmp         ?for_100
+           ?for_101:
```

The Pseudo *case* Macro

The last macro that we present in this chapter is the pseudo *case* macro, shown in Listing 1-17. Because the macro must have "foreknowledge" of the structures it supports, we don't consider this a structured control statement. Our case macro functions more like a dispatch block, something like FORTRAN's computed GOTO.

Listing 1-17.   Pseudo *case* Macro Definition

```
case    macro    key,case_list,jmp_labels
        ??tmp_1 = 0
        irp      match,<&case_list>        ;; sequence through cases
        ??tmp_1 = ??tmp_1 + 1              ;; set index number
        cmp      key,&&match               ; case match?
        ??tmp_2 = 0
        irp      retl,<&jmp_labels>        ;; sequence through jumps
        ??tmp_2 = ??tmp_2 + 1             ;; ... until index matches
        if       (??tmp_1 eq ??tmp_2)
        je       &&&retl                   ; yes!
        exitm
        endif
        endm
        endm
        endm
```

This macro does provide a good example of the ability to parse two lists simultaneously. The outer loop, *irp match,<&case_list>*, sequences through the elements in the case list, whereas the inner loop, *irp retl,<&jmp_labels>*, selects the corresponding jump label. This technique may also be used to implement substitution macros.

In substitution macros, the outer loop sequences through elements of a list and looks for a match. Once a match is found, say, at the xth element, the macro enters the inner loop and sequences to the xth element of that list. One possible use of this would be to implement a jump-on-not-condition macro where the selected jump would be replaced by its opposite. Once again, remember that additional ampersands are required in nested macro blocks.

The expansion of the *case* macro in Listing 1-18 gives the expected results. The programmer is responsible for ensuring that the same number of elements appears in each list. Otherwise, an invalid control structure could be created.

Listing 1-18.   Pseudo *case* Macro Expansion

```
        case    al,<'A','B','C','D'>,<subA,subB,subC,subD>
+       cmp     al,'A'          ; case match?
+       je      subA            ; yes!
+       cmp     al,'B'          ; case match?
+       je      subB            ; yes!
+       cmp     al,'C'          ; case match?
```

Listing 1-18. cont.

```
+                  je      subC          ; yes!
+                  cmp     al,'D'        ; case match?
+                  je      subD          ; yes!
                   jmp     default
subA:
                   jmp     merge
subB:
                   jmp     merge
subC:
                   jmp     merge
subD:
                   jmp     merge
default:
merge:
```

Summary

Our presentation of the world of MASM macros and conditional assembly is completed. From the examples contained in this chapter, you have gained a feel for the design and use of the usually frustrating, often complex, but ultimately rewarding features of the Microsoft Macro Assembler.

In this chapter, we have presented a variety of examples of each feature, from the simple to the complex, so that some measure of the usefulness of these features has been conveyed. By using these examples and doing some experimentation on your own, you can define the boundary between the possible and the impossible in the MASM assembler.

But you shouldn't lose sight of the reason for exploring macros and conditional assembly. We contend that the proper use of these features can help you program in a more organized manner, thus enhancing the readability and reliability of your programs and reducing the amount of time you spend debugging your programs. We hope that the examples presented, along with friendly tips, comments, and some warnings, have given you a sense of how to apply these two features to advance your programming skills.

Structured Programming 2: The Design and Implementation of Modular Programs

Chapter 2

The discussion in Chapter 1 focused on the tools of structured programming as they can be applied to the MASM environment. In Chapter 2, we present the methods of structured programming as they apply to MS-DOS and the 8086/8088.

Our presentation consists of two separate yet interrelated topics. These topics deal with the design of modular programs in assembly language and with the implementation of that design using MASM, macros, and whatever else may be at hand. Both these topics affect the writeability, readability, reliability, and maintainability of your programs. In short, these methods, separately and together, can be used to structure your programs to produce better programs.

Principles of Modular Programming

When impartial analysis is made of assembly language programs, the most glaring deficiency usually discovered is lack of recognizable structure. Despite the best intentions of most assembly language programmers, their programs tend to be intricately connected, unwieldy conglomerations of code that require almost divine insight to fully understand. This statement is not intended as a slight upon these dedicated people. The lack of structure is the result of their having to simultaneously deal with a large number of details. There are two directions in which to approach this problem. One is to simplify the code, replacing long complicated instruction sequences with more understandable structures. The techniques developed in Chapter 1 go a long way toward relieving the burden of detail implicit in assembly language programming. However, the programmer is still left to cope with a sometimes staggering number of functional details.

The way out of this rat's maze is to apply the same techniques that rescued higher level languages a decade ago. The concepts of decomposition and modular design should be applied to assembly language programming. These concepts, referred to under the collective heading of *structured design,* allow the programmer to segment the total programming task so that he or she need only deal with a manageable number of details at a time. This is the topic for our next discussion.

Designing Options

Modular design and "decomposition" refer to the process of breaking up a large problem into smaller, more manageable, subproblems. The first design step is deciding where to draw the lines between these subproblems.

In order to derive the maximum benefits from the use of modular programming each subproblem or *module* must have a single entry and a single exit. The flow of control in a program then may be readily traced. At any point in the module it should be possible to look at the module's entry point and say, "I know the values of registers X, Y, and Z at this point because they are specified as ...," then trace the operation of the module without worrying about rogue program flows intruding. The single exit ensures that when a module is invoked, the flow of control returns to the point of invocation. For this reason, modular programs are nearly always implemented with a CALL-RET structure.

Using multiple RET statements in a module does not violate this rule of single exit because all the RET instructions return to the same point. Similarly, jumping to a common RET at the end of a module does not add to the structure of the module but only adds code and complexity. On the other hand, jumping into or out of a module is strictly against the rules, for it negates the greatest advantage of modular programming: clean, maintainable program structure.

There is an exception to the rule of not jumping into a module. This arises when jump tables are used to decide the flow of control within a program. A jump table is used by pushing a return address of the stack, calculating the index of the desired jump address in the table, and performing a jump through memory. An example of this technique appears in the device driver program listings given in Chapter 5.

When practicing modular decomposition, you will find that a number of alternatives present themselves. Before we are able to intelligently choose, we must know the alternatives. The goal is to choose among alternatives those choices that give the most workable design.

Designing for Functional Separation

When approaching a problem in the design stage, the first alternative chosen should be functional decomposition, that is, the breaking up of a problem into small, manageable, functional units where each unit performs a complete, readily identifiable, task.

There are many ways of determining what should be contained in a task. Some common examples are units that perform an explicit function, such as obtaining the square root of a number; units which perform all operations relating to a specific device, such as disk or keyboard I/O; units which perform a common group of actions at a specific time, such as initializing data areas; and units which are related in sequence or their use of common data elements, such as reading and converting keyboard data to integers.

In today's world of high-level language programming value judgments often are made about which is the best method to use for segmenting programs. In assembly language programming, we usually cannot afford to be so critical. Each of the methods listed above gives at least a starting point for breaking up the problem. Often, you find that some modules are related by one set of criteria and other modules by another set. As long as each module encompasses a section of code that can be readily understood (usually of two pages or less), you're off to a great start.

Designing To Minimize the Number of Parameters Passed

Sometimes, you find that after defining the modules for your program, you have created something unwieldy. This is often the case when a module requires access to an extensive amount of data in order to accomplish its task. This might easily occur if you're writing an integrated package that supports many options. The module must accept many different variables to know the state of the program at a given time. If this happens and you find yourself with a module that accepts a large number of parameters, you must then ask two questions.

First, are you attempting to perform more than one function in that module? Does the module require parameters that are used in unrelated sections of the module? If either applies, you must segment the module again. Second, are you cutting across functional lines? Are the calling module and the called module actually part of the same function? If so, put them together even if the result looks too large. Try to segment them again in a different way.

Segmenting modules across functional lines often occurs when the programmer notices that two sections of code are identical or strongly similar. The programmer then attempts to create from them a single module. This is not modular programming because the resulting module has no functional cohesion.

If you find that you can do nothing to avoid using many common data references or passing scores of parameters, go back to the original design and check whether you have specified the problem correctly.

Designing To Minimize the Number of Calls Needed

Speed Optimization

One of the great advantages of modular programming is that the main level program can often be constructed to read as a sequence of procedure calls. This enhances understanding of the program because the reader can become familiar with its basic flow and operation after reading only a page or two of code. However, this feature can also have drawbacks. One of the most overquoted statistics of programming is that typical programs spend 90 percent of their execution time in 10 percent of the code. The implications are that if this 10 percent contains a large number of chained procedure calls, the amount of time spent in program flow control can be a handicap to a program with severe time constraints.

Before giving up on modularizing your programs, examine just what these time-related statements mean. First, most programs spend the majority of execution time waiting for something to be entered from the keyboard. Once a key has been typed, the required functions are not usually time-consuming in a way that humans think of time. The difference between 100 microseconds and 100 milliseconds (a 1000 times difference) is not going to be noticeable to the average user.

Contrary to some beliefs, the actual mechanism of the CALL-RET pair is not overly time-consuming. When compared to the jump instructions, the CALL takes about 30 percent to 50 percent longer and the RET averages 1 cycle longer. Only when the overhead of pushing parameters, saving registers, and what is euphemistically called *housekeeping* is considered do modular programs begin to look slow by comparison. In addition, because the modules of a modular program are usually more general than their unstructured counterparts, modules may use memory or stack references with greater frequency. The additional time required by effective address calculations may result in the body of the module executing more slowly than a linearly coded specific routine.

The advantages of housekeeping and generality are that the module may be used virtually anywhere in the program. When writing non-modular programs, you may spend hours attempting to discover whether a register is in use, or worse, just what its contents are supposed to be. In modular programming, the programmer is not concerned with what registers are currently in use as long as the called module takes its parameters off the stack and saves the entire register set on entry. With these kinds of advantages, it makes sense to use these modular techniques initially to speed coding, then rework the program to remove bottlenecks.

For those areas that are speed sensitive, the best recommendation is to selectively mainline the code. If a module is referenced only in the speed sensitive section of the code, the module may be included "inline" within the calling module. If other sections use the module, it may be copied to the calling module and fit into place. Because the main calling module grows larger, add comments that mark the included module as a block of its own. A future reader may then read the comments to determine the module's function and skip past it to resume reading the main code.

Rules for Modularization

We can summarize the more notable concepts of modular programming in the following rules:

- Divide and conquer. Divide the problem into smaller functional tasks, each one independent of the others except for its necessary parameters.

- Single entry-single exit. The module should have only one entry point where all calls begin. It should return control to the point in program flow where control was invoked. (The return address may be modified as discussed in the section on parameter passing below.)

- KISS—keep it sweet & simple. Avoid complexity in coding. Handle complex logic in a well documented way that explains each step and why it was designed that way.

- Hide details. Confine the details of register usage, local data structure, etc., to the internals of the modules. Don't let a module's implementation spill over into the rest of the program.

- If a module uses a particular variable, make that variable a documented parameter. Document all effects that a module has on global data.

- Plan for error detection and the actions to be taken if errors occur. Responsibility for *exception processing,* as it is known, must be assigned to the individual modules. Normally, lower level modules report errors to the calling module. The responsibility for decisions about those errors normally is reserved to the upper level modules.

References

What we have presented here has been a quick overview of the concepts of structured programming and modular design. We have neither the space nor the inclination to provide a full treatment of the subject and sincerely doubt that we could do justice to it in less than a full book. A wealth of literature is available. For those whose goal is to be a software professional, purchase some of these books and read them. The following titles reflect a small sample of the excellent professional level works published today.

DeMarco, T. *Structured Analysis and System Specification.* New York: Yourdon, 1978.

Kane, G., Hawkins, D. and Leventhal, L. *68000 Assembly Language Programming,* Berkeley: Osborne/McGraw-Hill, 1981.

Tausworthe, R.C. *Standardized Development of Computer Software.* Part I. Englewood Cliffs, N.J.: Prentice-Hall, 1977.

Yourdon, E.U. and Constantine, L.L. *Structured Design.* Englewood Cliffs, N.J.: Prentice-Hall, 1977.

Yourdon, E.U. *Techniques of Program Structure and Design.* Englewood Cliffs, N.J.: Prentice-Hall, 1975.

Implementing Modular Programs in Assembly Language

Parameter Passing Techniques

To this point, we have been speaking in the abstract about modules, parameter passing, and other such terms. Now is the time to begin relating this information to the concrete world of MS-DOS, MASM, and 8086 assembly language.

Modules in the MASM environment are best handled by the MASM PROC directive. We have been using this all along as a method of defining the entry and exit points of the program. We now extend its use to define the boundaries of the individual modules. PROC is used by MASM to define a label in the code and to give that label either a *near* or *far* attribute. This attribute is used both to generate the correct type of CALL instruction and the correct type of RET instruction. A detailed presentation of these types of instructions is given in the section on *Types of Coding.* What we are concerned with at this point is that the PROC directive is a convenient way to denote a block of code with a single unique entry and constant exit that forms the basis of the module.

Definition of *Parameter, Argument, Variable,* and *Constant*

We have been tossing the words *parameter, argument,* and *variable* around like so many ping-pong balls. For the most part they have had interchangeable meanings. Now we need to start drawing some distinctions, although some undoubtedly call it *splitting hairs.* After this chapter, we can all go back to our slothful ways, but for the moment, we need to be clear headed and clear thinking.

The dictionary sense of *parameter* is "a characteristic element." In common use, *parameter* is a reference to any piece of data used by a module that is not totally contained within that module. Why the added words, *reference to*? Because a parameter is not the data itself nor even an address of the data. Rather a parameter is a place holder (the characteristic element). For example, consider the equation $Y + 1$. No module can be written to evaluate that equation because Y is not a value! Y is a parameter that is replaced by an actual value when it is time to evaluate it. The actual value is called an *argument.*

We still have not defined *variables.* Strictly speaking, variables are register or memory locations that hold a piece of changeable data. In the example above, Y is also a variable because it changes to fit the required circumstances. Thus parameters are automatically variables (but not vice versa).

To recap, if a data object can be modified, it is a variable. If that variable is required for a module to perform its task, it's also a parameter. The argument is the actual value that the variable takes on when the module is invoked.

We also need to consider the special case of constants. A *constant* is a data object whose value never changes. In assembly language, constants can appear in two ways. They may be part of the immediate data for an instruction (as in "mov al,4"), or they can be located in memory like other data. When constants are placed in memory they differ from variables solely because they are only read, never written.

Can a parameter also be a constant? If the constant is of the memory type, unequivocally yes. But you encounter a problem when you try to use immediate data constants as parameters. Immediate data may not be passed by itself to a subroutine. Immediate data must be contained in something, either a register, memory location, or the stack. In higher level languages, the compiler takes care of converting constants to locations. In assembly language you have to do it yourself.

Parameters and Modules

So we have determined that a parameter is any data that a module requires to accomplish its task, which is located outside the module. We have also determined that parameters are by definition variables. This brings up the second great strength of modules. Because the inputs to a module are variables, they may be changed to fit the specific case at hand. This gives great generality to modules, enabling them to be reused in many places and in many programs.

In reality, parameters are an optional component of modular programming. You can have a module that accepts no outside parameters and operates solely on internal data. A simple routine to beep the console would have no parameters. A more common example is a simple routine to read numbers from the keyboard. Although the number reading routine would return a value, that routine would not necessarily need any arguments passed to it.

In combination, requiring input parameters and producing output values form four types of modules. These are

1. modules that accept no inputs and produce no outputs

2. modules that accept inputs and produce no outputs

3. modules that accept no inputs and produce outputs

4. modules that accept inputs and produce outputs

We typically call the first two types, which produce no output data, *subroutines* and the last two types, which do produce output data, *functions*. Note that no distinction is made as to whether they require input parameters, although as a programmer, you are aware of the difference.

Parameter Passing Options #1

For those routines, be they subroutines or functions, that accept input parameters, the problem of passing data to them must be resolved. When programming in a high-level language, the programmer typically has no choice in the matter. In assembly language, many options exist. We have presented all options for consideration, although the use of some is strongly discouraged.

Passing through Registers

The most common method for passing data in assembly language programming is via the registers. Instant accessibility and high speed makes them prime candidates for this task, for no matter what the program environment, registers are always an opcode away. Nearly all MS-DOS function calls pass their data in this manner. Short assembly language routines that interface to MS-DOS often use the same registers to manipulate data as those required by the MS-DOS functions they call. It makes sense to create a parameter in the same register that MS-DOS expects it.

One disadvantage of this method is that there are a limited number of registers. If you have a routine that requires more variables than you have registers, you're in trouble. Newer microprocessors have less restrictions than older ones, but the number of registers is still finite. In addition, if you ever think of "porting" your code, that is, moving it from one type of processor to another, that the two processors share the same register set is very unlikely. You could end up redesigning all the module interfaces.

Another drawback is that you must continually keep track of what use each register is put to. This game of "who's on first" can tire even the most dedicated bit pusher. Especially frustrating is the case when you decide that register X is free and code your module accordingly. Later you decide you can use the same module in another place, only register X is no longer free. So PUSH goes X, in goes the value, the call is made, and POP goes X. Whoops, X contained a returned value. Let's see, what's free now? And so it goes.

A practical limitation of passing parameters in registers is that the information is usually limited to 16 bits, the size of the largest register. Because most variables tend to be either bytes or words, size isn't a big problem. When the data to be passed exceeds the size of a register, the calling routine may pass the address of the data instead. Of course, the called routine must know what type of data is being pointed to in order to use it properly. MS-DOS function calls use this pass-by-address technique whenever they require large amounts of data.

Passing through Common

The next choice for most programmers is using a prearranged data area. We use *prearranged* in the sense that both the calling and called routine have "agreed" that their data is passed in some area of general memory. Routine A knows to put last month's receipts in the area labeled FOO, and routine B knows to go look for them in FOO. FOO is then known as a *common area.*

Passing through common has at least one thing going for it. Within the physical limits of your computer, you can put as much data as you want into memory. Passing through common puts an end to the shell game of free registers and allows data of any size to be passed, from one byte to kilobyte buffers.

In addition, passing through common makes the data available to any module that needs it. This is a great advantage when the data in question is being passed from a high-level module through many intervening modules to a low-level module. Each module doesn't have to handle data that it does not use.

On the negative side, depending on common memory can restrict the generality and reusability of the modules. Consider a series of modules designed to read and write files. If the modules are coded to use a common block of memory for a data buffer, having two files open at the same time can be a problem. If the program were designed to do a compare, the program would have to copy one set of data from the buffer into a storage area to prevent the buffer from being overwritten. Granted, the example is simplistic, but we trust that the implications are clear.

The last drawback to common memory results from one of its strengths. Because the area is available to any module, it is in a way "fair game." Protecting the data from accidental destruction is nearly impossible. This is not normally a great risk (unless program errors are common) but becomes a factor in the consideration of reentrant programming (covered in a subsequent section, *Types of Coding*).

Passing through Program Memory

Passing through program memory is a variant of passing data through common data memory. The differences are one, the data resides in program space (code segment); and two, the location of the data is determined by the CALL instruction because the data is located directly after the call.

The called routine takes the return address off the stack, uses that as a pointer to the memory area, adds the size of the memory area to the return address, and places it back on the stack. When the routine returns to the calling program, the return address is the first location after the data area.

This seems convenient until we consider that the 8086 is specifically designed for separate code and data areas. Passing through program memory requires that the code segment and the data segment be set to the same value, as the return address is code segment relative.

The worst problem with this method of passing data is that it requires manipulation of the stack in what comes very close to being self-modifying code. One rule that you should always remember is *never, never modify program memory!* If you succumb to the temptation, you find that your program becomes nearly impossible to debug without expensive hardware logic analyzers.

Passing on the Stack

The method used by most high-level languages for implementing procedure calls is passing the data on the stack. In this method all required parameters are pushed onto the stack before the call is made. After the call is made, the calling routine accesses the data without removing it. The designers of the 8086 family encouraged this method by providing the BP (base pointer) register. The BP has the wonderful feature of addressing its operands relative to the stack segment. This means that by setting the value of the BP to the proper location the contents of the stack may be addressed using indexed addressing.

What is the proper location to load into the BP? This is not the SP (stack pointer) itself because the SP is pointing to the return address on the stack. The data actually starts at either location SP + 2 or location SP + 4. Why plus two or plus four? Because for NEAR procedure calls, the processor stores only the current offset (instruction pointer) on the stack (2 bytes), whereas for FAR procedure calls, the processor stores the offset and the code segment on the stack (4 bytes). The called routine may be coded to start access at the proper location (depending on the type of routine) by using the following addressing:

```
NEAR                           FAR
mov bp,sp                      mov bp,sp
mov <1st arg>,[bp+2]           mov <1st arg>,[bp+4]
:                              :
:                              :
```

Note that if the contents of the BP must be saved, you must push the BP on the stack also, changing the addressing to BP + 4 for near calls or BP + 6 for far calls. However, these decisions can be avoided if the value of the BP is pushed before the parameters are pushed onto the stack. After the parameters are on the stack, the value of the stack pointer may be copied to the base pointer before the call. The called routine thus starts executing with the BP already set to the proper value.

When the called routine returns, the original parameters must be removed from the stack. This can be done by the called routine, with a RET *n* instruction or by the calling routine through POPping the parameters or incrementing the stack pointer. The example in Listing 2-1 uses RET *n*. After the stack has been cleaned up (by either method), the calling routine POPs the value of the base pointer back to the BP. Remember that the value of "n" used in the RET *n* instruction is equal to the number of parameters pushed times two because each parameter occupies two bytes and the RET *n* instruction adds "n" directly to the stack pointer.

Listing 2-1.　Passing Parameters on the Stack

The Calling Procedure

```
      :       :
push    bp               ; save current base pointer
push    <argument 1>     ; place last parameter on stack
      :       :              :
push    <argument N>     ; place 1st parameter on stack
mov     bp,sp            ; set up pointer to arguments
call    <myproc>         ; invoke procedure
pop     bp               ; restore value of base pointer
      :       :
```

The Called Procedure

```
<myproc> proc near               ; near or far, doesn't matter
       mov    <dummy 1>,[bp]    ; get 1st parameter
       mov    <dummy 2>,2[bp]   ; get 2nd parameter
        :       :                  :
       mov    <dummy N>,2N[bp]; get last parameter
        :       :                  :
       ret    2N               ; return--removing parameters
<myproc> endp
```

This seems like a lot of extra coding, what with PUSHes, MOVes, POPs, etc., in place of a simple call. This is one place to put our knowledge of macros to use and write a simple macro to perform these chores. The macros in Listing 2-2 help the calling program maintain the stack during parameter passing. Similarly, the macros in Listing 2-3 assist the called program in accessing and returning parameters on the stack. All registers used in these macros must be word length because the PUSH and POP instructions do not operate on 8-bit registers.

Listing 2-2.　CALLS & FCALLS Macros for Parameters on the Stack

```
;; **** PUSH_IM Macro: Push Immediate Data through BP register
push_im MACRO     arg
        mov     cs:mem_16,&arg
        push    cs:mem_16
        ENDM

;; **** CALL SUBROUTINE Macro:   calls    name,<arg1,arg2,...>
calls   MACRO     routine_name,arg_list
?count  =         0
        IRP       argn,<&arg_list>
        push      &&argn                 ; push parameters
?count  =         ?count + 1
        ENDM
        push_im %?count                  ; push number of parameters
        call    &routine_name            ; call routine
```

Listing 2-2. cont.

```
        add     sp,2*(1+?count) ; clear stack
        ENDM
;; **** CALL FUNCTION Macro: fcalls name,<arg1,arg2,...>,ret
fcalls  MACRO   routine_name,arg_list,return_val
?count  =       0
        IRP     argn,<&arg_list>
        push    &&argn          ; push parameters
?count  =       ?count + 1
        ENDM
        push_im %?count          ; push number of parameters
        call    &routine_name    ; call routine
        pop     &return_val      ; get returned value
        IF      ?count           ;; If nonzero ...
        add     sp,2*?count      ; clear stack
        ENDIF
        ENDM
```

**Listing 2-3.   ACCEPT, RET__VAL & CRET Macros for Taking
and Returning Parameters on the Stack**

```
;; **** RET_VAL Macro: ret_val register
ret_val MACRO   return_value
        mov     [bp+4],return_value      ; return word result
        ENDM
;; **** ACCEPT Macro:   pnum,<reg1,reg2,...>
accept  MACRO   reg_list
        push    bp              ; save base pointer
        mov     bp,sp           ; set BP to access parameters
        mov     &pnum,[bp+4]    ; get number of parameters
?count  =       0
        IRP     reg,<&reg_list>
?count  =       ?count + 1
        push    &&reg           ; save register for new value
        mov     &&reg,[bp+4+?count*2]    ; get parameters
        ENDM
        ENDM
;; **** CRET    Macro: <reg1,reg2,...>
cret    MACRO   reg_list
        IRP     reg,<&reg_list>
        pop     &&reg           ; restore the saved registers
        ENDM
        pop     bp              ; restore base pointer
        ret                     ; return from program
        ENDM
```

The *push__im* macro allows the 8086/8088 user to push immediate
data on the stack. To use the macro, you must first define somewhere in
the code segment the word location "mem__16." Although using a mem-

ory location to transfer immediate data to the stack is slower and takes more code, doing so allows more freedom of register use.

In the *calls* and *fcalls* macros, the symbol "?count" is used to inform the called routine of the number of parameters provided and to keep track of the number of bytes pushed on the stack for use in clearing the stack after the call. If the target, or called, routine already "knows" how many parameters are being passed to it (which is usually the case), these macros may be modified to dispense with pushing and clearing the parameter count. Note that the parameter count also serves as a way of returning a value for function calls (the *fcalls* and *ret_val* macros).

The *ret_val* macro is for use with the *fcalls* macro and replaces the parameter count pushed on the stack by *fcalls* with a 16-bit value to be returned to the caller.

The target routine macro *accept* works with either *calls* or *fcalls* to transfer the parameters from the stack to registers. This macro saves the registers it uses as it progresses. *?count* is used here to determine the offset of the next parameter within the stack. Because *accept* works its way up the stack (increasing offsets), this macro removes the parameters from the stack in the reverse order from which they were pushed! Note also that both *accept* and *ret_val* expect a NEAR call because they only allow for a two-byte return address.

The last target macro *cret* restores the registers that were saved by *accept*. Because POPs must be in reverse order from PUSHes, the argument list for *cret* must be in reverse order from that in *accept*. The last action *cret* takes before RET restores the base pointer saved by *accept*.

These macros are presented more as examples than as working copies and can be enhanced to provide more general coverage. For example, the parameter push, *push &&argn*, can be replaced with the more general *push_op* macro from Chapter 1 to handle immediate data parameters. A limitation of the current version is that the "mov [bp + 4],return_value" instruction in macro *ret_val* cannot return memory variables on the stack because the 8086 family does not support a memory-to-memory move instruction. This macro could be enhanced to recognize a memory-to-memory move and generate a transfer through an intermediate register.

For the called routine, MASM provides some tools to simplify accessing the data on the stack. By defining a *structure* that represents the data on the stack and aligning the base pointer (BP) with the beginning of the structure, data on the stack may be accessed symbolically, that is, by name. This helps prevent disastrous coding errors, which result from specifying an incorrect offset. Listing 2-4 demonstrates the use of the MASM STRUC directive in this context.

Listing 2-4.   Accessing the STACK Symbolically with the STRUC Directive

The Called Procedure

```
<myproc> proc near              ; procedure entry
stack_data      struc           ; define the ''template''
param_N dw      ?               ; last parameter pushed
   :     :      :                  :        :
param_2 dw      ?               ; 2nd parameter pushed
param_1 dw      ?               ; 1st parameter pushed
stack_data      ends
base    equ     [bp+4]          ; define structure base as BP+4
        push    bp              ; save old base pointer
        mov     bp,sp           ; point to stack
        mov     <dummy 1>,base.param_1    ; get 1st parameter
        mov     <dummy 2>,base.param_2    ; get 2nd parameter
         :       :                  :
        mov     <dummy N>,base.param_N ; get last parameter
         :       :                  :
        ret     (Nx2)           ; return--removing parameters
<myproc> endp
```

If this structure is used with a FAR procedure, *base* should be defined as [*bp* + *6*]. If this structure is used with an interrupt routine, *base* should be set to [*bp* + *8*]. Each case reflects the fact that *base* must account for the BP pushed on the stack and the proper number of return arguments.

Listings 2-1 and 2-4 demonstrate a peculiar property of using the stack for passing parameters. Whatever goes on the stack comes off it in reverse order. Listing 2-1 lists the order of the parameters as they are removed so that the "first" parameter is pushed last. In Listing 2-4, we have used the structure to correct this for readability so that the first parameter pushed is called *param__1*.

The STRUC directive does not add any code to the finished program. This directive only defines offsets that are used with the BP to ease the task of referring to parameters. In all other ways, STRUC is identical to Listing 2-1.

The stack also provides a convenient place to store returned values, but we delay discussion of that topic until we have discussed the differences between Functions and Subroutines, which we do in following sections of this chapter.

Parameter Passing Options #1 Summary
There are three proper ways to pass data to modules. These methods are

1. passing through registers—few number of parameters allowed; best for simple interfaces and for exception handling or returning values

2. passing through common—limited flexibility and generality but has the advantage of making the data available to all modules

3. passing on the stack—preferred method for handling data; excels in generality (reusable modules) and production of modular code; necessary for interfacing with most high-level languages; demonstrates that you're a member of the "in" crowd.

Additionally, when data is passed by any method other than common, each module must accept as parameters the data it needs not only for itself but for any modules that it calls in turn. This can sometimes lead to large parameter lists for upper level modules.

In actual use, you probably want to use a combination of these techniques (with the exception of passing data in program memory).

Parameter Passing Options #2

Once a decision on how to pass the parameters has been made, you must answer the question of what form of argument to use. You remember that argument is what we have decided to call the value that is given to the parameter. This value may be either the data itself or the address of the data.

Pass by Value
Most parameter passing in assembly language is done with *pass by value*. In this method, the actual data (its value) is passed to the calling routine. The target routine receives a number, either stored in a register or pushed onto the stack.

Data that is stored in common memory is something of a special case. In one sense, it is passed by address because the calling and called routine access the data by means of a common address. In another sense, the data in the common area may be either values or addresses, and the problem is simplified by basing the decision on the nature of the data in the common block. If the data is a value, data is passing by value. If it is an address, data is passing by address.

If parameters consisting of immediate data are to be passed on the stack, users of the 8086 or 8088 face some additional effort when transferring the value to the stack. Users of the iAPX188, iAPX186, or iAPX286 processors can use the PUSH < immediate > instruction, but for users of the older processors, the data must be transferred to the stack through an intermediate register. The *push_im* macro presented in Chapter 1 could be used, but its complexity is not called for in this application. If the calling procedure shown in Listing 2-1 is used, the BP register is available for transferring immediate data to the stack. Any pushes of immediate data may be accomplished with two lines of assembly code:

```
mov     bp,<immediate data>
push    bp
```

Passing parameters by value inherits the limitations of register and stack passing—restriction of the value to 16 bits. Indeed, eight-bit data may not be pushed onto the stack at all. There are ways around this, of course, of which the *push_op* macro from Chapter 1 is one example. Data belonging to large structures may be pushed a word at a time, but unless the called routine must receive its parameters from the stack, to pass the address of the data is much easier.

Pass by Address
In *pass by address,* the called routine receives only the address of the data. All accesses to the data are made using this address. There are a number of immediate advantages. One, unless the data resides in a different segment all addresses may be contained in one 16-bit value, which is convenient for using registers or the stack. Two, the routine becomes completely general because specifying a different address yields a new set of data. Three, the data may be directly manipulated by the called procedure to return a value to the calling routine in the same location that contained the original value.

Sometimes a problem is encountered if the values to be passed are not located in memory (that is, immediate data). For this case (or if you find it simply inconvenient to push all the required addresses onto the stack) a type of hybrid parameter can be used: the argument block.

The *argument* or *parameter block* is a special form of pass by address. In this case, the required arguments are contained in a contiguous piece of memory. However, unlike passing through common, the called procedure has no implicit knowledge of this block. When the procedure is called, it is passed the address of this block as a parameter. It still may not be convenient to place all the required arguments into the block, but this does avoid the necessity of pushing all those values onto the stack. If the block already exists for another purpose, passing parameters through an argument block makes a lot of sense.

Protecting the Integrity of Passed Data

There is another aspect of the *pass by ...* option that is equally as important as questions of ease of use. This aspect relates to the integrity of the data or its protection from unintentional change or corruption.

In typical use, data that is passed by value is a copy of the actual data. As such, the called routine may manipulate the data in any way without changing the data in the calling routine. On the other hand, if the called routine receives the address of the data, that routine may then alter the data, possibly changing the operation of the calling routine. Data that is passed by value is then considered to be protected, whereas data that is passed by address is considered to be at risk.

Surprisingly, variables that are passed in a register are sometimes considered to be passed by address because registers are simply specialized addresses in hardware. This distinction is made because the data in the register is at risk if the subroutine or function alters the data in the register and that alteration has an effect on the main routine.

There are no hard and fast rules regarding the degree of exposure of the data. Concepts such as pass by value and pass by address may help us to evaluate the situation, but the actual decisions of the type of passing to use depend on how valuable the data is to the calling routine (the degree of risk) and whether the called routine has access to the original data. This in turn determines how much protection is required for that data.

Functions versus Subroutines

It is often desirable for the called routine to return new data to the caller. As indicated earlier, those routines that return values are called *functions*; those that don't, *subroutines*. In high-level languages, functions are usually restricted to returning only one value. Any other information that must be returned to the calling procedure is passed back by modifying one or more of the parameters. In assembly language no such restrictions apply. Let's examine the options.

Returning Values in Registers

Once again, the simplest way to return a value is in a register. As with passing parameters, this option can be limited by the number of available registers and by the size of the data to be returned. On the positive side, the data is readily accessible and can be tested or manipulated quite easily.

For frequently called functions, returning values in the registers makes sense. It requires no special set up and no anticipation of memory buffers or such. Most MS-DOS functions return their values this way. However, if all functions in a program returned their data via the registers you would be faced with a major bookkeeping and shuffling task. In addition, because the registers are where most computations take place, there is fierce competition for their use.

Rather, the registers should be used for those small, frequently called routines that return only a few values and for routines whose returned value must undergo immediate calculations. A function to read character values for transformation into a number would be one example of the later case.

Returning Values in Common

When a routine returns values in common, no one thinks of it as a function. Nevertheless, this "side effect" method provides a reasonably simple means for returning large amounts of data. We call it a side effect method because the transfer operation is not readily apparent from reading the "call" section of the calling routine and appears to take place as an incidental result of the procedure. Because this is not readily apparent from the call, clear documentation must be added describing what values are returned and why.

However, if the address of the common area is instead passed in a parameter in either a register or the stack, the fact that returned values are expected in that particular memory area is made more apparent to the reader. In addition, the benefits of generality are gained because the procedure may be directed to return its values in any buffer location.

Returning Values on the Stack

The last method of returning values is to place them in the stack (as opposed to on the stack). This operation requires use of the BP to address the stack (in the same manner as passing parameters on the stack). To return a value, the value is loaded onto the stack in one of the memory locations above the return address. If the procedure is called with parameters, one of the parameter locations may be used to store the return value. If the procedure is called without parameters, the calling procedure must push a dummy argument on the stack in order to make room for the returned value.

When values are returned on the stack, the called routine should not clear the stack with a RET *n* instruction. Instead, the calling procedure should be used to clear the stack, retrieving the returned values through simple POPs.

If the returned values are too large to conveniently fit on the stack, the called routine may return a pointer to a memory location where the values that are returned may be found. Then that memory location would contain the actual returned values. In these cases, the calling routine should "decide" the location of the buffer area.

Exception Reporting

During this discussion, we have alluded to returning status indications or detecting and reporting errors. In many applications, a desirable option is to have called procedures, functions and subroutines provide some type of error indication or status code. You probably have noticed that many MS-DOS function calls return a status code upon completion. Frequently the carry bit is used to indicate the presence of an error with one or more of the registers, usually the AX, containing detailed information on the type of error.

The carry bit is used for a number of reasons. It is easy to check (with JC or JNC); easy to set, complement, or clear (with STC, CMC, and CLC); and easy to save and restore (with PUSHF and POPF). Access to the carry flag is more complete than for any other status bit in the 8086/8088 architecture. This combination provides an ideal mechanism for indicating the presence of an exception. Of course, the programmer must remember to clear the carry bit to indicate a proper completion if no errors occurred because the carry bit may be set already by a normal operation.

Once the calling routine has determined that an error exists, the routine must discover the nature of the error. Sometimes no further information is required. When more information is needed, a dedicated register for completion codes is helpful. A logical choice is the AX register, but because so many other operations depend on it (MUL and DIV for example), it may not be available. Whatever choice is made, the register should contain not only error codes but also a normal completion code. This way, if the original error indication is lost, the program may retest the register to discover the completion status. If the information is critical, choose a value for normal completion that is not a normal result. What this implies is that you should not use a value of zero for normal completion because another error could easily clear the status codes.

MS-DOS provides an error reporting service for use with programs that run other programs. If a subprocess wishes to return an error code to the process that invoked that subprocess, it may do so as part of the Terminate Process function call, Function 4Ch. The parent process then may obtain that return code through MS-DOS Function 4Dh, Retrieve the Return Code of a Child. This mechanism is for use only with programs run under the Load and Execute Program function, 4Bh, which is introduced in Chapter 3.

Types of Coding

For most basic programming in any language, the programmer is rarely concerned with the details of how the processor is executing the program. Details of I/O handling, memory management, and where in memory the program is executing are left to the operating system to manage. However, there are times when more direct control of the program environment is desired. At these times the programmer may need to know about, and take responsibility for, the mechanism used to load, position, and execute the program. Examples of this occur when writing stand-alone programs that operate without MS-DOS present, supporting program overlays to fit large programs into limited physical memory, and when writing interrupt driven or recursive programs.

During execution a program's position in memory is reflected in two ways. One of the segment registers is used to relate the program counter (also known as the instruction pointer) or memory reference address to a block of physical memory. Then, within that block, the actual memory reference is formed, using an offset from the beginning of the block. This offset appears in the program counter, in memory references, and within indirect memory references through registers.

What does this have to do with different types of coding? These types of references and the way that they are used determine how a program is loaded into memory, what types of features it can use, and how the program may be structured. We examine how these references are created and how to use the right ones to allow us to write the best possible programs.

Program Code Positioning

Understanding the alternatives in positioning program code requires a clear understanding of both program flow control instructions (CALL, RET, and JMP) and memory accesses in the 8086 processor. Both of these can restrict the options available to the programmer in locating code in the available memory space.

Program flow control instructions, often called *control transfer* instructions, come in two basic forms: the CALL and the JMP. Each causes the program to begin executing code from a new place in memory, called the *destination*. Each of these instructions has three implementation options for specifying the destination location. They are: current location relative, current segment relative, and absolute addressing.

Location Relative

Current location relative, sometimes called *PC relative* (program counter relative), calculates the destination address from the current address and a displacement. The displacement is added to the current location to form the destination address. Because the entire operation is totally independent of the absolute location of the code in memory, the resulting address is position independent. If the entire block of code is moved in memory, the new destination address created correctly points to the new location of the destination instruction.

This method of calculating transfer addresses is used with all conditional jumps, all intrasegment (SHORT or NEAR) direct JMPs, and all intrasegment (NEAR) direct CALLs. *Direct* means that the CALL instruction contains a displacement as immediate data. The alternative, *non-direct*, is a CALL to an address contained in a 16-bit register (offset only) or to an address contained in a 16-bit or 32-bit memory location (offset or offset and segment).

Because direct transfers involve no actual addresses, they may be located anywhere in memory and may even be moved about within a segment as long as both the source instruction (JMP or CALL) and destination routine are moved together.

Segment Relative

Current segment relative addressing specifies an actual offset value to be loaded into the instruction pointer (as in the non-direct CALL) or used as a pointer to data. References made using this method always point to the same location within the block of memory addressed by the relevant segment register. As such, the code or data may not be moved within the segment. However, such code may be moved in memory if the segment register for that block is also updated. Because segments must be aligned on paragraph boundaries (address XXXX0 hex), the code may be moved only by increments of 16 bytes (one paragraph).

This type of addressing is used by intrasegment (NEAR) indirect JMPs and CALLs where a new destination instruction pointer value is fetched from a register or memory location. This addressing is also used with all data references, regardless of the segment used (DS, ES, or SS).

Code that uses this type of reference is still considered relocatable as long as the segment registers are updated to reflect the position of the code.

Absolute

Absolute addressing occurs when the entire physical memory address is explicitly specified. To accomplish this in the 8086 family, both the segment address and offset may be explicitly specified. These references point every time to the same location in memory. Absolute addresses in the 8086 are rare. Only a few instructions have the ability to generate absolute addresses in the 8086. These instructions are intersegment (FAR) JMPs and CALLS and the LDS and LES instructions (load pointer using DS or ES). The JMP and CALL instructions, either direct or indirect, update not only the offset (instruction pointer) but the Code Segment register as well. This specifies a physical address in memory. Likewise, the LDS and LES instructions load not only an offset into a 16-bit register but load either the Data Segment register or Extra Segment register. Once again, this is a physical address.

One other way to create an absolute address is to use a MOV or POP instruction to directly load one of the segment registers with a constant. However, note that POPping a value into the CS register is not allowed in the iAPX186, iAPX188, or iAPX286 processors and should not be done if only for compatibility reasons.

Types of Program Code

When discussing the properties of a program, we refer to it by the least flexible type of addressing that it contains. If only a single absolute reference is contained in a program, that program is said to have absolute addressing or be nonrelocatable. It may not be moved in memory.

Attentive readers may believe that an error has been made. After all, the entry point of a MASM program is specified as FAR, and all .EXE programs load the DS and ES with a MOV instruction. Both of these facts would seem to imply a nonrelocatable program, yet MS-DOS does load our programs into memory at different addresses as required. The key to this dilemma is that the values used are not constants in MS-DOS. MASM and LINK treat segment and FAR procedure names in a special way, producing what is called a *relocation map*. When a program is loaded into memory, MS-DOS reads the relocation map, and changes the values of those references that contain segment addresses. The important note for us as programmers is that MS-DOS does not extend such courtesies to standard data values, and loading one of the segment registers with a constant is not the same as using a segment or FAR procedure name.

Relocatable Code

MASM and LINK normally produce relocatable code. That is, in normal use, they create programs that may be moved in memory by MS-DOS and still operate correctly. Only the contents of the segment registers change. This has use in a number of applications. Programs may load other programs into any area of memory using MS-DOS Function 4Bh (useful for program overlays). Multiple programs may be loaded into memory concurrently (useful for multitasking systems or memory resident programs, such as print spoolers).

As indicated, MS-DOS accomplishes this feat by changing only the values of the segment registers and any locations in the program code that reference the segment name or a FAR procedure. We can also extend these concepts of flexibility to the data areas used by a program. Normally relocatable programs contain relocatable data areas. When the MS-DOS loader brings a program into memory, the loader assigns values to all segment references rather than just code segment references. Listing 2-5, which is taken from a standard .EXE type program file, shows the data segment reference used to load the data segment register. Listing 2-6 shows the equivalent code produced by MASM.

Listing 2-5. Source for .EXE Program Header

```
data_seg segment                        ; define the data segment
         :                              ; data area & values
data_seg ends
code_seg segment                        ; define the code segment
         assume cs:code_seg
         assume ds:data_seg
main     proc    far                    ; entry point for the program
start:
         mov     ax,data_seg            ; transfer data segment address
         mov     ds,ax                  ; ... to AX and thence to ...
         mov     es,ax                  ; ... segment registers
         :       :
         :       :
```

Listing 2-6. Listing for .EXE Program Header

```
0000                          code_seg  segment
                                        assume   cs:code_seg
                                        assume   ds:data_seg
0000                          main      proc     far
0000                          start:
0000 B8 ---- R                          mov      ax,data_seg
0003 8E D8                               mov      ds,ax
0005 8E C0                               mov      es,ax
```

In standard use, the variable *data_seg* is not a constant. Rather, this variable is a segment relocatable value, which is indicated in the MASM listing by four dashes and the letter *R*. As it loads the program, MS-DOS inserts in the program the actual value to be used during execution. This value is the address of the location in memory where *data_seg* was loaded. So with the help of MS-DOS, a program's code and data areas may be moved around in physical memory.

Separate Data Area

If more than one data segment is defined in the program (using corresponding ASSUME directives), it is possible for routines to have separate data areas. But in typical programming style, each routine is limited to accessing the same data area every time that routine is called. The data area is dedicated to the routine and vice versa.

In normal use, dedicated areas are not a handicap because most routines execute in a sequential manner, one after the other. But what happens when we try to execute the same procedure more than once at the same time? Wouldn't the later call overwrite the earlier call's data because the routine uses only one data area? At this point, you may be wondering why the same procedure would be invoked more than once simultaneously.

There are at least three cases where this occurs. First, multitasking systems may have multiple programs running, sharing common libraries of code called *run-time libraries* (because the code is accessed at run-time instead of being included during link time). Run-time libraries have only one copy of the code, located in memory, instead of having multiple copies, located in the program file. (See Chapter 3 for a more complete discussion of run-time libraries). Although they may all run the same code at the same time, run-time libraries must have separate data areas to avoid inadvertent sharing and corruption of data.

The second case where the same procedure may be invoked by two parties simultaneously occurs in interrupt driven systems. Assume that a routine is executing but is interrupted by some external event. The program that services the interrupt starts executing but needs to call the routine that was interrupted. Unless they have separate data areas, the interrupt procedure destroys the data that belongs to the interrupted routine. For this reason, interrupt service routines need to have separate data areas.

Recursive Code

The third use for separate data areas occurs when a routine needs to call itself. This is a common tool for problem solving and is given the name *recursion*. Calculating factorials is a good example of this technique. A sample recursive solution for calculating the value of a factorial appears in Listing 2-7. The solution is not very elegant and contains no overflow checks on the multiplication, but it suffices for values of N up to seven.

Listing 2-7. Recursive Solution for Calculating Factorials

```
factor  proc    near            ; find factorial N
        cmp     ax,2            ; reached end yet?
        jne     subfact         ; no, calculate (N - 1)!
        mov     ax,2            ; yes, start at the beginning
        ret
subfact:
        push    ax              ; save current value of N
        sub     ax,1            ; get N - 1
        call    factor          ; request (N - 1)!
        pop     bx              ; restore value of N
        mul     bx              ; N × (N - 1)! = N!
        ret
factor  endp
```

Reentrant Code—Local Storage Requirements

For all these cases, a routine's data must be preserved separately from its code in such a way that more than one procedure, each with its own data areas, may be executing the code at the same time. If this criteria is met, the routine is said to be *reentrant*. That is, the routine may be invoked (entered) by one program flow while another program flow is still executing it. We say *program flow* because we don't really care whether the routine is called by another program, another routine, or even by itself (recursion).

In *factor*, the data to be preserved is saved on the stack by the calling routine. This is only possible in recursion because the programmer knows when control is given to the new routine and may anticipate the need to set up a new data area. For multiuser and interrupt handler applications, this is not sufficient, and the routines must have their data protected at all times. Control may be taken away at any time. In these cases, set up a local data area when the routine is first entered. This storage may be allocated in one of two ways: on the stack or in memory.

Local Storage on the Stack

A block of the stack may be reserved for local storage by decrementing the stack pointer. Then any interrupts or calls that occur continue to build on the stack, preserving any local data belonging to the routine that was interrupted. This is the easiest method but requires that all local variable access take place through the BP register. (See the preceding section entitled *Parameter Passing Techniques* for a discussion of this.) Listing 2-8 contains an annotated example of this method.

ing section entitled *Parameter Passing Techniques* for a discussion of this.) Listing 2-8 contains an annotated example of this method.

Listing 2-8.   Allocating Local Storage on the Stack

```
stack_example    proc    near   ; start of procedure
stack_data       struc          ; dummy data structure
local_1 dw       ?              ; ... 1 word of local storage
local_2 db       14 dup (?)     ; ... 14 bytes of local storage
bp_save dw       ?              ; space for storing BP
ret adr_dw       ?              ; return address (NEAR proc)
param_2 dw       ?              ; 2nd parameter pushed
param_1 dw       ?              ; 1st parameter pushed
stack_data       ends
base      equ    [bp-offset bp_save] ; define position of BP
          push   bp                 ; save old base pointer
          mov    bp,sp              ; load BP ...
                                    ; ... points at BP_SAVE
          sub    sp,offset bp_save  ; reserve space on stack.
          mov    ax,base.param_1    ; access to 1st parameter
          mov    ax,base.param_2    ; access to 2nd parameter
          mov    ax,base.local_1    ; access to local storage
          mov    al,base.local_2    ; access to local storage
          mov    sp,bp          ; restore SP--free local store
          pop    bp             ; restore BP
          ret    4              ; remove passed parameters
stack_example    endp           ; end of example procedure
```

Because the structure *stack_data* is defined in the current segment, no segment overrides are necessary. If offsets from another segment are used, as in attempting to use a template from the data segment, you have to use the SS: override in the references. Failure to do so results in the MASM error message **Can't reach with segment reg.** If you ever see this message, an explicit segment overrides to define what segment you are accessing and see whether this solves the problem.

If local storage is allocated on the stack, that storage must be freed prior to returning from the routine. This may be accomplished by either adding the size of local storage to the stack (reversing the "sub sp,offset bp_" or restoring the SP from a saved value (mov sp,bp). It may not be freed by using the RET n because the current top of stack does not contain the return address!

The ENTER and LEAVE Instructions for Local Stack Storage

In the more advanced members of the 8086 family, Intel has provided two new instructions to aid in using local storage on the stack. The iAPX186, iAPX188, and iAPX286 processors all support the ENTER and LEAVE instructions. ENTER is used to set up local storage on the stack when first entering a routine, and LEAVE deallocates this local storage when exiting the routine. In addition, ENTER and LEAVE have the capability of maintaining frame pointers, which are used in certain block structured high-level languages such as PASCAL.

Due to the complexity of these instructions, we have presented their macro equivalents in Listing 2-9. This also allows 8086/8088 users to take advantage of these instructions in anticipation of an upward migration to one of the more advanced processors.

Listing 2-9. Macro Equivalents for the ENTER and LEAVE Instructions

```
;; MACRO DEFINITIONS FOR ENTER & LEAVE INSTRUCTIONS
;;
;; Base addressing definitions for use in accessing
;; elements in the stack frame created by ENTER.
;;
pbase equ      [BP + 4]        ;; access to parameters
lbase equ      [BP - ??tsize]  ;; access to locals
fbase equ      [BP - ??fsize]  ;; access to frame pointers
;; Form: ENTER    local <immediate 16>, level <immediate 8>
;;
;; ENTER--Create stack frame and allocate local storage
;; Copies stack frame pointers from previous routine into
;; a new stack frame for this routine and opens up space
;; on the stack for new local storage.
;;
enter  MACRO   local,level
       ??tsize = local + level * 2
       ??fsize = level * 2
       push    bp
       IF (level NE 0)
         IF (level GT 1)
           REPT level - 1
             sub         bp,2
             push        [bp]
           ENDM
         ENDIF
         mov bp,sp
         IF (level GT 1)
           add bp,(level - 1) * 2
         ENDIF
         push bp
       ELSE
         mov     bp,sp
       ENDIF
       sub     sp,local
       ENDM
;; Form: LEAVE
;;
;; LEAVE--Execute procedure return removing stack frame
```

Listing 2-9. cont.

```
;; and local storage set up by ENTER instruction.
;;
leave   MACRO
        mov     sp,bp
        pop     bp
        ENDM
```

The ENTER instruction performs three actions on the stack when the instruction is executed. It always pushes the value on the BP onto the stack. If the value of *level* is one or greater, the instruction copies the previous values of the BP onto the stack. If the value of *local* is one or greater, the instruction opens up space for local storage on the stack by subtracting *local* from the stack pointer. The BP is always set to the location of the old BP on the stack (the first PUSH).

The LEAVE instruction reverses the action of ENTER as long as the BP is left at or reset to the original value of the BP as set by ENTER.

The most confusing phase of this operation is that relating to the frame pointers. Figure 2-1 shows the state (and contents) of the stack for a series of operations that consisted of four successive ENTER instructions.

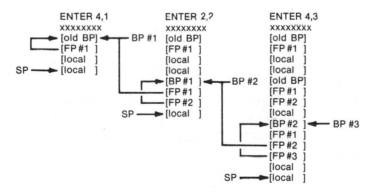

Fig. 2-1.   Effects of ENTER on the stack.

Each stack entry in Figure 2-1 symbolizes two bytes. (For this reason all *local* parameters for ENTER are multiples of two bytes. This is not a restriction of the ENTER instruction.) The arrows in the figure symbolize that an entry points to another entry (contains the address of that entry).

The first ENTER (level one) sets up a single frame pointer, pointing to its own frame, and opens up space on the stack for four bytes of storage. The second ENTER (level two) not only creates its own frame pointer (FP #2) but copies the frame pointer from the previous frame (FP #1). The second ENTER only creates two bytes of local storage. The last ENTER (level three) carries the operation one step further, copying the frame pointers of the previous two levels (FP #1 and FP #2).

Why does the example sequence start with a level one ENTER rather than a level zero ENTER? A level zero ENTER simply pushes the BP onto the stack and subtracts the value of *local* from the stack pointer, setting the BP to point to the value of the BP just pushed. No frame pointers are copied. A level zero ENTER is thus ideal for creating local storage on the stack. When used in conjunction with the STRUC directive, ENTER can almost automatically create local stack storage that is easy to access. Listing 2-10 demonstrates further.

Listing 2-10.   Creating and Referencing Local Stack Storage with ENTER

```
?data_1          struc
my_var dw        ?
?data_1          ends
test   proc      near
       ENTER     %(size ?data_1),0   ; allocate local storage
       mov       lbase.my_var,10     ; store a value in local
```

This program fragment defines, allocates, and uses local storage from the stack. ENTER is instructed to reserve the proper amount of space through the MASM SIZE operator. The percent mark (%) is only required with the macro implementation of ENTER. When using the machine code version (supported by MASM 2.0 and higher by specifying the ".286C" switch) the "%" should be omitted.

The symbol *lbase* is defined in Listing 2-9 as the base address for all local variable accesses. The actual reference created in the MOV instruction is

```
mov     [BP - ??tsize].my_var,10
```

The symbol *??tsize* is set by the macro implementation of ENTER to the number of bytes added to the stack by the ENTER instruction, not including the BP. This symbol is calculated as *local + level * 2*. When *??tsize* is subtracted from the contents of the BP, the result is the address of the top of the stack. All structure references are thus positive offsets from *lbase*. Even if you use the machine code version of ENTER, you can easily write a macro that calculates *??tsize* and creates the ENTER instruction so that this technique can be used on the 186/188/286 processors as well.

Another symbol defined in Listing 2-9 is *pbase*, the base address for all access to variables passed on the stack. The value of *pbase* is [BP + 4] to cover the two bytes pushed on the stack as part of a "near" CALL instruction and the two bytes required for the BP pushed on the stack by the ENTER instruction. Once a structure has been defined for the stack parameters, *pbase* can be used with their field names for symbolic access as in *pbase.my_param*.

Having described the simpler uses of ENTER, we return to the question of the frame pointers. What are they for? Each frame pointer points to the beginning of the previous routines' stack frames. By loading the BP with the contents of one of the frame pointers located in the current frame, access can be gained to the previous level's local variables. This is primarily designed for implementing high-level languages, such as PASCAL, where a routine has automatic access to the parent routine's variables. Unless you are very serious about high-level structured programming in assembly languages, you probably pass using the frame pointer capabilities of ENTER. If you decide to try using ENTER with frame pointer anyway, a little experimentation should give you a feel for the operation.

Allocation and Use of Local Storage in Memory

Returning to our major topic of allocating local storage, you may also allocate a block of memory from the unused memory in the system (often called the *memory pool*). MS-DOS may be used to accomplish this, or the programmer can implement a personal memory management scheme. The latter can be a dangerous proposition unless all programs use the same memory allocation method. Otherwise memory that is actually in use can be allocated with disastrous results! For our applications, using MS-DOS Function 48h, Allocate Memory, is easier.

Once the block of memory has been obtained, the program must be able to address it. Memory that has been allocated through MS-DOS comes in 16-byte chunks called *paragraphs*. MS-DOS returns a pointer to this memory that contains the high 16 bits of the block's memory address. Segments are also addressed as paragraphs, so the pointer should be loaded into one of the segment registers (but not the CS register!). Usually either the data segment or extra segment is used to gain access to the block of memory. If the routine that allocated the memory is not the main routine of the program, the old segment register value must be saved and restored before the routine exits. In addition, the memory that was allocated should be returned to the system before the routine exits. Return is accomplished by using MS-DOS Function 49h, Free Allocated Memory. Listing 2-11 shows how a routine from a .EXE type program would allocate, use, and free memory for use as local storage.

Listing 2-11.   Allocating Local Storage through MS-DOS

```
                common    segment              ; common data used by all
                com_1   dw     ?
                com_2   db     14 dup (?)
                common    ends
                dummy_dat  struc               ; structure definition ...
                dummy_1 dw     ?               ; ... used with the ...
                dummy_2 db     14 dup (?)       ; ... allocated memory
                dummy_dat ends
                        assume   ds:common    ; access to COMMON data
                local_example    proc     near; example procedure
                push    ds                    ; save previous DS
B8 ---- R       mov     ax,common             ; COMMON is MS-DOS relocatable
                mov     ds,ax
                push    es                    ; save previous ES
                mov     ah,048h               ; allocate memory
                mov     bx,1                  ; request 1 block (16 bytes)
                int     21h                   ; call MS-DOS
                jc      not_alloc             ; carry means allocate failed
                mov     es,ax                 ; if allocated, address it
                ;
                ; Three examples of addressing
                ;
A1 0000 R       mov     ax,com_1              ; proper seg.--DS assumed
B8 0000         mov     ax,dummy_1            ; wrong seg.--immediate
26: A1 0000     mov     ax,es:dummy_1         ; proper seg.--overridden
                ;
                mov     ah,049h               ; free allocated memory
                int     21h                   ; call MS-DOS
                jnc     free_ok               ; no carry means worked
                not_alloc:
                ; Error messages, if failed, allocate or deallocate
                free_ok:
                pop     es                    ; restore ES
                pop     ds                    ; restore DS
                ret
                local_example    endp         ; end of example
```

Listing 2-11 contains both the Allocate Memory and Free Allocated Memory MS-DOS function calls. Instead of using the DS register to point to the newly allocated memory, we have used the ES register, reserving the DS for access to an area of common program variables. Note that unlike the stack example, accesses using the structure defined here do require the segment override operator (:). Without a segment override "mov ax,dummy_1" does not generate a memory reference involving the ES but instead generates an immediate load of the offset (zero here) into register AX. When the segment override is added to the instruction, "mov ax,es:dummy_1," MASM generates a memory transfer from offset *dummy_1* in the extra segment. The segment override is shown in Listing 2-11 with the prefix byte "26:."

When using multiple data segments in a program, the programmer's responsibility is to manage the data areas in use. For example, if routine X allocates local storage and updates the DS register to access this area, the programmer must remember that this data area is now the default data area for all routines called by X. Common data areas that have been defined in the program are still accessible by loading either the DS or ES registers from a segment variable as shown in Listing 2-6. Those routines that modify their segment registers must save and restore the original segment registers to prevent confusing their parent routines.

Whenever more than one data or extra segment is used by a program, the programmer must pay careful attention to the ASSUME directives used in the program. In assembling a typical memory reference, MASM first searches its internal symbol table for the name of the variable being accessed. If MASM finds the variable in the symbol table, MASM tries to create the reference using the segment in which the variable was defined. If that segment isn't present (through an ASSUME), MASM generates the error message **Can't reach with segment reg.**

If MASM can't find the variable in the symbol table, MASM assumes that it's in the data segment. If this turns out to be wrong, MASM attempts to fix the error during pass two by attaching a segment override prefix to the instruction. Unfortunately, inserting this byte causes another error message **Phase error between passes.**

In case of confusion or of a forward reference where the variable name is not yet in the symbol table, the programmer must use the segment override operator (:) to more clearly define to MASM which segment is to be used. The SEG operator is also useful for controlling accesses in a routine. This operator allows the programmer to obtain the segment value (base address of the segment) for any defined variable. The references that SEG creates are MS-DOS relocatable and useful for creating relocatable references in place of absolute ones.

A Diversion on MS-DOS Memory Allocation

The example in Listing 2-11 only works if free memory is available to be allocated. Unfortunately for us, in the normal MS-DOS program environment, no free memory is available! When MS-DOS loads a normal program, the system allocates all available memory to that program. If a program wants to use the Allocate Memory function, some of the memory allocated to that system must be freed, preferably all memory that is not occupied by the program's code, data, or buffers. So for all applications that require free memory, MS-DOS provides function 4Ah, Modify Allocated Memory Block. (Another method of freeing memory is still to be discussed, but we delay its presentation until Chapter 3 when we have introduced program loading and MS-DOS program files.)

The parameters required for the Modify Allocated Memory Block function are the segment address of the block to be modified and the new size of the block. The segment address of the block that contains the program (whose size we wish to modify) is given by something called the PSP (program segment prefix). The PSP is a section of memory that begins every program in the MS-DOS environment. The details of the PSP's contents are described in Chapter 3. For now, our only concern is that the segment address of the PSP is the segment address of the block to be modified, and we need that address.

Just how we go about determining these parameters is different for .COM type files and .EXE type files. Figure 2-2 shows the arrangement of memory for both .COM and .EXE files. The PSP is the first entry for each type. In the .COM type program, the PSP is contained in the first 256 bytes of the program segment, and the program's segment address (in all segment registers) is the segment address of the PSP.

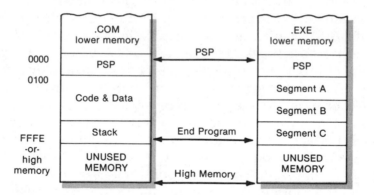

Fig. 2-2. MS-DOS program memory map and the program segment prefix.

For .EXE files, the PSP resides in its own segment. However, whenever a .EXE program is loaded and receives control from MS-DOS, both the DS and ES registers contain the segment address of the PSP. So for either type of program, the PSP address may be obtained from at least the DS and ES registers. In addition, users of MS-DOS version 3.0 (or higher) may use the Get Program Segment Prefix Address, Function 62h, to determine the PSP address. MS-DOS returns the value in the BX register.

Because the Modify Allocated Memory Block function expects the block address in the ES register, the function may be called immediately upon the program starting execution because the ES already has the PSP address.

Once the memory block address is found, we must determine the amount of memory that must be saved. The difference between .COM programs and .EXE programs becomes much more marked here. For .EXE. programs the size can be determined by subtracting the starting segment address of the PSP from the segment address of a dummy segment located at the end of the program as shown in Listing 2-12. Why are segment addresses used? Function 4Ah expects the size in paragraphs, and segment addresses are actually paragraph addresses.

Listing 2-12.   Function 4Ah—Modify Allocated Memory Block RESIZE for .EXE Programs

```
resize proc near
        mov     ax,es           ; get PSP address
        mov     bx,seg end_addr ; get next segment address
        sub     bx,ax           ; difference is prog size
        mov     ah,04Ah         ; modify allocated memory
        int     21h             ; ... MS-DOS call
        jnc     short resize_ok ; no carry => re-sized okay
        mov     ax,04C00h       ; carry => failed--abort
        int     21h
resize_ok:
        ret
resize endp
;
; The remainder of the code goes here with END_ADDR as the last
; entry in the program file before the END statement. Take care
; to ensure that END_ADDR is linked as the last segment if more
; than one source file is used.
;
end_addr segment
end_addr ends
        end
```

For .COM type programs, a little forethought is required. Unlike .EXE programs, which have a definite size set by the linker, .COM programs can vary in size. The location of the stack in a .COM program, which is set by MS-DOS, can vary from the end of the segment (FFFE) to 256 bytes longer than the program (the minimum size required by MS-DOS for the stack). The user can choose between 1) accepting what MS-DOS has provided and resizing the stack provided by MS-DOS (set size 64K [1000 hex paragraphs] or whatever remains or 2) moving the stack and resizing based on that. The second choice frees more memory and so is preferred and recommended by Microsoft and IBM. Listing 2-13 contains an example of a .COM program that sets up its own stack and resizes its initial allocation block to the more moderate size.

Listing 2-13.   Function 4Ah—Modify Allocated Memory Block RESIZE for .COM Programs

```
code_seg    segment
            assume  cs:code_seg
            ORG     0000h
seg_org     equ     $
            ORG     0100h
main        proc    far
start:
            mov     sp,offset stack
            call    resize
;
; The remainder of the program can go here.
;
main        endp
resize      proc    near
            mov     bx,(offset last_byte - seg_org + 15) shr 4
            mov     ah,04Ah             ; modify allocated memory
            int     21h                 ; ... MS-DOS call
            jnc     short resize_ok ; no carry => re-sized okay
            mov     ax,04C00h           ; carry => failed--abort
            int     21h
resize_ok:
            ret
resize      endp
            db      32 dup ('stack     ')
stack:
last_byte   equ     $
code_seg    ends
            end     start
```

The only interesting part of this routine is the way that it determines the size of the resultant program. The MASM operator SHR is used to convert the number of bytes in the program to the number of paragraphs through what is essentially a division by 16. What is not so obvious is why *seg_org* is subtracted from the offset of *last_byte*. The SHR operator doesn't work when applied to an offset and produces the error message **Constant was expected.** However, the difference between two offsets is considered a constant, making the expression palatable to MASM. Note that *seg_org* must have an offset of zero so that the size is relative to the beginning of the segment. Were *start* used instead, the last 100 hex bytes of the program would be lost. (Note that "last_byte:" works just as well as "last_byte equ $" for calculations.)

In addition to being useful for freeing memory, the trick of subtracting two offsets (either Label or Number) to get a constant can be useful for all types of operations where sizes are required in expressions that demand constants. We'll see this applied to the task of aligning a data buffer on a paragraph boundary in Chapter 5.

Code Positioning Summary

Note that reentrant routines are not necessarily relocatable, nor are re-locatable routines necessarily reentrant. Relocation applies to the ability to position the program in memory. Reentrant applies to a routine having secure "local" data storage. Recursive routines are a type of re-entrant routine with the relaxed restriction that the programmer knows at what point data must be preserved in preparation for the next call.

In addition, when writing reentrant routines, don't forget that the routines' parameters must be reentrant also. Data must be passed to the called routine in an area that is either protected (such as the stack) or that is always saved when a new procedure or task takes control (for instance, all interrupt service routines save all registers when invoked).

You also should remember that there are two types of relocatable code. The first type is MS-DOS relocatable where MS-DOS, using the relocation map, alters the values of segment variables in order to relocate the program. The second type is self-relocatable, which simply means that no relocation map is required. Only programs that use only displacement addressing in CALLs and JMPs may be self-relocatable.

Protecting Data and Controlling the Scope of Data

The techniques used in reentrant coding lead us into another aspect of modular programming: protecting the data in the program from accidental alteration. Destruction of important data most often occurs when one part of the program mistakenly alters the data that belongs to another part of the program. The possibility of this happening can be reduced by following some basic rules. The foremost of these rules is to modularize the data in a program as well as the code, that is, controlling the range of data that a routine may access. This is often called the *scope of data*. Let's review what we have just learned and see how it may be applied to our new problem.

Local Storage versus Global Storage

The human mind can only deal with a limited number of concepts at any given time. The implication of this for programmers is that as the number of elements to be manipulated and remembered grows, so does the number of errors. By using local storage for subroutines, the programmer reduces the number of data elements that must be remembered. Rather than data areas containing hundreds of variables, the programmer now need only deal with a data area that contains a handful of variables. Many small data areas may exist, each one may be verified with the routine that uses it because each is secure in the knowledge that no other routine interferes with it. Either of the methods presented for reentrant routines serves for the allocation of temporary local data storage.

Global storage areas, also known as common areas, may be modularized. In this case, a number of smaller data areas are created in place of a monolithic one. Routines then can access only those portions of global data that they require. This necessitates careful attention on the part of the programmer to ASSUME directives in the contents of the segment registers, but such explicit handling of common data also makes clearer what is accessing and thus altering critical data. For example, a common data area containing text strings and character constants need not be part of a numerical calculation routine, just as a table of sine and cosine values is not needed by a terminal input routine.

Parameters should be passed on the stack as much as possible, reducing the number of interroutine data accesses. Whenever multiple routines must access common data areas for parameter passing purposes, the likelihood of a mistake increases.

Common data usually should be defined with DEFINE DATA directives so that the contents of the area are static and not subject to accidental deletion if a routine makes a mistake with Free Allocated Memory.

Using Segment Registers

The segment registers allow the programmer to restrict the range of possible data references. By changing the base of the segment that contains the data, the architecture of the machine automatically constrains the program to a 64K-access window. If more sensitive data is located in the lower areas of memory, then as the segment register is changed to point to a higher addressed block of memory, the data in the lower area is totally protected against any unauthorized access.

Controlling the Size of Data Access

The programmer may further constrain this window on the data by setting up bounds-checking on array accesses. One of the most typical data errors occurs when an array access runs across its boundaries. Whatever data happens to border on the array is lost. Bounds-checking may be accomplished by a simple macro as shown in Listing 2-14. For those programmers who are working with a 188, 186, or 286 processor, the BOUND instruction has been provided to accomplish this checking. The *bound* macro shown in Listing 2-14 has been written for compatibility with the BOUND instruction.

Listing 2-14.   Checking Array Bounds with Macros

```
;; BOUND-Check the contents of the general register REG
;; against the two consecutive values located in memory at
;; address MEM32. This is a signed integer compare.
bound   macro   reg,mem32
        local   out_bound,in_bound
        pushf                             ; save flags
        cmp     reg,word ptr mem32        ; check lower limit
        jl      out_bound                 ; index underflow
        cmp     reg,word ptr mem32 + 2    ; check upper limit
        jle     in_bound                  ; index is okay
out_bound:
        popf                              ; clean up stack
        INT     5                         ; ACTION TO BE TAKEN
in_bound:
        popf                              ; restore flags
        endm
```

The *bound* macro compares the contents of a general register containing the array index against two successive memory locations. The first memory location is assumed to contain the lower limit of the index, and the second memory location is assumed to contain the upper limit of the index. The BOUND instruction executes an interrupt type 5 (INT 5) if the index tested is out of bounds. Macro version users may modify *bound* to take whatever action they desire.

Protecting the Integrity of the Stack

The other area that is susceptible to destruction is the stack. Because the stack mixes code and data, an error here undoubtedly will result in total failure of the program as the processor attempts to use data as an instruction reference.

The two most common ways to destroy the stack are problems of faulty alignment. One way is caused by mismatching PUSH and POP operations and the other is through attempting to POP data that was PUSHed on the other side of a CALL or RET. These problems may be avoided only by paying close attention to pairing the PUSHes and POPs used in a program and making sure that such pairings do not cross routine boundaries. When reading source code, remember that macros often contain PUSH and POP instructions that must be taken into account.

In the case of parameter passing, the question of what routine clears the stack arises. Normally the rule for such occasions is that the routine that pushed the data gets to pop the data from the stack. If this rule is followed, the programmer can verify that the stack is aligned by reading one routine's listing rather than two. However, rigidly following this rule prevents use of the 8086's RET *n* instruction. If the interface between two routines is fully debugged and dependable, an acceptable risk is to use the RET *n* instruction.

Whenever a routine must be coded to accept a variable number of parameters, the RET *n* instruction should not be used. There are various ways to get around the limitation of being able to clear the stack only of a set number of variables, but all of them involve tricky manipulations of the stack that are difficult to understand and even more difficult to debug. If a routine must take a variable number of parameters, the calling routine should clear those parameters from the stack. In addition, the calling routine must clearly indicate to the called routine, the number of parameters that have been passed to it.

All operations that are performed on the stack, except PUSH and POP, should take place under the umbrella of the stack pointer and use the BP register to access the stack. What this means is that the stack pointer should be set to a value below the elements being manipulated. Should an interrupt take place, the data being manipulated remains untouched. For the same reason, the stack pointer should not be directly manipulated unless switching stacks or opening storage on the stack. If an interrupt takes place at a time when the stack pointer is not pointing at the true top of stack, data on the stack could be lost. What this all adds up to is a warning not to use clever manipulations of the stack.

Summary

In this chapter, we have covered a variety of topics ranging from the theoretical nature of structured programming to the details of MASM, MS-DOS, and 8086 family processor operation. We have tried to give you some alternative approaches for your structured programming needs. Although it is most unlikely that all or even most of these techniques will appear in your small assembly language programs, we think that many of them will find uses in your larger projects. And if only one point is remembered, let it be this: think first, code later.

Most of the more practical points about MASM and MS-DOS resurface in subsequent chapters. Try out the examples in our sample programs and get comfortable with their use. You'll need many of them. Most particularly, our introduction to MS-DOS memory management forms the stepping stone for Chapter 3, *Program and Memory Management in the MS-DOS Environment.*

Program and Memory Management in the MS-DOS Environment Chapter 3

Among the more advanced features of MS-DOS are functions intended for the management of programs and program memory. These functions and some of their possible applications are the topics of this chapter.

We briefly introduced some of these functions in Chapter 2 where Modify Allocated Memory, Allocate Memory, and Free Allocated Memory were used to implement temporary local storage. In Chapter 3, these functions are used to position programs in memory. When combined with MS-DOS' program management functions, these functions are a powerful tool for the creation of memory resident programs, run-time libraries, and program overlays. Also included in this chapter are short explanations of the methods used by MS-DOS to load both .EXE and .COM program files, including an explanation of the method MS-DOS uses to locate (or *relocate*) these programs in memory.

Memory Resident Programs

What Is a Memory Resident Program?

In typical use, MS-DOS is a single-task operating system. Only one program executes in memory at one time. In fact, MS-DOS is capable of supporting multiple programs in memory at any given time. Only one program is actually executing at a time because the processor can only execute instructions one at a time, but programs may be configured so as to give the appearance of executing simultaneously. These multiple programs are created by having MS-DOS load a program into memory, then return control to MS-DOS without removing the program from memory. Because the program doesn't leave memory when control is returned to the operating system, the program is called *memory resident*.

The first step in the implementation of a memory resident program is the installation of the program in memory. One of the simplest types of memory resident programs is the run-time library, and we use that as our first example.

What Is a Run-Time Library?

What is a run-time library? You know that libraries are collections of useful routines that may be called from a program. Most libraries are link libraries where the desired routines are included in the program file (.EXE or .COM) at link time. Because they are part of the program file, the linked library routines are loaded with the program when the program file is loaded. An RTL (run-time library) is not linked with a program but is included at execution time, also called *run-time*. The RTL must already be in memory or it must be brought into memory when needed, but an RTL is not part of the program file itself.

An RTL is not directly connected to a program, so how does the program call it? The program must somehow signal either the operating system or an RTL support process that the program has a request for the library. This signaling can take place via calls, traps, exceptions, or interrupts, depending on the complexity of the hardware and operating system. In the MS-DOS/8086 environment, the most convenient way is through interrupts.

Why use RTLs if they require the additional effort of loading, calling, etc.? First, RTLs are often used to develop applications that have a large number of programs which share common routines or to provide a common resource to all users of a particular language. By using RTLs, the developers need only store a copy of the library once instead of making sure each program contains a copy. As long as the interface between the programs and the RTL remains the same, the routines in the RTL may be updated without modifying or relinking the programs that call them. Thus, an RTL may be viewed as an extension of the operating system because an RTL provides those facilities that the developers deem necessary but the system does not support. Second, additional benefits of RTLs include reduced disk storage and faster program load time because the RTL doesn't have to be loaded with each program.

Loading Memory Resident Routines from the Command Line Example: Run-Time Libraries (RTLs)

There are a variety of methods that may be used to load a program image in MS-DOS. The methods range from using MS-DOS to load a program from the command line to the lower level boot routines that transfer program code from absolute disk locations to fixed locations in memory. The easiest method to use is the MS-DOS command line loader, which is simply a request to run a program. Memory resident programs, such as RTLs, are loaded like any other program. However, once a memory resident program has been loaded and after it runs through its initialization sequence, the program terminates by using a special exit: MS-DOS Function Code 31h (Keep Process) or Interrupt Vector 27h (Terminate But Stay Resident). The recommended procedure is to use Function Code 31h of INT 21h, which is demonstrated in Listing 3-1.

Listing 3-1.   Keep Process—Function Code 31h

.COM Type Use

```
program   segment
          ORG     0
seg_org   equ     $
          ORG     0100h
start:
          :       :
          mov     dx,(offset last_byte - seg_org + 15) shr 4
          mov     ah,31h                  ; keep process
          int     21h                     ; call MS-DOS
          :       :
last_byte:
program   ends
          end     start
```

.EXE Type Use

```
          :       :
          mov     ax,es                   ; get PSP address
          mov     dx,seg end_addr         ; get last segment address
          sub     dx,ax                   ; difference is program size
          mov     ah,31h                  ; keep process
          int     21h                     ; call MS-DOS
          :       :
program   ends
end_addr  segment
end_addr  ends
          end     start
```

Function Code 31h has two parameters: an optional return code used to signal the exit status and a required value indicating the size of the memory block to remain allocated to the process in paragraphs. When the function is called, MS-DOS reserves the requested amount of space, starting at the address of the PSP (program segment prefix). This is almost exactly what happens when the Modify Allocated Memory Block function is called with the PSP address and desired size. In the case of the Keep Process function, MS-DOS knows that the block to be resized has to start at the PSP address, so that parameter is not needed.

In Chapter 2 we presented a set of formulas for calculating the size of a program in paragraphs. Those formulas can be used with the Keep Process function as well as the Modify Allocated Memory Block function. When we use them in memory resident programs, the proper equations appear as shown in Listing 3-1. Note that even though the Keep Process function doesn't require the PSP address, .EXE-type programs need to save the PSP address until the exit call. These programs need to save the PSP address for the purpose of calculating the size of the program.

Because space is reserved from the start of the PSP, memory resident routines must not be loaded into the upper part of a memory block (by using MS-LINK switch /high, for example). If the routine is loaded into high memory, that routine is left unprotected when the memory resident routine terminates, because the block of memory saved is located at the start of the memory block. The routine itself would be located above the reserved memory space. When routines are thus unprotected, MS-DOS could load another program or the transient part of COMMAND.COM in the same space, overwriting the memory resident routine.

In any case, the MS-LINK switch /high only affects .EXE programs. When converting a program to a .COM file, EXE2BIN removes the "load high" marker. MS-DOS then loads the program at the beginning of the PSP.

The other method for installing memory resident programs, the Terminate and Stay Resident interrupt, INT 27h, is a holdover from earlier versions of MS-DOS. INT 27h has a number of disadvantages that make it a poor choice. Unlike Keep Process, INT 27h *does* require the memory block address (given by the PSP address), and INT 27h requires this address in the CS register. Only .COM type files have the PSP address in the code segment register, making this function difficult to use in .EXE type programs. (How do you change the CS and still execute code?) In addition, the size parameter is specified in bytes rather than paragraphs, which limits the size of program that can be saved to 64 Kbytes (the maximum size of a .COM program). The only advantage to this function is that the offset of the last address can be used as a parameter with no conversion as shown below.

```
        :       :
    mov     dx,offset last_byte     ; get number of bytes
    int     27h                     ; terminate & stay resident
```

```
              :        :
last_byte:
program   ends
          end      start
```

Microsoft recommends that this interrupt be converted to Function Code 31h for all new programs written and for all existing program upgrades. When performing the conversion, remember to modify the size parameter from bytes to paragraphs.

Accessing Memory Resident Routines via INT

If you were to run the program shown in Listing 3-1, you would install a memory resident program on your system. Unfortunately, as this program now stands, all it would do is take up space in memory. To turn this program into an RTL, we need to give it a purpose, and we must make it available to other programs.

An RTL may contain any function and make any call to MS-DOS (for example, INT 21h) as long as the library is only called by the currently executing program. This restriction is intended to prevent inadvertently reentering MS-DOS, which causes system failure. The next program, shown in Listing 3-2, contains an example interface to an RTL that could support many separate functions, much like the MS-DOS INT 21h handler.

As shown in Listing 3-2, this sample framework can be extended to support math routines, table lookups, I/O conversions, or even a common area for multiple programs, all by adding the necessary "personality" code. We have attempted to include some examples of the techniques outlined in Chapter 2, such as stack parameters, error reporting, etc. If this routine is used to support a large number of functions, you may wish to replace the *case* macro with a jump table as demonstrated in Listing 5-3 (the RDISK Ram Disk driver) in Chapter 5.

The MACRO library referenced in the EXRTL program contains the *case* macro introduced in Chapter 1 and the *dis_chr* (display character) and the *dis_str* (display string) macros as presented in the *MS-DOS Technical Reference* manual. *Doscall* is, of course, a macro for interrupt 21h.

Listing 3-2.   Example Run-Time Library Installation

```
;****** EXRTL.ASM--This file produces a .COM file ****************
cr       equ     0Dh              ; carriage return
lf       equ     0Ah              ; line feed
v_num    equ     40h              ; this RTL uses vector 40 hex
```

Listing 3-2. cont.

```
            ORG     2Ch
    env_adr         label   word      ; offset of environment in PSP
    ;
    INCLUDE         STD.MLB           ; include macro library (MLB)
    ;****** PROGRAM CODE SECTION **********************************
    ;
    frame   struc                     ; layout caller's stack structure
    old_bp  dw      ?                 ; pushed base pointer
    ret_IP  dw      ?                 ; return address (IP)
    ret_CS  dw      ?                 ; return address (CS)
    flags   dw      ?                 ; caller's flags
    funct   dw      ?                 ; function number to perform
    frame   ends
    ;
    code_seg segment
            assume cs:code_seg
            assume ds:code_seg
    main    proc    far
            ORG     0
    seg_org equ     $
            ORG     0100h
    start:  jmp     install
    entry:  push    bp                ; save base pointer
            mov     bp,sp             ; get stack address
            push    ds                ; save data segment
            push    ax                ; save register
            push    bx
            mov     ax,cs             ; set up data segment
            mov     ds,ax
            mov     ax,[bp].flags     ; transfer caller's flags to AX
            sahf                      ; ... and to my flags
            clc                       ; clear carry (no error)
            pushf                     ; and save copy of flags
            mov     bx,[bp].funct     ; get function code
    case    bl,<1,2>,<f1,f2>
            popf                      ; get copy of flags
            stc                       ; set carry--illegal function
            pushf                     ; save copy of flags
            jmp     short exit
    f1:     dis_str f1msg
            jmp     short exit
    f2:     dis_str f2msg
    exit:   pop     ax                ; put flags back in stack
            mov     [bp].flags,ax     ; ... through ax
            pop     bx                ; restore registers
            pop     ax
            pop     ds                ; restore data segment
            pop     bp                ; restore base pointer
            iret                      ; return from interrupt
    main    endp
    ;
    f1msg   db      'Function # 1 performed',cr,lf,'$'
    f2msg   db      'Function # 2 performed',cr,lf,'$'
    lst_byt:                          ; last byte to save
    ;
```

Listing 3-2. cont.

```
; This is the installation code. All code following this point
; is thrown away after installation is complete.
;
; See the section on MEMORY MANAGEMENT TIDBITS for an
; explanation of why the environment block is being removed.
;
; Remove environment block--DS points to current segment
; Set ES to point to environment block
;
install:
        mov     es,env_adr      ; get address of environment
        mov     ah,49h          ; free allocated memory
        doscall                 ; call MS-DOS
        jnc     setvect         ; branch if no error
        dis_str fail49          ; inform if was error
        mov     ah,4Ch          ; terminate process
        doscall                 ; abort on error
;
; Set vector--DS points to current segment
setvect:
        mov     dx,offset entry ; get RTL entry point
        mov     al,v_num        ; set vector number
        mov     ah,25h          ; set vector
        doscall                 ; call MS-DOS
;
; terminate & stay resident
        mov     dx,(offset lst_byt - seg_org + 15) shr 4
        mov     ah,31h          ; keep process
        doscall                 ; call MS-DOS
;
fail49 db       'Failed to Free Environment Block',cr,lf,'$'
code_seg ends
        end     start
```

A peculiarity of the EXRTL routine is that no memory for a local stack is provided when the Keep Process executes. This would be a fatal mistake were EXRTL a program because the program stack would then be totally unprotected and subject to destruction. EXRTL, however, is not a stand-alone program but is called by other programs, which do have local stacks. The EXRTL routine performs all of its operations using the calling routine's stack.

Once we have written the RTL, we must provide some means of accessing it. Because it is impossible to determine in advance where MS-DOS will load the procedure in memory, we cannot CALL the library directly from a program that wishes to access it. The 8086 family provides one solution in the form of interrupt vectors. By setting an interrupt vector to point to the address of the library, any program that wishes may access the library by the use of the INT instruction.

The 8086 family supports 256 interrupt vectors of which 64 (00h through 39h) are reserved for the use of the system hardware or MS-DOS. (See Table 3-1 for a listing of Intel and MS-DOS interrupt vector use). This still leaves INT 40h through INT 0FFh available for our use, a total of 192 interrupt vectors. We have chosen to use vector 40h for our RTL.

CAUTION

Some systems may use interrupt vectors other than those defined for MS-DOS. Check your system's manual before using any of the vectors. Complete system failure may result from altering a vector that is already in use.

Table 3-1.   INTEL & MS-DOS Reserved Interrupt Vectors

Interrupt	Reserved By	Use
Type # 0	Intel	Divide by zero error interrupt
Type # 1	Intel	Single step "trace" interrupt
Type # 2	Intel	Non-maskable hardware interrupt
Type # 3	Intel	Breakpoint interrupt
Type # 4	Intel	Multiply overflow interrupt
*†Type # 5	Intel	BOUND exception
*†Type # 6	Intel	Undefined opcode exception
*†Type # 7	Intel	ESC opcode exception
*‡Type # 8-0F	Intel	Used by 186/188 for peripherals
* Type # 10 & 11	Intel	Reserved by Intel
*‡Type # 12 & 13	Intel	Used by 186/188 for peripherals
* Type # 14-1F	Intel	Reserved by Intel
Type # 20	MS-DOS	OLD program terminate function
Type # 21	MS-DOS	MS-DOS function call
Type # 22	MS-DOS	Program terminate address
Type # 23	MS-DOS	<**CONTROL-C**> exit address
Type # 24	MS-DOS	Fatal error abort address
Type # 25	MS-DOS	Absolute disk read function
Type # 26	MS-DOS	Absolute disk write function
Type # 27	MS-DOS	Terminate & stay resident function
Type # 28	MS-DOS	Used internally by MS-DOS
Type # 29-2E	MS-DOS	Reserved for MS-DOS
Type # 2F	MS-DOS	Printer control MS-DOS version 3
Type # 30-3F	MS-DOS	Reserved for MS-DOS

All vector numbers given in hexadecimal.
* Used by some BIOS; check your manual for conflicts
† Used by the iAPX186, iAPX188, & iAPX286 processor family for advanced instructions
‡ Used by the iAPX186 & iAPX188 Integrated Microprocessors for hardware support

Under MS-DOS, interrupt vectors may be set through the use of MS-DOS Function Code 25h, Set Interrupt Vector. The installation operation is very simple: the vector number is provided in the AL register, and the address to be loaded into the vector is provided in the DS:DX register pair (segment:offset). Because the DS register is set to the same value as the CS register in .COM programs, the DS register's contents are already correct for the call. The remaining registers are loaded and the call is made with the following code:

```
        mov     dx,offset entry ; get RTL entry point
        mov     al,v_num        ; set vector number
        mov     ah,25h          ; set interrupt vector
        doscall                 ; call MS-DOS
```

Once the EXRTL routine has been installed in memory and its access interrupt vector installed in the interrupt vector table, the RTL is ready for use. To call it, a routine uses the INT 40h instruction, and control is transferred to the EXRTL routine. The program RTL_TEST shown in Listing 3-3 is one example of a routine that accesses this particular RTL.

Listing 3-3.   Exercise Program for RTL

```
;****** RTL_TEST.ASM--This file produces a .COM file ***********
cr      equ     0Dh             ; carriage return
lf      equ     0Ah             ; line feed
v_num equ       40h             ; this RTL uses vector 40 hex
;
INCLUDE         STD.MLB         ; include macro library (MLB)
;****** PROGRAM CODE SECTION **********************************
;
code_seg segment
        assume cs:code_seg
        assume ds:code_seg
main    proc    far
        ORG     0100h
start:          mov     cx,3    ; start at illegal value
loop:   push    cx              ; function code
        int     v_num           ; call RTL
        pop     cx              ; clear return param
        jnc     nxt             ; branch no error
        dis_str caserr          ; show error
nxt:    dec     cx
        jge     loop            ; loop through 0
        mov     ah,4Ch          ; terminate process
        doscall
;
caserr db       'Case Error-Illegal Function Code',cr,lf,'$'
main    endp
code_seg ends
        end     start
```

The interface between EXRTL and RTL_TEST is all through the stack. RTL_TEST pushes a function code on the stack and executes the INT 40h instruction. Note that the stack layout in *RTL* differs from that of a CALL interface in that the interrupt pushes the flags on the stack as well as the return segment and offset.

The flow of control between the two sections is illustrated in the flowchart in Figure 3-1. The INT 40h instruction transfers control through the interrupt vector table to the EXRTL routine. The EXRTL routine then extracts the function code from the stack, assisted by the stack structure definition *frame*. EXRTL analyzes the function code to check whether it is legal, and if it is, branches to the proper function handler through use of the *case* macro. Once the function has been performed, EXRTL returns control to RTL_TEST with an IRET (Return from Interrupt) instruction.

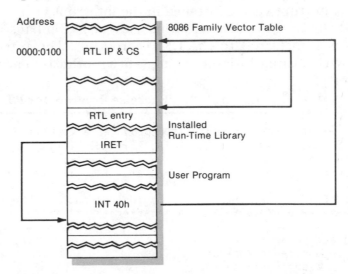

Fig. 3-1.   Flowchart of run-time library access.

The stack structure *frame* also provides EXRTL access to the caller's flags, which are stored on the stack by an INT. By copying the flags from the stack into its own flags register, EXRTL can change the value of the carry bit, then before exiting, copy the flags back into the stack (including the new value of the carry flag). This operation allows EXRTL to use the carry flag to signal error conditions to the calling routine, using the IRET instruction to restore the flags from the stack.

The last point is that EXRTL may make full use of MS-DOS as control is passed directly to it by a program. This isn't the case in some of the other memory resident programs presented in following sections of this book. Those programs receive control via hardware or MS-DOS interrupts.

How To Tell whether a Memory Resident Program Is Installed

So far we have assumed that the RTL would be loaded into memory and then the programs that use it would be started. In some circumstances, the RTL may already be present in memory. Rather than loading two copies of the RTL, the loader should first determine whether the RTL is loaded, and load it only when it is not present. There are two ways for determining whether an RTL is present, both of which depend on having used a preassigned INT vector to access the RTL.

The first method involves reading the interrupt vector contents via Function Code 35h, Get Interrupt Vector, to determine the starting address of the interrupt service routine. The next step is to place the starting address of the existing routine into the ES and DI registers and the starting address of the routine to be installed into the DS and SI registers. A CMPS instruction is executed for some number of bytes (in CX) to compare the two sections of code. If a match results, the routine is already present. If the compare fails, the routine hasn't been installed.

The effectiveness of this method is greatly decreased if all of your RTLs (or memory resident routines) begin with the same sequence of instructions. Conversely, the effectiveness can be greatly increased if all memory resident routines contain the header block shown in Listing 3-4, which uniquely identifies each memory resident routine.

Listing 3-4.   In-Line Routine Identification

```
enter:    jmp   start              ; bypass the data area
          db    '< routine name >' ; your routine's name goes here
          :     :                  ; data area ...
start:    < beginning of the code >
          :     :
```

The second method for checking to see whether an RTL or memory resident routine is present requires that all unused vectors (vectors 40h through 0FFh on most systems) be set to a known state. This known state can be either high or low memory (0000:0000 or FFFF:FFFF) or the address of an IRET instruction. In MS-DOS version 2.0 and higher, vector 28h, an MS-DOS vector, seems to always point to the location of an IRET instruction, although this is not guaranteed! A more elegant solution is to install a pseudo-device driver to handle unsolicited interrupts and to initialize all unused interrupt vectors to point to this routine. (See Chapter 5 on Installable Device Drivers.) This driver can then contain an IRET instruction, report an error to the console, or whatever else is desired. By permanently allocating one vector to always point to the unsolicited interrupt handler (for example, vector 40h), an installation program can read and compare that vector and the vector of the memory resident routine to see whether the memory resident routine has yet been installed in memory.

Removing Memory Resident Routines

When a program is through using an RTL or when a memory resident routine is no longer needed, you want to be able to recover the memory that was allocated to that routine. The simplest way to remove a memory resident routine is to reboot your system. This restores all the vectors that the system requires and returns all allocated memory to the system. However, this is a rather drastic step and is best reserved for desperate situations.

Without rebooting, removal of the routine should take place in two steps: 1) disable the routine and 2) recover the memory.

The first step is to reset to a null state the vector that points to the routine. The null state indicates to any potential users that the routine is no longer available. If you have patched the memory resident routine to a preexisting vector, the vector must be restored so that it points to the original location. You can write a program to restore the vector if the value of the old vector is stored somewhere in the memory resident routine where the restore program can find it. Programs INIT28 (Listing 3-9) and REMOVE (Listing 3-10) demonstrate this process of saving the vector for later restoration.

If the memory resident routine is driven by its own hardware interrupt (not patched), you must be sure to disable interrupts from that device before you remove the memory resident routine. You can change the value of the vector in the table or leave the vector as it is.

Once the memory resident or RTL routine has been disabled, step two is to recover the memory. Memory is recovered from MS-DOS through the Free Allocated Memory function, Function 49h. MS-DOS doesn't seem to care whether you deallocate memory that doesn't really belong to the program, so if the starting address of the block of memory that is occupied by the memory resident routine can be determined, the memory can be freed and recovered. The installed routine can usually determine this address, so one option is to provide a function code to call the routine and tell it to disable and remove itself. For routines that have been installed through the use of the interrupt vectors, a second interrupt vector may be allocated for the purpose of instructing the routine to remove itself.

If you know that the routine's interrupt vector segment address and the routine's memory block segment address are the same, another method is to write a program to read the vector, determine the memory block segment address from it, and instruct MS-DOS to free the memory.

For some reason neither of these methods always works because MS-DOS may not recover all of the memory. The problem seems to be internal to MS-DOS, so currently we can give you no advice for doing something about the inconsistency. Some hints for dealing with this problem are given in the section on *Memory Management Tidbits* in this chapter.

Function 4Bh—Load and Execute Program

Memory resident routines and RTLs often are initiated by a user entry or batch file, but on occasion a program may need to load another program into memory, either for use as a program overlay or as part of a memory resident routine installation process. In either case, the original program is called the *parent* and the other program is called the *child*.

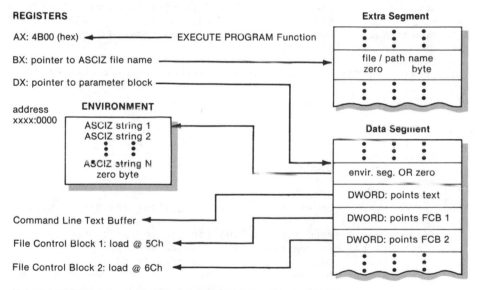

Note: All DWORD pointers are stored as OFFSET followed by SEGMENT.

**Fig. 3-2.   Parameter block for function 4Bh
(AL = 0)—EXECUTE.**

MS-DOS provides for these occasions through the Load Program and Execute function, Function Code 4Bh. This function can operate in either of two modes. The first mode, Execute Program, is designed to load a program file into memory and execute that program. The child program runs without control from the parent program. This mode is chosen by setting register AL equal to zero and setting the appropriate parameters in the parameter block. The parameters required for this operation are shown in Figure 3-2, and an example of loading and executing a program is contained in the LOAD program, shown in Listing 3-5. The macro library referenced in LOAD is the same one that was used for the EXRTL program (Listing 3-2).

Listing 3-5.   Loading Programs with MS-DOS Function 4Bh (AL = 0)

```
;****** LOAD.ASM--This file produces a .COM file ***************
; LOAD has the ability to load and execute another program.
; LOAD is invoked by typing:
;        "LOAD <filename> <program arguments>
; There must be only one space between LOAD and the file name
; and between the file name and arguments. The file name must
; include the extension.
;
cr      equ     0Dh             ; carriage return
lf      equ     0Ah             ; line feed
newprog         equ     82h     ; addr of load command line in PSP
newstr equ      81h             ; addr of string in PSP (blank 20h)
newlen equ      80h             ; addr of command line length
;
INCLUDE         STD.MLB         ; include macro library (MLB)
;****** PROGRAM SECTION ****************************************
;
code_seg        segment
        assume  cs:code_seg
        assume  ds:code_seg
        ORG     0
seg_org equ     $
        ORG     0100h
main    proc    far
start:
        mov     sp,offset top_stk       ; set the top_of_stack
;
; parse the command line looking for the end or a space.
; convert the program name into an ASCIZ string.
        mov     bx,0            ; clear upper BX
        mov     bl,newlen[bx]   ; get length of command string
        or      bl,bl           ; check length of string
        jnz     cmd_ok
        dis_str bad_cmd         ; command line error
        jmp     exit
cmd_ok:
        dec     bx              ; subtract 1 for leading space
        mov     cx,bx           ; copy length into count
        mov     di,newprog      ; search address (1st nonblank)
        mov     al,' '          ; search value (blank)
        repne   scasb           ; search for file extension
        pushf                   ; save results of search
        sub     bx,cx           ; get remaining count
        popf                    ; ... and get search results
        jz      set_zb          ; zero flag => params. (found space)
```

Listing 3-5. cont.

```
        inc     bx                      ; not zero flag implies end of string
set zb:                                 ; convert command line to ASCIZ
        mov     byte ptr newstr[bx],0
        mov     cmd_buf,cl              ; set length of parameter string
        cmp     cl,0                    ; check whether end of string reached
        jle     free_mem               ; no command parameters
;
; Take the remainder of the line and transfer it to the
; command line text buffer for the called program.
        inc     cl                      ; transfer the CR also
        mov     si,di                   ; transfer source index
        mov     di,offset cmd_txt       ; & set destination index.
        rep     movsb                   ; transfer remainder of line
        add     cmd_buf,1               ; inc. length for leading space
;
; Free system memory for the Loader and the invoked program.
; Cut down allocation block to minimum necessary
free_mem:
        mov     bx,(offset lst_byt - seg_org + 15) shr 4
        mov     ah,04Ah                 ; ES contains address of PSP
        doscall                         ; modify allocated memory
        jnc     modify_ok
        push    ax                      ; (push expected by error)
        dis_str fail4A                  ; error message & terminate if fail
        jmp     error
;
; Set up the parameter block and register parameters for the
; Load & Execute Program function call.
modify_ok:
        mov     ax,cs                   ; set all parameter segments to
        mov     p1,ax                   ; this segment.
        mov     p2,ax
        mov     p3,ax
        mov     dx,offset newprog
        mov     bx,offset param_block
        mov     spoint,sp               ; save stack pointer
        mov     ax,4B00h                ; load & execute program func.
        doscall
;
; Restore the Segment Registers and Stack Pointer after call.
        mov     cx,cs                   ; duplicate CS into all segs.
        mov     ss,cx                   ; stack restored first
        mov     sp,cs:spoint            ; restore stack pointer
        mov     ds,cx
        mov     es,cx
        jnc     exit                    ; exit program if all okay
        push    ax                      ; save error code
        dis_str fail4B                  ; display error if failed
;
; Parse the error code returned from the system and
; display the corresponding text message
error:
        pop     ax                      ; get back error code
        case    ax,<1,2,7,8,9,10h,11h>,<em1,em2,em7,em8,em9,em10,em11>
        mov     dx,offset err0          ; bad error code--no match
```

Listing 3-5. cont.

```
        jmp     merge
em1:    mov     dx,offset err1   ; invalid function
        jmp     merge
em2:    mov     dx,offset err2   ; file not found
        jmp     merge
em7:    mov     dx,offset err7   ; memory arena trashed
        jmp     merge
em8:    mov     dx,offset err8   ; not enough memory
        jmp     merge
em9:    mov     dx,offset err9   ; invalid memory block
        jmp     merge
em10:   mov     dx,offset err10  ; bad environment
        jmp     merge
em11:   mov     dx,offset err11  ; bad .EXE file format
        jmp     merge
merge:  mov     ah,09h           ; display string
        doscall
exit:   mov     ax,04C00h        ; terminate when finished
        doscall
main    endp
;
bad_cmd         db       'Error in Command Line',cr,lf,'$'
fail4A db       'Failed to Modify Allocated Memory Blocks',cr,lf,'$'
fail4B db       'Failed to Load Program Overlay',cr,lf,'$'
err0   db       '<<< UNKNOWN ERROR CODE >>>',cr,lf,'$'
err1   db       '<<< invalid function >>>',cr,lf,'$'
err2   db       '<<< file not found >>>',cr,lf,'$'
err7   db       '<<< memory arena trashed >>>',cr,lf,'$'
err8   db       '<<< not enough memory >>>',cr,lf,'$'
err9   db       '<<< invalid memory block >>>',cr,lf,'$'
err10  db       '<<< bad environment >>>',cr,lf,'$'
err11  db       '<<< bad .EXE file format >>>',cr,lf,'$'
;
spoint dw       ?                ; space for stack pointer
param_block     label word
        dw      0                ; use parent environment
        dw      offset cmd_buf
p1     dw       ?                ; cmd. line segment
        dw      5Ch              ; FCB #1 segment & offset
p2     dw       ?
        dw      6Ch              ; FCB #2 segment & offset
p3     dw       ?
cmd_buf         db       ?            ; length of command string
        db      ' '                  ; space always expected
cmd_txt         db       80 dup (?)   ; 80 characters
; Local Stack Definition
even                             ; word align the stack
stack db         32 dup ('stack   ')  ; local stack
top_stk          equ     $-2     ; set top stack address
lst_byt          equ     $       ; last byte in program
;
code_seg         ends
        end     start
```

The second mode is called Load Overlay. Although it loads a program file, Load Overlay does not invoke the program. Instead, control is immediately returned to the calling program. This mode is selected by setting register AL equal to three, and its parameter block is shown in Figure 3-3.

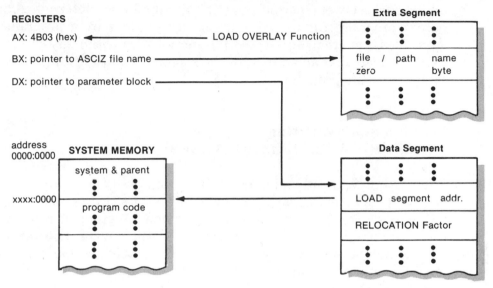

Fig. 3-3. Parameter block for function 4Bh (AL = 3)—LOAD OVERLAY.

In either mode of operation, before the Load and Execute Program function may be executed, the initial allocation block of the calling program must be reset to free up memory space. The reason is that MS-DOS loads programs by using the COMMAND.COM program loader, which is not in the memory resident part of COMMAND.COM. Instead, the program loader must itself be read into memory from the disk before it can load a user's program or program overlay. (This also implies that a disk containing the file COMMAND.COM must be in the system for this function to work.)

A quick refresher on memory allocation is called for. From Chapter 2, you know that current MS-DOS programs (produced by LINK) allocate all the user memory to the currently running program and that the initial memory allocation block for the current program may be reset to a more reasonable size through Modify Allocated Memory, Function 4Ah. Also remember that the memory block address (program segment prefix address) can be found on startup in all segment registers in a .COM program, in the DS and ES registers for a .EXE program, or obtained from MS-DOS version 3.0 by Get Program Segment Prefix, Function 62h (INT 21h).

There is an important difference between loading program overlays and loading and executing programs. Program overlays are loaded under control of the parent program, at an address determined by the parent program, and are considered part of the parent program. Program files that are to be executed (Function 4Bh with register AL equal to 0) are loaded at an address of the system's choosing and are considered a separate program.

Loading and Executing Programs via MS-DOS (Code 4Bh with AL = 0)

When using the Load and Execute function, MS-DOS requires not only enough free memory to load the COMMAND.COM program loader but also enough free memory to contain the new program. This memory is used to create an initial allocation block for the new program also.

Remember that the initial allocation block of the parent program must be set large enough to preserve the current program, or MS-DOS overwrites the block when the new program is loaded. In addition, most of the memory resident routines or RTLs are written in .COM format. For .COM programs, MS-DOS sets the stack to start at the highest available memory address in the common segment that is used for code, data, and the stack. Unless the top of the stack is relocated downward in the segment, up to 64K of the parent program must be preserved. If the stack is relocated downward, whatever was on the stack (such as the return to MS-DOS) is lost. Of course, the return to MS-DOS on the stack is not needed if you exit from your programs by using Function Code 4Ch.

Each time a program is loaded with the Execute function, that program is allocated all of free memory. If a newly loaded program uses memory allocation or needs to load yet another program, the newly loaded program must first call the Modify Allocated Memory function to return memory to the system.

Controlling the Child Program

In spite of the fact that the child program is autonomous, the parent program still has a measure of control. Control is exercised through the parent's ability to control the child's environment and its PSP parameters.

Control can be exercised at different levels, depending on the amount of integration between the programs. At the most basic level the parent program can control the values contained in the child's FCBs (file control blocks) and command line text buffer. These values allow the parent to invoke virtually any program and instruct it to operate on files of the parent's choice with the command line providing any switches (for example, / <option>) that the child program requires.

When passing file names to the child program, remember that the FCB file name cannot contain a directory path. Instead, the complete file name and pathname are to be placed in the child's copy of the command line text buffer so that if the child wishes to use the file handle method of accessing files in a different directory, the child program may obtain the complete name and use it.

If the parent program wishes the child to either input or output to a device, the parent program can pass the child the device's name in the proper FCB file name field and the command line text buffer. Note that neither the FCBs nor the command line text buffer reflect any redirection that has occurred, so the parent's ability to control those fields does not provide the parent program with the ability to perform redirection of the child's input or output.

One other way exists in which the parent process can control the child's view of the system. The first entry in the Load and Execute parameter block is a pointer to the child's *Environment Block*. The environment block is made up of a series of ASCIZ strings (ASCII text terminated with a zero byte), which contain entries for the COMMAND. COM search path (COMSPEC = <path>), the current path in effect (PATH = <search path>), and various other parameters. If the pointer in the Load and Execute parameter block is a zero, the parent's environment is duplicated for the child. If it is nonzero, the block that it points to is loaded as the child's environment.

What does this mean for you? You can write a program to search the environment block for particular entries, then use those values to establish the program's run-time parameters. Entries may be inserted in the system environment block with the SET command to control the actions of programs that read and act on their environment block. Because the parent process can change the block, the parent process can change the behavior of a child process that reads the block.

An executing process can access its environment block through a pointer stored at offset 2Ch in the PSP. The pointer is used as a segment address with offset zero pointing to the start of the block. If this address is transferred to the extra or data segment register, the program can do a string search to find those parameters that the program requires. Be careful when you do this so that you don't lose the PSP address.

The information contained in the PSP is equally valid for .COM and .EXE format files, and either type may be used with the Load and Execute Program function.

Executing MS-DOS Commands with Function 4Bh

One of the Load and Execute function applications is loading COM-MAND.COM. Consider that COMMAND.COM may be given commands through the command line text buffer, and you can see that you can invoke built-in MS-DOS commands from within a user's program. In addition, the command line passed to COMMAND.COM may contain redirection, pipes, and filters. The format of the command text used with this method is nearly the same as that used on the initial command line, except that when invoking COMMAND.COM from a program, the text must begin with "/c."

Loading two files (COMMAND.COM and the application program) to execute just one is not a terribly efficient way of running programs. However, the flexibility and power gained by using this method are worth considering.

An Important Warning

The implementation of the Load and Execute Program function in version 2.0 of MS-DOS has a serious bug. It causes the function to "trash" all the segment registers with the exception of the Code Segment, to destroy the stack pointer, and to destroy the majority of the general registers. If this function is used with any of the subversions of MS-DOS version 2.0 (that is, 2.00 or 2.10), you must save the stack pointer and any needed general registers in memory before the call, and you need to restore the segment registers, stack pointer, and needed general registers after the call. The code sequence appearing in Listing 3-6 seems to do the job for .COM programs.

Listing 3-6. Recovering from the Load and Execute Program
Function in MS-DOS Versions 2.XX

```
        :          :
        < set up calling parameters >
        :          :
        mov     spoint,sp      ; save stack pointer in memory
        mov     ax,4B00h       ; load & execute program function
        int     21h            ; call MS-DOS
; Registers are unchanged if the load fails--don't recover
        jc      error          ; jump if error
        mov     ax,cs          ; get common segment ...
        mov     ds,cx          ; ... for data segment ...
        mov     es,cx          ; ... for extra segment ...
        mov     ss,ax          ; ... and for stack segment
        mov     sp,spoint      ; stack is now realigned
        :          :
```

Listing 3-6. cont.

```
< recover general registers >
  :           :
```

For .EXE files, recover the proper segment values from the values established by LINK (for example, "mov ss,stack") or from memory located within the Code Segment. To protect the stack, remember to restore the stack segment and stack pointer in that sequence, one right after the other.

Beginning with version 3.0 of MS-DOS, this problem appears to have been corrected. The Load and Execute Function returns with all registers intact.

Loading Program Overlays via MS-DOS
(Code 4Bh with AL = 3)

The ability to execute one program from within another is indeed powerful but has the disadvantage of having the invoked program run once, then terminating. On many occasions, the developer wants to invoke another program to perform some sort of function but in addition wants greater control of the child program, a higher degree of communication with the child, or just wants to be able to call the child program repeatedly without having it reloaded each time. For these circumstances, MS-DOS provides the Load Overlay option for Function 4Bh.

One difference between the Load and Execute function and the Load Overlay function is that when loading overlays, the parent program has no means to modify the parameters of the child program. This is because the parent and child are really part of the same program. All that the Load Overlay function accomplishes is to load additional program code (and/or program data) into memory.

Another way in which Load Overlay differs from Load and Execute is that Load Overlay does not require a memory block of its own. It is not given an environment or initial allocation block, as with the Load and Execute Program function. Load Overlay simply loads the requested file in memory, relocating the program's segment values based on the parameters that are provided in the Load Overlay function call (as shown in Fig. 3-3). The resulting code may be run as a subroutine but should not be executed as a separate program.

If the overlay terminates through one of the MS-DOS Terminate Program functions, both the overlay and the parent program are terminated. If either Function 31h or Interrupt 27h (Terminate and Stay Resident) are used to exit, the initial allocation block of the parent routine is modified and the parent program stays in memory. The child only stays resident if the requested memory block is large enough to cover both parent and child. If one of the other Terminate Program functions is executed, both programs are removed from memory.

Figure 3-3 shows that the relocation factor specified as part of the Load Overlay function does nothing to affect the load address of the overlay. Instead, the relocation factor is used to modify offset references within the code being loaded. If the overlay to be loaded is in .COM format, the relocation factor has no effect on the loaded overlay and should be set to 0.

For .EXE files, the relocation factor is added to the values of the segment references that appear in the load file. When loading most .EXE format overlays (which usually default to origin 0000:0000), the relocation factor should be set to the same value as the load address. Further details about loading both .COM format files and .EXE format files are found in the section on Loading Program Files, toward the end of this chapter.

Accessing Program Overlays from the Parent Program

Once the program overlay has been loaded, the parent program must access it. Because the parent knows the address at which the overlay was loaded it can either CALL the overlay or JMP to it. Calling is recommended for the reason that the overlay may then return to the parent by using the RET instruction rather than having to know the return address to JMP to in the parent. If control doesn't need to be returned to the parent program, a JMP is recommended. The overlay then contains the Terminate Program function call.

All accesses, by either CALL or JMP, to the overlay must be FAR references. The code that has been loaded in the overlay is relative to its own segment address and may not be run in the same segment as the parent routine (although it can be loaded into the same memory space). In addition, no PSP is built by the Load Overlay function. Because there is no additional information placed in memory by the loader, the code and data are loaded from the overlay file beginning at the exact load address specified.

Let's consider the simplest case: overlays that are loaded from .COM format files. All .COM files have origins of 100 hex. That is, their code starts at address 100 hex relative to their segment. All references contained in the program are relative to that address. Because the .COM file is loaded right on the load address, you would be incorrect to use the load address as the segment value for the overlay. Figure 3-4 shows that if the load address is used as the segment, the offset values in the code are misplaced by 100 hex. The correct program segment address to use is the load address minus 10 (hex), which translates the code offsets by 100 hex.

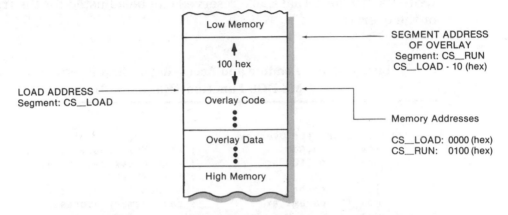

Fig. 3-4.   Relationship of segment and load addresses for .COM format overlays.

A different problem exists for .EXE format programs. When a .EXE file is loaded for execution, MS-DOS initializes the Code Segment and Stack Segment to point to the proper segments and the Instruction Pointer to point to the first instruction of the program. When a .EXE file is loaded as an overlay, MS-DOS doesn't provide these values. How then does the parent program know where to enter the program?

Because .EXE files usually have an origin of zero, couldn't we just call or jump to the load address? That would depend on how the program was written. For .EXE files created from a single source file, LINK and MS-DOS load the segments in memory in the same order in which they appear in the source program! A common order for defining segments is stack segment, then data segment, then code segment. (The reason is to minimize forward references in the code segment.) For a .EXE program to be callable at its load address, the code segment must be the first segment in the .ASM file, and the entry point must be the first instruction in the code segment. MASM and LINK have no problems handling this, although in some cases you may need to use override directives to resolve forward references for MASM.

Listing 3-7 shows how the load and call sequence could appear when using the Load Overlay function for a .COM file. The sequence for a .EXE type program is simpler. No translation from load address to run address is needed. We have assumed that all segment registers in the parent program are already initialized and that Modify Allocated Memory has already been called to free enough memory for the COMMAND

.COM loader. The sample program allocates the memory that is to contain the overlay code. This reserves that area of memory so that if the overlay also allocates memory, a virgin area is provided. Otherwise, the overlay could allocate the memory that it already occupies and overwrite itself. The actual space reserved can be adjusted for the true size of the overlay.

Listing 3-7.   Loading and Accessing a .COM Program with MS-DOS Function 4Bh (AL = 3)

```
        :         :
; Allocate memory for Overlay
        mov     ah,48h              ; allocate memory function
        mov     bx,1000h            ; assume 64K segment for now
        int     21h                 ; call MS-DOS
        jc      error               ; branch if error occurred
        mov     params,ax           ; save memory address
; Load overlay
        mov     dx,offset params    ; access parameter block
        mov     bx,offset filename  ; access ASCIZ file name
        mov     ax,4B03h            ; load overlay function
        int     21h                 ; call MS-DOS
        jc      error               ; branch if error occurred
; Call overlay
        mov     ax,params           ; get load address
        sub     ax,10h              ; translate to run address
        mov     run_seg,ax          ; and save it
        push    ds                  ; save data segment
        call    dword ptr run_adr   ; call overlay
; Free memory that was used for overlay
        pop     ds                  ; restore data segment
        mov     ah,49h              ; free memory function
        mov     es,params           ; get memory block address
        int     21h                 ; call MS-DOS
        jc      error               ; branch if error occurred
        :         :
params  dw      ?                   ; load address
        dw      0                   ; relocation value
run_adr dw      0100h               ; new instruction pointer
run_seg dw      ?                   ; new code segment value
```

The overlay may be changed as often as necessary for the execution of the program. The only warning that applies to all uses of the Load Overlay function is that MS-DOS does nothing to prevent you from loading the overlay on top of the currently executing program or anywhere else in memory, including the system itself! Although someone might find such a trick useful, it is definitely not recommended procedure, and care should be taken to prevent its inadvertent occurrence.

Loading Memory Resident Programs

Memory resident routines and RTLs to be installed from another program are best loaded through the Load and Execute Program function so that the new routine has its own memory block. In these cases, the calling program (the parent) receives control after the memory resident program's initialization section executes its Terminate and Stay Resident request.

If a stand-alone memory resident routine was loaded, the parent program terminates, leaving the memory resident program in place. This breaks up memory free space, but there is no risk of MS-DOS loading a subsequent program over the memory resident routine. If an RTL was loaded, the parent program would be ready to call the RTL as needed. When the parent routine terminates, it has the option of leaving the RTL in memory for subsequent use or of removing it by resetting its interrupt vector and freeing its memory block.

Because the Load and Execute Program function does not inform the calling routine of the load address of the memory resident routine and because that address cannot be passed back to the parent in the single byte reserved for the program's exit code (see Terminate and Stay Resident, Function 31h), the parent routine must resort to the tactics discussed in preceding text to determine the location of the memory block to be removed.

A Special Case: Part-Time Run-Time Libraries

One of the many features that can be implemented with the functions presented is a part-time run-time library. Part-time RTLs are resident only when required and the rest of the time reside on disk. A part-time RTL is implemented by installing the header part of an RTL exactly as described in this chapter. However, this header contains none of the code for executing the library functions, that is, it doesn't contain the library routines themselves, which are left on disk in another file. Flowchart 3-1 shows the sequence of events in the life of a part-time RTL.

When one of the routines in the library is accessed (via an INT), the header portion of the routine loads the library file into memory using Function Code 4Bh with AL = 3 (Load Overlay) and locks it into its own memory. The desired library routine is then called to execute the requested function. Either the header or the individual library routines can contain the IRET to return to the caller. From this point on, all subsequent calls access the library without having to wait for the load because the RTL stays resident in memory.

Flowchart 3-1.   Part-time RTL load sequence.

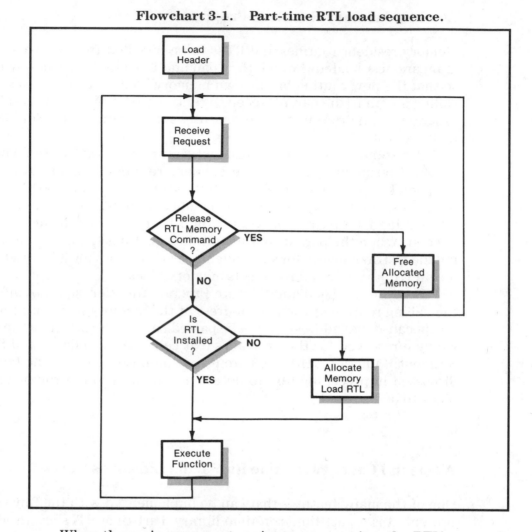

When the main program terminates, or requires the RTL's space, it signals the RTL entry point with a code to release the memory allocated to the RTL. Because the header portion specified the load address of the library routines when it loaded them and because the memory block they occupy is "owned" by the header, freeing the memory is no problem. After this is accomplished, the header goes back into hibernation and waits for the next call.

Program Files and the MS-DOS Loader

As you know, executable program files under MS-DOS come in two "flavors"—.COM and .EXE files. To the programmer, the differences between these two formats is summarized in Table 3-2.

Table 3-2.   Comparison of .COM and .EXE Files

.COM	.EXE
Only one segment allowed	Multiple segments allowed
No segment references allowed	Segment references allowed
No stack segment	Must have stack segment
Must be ORG at 100h	No ORG required
Must be less than 64Kbytes	May be any size

To the operating system the differences appear in another form. MASM doesn't know or care what type of file is being assembled. LINK detects that .COM format files have no stack segment but otherwise doesn't care. Only when EXE2BIN is run do the differences begin to show.

All files produced by MASM and LINK can contain segment relocatable references. The name that is given to these files is .EXE. They contain information telling MS-DOS where the program makes references to the current segment. When MS-DOS loads these files into memory, the system updates the locations in the program where segment references are made, which changes the values to point to the current segment.

When a .EXE file is converted to a .COM file, EXE2BIN scans the file looking for these segment references. If any references in the code are found, EXE2BIN produces an error message stating that the file cannot be converted. In addition, EXE2BIN checks to make sure that the code starts at address 100 hex relative to the segment. If these conditions are met, EXE2BIN strips the file of all relocation information and produces a .COM file. Because this information has been removed, the file is now smaller in size, and because no relocation need be performed during load, the file loads faster.

The Initial Allocation Block and .EXE Programs

In our examples thus far, we have been taking it for granted that when MS-DOS loads a program into memory, the system allocates *all* remaining memory to that program. Because of this, we have begun our programs by resizing the allocated memory block. However, another method of providing free memory for an executing program is available.

Although MS-DOS automatically allocates all remaining memory for .COM programs, MS-DOS doesn't cause .EXE programs to allocate all of memory. For .EXE programs, MS-DOS follows the control and relocation information contained in the program file header. The contents of this area are shown in Table 3-3. The information that concerns us is MAXALLOC, the maximum memory allocation word, at word 0C (hex).

Table 3-3.   .EXE Program File Header

Address (hex)	Contents
00-01	4D5AH (hex): .EXE program file type marker
02-03	Number of bytes in last page of file
04-05	Size of the file, including the header, in 512-byte pages
06-07	Number of relocation entries in the relocation table
08-09	Size of the header in 16-byte paragraphs
0A-0B	MINALLOC: minimum number of memory paragraphs required beyond the end of the program
0C-0D	MAXALLOC: maximum number of memory paragraphs required beyond the end of the program
0E-0F	Initial value for the stack segment (relative to the start of the program)
10-11	Initial value for the stack pointer
12-13	Two's complement checksum of the program file
14-15	Starting instruction pointer value
16-17	Initial value for the code segment (relative to the start of the program)
18-19	Relative byte offset from beginning of the run file to the relocation table
1A-1B	Number of the overlay as generated by MS-LINK

MAXALLOC is the number of memory paragraphs that the program desires be allocated to it. MS-LINK normally sets this value to FFFFh, which tells MS-DOS that the program wants all of memory. Conversely, MINALLOC (at word 0Ah) is the number of memory paragraphs that the program actually needs. By copying the value of MINALLOC to MAXALLOC in the .EXE file header, MS-DOS is instructed to allocate only what memory is actually required. This modification can be done with a small program or with DEBUG.

The Program Segment Prefix (PSP)

When MS-DOS loads a program file for execution (as opposed to overlay), be it either .EXE or .COM, the system begins by setting up a context for the file. The first thing that MS-DOS does is set up the Environment Block, writing into the block either a copy of the current system environment or, if loaded from another program, the environment specified by the parent. Once the environment has been set up, MS-DOS sets up the memory block for the program and proceeds to build the PSP for the program. After this has been completed, the program is read into memory, relocated by altering its segment references, and the various registers set to their starting configurations. The part that is of most use to us is the PSP, which appears in Table 3-4.

Table 3-4.   The Program Segment Prefix

Offset	Length	Contents
00 (hex)	2 byte	INT 20h instruction
02 (hex)	2 byte	System memory size in paragraphs (16-byte blocks)
04 (hex)	2 byte	Reserved
05 (hex)	5 byte	Long call to MS-DOS function dispatcher
06 (hex)	2 byte	Number of bytes available in the segment
0A (hex)	4 byte	Program terminate address (IP, CS)
0E (hex)	4 byte	<CONTROL-C> exit address (IP, CS)
12 (hex)	4 byte	Hard error exit address (IP, CS)
16 (hex)	22 byte	Reserved for MS-DOS
2C (hex)	2 byte	Segment address of the environment block
2E (hex)	34 byte	Reserved for MS-DOS
50 (hex)	12 byte	Code to call MS-DOS function dispatcher (Usually an INT 21h Instruction)
5C (hex)	16 byte	Unopened file control block #1 (The file name is not valid if the parameter contained a pathname, in which case only the drive number is valid.)
6C (hex)	16 byte	Unopened file control block #2 (The same conditions apply as for FCB #1. In addition, FCB #2 is overlayed if FCB #1 is opened.)
7C (hex)	4 byte	Reserved for MS-DOS
80 (hex)	128 byte	Default disk transfer area. Overlays the command line text string when used.
80 (hex)	1 byte	Length of the text string that was typed following the command, minus any redirection characters or parameters.
81 (hex)	127 byte	Text string that was typed following the command. Redirection characters (< and >) and their associated file names do not appear in this area. Redirection is transparent to the application.

The PSP can be best described as a collection of unrelated data elements, the repository for various pieces of information required by programs. We have already seen many of the PSP's uses, including obtaining the environment address and the command line text. Some of the contents that we have not covered are the parameters describing the total size of system memory and the number of bytes remaining in the segment. Both of these can be useful in determining how to distribute memory for internal buffers, managing program overlays, etc., or just for fiddling with memory.

Not covered also in this chapter are the transfer addresses provided for various error and exit conditions. The values that are stored in the PSP are not used by the system but rather are copies of the addresses appearing in the 8086/8088's interrupt vector table. Programmers should use the Set Vector (Code 25h) and Get Vector (Code 35h) functions to obtain and change these addresses.

Self-Relocatable Code

When any program is loaded into memory, MS-DOS determines that program's load address based on what memory is available and a set of rules for determining the best fit. This address is nearly always the first free memory block located after the highest addressed memory block that is still allocated. Sometimes the developer may wish to locate the routine at a different location in memory.

A routine coded to be segment relocatable can move itself. The move is accomplished by allocating the desired block of memory, setting the ES and DI registers to point to the new block of memory, setting the DS and SI registers to point to the code to be moved, and using the REP MOVS instruction to copy the routine to a new location. For any code that does not contain segment value references (for instance, .COM format), the new code can change its segment registers and begin execution. If the code is to be contained in another segment, however, and is supposed to be part of it, then the code must be fully relocatable, that is, the code must contain only relative addressing modes.

For the worst cases where a routine contains segment references and is not relocatable at all, a whole new copy of the routine may be loaded into a block of memory with the overlay option (AL = 3) of the Load and Execute Program function, Code 4Bh.

The case of code that contains absolute segment references need not be considered because MS-DOS won't load a routine that has been linked to execute at an absolute address.

Memory Management Tidbits

Memory management is probably the most important aspect of MS-DOS explained in this chapter. Why then have we left it to the end? To be able to explain the actions of MS-DOS regarding memory requires a sizable number of details. Details that have been provided over the course of the chapter. Now we're ready to fill in the gaps.

"Hidden" Memory Allocation and the Environment Block

By now you are familiar with the mechanics of sizing, allocating, and deallocating memory via MS-DOS. Some problems still may be encountered. One you may have noticed is the "stranded" memory problem that occurs when you attempt to free memory that was allocated to a memory resident routine. There are two points that may help. First, MS-DOS appears to deallocate memory in the reverse order from which it was allocated. This means that if you attempt to free a memory block that lies below another memory block which is still allocated, MS-DOS doesn't make that memory available to the system, and the memory doesn't appear when CHKDSK is run. Only after the higher addressed memory block has been freed does MS-DOS release the lower block.

Even if all the blocks that were allocated to memory resident routines are removed in reverse order, you notice that not all of the memory is returned. Where did this memory go? The answer is that the "missing" memory was allocated to provide space for the memory resident routine's environment block. The amount of memory allocated depends on the size of the environment at the time the memory resident routine was installed. You can recover this memory in one of two ways.

From the command line, run CHKDSK to determine the amount of missing memory. (You have to know the amount of memory that was available when the routine was first installed to be able to figure out how much is missing.) This amount must be converted to paragraphs (divide by 16). That number is subtracted from the segment address of the memory resident routine that was just removed. The resulting number is the address of the memory block to be removed to free up the environment block. We might call this method the *after-the-fact* method, and you can use it when something has messed up the memory allocation tables and rebooting isn't desirable.

The second method that can be used to free memory allocated to the environment block is to obtain its address from the PSP (offset 2Ch) and release that block of memory at the start of the program. This doesn't appear to have any ill effects because MS-DOS won't reuse the block until the routine that appears above it in memory has been removed. This is a cleaner method because it doesn't require any arcane calculations.

This method may also be applied to memory resident routines "after-the-fact." For .COM format routines, the address of the environment is read from the routine's PSP at offset 2C hex in the memory resident routine's segment. The release program can then release both the routine and its associated environment block.

For .EXE type routines, the address of the PSP is unavailable except on initial entry. In these cases, the memory resident routine must store the PSP address for access by the removal routine. The removal routine can then read the stored PSP addres to determine the addresses of the routine's memory block (the PSP) and environment block. This method is similar to that used to store a previous vector address for memory resident routines.

The Get Program Segment Prefix call (function 62h) supported by MS-DOS version 3.0 cannot be used by any memory resident routine to obtain its PSP address. This is because once the routine has executed a Keep Process or Terminate & Stay Resident function, MS-DOS no longer considers the routine active. The Get PSP function only applies to the program last loaded by MS-DOS, which MS-DOS considers to be the currently active program.

Memory Allocation and .COM Programs

When a .COM program is run, MS-DOS takes responsibility for setting up the stack. For most systems, the stack pointer is initialized to FFFE (hex), indicating that the top of the stack is at the top of the segment. However, what happens when the system doesn't have 64Kb of free memory left? MS-DOS sizes the stack downward. With a little thought, you may find this technique obvious, but it's one of those things that you don't think about too often. The upshot of this possibility is that the programmer should never assume that the stack begins at address FFFE in the segment. The minimum size required for the stack under MS-DOS is apparently 256 bytes and is aligned on a memory paragraph.

If you intend running programs that push your system's memory to the limits or require a larger stack, build a stack into your .COM programs. You can't use a stack segment, but you can set up a data area for the stack in your program and transfer the stack to that area on entry. This way if there isn't enough room for the stack you need, MS-DOS won't be able to load your program. At least you won't have the problem of a stack that's too small. That could result in having your stack extend into code or data sections of the program.

For an example of a local stack in a .COM program, look again at Listing 3-5.

Context Switching and Switching Stacks

Because so many of the topics that have been discussed in this chapter relate to operations between separate programs with separate stacks, the process of switching stacks deserves some attention. Stack switching, or changing from one stack to another, is part of a broader topic called *context switching*.

If you view the segments in which a program executes as its context, you can see that in many instances you need to change the entire context of a program. Examples are in invoking memory resident routines, calling RTLs, and in some type of overlays or co-routines. (A co-routine is a sort of special overlay where there is no parent-child relationship). In these cases, when one routine receives control, it wishes to set up its own data, extra, and stack segments for execution. At the time that it receives control from the other program, the only thing that is known for sure is that its code segment and instruction pointer are set to the proper values. Refer to Listing 3-6. We had to reset the program context after calling the Load and Execute Program function, and this listing shows one way to establish a context for a program. The example in Listing 3-6 unfortunately does not preserve the context of the previous program but simply overwrites it.

When you need to save the entire register set on receipt of control, the easiest way is to set up the new program's stack first, then proceed to stack the other registers. Because the values of the stack segment and stack pointer cannot be saved on the caller's stack (because there would be no way to retrieve them) and because they cannot be saved on the new stack (which hasn't been set up yet) the stack's parameters must be saved in memory. If you can stand mixing code and data in the same segment just this once, the sequence shown in Listing 3-8 can be used to store the old stack segment and pointer and set up the new stack segment and pointer.

Listing 3-8.   Stack Switching for a .EXE Program

```
enter:  mov     cs:old_stk_seg,ss    ; save old stack values
        mov     cs:old_stk_ptr,sp
        mov     ss,cs:new_stk_seg    ; load new stack values
        mov     sp,cs:new_stk_ptr
        push    ds                   ; stack segment registers
        push    es
        push    ax                   ; start stacking general regs.
          :     :
        push    bp
        push    si
        push    di
          :     :
body:   < body of the program >      ; your code goes here
          :     :
        pop     di                   ; start recovering general
        pop     si
        pop     bp
          :     :
        pop     ax
        pop     es                   ; recover segment registers
        pop     ds
```

Listing 3-8. cont.

```
        mov     ss,cs:old_stk_seg  ; restore old stack values
        mov     sp,cs:old_stk_ptr
        jmp     exit               ; bypass data storage
;
old_stk_seg  dw  ?                 ; caller's stack segment
old_stk_ptr  dw  ?                 ; caller's stack pointer
new_stk_seg  dw  segment stack     ; this routine's stack segment
new_stk_ptr  dw  top_of_stack      ; this routine's stack pointer
exit:                              ; exit position
        ret                        ; return to calling program
```

The code in Listing 3-8 depends on having the values for the stack segment and stack pointer already located in memory. This could be accomplished for a memory resident or run-time routine by the initialization process. For a .EXE program, MS-DOS places the proper values in memory during the relocation process.

Because .COM routines cannot contain segment values, these routines require another method for switching stacks. Embedding the value for the top of stack in memory causes no problem, except with determining the starting segment address. Because .COM routines share the same segment for all purposes, the stack segment value may be obtained from the code segment register. Unfortunately the 8086 family does not support moves from segment register to segment register, so the value must be passed indirectly. Because none of the registers have been saved as yet, the value is passed through memory using the code segment. To implement this modification, start the routine with the instruction:

```
mov     cs:new_stk_seg,cs ; get new stack segment
```

If you intend doing a fair amount of stack switching in your programs, you can set up two macros to include the necessary code. The first macro includes the code from *enter* to *body*, and the second macro contains the code from *body* to *exit*. Both macros must agree on the names of the stack variables in the data area, and the second macro must accept the label *top_of_stack* as a parameter to include in the "dw" statement for *new_stk_ptr*. The RET instruction should not be part of the macros, which allows them to be used with JMP and IRET exits as well as RET exits.

For .EXE files, the second macro must also accept the name of the stack segment as a parameter. Listing 3-9 (INIT28) contains an example use in a .COM format of the two macros just described.

Additional Considerations for Stack Switching

When swapping stacks or otherwise manipulating the stack segment, the program is vulnerable to interrupts. Should an interrupt occur when the stack segment but not the stack pointer has been changed, the system could very well crash. In the 8086 family, this is prevented by changing the stack pointer *immediately* following the instruction that loaded the stack segment. When an 8086 family processor loads a segment register (through either a MOV or POP instruction), interrupts are prevented from occurring until after the next instruction executes. This feature allows both the stack segment and stack pointer registers to be safely updated. This also explains why DEBUG appears to skip one instruction when tracing a MOV to a segment register. DEBUG single-steps the program by setting the trap flag, which generates a type #1 interrupt following most instructions. Because interrupts are disabled following a MOV to a segment register, DEBUG does not regain control until two instructions following the MOV.

In any case, you don't always have to go to the lengths demonstrated in Listing 3-8. Many times some registers may be pushed onto the caller's stack, either allowing the registers to be used in the program or at least to transfer new values into the stack register. The individual programmer must decide how much of the current context should be saved in a particular program.

If context switching is used with co-routines, each routine ends up saving the other routine's context. Although this is redundant, because only one routine needs to save the other's context, it is not really harmful. Co-routines that use this structure should only exit via Function Code 4Ch, Terminate Program, so that MS-DOS correctly terminates the program regardless of the state of the stack.

If parameters are to be passed from one program to another and each program maintains its own stack, the BP register cannot be used to access parameters on the stack. Instead the programmer needs to extract the caller's stack segment value and move it into either the DS or ES segment registers and perform the memory access relative to that register. The parameters may then be read from the caller's stack even though the called routine is using its own stack.

Considerations for Memory Resident Programs

The Parts of MS-DOS

In some ways, MS-DOS itself is implemented as a memory resident program. Look back at Figure 3-3 to see the memory layout for a typical MS-

DOS system that is running version 2.0 or higher. (Note that this does not necessarily apply to versions higher than 3.1). All of these parts, with the exception of a transient piece of COMMAND.COM, are resident in memory at all times. User programs access MS-DOS through interrupts or jumps to interrupts, just as we did for our memory resident routines.

Certain parts of this system are common to all MS-DOS systems and are compatible even among systems of different version numbers. Other parts of the system are unique to the particular version number or particular hardware that is running MS-DOS. Table 3-5 lists the different sections that make up the MS-DOS system and the attributes that are associated with each part. The names may change from system to system, but the functions are equivalent. Your user's manual tells you what files are for what part of the system. Note that some of the files may be "hidden" files that do not appear in a directory listing. These files are still on disk.

Table 3-5.   Components of the MS-DOS System

Name	Attributes	Function
COMMAND.COM	Compatible	Command processor
IBMDOS.COM or other	Compatible	System services
IBMBIO.COM or other	System dependent	ROM-BIOS interface or BIOS
ROM-BIOS	System dependent	ROM-based BIOS (some)

ROM BIOS versus a Loadable BIOS

There are two main areas of difference that may occur within the realm of MS-DOS systems. These differences drastically affect what can be done and what cannot be done in the way of memory resident systems. One of these differences is whether your particular hardware has its BIOS (basic input/output system) in ROM (read-only memory) or in a file that must be loaded from the disk. The effect of these alternatives is that a ROM based BIOS (often called a ROM-BIOS) provides a set environment for that particular machine, whereas a loaded BIOS is often inaccessible to the programmer. (Unlike CP/M systems, MS-DOS suppliers don't seem to be as willing to provide source listings for a loadable BIOS).

The importance of this option lies in the fact that MS-DOS is not *reentrant!* That is, if you have written a memory resident routine that is either interrupt driven or patches into the MS-DOS interrupt vectors, that routine may not call MS-DOS! MS-DOS apparently maintains only one set of internal data buffers and any attempt at reentering that set results in a total failure of the system. Because MS-DOS isn't reentrant, it cannot be used to perform I/O or support functions for interrupt driven memory resident programs. This restriction may be lifted whenever Microsoft releases a concurrent version of MS-DOS, which we hope will provide some method for handling such events. Until then, programmers who wish to write memory resident routines most likely will have to rely on a ROM BIOS or write driver routines themselves. All of these options result in non-portable code, but sometimes that is the price one pays for desired features.

If the BIOS is actually loaded from the disk during boot, you almost certainly will have to write your own routines to interface with the hardware. Unlike communications between normal programs and MS-DOS, which use the interrupt vectors, MS-DOS communicates with the BIOS through CALLs and JMPs. There is no MS-DOS standard jump-table for the BIOS (á la CP/M) that can be used by the application programmer, so you can see that having a ROM based BIOS can be a great asset in writing memory resident routines that need to access the hardware.

Interrupt versus Polled Systems

The second area of difference is whether the hardware is interrupt driven or polled. By *interrupt driven,* we mean a system that uses hardware interrupts to notify the BIOS of events that have occurred. By *polled,* we mean a system that must repeatedly ask, or poll, the hardware to check for the occurrence of events. Interrupt driven systems provide more flexibility and greater opportunity for installing some types of memory resident programs.

One of the temptations of interrupt driven systems is to use one of the hardware interrupts to drive a memory resident routine. This sometimes can be an easy way out and sometimes can be a nightmare. As long as you use a local stack and don't trash the system's stack, MS-DOS itself is usually insensitive to the presence of interrupts. However, your BIOS may not be so forgiving. Often the BIOS is not written with interrupts in mind, or at least not ones that the authors of the BIOS were expecting. Should an interrupt occur in a time-sensitive portion of the BIOS, as in reading or writing to a disk drive, the interrupt service routine could disrupt the operation of the BIOS with the result that the entire system may fail and hang.

Patching into the Interrupt Vectors

Memory resident routines are activated in one of two ways. They are 1) initiated by hardware interrupts (event driven) or 2) they must patch into the existing system (trap driven). A combination of these methods is also possible, where the patch point is one of the hardware interrupts. If the system that you are using does not support hardware interrupts, you must use the patch method.

Hardware interrupts that are unused by MS-DOS can be used to access with few complications a memory resident routine. As long as the program doesn't call MS-DOS, no system conflicts should occur. If the hardware of the system is accessed by the memory resident routine, it should check to make sure that no one else is accessing the hardware at that time and be careful to restore the hardware to its original state. An example of a minimal impact interrupt driven routine is a program to save all the registers of a currently running program in a reserved section of memory when an outside interrupt occurs. Such a routine is useful when debugging a program in real time. However, if the interrupt that is to be used is also used by the system, the routine should be considered trap driven because the memory resident routine is installed with a patch.

The patch method is a way of inserting a memory resident routine into the normal system flow at a given point so that all accesses to that point of the system pass through the memory resident routine. An example of patching that also involves a hardware interrupt is found when a keyboard driven memory resident routine is installed. To accomplish this, the keyboard interrupt vector is changed to point to the memory resident routine. The value of the previous keyboard vector is stored in the destination address of a FAR jump instruction that is used to exit the memory resident routine. When a keyboard interrupt occurs, the memory resident routine is entered. When the interrupt completes, the memory resident routine jumps to the keyboard handler. If the memory resident routine actually uses the keyboard input in some way that does not continue to the keyboard handler, the memory resident routine must service and clear the interrupt itself, then return to the calling program with an IRET instruction. In all cases the memory resident routine must preserve the context of the interrupted program.

Other possible patch points that do not use hardware interrupts are patches into one of the software interrupt vectors or into a jump address. Patching into MS-DOS is usually done via the software interrupt vectors because there is no recognizable jump table in the MS-DOS system. In addition, because no standard interface exists between MS-DOS and its BIOS interface, patching between MS-DOS and the BIOS is extremely difficult. Using software interrupts remains the solution.

One of the common places to patch into the MS-DOS interrupt vectors is at INT 28h. This is apparently an auxiliary interrupt used internally by MS-DOS. This also seems to be one patch point where frequent access is assured. A memory resident routine patched at this point must not call the MS-DOS function handlers or a system failure results. The memory resident routine should also use its own context to prevent altering the existing stack and registers. Listing 3-9 shows the code necessary to install a memory resident routine at Interrupt 28h and the accompanying memory resident routine.

**Listing 3-9.   Program INIT28—Patching into System
Interrupt Vectors**

```
; **** INIT28--This file produces a .COM program ****************
; **** Install Memory Resident Routine by patching into INT 28 **
        page    60,132
; **** EQUATES FOR INSTALL INTERRUPT ***************************
vect__num equ   28h             ; vector number to install
off     equ     0h              ; routine inactive
on      equ     0FFFFh          ; routine active
;
INCLUDE STD.MLB                 ; include macro definitions
; **** BEGIN PROGRAM SECTION *********************************
init28 segment
        assume cs:init28
        assume ds:init28
        ORG     0
seg_org equ     $
        ORG     0100h
main    proc    far
start: jmp      init            ; skip "old vector" storage
old_v  dd       ?              ; space to store old vector
entry: jmp      first           ; skip "identification"
        db      'TEST ROUTINE'
first: swap_new                 ; MACRO to swap to new stack
        cmp     go_switch,on    ; test if I am active
        jne     bypas           ; yes, continue to exit
        mov     go_switch,off   ; no, set active switch
;
;    < YOUR MEMORY RESIDENT ROUTINE GOES HERE >
;
        mov     go_switch,on    ; set inactive
bypas: swap_old tos             ; restore stack (and include data)
        jmp     cs:exit         ; goto Interrupt Service Routine
exit            dd      ?
go_switch       dw      ?
                db      32 dup ('stack   ')
tos             equ     $
last_byte       equ     $
;
; ***** INITIALIZATION SECTION--THROWN AWAY AFTER LOAD **********
;
init:   mov     go_switch,off   ; prevent activation
        mov     ah,35h          ; get vector address
        mov     al,vect_num
        doscall
```

Listing 3-9. cont.

```
        mov     word ptr exit,bx        ; save pointer IP for exit
        mov     word ptr exit+2,es      ; save pointer CS "    "
        mov     word ptr old_v,bx       ; save pointer IP " remove
        mov     word ptr old_v+2,es     ; save pointer CS "    "
        mov     ah,25h          ; set new pointer
        mov     al,vect_num
        mov     dx,offset entry ; set pointer IP (CS & DS same)
        doscall
        mov     go_switch,on
        mov     dx,(offset last_byte - seg_org + 15) shr 4
        mov     ah,31h          ; terminate & stay resident
        doscall
;
main    endp
init28  ends
        end     start
```

Other possible patch points depend on the type of memory resident routine and the frequency with which it must be called. For example, a print spooler routine (which prints files while allowing other programs to be run at the same time) must not only trap an interrupt to activate it to send characters to the printer, but must also trap any accesses to MS-DOS that use the printer so that conflicts do not occur. Figure 3-5 shows a print spooler trapping INT 28h to activate itself and trapping INT 21 to guard itself against printer access conflicts. Your particular system may require additional traps if it provides other means of accessing the printer.

In any use of trap vectors to implement some semblance of concurrency there is a risk of running afoul of programs that access the hardware directly. For example, if a keyboard trap vector is installed to provide some feature and another program bypasses the keyboard vector and instead reads the hardware directly, the memory resident routine is bypassed. These effects can occur quite easily if multiple memory resident programs are installed because each program must bypass MS-DOS to perform I/O. For example, if both a print spooler and a memory resident routine to print the contents of the video display are installed and both are activated at the same time, a conflict occurs. These problems can occur with commercially available memory resident routines also. The only way for users to protect themselves is to install one routine at a time, checking for conflicts.

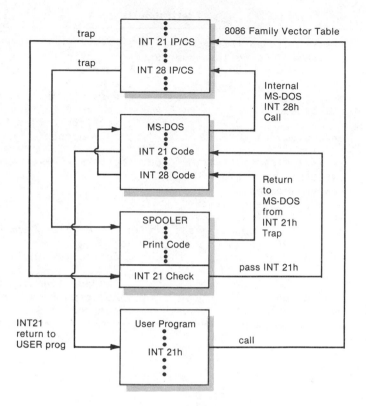

Fig. 3-5. Print spooler using trap vectors.

REMOVE—An Integrated Program Example

The REMOVE program (see Listing 3-10) is intended to "uninstall" a memory resident program based on the example given in INIT28 (Listing 3-9). REMOVE attempts to identify the memory resident program by dumping the bytes following the entry point and displays the four bytes preceding the entry point as a previous vector address. In addition, REMOVE assumes that the program is in a .COM format and attempts to locate the addresses of the PSP and environment block. REMOVE presents all this information to the user and prompts the user to decide to attempt removal or not.

Listing 3-10.   REMOVE—A Program To Remove Memory Resident Routines that Were Patched into Interrupt Vectors

```
        page 60,132
;***** REMOVE--This file generates a .COM program ***************
;***** Removes a memory resident program that has been patched **
```

Listing 3-10. cont.

```
;***** into an interrupt vector. *******************************
; (ISR refers to Interrupt Service Routine)
cr      equ     0Dh             ; carriage return
lf      equ     0Ah             ; line feed
old_ip  equ     -4              ; possible IP location in ISR
old_cs  equ     -2              ; possible CS location in ISR
id      equ     0               ; location of 1st byte in ISR
iretop  equ     0CFh            ; IRET opcode
;
;****** MACRO DEFINITIONS FOR UTILITIES ************************
INCLUDE         STD.MLB
remove segment
        assume cs:remove
        assume ds:remove
; Define needed addresses within the Program Segment Prefix
        ORG     2Ch
env_adr label   word            ; address of environment pointer
        ORG     80h
cmd_len db      ?               ; command line string length
new_len db      ?               ; buffered read string length
cmd_buf db      ?               ; command line string
;****** BEGIN PROGRAM CODE *************************************
        ORG     0100h
main    proc    far
start:
        mov     ch,byte ptr [cmd_len]
        cmp     ch,0            ; was argument provided ?
        jnz     have_cmd
; Argument not provided--prompt user to supply one
get_cmd:
        dis_str request         ; ask for vector number
        mov     byte ptr [cmd_len],80
        mov     dx,offset cmd_len
        mov     ah,0Ah          ; perform buffered read into
        doscall                 ; the command line buffer
        dis_chr lf              ; new line
        mov     ch,new_len      ; get size of text entered
        cmp     ch,0            ; see whether user responded
        jz      abort           ; if not, assume exit
        inc     ch              ; adjust response to conform
have_cmd:
        cmp     ch,3            ; check for proper # characters
        je      ok_cmd
        dis_str bad_cmd         ; if incorrect, flag error
abort:  jmp     finis
ok_cmd:mov      bx,offset cmd_buf
        mov     ch,2            ; parse two characters
        call    get_hex         ; convert # in buffer to binary
        jc      abort           ; exit if error in parse
        mov     vec_num,al      ; save vector address
        mov     ah,35h          ; get vector pointer from MS-DOS
        doscall
        mov     vec_ip,bx       ; store the vector IP
        mov     al,vec_num      ; restore vector number
        call    show_vector     ; display contents of vector
```

Listing 3-10. cont.

```
            dis_str askresv
            call    yesno
            jc      no_restore          ; don't wish vector restored
;
; RESTORE THE VECTOR FROM ADDRESS IN ROUTINE
            mov     bx,vec_ip           ; get address of routine
            mov     dx,es:old_ip[bx];   get old vector IP
            mov     cx,es:old_cs[bx];   get old vector CS
            mov     al,vec_num          ; get the vector number
            push    ds                  ; save current DS
            mov     ds,cx               ; set vector destination
            mov     ah,25h              ; set vector address
            doscall
            pop     ds                  ; restore data segment
;
; Display environment address and ask whether wish removed.
; The environment address is only valid if this is a .COM
no_restore:
            dis_str askremb             ; display environment address
            mov     ax,es:env_adr       ; get address of environment
            mov     ch,4
            call    bin2hex             ; display possible envir. seg.
            dis_str ip0
            call    yesno
            jc      no_env              ; bypass removing the environment
;
; REMOVE ENVIRONMENT BLOCK
            push    es                  ; save main routine segment
            mov     cx,es:env_adr       ; get address of environment
            mov     es,cx               ; and prepare to remove
            call    rem_mem             ; attempt to remove block
            pop     es                  ; restore address of main routine
;
; Display Main Routine Segment Address and ask whether want removed
no_env:dis_str askremm                  ; display main block address
            mov     ax,es               ; address of main block
            mov     ch,4
            call    bin2hex
            dis_str ip0
            call    yesno
            jc      finis               ; don't want to remove main block
;
; REMOVE MAIN MEMORY RESIDENT ROUTINE MEMORY BLOCK
            call    rem_mem             ; attempt to remove block
;
finis: mov     ax,4C00h                 ; terminate program
            doscall
;
vec_num db      ?                       ; space to store vector number
vec_ip dw       ?                       ; space to store vector IP
;
request   db    'Vector number to remove: $'
bad_cmd   db    'Command line format error - aborting',cr,lf,'$'
askresv   db    'Restore Vector from Old? $'
askremb   db    'Remove Environment Block: $'
```

Listing 3-10. cont.

```
askremm  db        'Remove Main Program Block: $'
ip0      db        ':0000 $'
;
main     endp
;
; ***** ROUTINES **********************************************
; ===== REM_MEM uses MS-DOS Function 49 (hex) to attempt to    ==
; ===== deallocate the memory block addressed by ES.           ==
;
rem_mem proc     near
         push     ax                 ; save registers
         push     cx
         push     dx                 ; used by dis_str & dis_chr
         mov      ah,49h             ; free allocated memory
         doscall
         jnc      free_ok            ; no errors--give success msg
         push     ax                 ; save error code
         dis_str fail                ; inform that it failed
         pop      ax                 ; and give the error code
         mov      ch,4               ; (all 4 digits)
         call     bin2hex
         dis_chr cr
         dis_chr lf
         jmp      rem_exit
free_ok:
         dis_str pass
rem_exit:
         pop      dx                 ; restore registers
         pop      cx
         pop      ax
         ret
pass     db        'Successful Free Allocated Memory',cr,lf,'$'
fail     db        'Failed to Free Allocated Memory - Error Code: $'
rem_mem          endp
;
; ===== YESNO prompts the user for a Y or N. If Y is entered   ==
; ===== YESNO returns w/o carry (NC). If N or <RET> is         ==
; ===== entered, YESNO returns w/carry (CY).                   ==
yesno   proc     near
         push     ax
         push     dx
         dis_str prompt              ; prompt user for input
retry: mov      ah,08h              ; get response (no echo)
         doscall
         case     al,<'y','Y','n','N',cr>,<yes,yes,no,no,no>
         dis_chr 07h                 ; illegal response--beep
         jmp      retry              ; and wait some more
no:    dis_chr 'N'
         stc
         jmp      yn_exit
yes:   dis_chr 'Y'
         clc                         ; clear carry
yn_exit:
         dis_chr cr
         dis_chr lf
```

Listing 3-10. cont.

```
        pop     dx
        pop     ax
        ret
prompt db      ' (Y/N): $',
yesno endp
;
; ===== SHOW_VECTOR displays the contents of location pointed ==
; ===== to by ES:BX in both HEX and ASCII format. Because it's =
; ===== intended for use in displaying vectors, it also shows ==
; ===== AL in hex as a vector number and informs the user     ==
; ===== whether the first byte pointed to is an IRET          ==
; ===== instruction. SHOW_VECTOR also displays the two words  ==
; ===== located before the vector address as CS:IP in case    ==
; ===== the user has stored the old vector address there on    ==
; ===== installation.                                          ==
;
show_vector     proc    near
        push    cx              ; save registers
        push    dx
        push    ax              ; used by dis_chr & dis_str
        dis_str vmsg1           ; start displaying messages
        pop     ax              ; restore value of AL
        push    ax
        mov     ah,al
        mov     ch,2            ; display 2 digits of hex
        call    bin2hex
        dis_str vmsg2           ; show potential restore address
        mov     ax,es:old_cs[bx]; get possible CS value
        mov     ch,4
        call    bin2hex         ; display possible old CS
        dis_chr ':'
        mov     ax,es:old_ip[bx]; get possible CS value
        call    bin2hex         ; display possible old CS
        cmp     byte ptr es:id[bx],iretop
        jne     noiret          ; is this an IRET instruction ?
        dis_str vmsg3
noiret:dis_chr cr
        dis_chr lf
        mov     cl,16           ; dump 16 bytes
        call    dump            ; show HEX and ASCII values
        pop     ax
        pop     dx
        pop     cx
        ret
vmsg1   db      'Vector # $'
vmsg2   db      ' Old Vector: $'
vmsg3   db      ' IRET$'
show_vector     endp
;
; ===== DUMP displays the contents of location pointed to by  ==
; ===== ES:BX in both HEX and ASCII format. CL contains the # ==
; ===== of bytes to display.
dump    proc    near
        push    ax              ; save registers
        push    dx              ; used by dis_chr & dis_str
```

Listing 3-10. cont.

```
        push    bx
        push    cx
        dis_str dmsg1           ; start displaying messages
        mov     ch,2            ; 2 hex digits per byte
h_dump:mov      ah,es:[bx]      ; get byte
        inc     bx              ; next byte
        call    bin2hex
        dis_chr ' '
        dec     cl              ; loop count -1
        jnz     h_dump          ; repeat until count 0
        dis_str dmsg2           ; next section
        pop     cx              ; restore values of
        pop     bx              ; ... BX (index) ...
        push    bx              ; ... and ...
        push    cx              ; ... CX (count)
t_dump:mov      al,es:[bx]      ; get byte
        inc     bx              ; next byte
        cmp     al,' '          ; check for printable range
        jb      no_prnt         ; ? < space
        cmp     al,7Eh          ; DEL is not printable either
        ja      no_prnt
        dis_chr al              ; is printable--do so ...
        jmp     nxt_txt
no_prnt:
        dis_chr '.'             ; use "." for non-printable
nxt_txt:
        dec     cl              ; loop count -1
        jnz     t_dump          ; repeat until count 0
; All done--clean up & exit
        dis_chr cr
        dis_chr lf
        pop     cx              ; restore registers
        pop     bx
        pop     dx
        pop     ax
        ret
dmsg1   db      'HEX: $'
dmsg2   db      ' ASCII: $'
dump    endp
;
; ===== GET_HEX parses the buffer pointed to by BX for a hex  ==
; ===== number and returns the number in AX. The # of digits  ==
; ===== to parse is contained in CH, and BX is incremented by ==
; ===== the # of digits processed.                            ==
;
get_hex proc    near
        push    dx              ; save DX register
        push    cx              ; save CX register
        mov     ax,0            ; clear accumulated #
        mov     dh,0            ; clear upper workspace
        mov     cl,4            ; set shift count for later
nxt_digit:
        mov     dl,[bx]         ; get character
        sub     dl,'0'          ; ? < '0'--illegal
        jb      bad_digit       ; ? < '0'--illegal
```

Listing 3-10. cont.

```
        cmp     dl,0Ah
        jb      ok_digit        ; '0' through '9'--okay
        sub     dl,'A'-'0'
        jb      bad_digit       ; '9' < ? < 'A'--illegal
        add     dl,0Ah
        cmp     dl,10h
        jb      ok_digit        ; 'A' through 'F'--okay
        sub     dl,'a'-'A'-0Ah
        jb      bad_digit       ; 'F' < ? < 'a'--illegal
        add     dl,0Ah
        cmp     al,10h
        jae     bad_digit       ; 'f' < ?--illegal
ok_digit:
        add     ax,dx           ; accumulate digits in AX
        inc     bx              ; next digit
        dec     ch
        jnz     more_digit      ; more digits to accumulate
        clc                     ; no error--clear CY
        pop     cx
        pop     dx
        ret
more_digit:
        shl     ax,cl           ; open room for next digit
        jmp     nxt_digit       ; loop for next digit
bad_digit:
        dis_str digit_error     ; inform of entry error
        stc                     ; error--set carry
        pop     cx
        pop     dx
        ret
digit_error db 'A two-digit hex number was expected',cr,lf,'$'
get_hex endp
;
; ===== BIN2HEX displays the value contained in AX as a hex #. =
; ===== No registers are destroyed. CH contains the # of      ==
; ===== digits to display, taken left to right in AX. (AH is  ==
; ===== displayed if CH equals 2).                            ==
;
bin2hex proc near
        push    ax              ; save all registers
        push    bx
        push    cx
        push    dx
        mov     cl,4            ; set rotate count
        mov     bx,ax           ; copy ax for work
; Begin DIGIT loop to process digits
moredig:
        rol     bx,cl           ; convert binary to hex
        mov     al,bl
        and     al,0Fh
        add     al,90h
        daa
        adc     al,40h
        daa
; Display the digit & check for more--restore if done.
```

Listing 3-10. cont.

```
        dis_chr al
        dec     ch
        jnz     moredig
        pop     dx
        pop     cx
        pop     bx
        pop     ax
        ret
bin2hex endp
;
remove ends
        end     start
```

The section that displays the contents of the location addressed by the vector may be extracted and made into a program. This program can be used to display the contents of any of the interrupt vectors and their possible service routines.

REMOVE serves as an example of many of the topics discussed in this chapter and helps to demonstrate recommended installation and removal techniques.

Summary

In this chapter, we have presented material about many separate topics. In addition to the promised material on program and memory management, we also have included material on how to organize programs, on the structure and contents of MS-DOS programs, and more examples of the way MASM operates.

Although some of the material covered may seem only occasionally useful, we think that you will find applications for most of it. Especially important to the systems and applications programmers are the PSP and the organization of programs in memory.

We encourage you to try your hand at writing memory resident programs. Many interesting applications are waiting out there. A little effort can greatly enhance your system and your productivity. If you are the owner of an "orphan" MS-DOS system that everyone seems to have passed by (like the authors' CompuPro system), you can now write your own memory resident programs for those features that you've always wanted but that just weren't available for your machine.

In the next chapter we'll take a break from the "nitty-gritty" of MS-DOS and look at the concepts of real-time programming for MS-DOS and the Intel family of processors.

Real-Time
Programming Under
MS-DOS
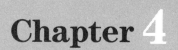

Chapter 4

The Place of Real-Time Systems in Computing
Why Have Real-Time Systems?
Some Examples of Real-Time Systems
The Hardware Environment of Real-Time Computing
Help for Implementing Real-Time Systems Under MS-DOS
Summary

eal-time computing is one of those terms that everyone seems to use but no one seems to know the real meaning of. Rather than attempt an all-inclusive definition of the term, it may be better to approach it obliquely, like a tiger stalking a stag. By contrasting real-time computing with related options, we may gain a better understanding of what real-time computing really is.

In the early days of computer systems, cost was the most important factor governing use, and maximum utilization was demanded from every system. To achieve these goals, computers were supplied with a constant backlog of work, and the computer waited for no one. All human activities were accomplished "off-line" so that the inevitable human delays did not waste expensive computer time. The name given to this type of computing is *batch-processing* because the computer is given complete jobs to process, like an assembly line stamping out parts. The result of this philosophy was long delays for humans, who spent hours waiting for the computer to complete a job.

As the cost of computing came down, it was no longer economical to have highly paid professionals sit on their hands waiting for the computer. More computers were purchased, and users were allowed to work directly with computers. This was called *on-line* processing. Because humans still tended to waste a lot of time thinking and such, computer systems were designed to handle more than one job at a time. When the human held up the work, the computer simply switched its attention to another job that was ready to be processed. This was the birth of *time-sharing* systems, where one computer gave each user a small "slice" of time often enough to give the impression of continuous processing. Time-shared systems were a vast improvement over batch systems but were still subject to lengthy delays.

At long last came the microcomputer revolution. Computing power is no longer for the rich or powerful, and the cost of the actual computer system is equal to only a fraction of the value of the user's time. Now we have arrived at the other extreme: The computer "waits hand and foot" on the human. The philosophy of one person, one computer is not uncommon.

The Place of Real-Time Systems in Computing

From the earliest batch systems to the most recent personal computers, constant progress has been made toward faster and faster response. At some point this response time approaches the time scale of the real world, allowing the computer to process events as fast as they occur. Does fast response time make a system real-time? Although a necessary part of real-time, fast response time isn't the entire answer. The total architecture of the system must be designed for real-time computing.

What's wrong with the systems just described that disqualifies them from being real-time? Batch processing systems aren't real-time, no matter how fast they are because a completely artificial boundary exists between the real world and the system.

What about time-shared computing? Although much faster than batch systems and with normally imperceptible delays, these interactive on-line systems sometimes do slow down, and one user's process can be blocked from execution by the activities of another user's process.

Is the answer a dedicated system like a microcomputer? Not necessarily, for the operating system of that computer may not be equipped to deal with external events as they occur.

The problem with these systems is that no matter how fast, they have no commitment to a specified response time. True real-time processing requires that the response time of the computer system be tied to the time scale of events occurring outside the computer. The computer must be able to accumulate, process, and output data within a critical specified time period. Accomplishing this requires guaranteed response from each part of the computer system: peripherals, processor, operating system, and the user's program.

When we apply this definition, even a batch processing system is capable of real-time performance if the response criteria is long enough. If the Internal Revenue Service says that refund checks will be delivered within X days, and their batch processing computers can manage the task, they have a real-time system. To prevent this absurdity from occurring, we add to our definition of real time that the response time must be in the range of seconds to nanoseconds (billionths of a second).

Why Have Real-Time Systems?

The purpose behind real-time computing is that many complex activities (processes) in the real world would benefit from computer control but they cannot be made to slow down or stop to wait for instructions from a computer. The computer must keep up with changes in the process as they occur and be able to control the process before it can go astray. Most examples of real-time systems occur in industry or utilities (power and telephony), but some are suited for the personal computer user. We have included three examples in this chapter: a laboratory measurement system, a home control system, and a robotics system. Each example has modest requirements that can be met with the average personal computer.

How fast is the average personal computer? The fastest ideal response time of which an 8086 or 8088 is capable is around two microseconds (a microsecond is a millionth of a second), which is the amount of time required for one IN and one OUT instruction at 8 MHz, allowing no time for decision making. Given our two approximate boundaries, ranging from seconds to microseconds, what can be done with our system, what can't be done, and how can we make a personal computer do what it can do?

Some Examples of Real-Time Systems

Real-time systems are used in many applications, and there are very few people who do not interact with one every day. Modern telephone switching equipment is all computer controlled and so are most utility company power generation and distribution systems. Many large metropolitan areas have computer controlled rail transit systems. The automatic tellers that many banks have installed are, to some degree, examples of real-time systems. The list stretches on: oil refinery systems, electronic component manufacturing, automated assembly plants, signal processing (e.g., radar), military applications, etc. Within this broad area are many subdivisions. We examine three examples of real-time applications for microcomputers to demonstrate some of the trade-offs and requirements in real-time systems.

Let's first define some terms to use in our analysis of the systems, then proceed to see how our first example, a laboratory measurement system, fits in. The categories that we are going to use for evaluation are shown in Table 4-1. Each category stresses some particular aspect of a real-time system. The decision of whether MS-DOS can support the application is a result of which categories are stressed.

Table 4-1. **Analysis and Evaluation Categories for Real-Time Systems**

Category	Definition
Process	The real world events and activities that are occurring outside the computer and that the computer is measuring, controlling, or otherwise interacting with.
Data Acquisition	The input of digital measurement data (or event signals describing the process) into the computer's memory or storage devices. In this use, data acquisition serves as the "senses" of the computer.
Data Analysis	The calculations that the computer must perform on the input data for the purpose of arriving at a conclusion or reducing the data to a meaningful form.
Process Control	The output of data for the purpose of controlling the process being observed or for otherwise affecting the real world.
Process Monitoring	The output of data to some form of display device for the purpose of informing the operator of the status of the process being observed. Even though a subset of process control, process monitoring is separate from process control in the sense that process monitoring is tied to the time-scale of the operator rather than the time-scale of the process.
Time Base	A real-time clock, device, or software routine that provides a means of determining the timing relationship between data input elements. Time base may also be used to describe the interval between "ticks" of the clock, as in the phrase *a one-second time base*.
Multitasking	The ability of the computer to handle more than one task simultaneously and where the sequence of tasks is a function of outside events instead of being pre-determined by the nature of the process.

The term *process control* does double-duty in our definition, for, in addition to its definition as expressed in Table 4-1, the term is often used to describe real-time systems that are dedicated to the purpose of controlling external events. Most of the examples of real-time systems described previously are applications of this second kind of process control, with the systems being dedicated to controlling switching functions, subway cars, or whatever. In this chapter, we have used the term *process control* to describe only that portion of a real-time system dedicated to such control functions, and our definition is logically consistent in that a real-time system with a high process control content is a process control system.

Our definition of *multitasking* is necessarily rigorous in that it makes a distinction between processes that may be monitored or controlled in a sequential manner and those where multiple events must be handled in an unknown order. For example, a software program that takes input from the keyboard and sends it to a printer is handling two simultaneous events, typing and printing, yet both events are accomplished one step at a time with a read/write cycle. Such a program is not multitasking. On the other hand, a system that controls a nuclear reactor must respond to a number of different events of various priorities so that if a critical event occurs while the system is processing a non-critical event, the system switches to processing the critical event. This type of operation demands multitasking ability, allowing one task to be put on "hold" so that a more important task can be attended to.

A Laboratory Measurement System

A common industrial and educational application for microcomputers is providing intelligent support for the measurement of a process. Whether the application is measuring electronic wave forms or performing a spectral analysis, the computer's basic job is to measure the ongoing process, reduce the data according to some transformation, and present the results to the operator in an understandable form.

What are some of the common elements in this application? By applying the categories contained in Table 4-1, we can estimate the requirements as follows:

- Data Acquisition: usually very high data rate required

- Data Analysis: ranges from simple display of raw data to complex analysis; analysis typically handled in a "batch" mode, which consists of a two-stage acquire/analyze loop

- Process Control: none required for most applications

- Process Monitoring: moderate data rate usually required

- Time Base: a necessity

- Multitasking: some applications but not usually

The basic operation of our laboratory measurement system consists of the rapid (geared to the time scale of the process being monitored) accumulation of data followed by a more leisurely (geared to the time frame of the operator) analysis and display of the results. A simplified version of this process can be seen in Figure 4-1.

The critical factors for laboratory measurement are then high speed data acquisition coupled with a moderate rate of data analysis. It is also critical that the system have a means of determining the time interval between samples (the time base), although this can be built into the sampling mechanism.

The requirement for multitasking in laboratory measurement systems comes from such applications as logic analyzers, telescope controllers, etc., where the system is required to monitor more than one event. For example, a logic analyzer may be updating displayed wave forms while waiting for a sampling breakpoint to occur. A telescope controller may be accumulating spectral data when the tracking mechanism senses that the telescope mount must be advanced to a new position. In these cases, the capability of the operating system to multitask, although not an absolute requirement, makes life easier for the programmer.

When we examine the environment of a real-time system, we concentrate on the data acquisition methods and are able to make judgments as to the implementation of such a system, but for now, let's look at the other examples.

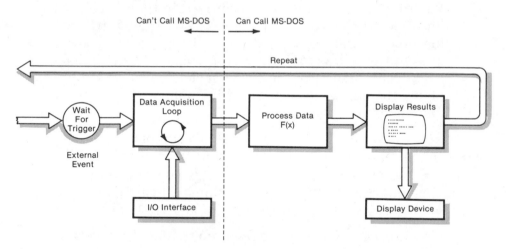

Fig. 4-1.   Program flow in a laboratory measurement system.

A Home Control System—Security and HVAC (Heating, Ventilation, and Air Conditioning)

Although you probably would not dedicate your MS-DOS development system to the task of guarding your home or keeping your goldfish warm, you may be considering using an inexpensive battery backed-up system for such a task, and some of these systems come supplied with MS-DOS in ROM (read-only memory).

Once again, we apply our evaluation criteria to analyze total system requirements and discover where the critical areas are.

- Data Acquisition: low data rate, usually on/off inputs, but may require some digitized inputs of temperature, fan speed, damper position, etc.

- Data Analysis: usually yes/no questions of low complexity; analysis usually handled in a polled loop, checking the inputs in sequence

- Process Control: moderate, usually in form of binary on/off outputs for devices such as fans, furnaces, lights, alarms, etc.; can be more complex for telephone auto-dialers

- Process Monitoring: usually unattended operation

- Time Base: not required, although may be useful to have real-time clock to determine time of day for changing settings, etc; a delay timer is required for the HVAC section to avoid oscillation of system

- Multitasking: not required

This system differs from the first in that we now have to consider output to external devices as well, which is offset by the consideration that in this application, blinding speed is not of real importance. For the majority of the time, a home control system idles as it "watches" for changing events. Once an event occurs, the system checks to see what it should do, then activates the proper equipment. Because of the low data rate, this system doesn't have to process all its inputs and outputs at one time. The system flow as diagrammed in Figure 4-2 shows that each process can perform its own I/O. The main concern for this system is reliability so that you don't return to a hundred degree house with a roaring furnace.

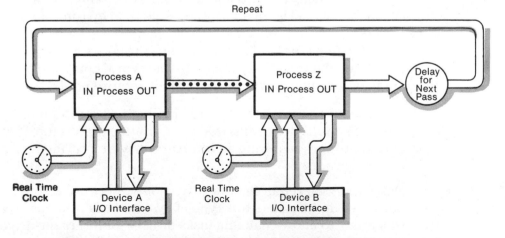

Fig. 4-2.   **Program flow in a home control system.**

The type of time base in this system also differs from a laboratory measurement system. Although the lab system's time base is used to guarantee that data samples are properly spaced, the home control system's time base is used to generate events, such as *lower temperature of house at night* or *turn up water heater in morning*. The other use of time in a home control system is to slow the controller's decisions to the rate of the equipment that it controls. When an action is initiated by the system, it must allow sufficient time for the results of the action to happen. Our last example illustrates this principle of feedback loops in greater detail.

A Robot Control System

The increasing popularity of robotics both at home and in industry makes it likely that many users get their first taste of real-time computing in this field. The degree of support required for a robot control system depends on the environment that it is to be used in, but some common elements can be identified. The most unique trait for our purposes is a nearly equal balance between data acquisition rates and process control rates (leaving aside vision or voice recognition systems). This balance is a reflection of the need for most robotics systems to implement a true feedback loop design.

A feedback loop is a design in which the outputs from the system are being constantly updated by new inputs into the system. When controlling the speed of a motor for example, simply switching it on is rarely accurate enough. Rather, the speed of the motor is constantly monitored, and new commands are issued to either increase or decrease the speed to compensate for changing loads, power supply variations, etc. The process of steering an automobile is another example of a feedback loop because the wheel is constantly adjusted to keep the vehicle on the proper course.

Due to the need for feedback loops, most robotics applications cannot use the "set and forget" approach to real-world control. The following generalizations may be made about their requirements.

- Data Acquisition: moderately high to high data rate, usually requiring multiple bit digitized data; inputs are often prioritized and sometimes requiring an interrupt-driven interface for high priority events

- Data Analysis: requirements vary widely; because of the random nature of input events this type of system either embodies a scheduler to allow changing tasks or uses an interrupt-driven structure to activate event handlers

- Process Control: depending on the sophistication of the control hardware, moderately high to very high output data rates are required; output must often be immediate instead of waiting for a common output phase

- Process Monitoring: very low data rate in comparison to the acquisition/control requirements, usually composed of summary information

- Time Base: required for both acquisition and process control (determining parameters such as speed, etc.).

- Multitasking: the random nature of events occurring in the system requires as least the ability to emulate multitasking systems.

We've already discussed the reasons for the high input and output data rates. What may not be so obvious is the need for multitasking. A robot control system is more than just a single electric motor. Such a system usually consists of dozens of motors, sensors, valves, etc. Were the approach that was used in the home control system applied here, the system could find itself swamped in data, unable to respond to the more important items in time. (Crash! Your robot just hit the wall!) The approach that is used instead in such systems depends on prioritizing the input data in hardware. In a home robot for example, a proximity sensor could be tied to a high priority interrupt and allow the program to respond to the danger of hitting the wall by stopping the robot before damage is done.

Because of this prioritization and because these events are often random in sequence, the system must be capable of switching tasks on demand in a short length of time. Figure 4-3, which shows an example control flow for an interrupt driven system, demonstrates the dynamic nature of processing in this type of system. In Figure 4-3, each task executes at a particular priority or level. If something more important should occur, the executing task is suspended and the more important event is handled. When the new task is finished, the old task resumes.

Each task also has the option of processing its own I/O to the devices that task is responsible for. Note that using interrupts does not preclude the use of the more conventional technique of polling. With the proper support each level can execute as a normal task, unaware of the presence of other tasks.

What type of support is required? Besides supporting task switching, the system should not allow one task to interfere with another. Interference can be either overt (corrupting another task's data, registers, or stack, illegally writing to its device, etc.) or indirect (preventing a task from taking required actions by tying up processing time, an I/O channel, or other needed resource). Overt interference can only be controlled through careful design and coding of the tasks themselves. Indirect interference is controlled by letting the operating system manage the available resources. These requirements indicate the need for a multitasking system with intelligent control of resources, including that most important of resources, time.

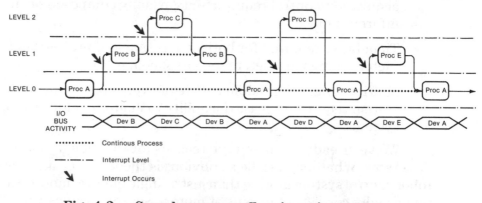

Fig. 4-3.   Sample program flow in an interrupt driven system.

Time bases are typically required to allow the system to determine the rate at which an outside action occurs or to gear the system's command to the rate of the equipment. To some extent the requirement for a time base can be reduced through building sampling rates into the hardware (as in the laboratory measurement system) and through the use of feedback loops, which let the system adjust its actions to the responses of the process and its equipment.

Feedback loops can have negative effects also, which a good design and system time base can diminish. Consider the example of a computer steering a car. Now assume the computer decides to turn right and issues the command *turn right*. The wheels begin to turn, but suppose the computer is sampling the input data at its own much higher rate. It decides that the car is not turning right and so re-sends the command *turn right*. Before "realizing" that the car *is* turning, the computer issues enough *turn right* commands to put the car in a skid. To avoid this type of negative feedback loop, the computer must be programmed to respect the slower pace of the physical world, and a time base is required to let the computer know how long to wait. Indeed, the robot control systems used in automated stockrooms and warehouses are programmed with information regarding the maximum acceleration, braking speeds, etc., of the systems they control, all in order to prevent the dangerous and costly accidents that can result from negative feedback loops.

The result is that a time base is nearly always required in robotics systems so that at the very least the system can effectively model the world being controlled by interpreting its events and anticipating its reactions.

Specialized Systems for Process Control

The systems we have described are all capable of being implemented on a general purpose microcomputer, and the examples are structured with that in mind. Entirely different system architectures are used in the design of industrial systems for controlling processes. Often these systems, called *programmable controllers*, contain special purpose hardware dedicated to performing input and output operations. The operating systems are written to enable rapid processing of input data with few of the "bells and whistles" of a more general purpose system.

To meet strict timing requirements, programmable controllers use polled I/O rather than interrupt driven input. They continually repeat a INPUT-PROCESS-OUTPUT cycle: acquiring all input data at one time, analyzing the information, and writing all output data. A polled I/O system is chosen because it has a lower overhead when reading multiple inputs than interrupt driven input. By repeating the cycle at extremely high rates (up to once every millisecond) the system guarantees a fast response time.

Why then have we recommended using interrupts for our robot control example? For one, programmable controllers depend on special hardware that isn't present in your everyday personal computer. For another, the high cycle rate that a polled I/O system requires virtually prevents use of a standard operating system such as MS-DOS. By using interrupts, we allow the I/O to take place at a different rate than that imposed by the operating system. Events establish their own rate through the interrupt system, and the program can still take advantage of the support that MS-DOS offers.

Of course, the interrupt driven system must pay the penalty of having a substantially smaller capacity. This system is able to control only a few devices rather than the thousands that may be connected to a programmable controller.

The Hardware Environment of Real-Time Computing

Having outlined the requirements for some examples of real-time systems, we now proceed to the methods that can be used to implement the various requirements. The same list of criteria that we used to evaluate our example systems is used to evaluate ways of meeting those requirements.

For nearly all real-time applications, specialized hardware is required to accomplish the physical interface between the real-world and the computer system. Luckily for us, this hardware is available from manufacturers for most of the popular computer systems. The scope of this book precludes detail regarding exactly what boards are available and from whom, especially as the current boards only work with particular types of systems, and new boards are being designed every day. Rather, we discuss the generic types of boards available and their relative strengths and weaknesses. We leave to the reader the decision of which particular manufacturer makes the board best suited to his or her system.

Timing Differences in the 8086 Family of Processors

At the time this book was written, MS-DOS was available on five members of the Intel 8086 family of processors; the 8086, 8088, the enhanced multifunction iAPX186 and iAPX188, and the still more enhanced iAPX286. Unless stated otherwise, all timing information given in this chapter is for the 8086 and 8088 processors, and all execution times are based on instruction times given in the Intel *iAPX 86/88, 186/188 User's Manual Programmer's Reference*.

Execution times for the INS instruction are given for the iAPX 186/188 processors. Note that with an 8-MHz clock, the iAPX186/188 processors were designed to execute about 30 percent faster overall than the 8086/8088 processors.

Because all 8086 family processors have pre-fetch queues, the actual execution time of any sequence of instructions may be different from that calculated solely on the basis of individual instruction execution times.

Data Acquisition

Data that is acquired by real-time systems falls into one of three groups. First, the data may be represented by single bits that record the current state of a two-state device. Second, the data may represent the digitized value of analog signals produced by analog to digital converters (abbreviated A/D and pronounced *A to D*). Third and last, the data may be digital information sent from another piece of equipment (which could have obtained the data in one of three ways).

Our discussion here pertains to data obtained in any of these three ways but does not fully cover the third method. Data that is being transmitted from another computer or device may also be acquired over a serial line (for example, RS-232 and RS-422), an interface bus (for instance, IEEE-488 bus or the GPIB and HPIB buses), or though shared memory. Using one of these techniques can greatly reduce the effort of building an interface for a real-time system and should definitely be considered by users contemplating a laboratory measurement system. However, because there are more comprehensive texts dedicated solely to that subject, we don't cover these techniques in this chapter.

An MS-DOS computer system can acquire data about the outside world in three ways: through the IN instruction (or the INS input string instruction on the iAPX188, iAPX186 or iAPX286 processors), through DMA (direct memory access) operations, and through an interrupt line.

IN instructions may be used to input data into the system from virtually any device. All I/O using these instructions, however, is performed as a programmed transfer, with the system giving its full attention to the job of moving data into or out of memory. When using the REP INS instruction on the iAPX186/iAPX188/iAPX286 processors, transfers into memory may take place at the system's full bus bandwidth, one transfer every 8 clock cycles. (With an 8-MHz processor this results in a 1-MHz transfer rate when no wait states are inserted.) For the iAPX188, the transfer rate for word-wide moves is only 500 kHz because data may be moved only a byte at a time and so an additional four clock cycles per transfer are required. The INS instruction uses two transfers so the overhead is incurred twice (8 additional clock cycles per transfer).

For the 8086 and 8088, a much different rate is obtained. For repeated programmed I/O to be performed requires at least the four instructions shown below (the number of cycles given is for an 8086):

```
read:    in  ax,dx      ; read data--8 cycles
         add di,2        ; next destination--4 cycles
         mov [di],ax     ; store data--14 cycles
         loop read       ; loop until done--17 cycles
```

The instruction count can be decreased by one if the same register is used for the destination index and counter, but this is offset by the increased effective address calculation time required for the MOV instruction and precludes use of the LOOP instruction (the CX register may not be used for addressing).

For an 8086 running at 8 MHz, the 43 clock cycles take 5.375 microseconds, resulting in a transfer rate of 186 kHz. Timing for the 8088 is eight clock cycles longer because two transfers are involved, which require a total of 51 clock cycles to perform the same operation. If the 8088 were run at 8 MHz, the input loop would take 6.369 microseconds per pass, which results in a transfer rate of 157 kHz.

Even with the lowly 8088, these rates are often sufficient for most applications, but there is another problem to consider: When the processor is reading data at these rates from the interface into memory, the system must be totally dedicated to the task at hand. No disk accesses are allowed, no terminal I/O may be performed, and usually no time is available for data reduction. If the application consists of separate sample and calculate steps, all sampling takes place without any use of the operating system, and the subsequent calculation step uses system resources as it requires (for data storage, display, etc.).

What if the application requires that data processing occur simultaneously with sampling? When data transfers into memory must take place simultaneously with the processing of the data, DMA techniques are used. In a DMA transfer, the device places the processor on hold, transfers the data into or out of memory, then allows the processor to continue where it left off. Because the processor is not involved, transfers take place at the full speed of the bus and memories. When high data rates are required or the processor has other tasks to attend to, DMA makes perfect sense. Another advantage of DMA transfers is that transfers are not limited to the data bus width of the processor. (One of the authors' systems is an S-100 bus system with a 16-bit wide data bus, even though the processor is an 8088. DMA transfers may take place in either byte or word mode.)

The iAPX186/188 processors contain on-chip support for two high-speed DMA channels, which are capable of moving data at full bus bandwidth. The transfer times are equal to that of the REP INS instruction. Each DMA cycle takes two to four bus cycles (eight to sixteen CPU clock cycles).

For very high speed data acquisition needs, specialized boards are available that offer on-board local memory for local storage (allowing acquisition at rates higher than the system's memory) or on-board processors for reduction of the data. These types of boards usually contain microcontrollers, a specialized microprocessor dedicated to servicing the external device. The level of sophistication of these boards varies widely from manufacturer to manufacturer.

The details of DMA transfers (rates, word widths, etc.), are determined by the system's bus type and the interface board that is installed. In nearly all cases, an interface board capable of performing DMA transfers is faster than using programmed I/O methods.

The last method of data acquisition we discuss is through an interrupt line. Although interrupts can be used in conjunction with either programmed I/O or DMA transfers to signal the start of a transfer, the interrupt alone can be used to convey single bits of data. Unfortunately, whereas use of an interrupt may simplify interfacing, this method is not particularly fast due to the requirement of pushing three words of data on the stack (Flags, CS, and IP) and reading two words from the interrupt vectors. Overhead on servicing an interrupt takes 51 clock cycles on an 8086 and 71 clock cycles on an 8088.

Data Analysis

Once the data has been entered into the system through any of these three methods, the next question arises: What to do with the data?

There are as many different types of data analysis as there are applications for real-time computing. Even with so broad a scope, we can distinguish two major divisions of real-time data analysis.

The first, used in laboratory measurement systems and such, involves the reduction and interpretation of data. The collected raw data is transformed by the system to understandable results. Many of these transformations involve advanced mathematics and complex calculations (digital filters, Fourier and Laplace transforms, splines, etc.). Because of this, advanced data analysis is often receptive to the addition of a numeric coprocessor, such as the 8087 or 80287. For operations involving a large amount of precision math, real numbers, multiplications, or divisions, the addition of an 8087 may speed throughput by orders of magnitude. (Intel, the manufacturer of the 8087, has benchmarks showing over a thousand times speed increase in certain math operations using the 8087 in place of software math routines). In one of the authors' applications, involving probability calculations coded in a high-level language, use of the 8087 resulted in a twenty times increase in execution speed.

The second main application of data analysis in real-time systems is decision making, the process of interpreting the incoming data for the purpose of controlling the actions of the equipment. For tasks in which this chore becomes onerous, one of the possible solutions is to use decision tables in place of IF-THEN structures. The difficulty with IF-THEN coding is that if the chain of questions and decisions becomes long, the execution time becomes unpredictable, depending as it does on the placement of the operative question in the chain of decision making. Decision tables, on the other hand, have a discrete execution time, based on the amount of time required to index into the table. In addition, the 8086 family has an instruction that can aid this process, XLAT. The XLAT instruction provides a quick way to index into a 256-byte table and obtain the contents at that location (see Fig. 4-4). By chaining XLAT instructions together, larger table lookups can be handled.

The individual use of decision tables is best left to the application's implementor. Reference works are available that do much more justice to the subject than is possible here.

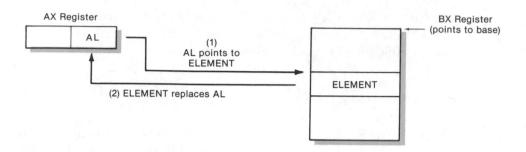

Fig. 4-4.   Operation of the XLAT instruction.

Process Control

Process control is nearly always achieved through programmed I/O (either the OUT or OUTS [output string] instructions) or through memory mapped I/O (where the output port appears as a memory location to the processor). Timing for the OUT and OUTS instructions is identical to the IN and INS instructions. DMA may be used to output large amounts of data, especially for programmable controllers, which typically read all inputs, process all decisions, and write all outputs in separate steps. However, in most general purpose systems, DMA is usually reserved for peripheral devices, such as graphics displays, disks, and high speed communications (for example, X.25 protocol or Local Area Networks).

Because MS-DOS computers are either byte or word oriented, all control of the process is done in terms of either eight or sixteen bits. The interface hardware usually translates process control data into either analog signals or single bit control lines. Analog signals are most often created using a DAC (digital to analog converter and pronounced *dak*). DACs are available for either voltage control or current control. They translate a multibit input (usually in the range of four to twelve bits), into an analog signal whose voltage level or current level is proportional to the binary number used as input. Your computer probably contains at least one DAC to control the video display.

Other available multibit control circuits are frequency generators (the input value represents the desired frequency of an analog signal); stepper or brushless DC motor controls (the input value representing speed is translated into a pulse train for the motor); phase shift circuits, such as those used in modems; and variable power supplies, where the input value controls a switching power supply.

Single Bit Control Circuits
Circuits that have only two states (usually representing on/off) are controlled by a single bit. Interfaces for these applications usually group four or eight such circuits in a single control port. Setting or clearing the

corresponding bit in the interface port closes or opens the circuit associated with it. Interface circuits are available for relay closure, AC or DC power control, TTL level control (usually ground and plus five volts), etc.

Single bit interface circuits can be grouped in control ports in a number of ways. A single port address may serve as an 8-bit input when read and with no effect when written. The reverse may be true so that the port allows output and no input. Another option is that the port may support both input and output operations. The type of port being used makes a difference in the operation required to control it.

When the single bit controls are grouped into bytes, the programmer must take additional steps to ensure that only the desired bits are affected. If the interface allows reading the current settings in the control byte, a single value can be set by the following code. (Assume the number of the bit to be affected is contained in the CL register on entry.)

```
mov   ah,1          ; set bit for circuit 0
shl   ah,cl         ; and shift to select circuit
in    al,port       ; read current settings
or    al,ah         ; set required bit
out   port,al       ; send new setting
```

Clearing a bit is accomplished similarly—by building a mask with 1's in the "don't care" positions and a 0 in the position of the bit to be cleared.

```
mov   ah,1          ; set bit for circuit 0
shl   ah,cl         ; and shift to select circuit
not   ah            ; flip to 0's bit mask
in    al,port       ; read current settings
and   al,ah         ; clear required bit
out   port,al       ; send new setting
```

If the interface does not allow the reading of the current settings, the program has to maintain a table of the settings and refer to the table whenever the status of a line must be changed. The required code to set a bit must be changed as follows (where OLD_VAL is a memory location with the current settings):

```
mov   ah,1          ; set bit for circuit 0
shl   ah,cl         ; and shift to select circuit
OR    OLD_VAL,AH    ; UPDATE CURRENT SETTINGS
MOV   AL,OLD_VAL    ; RETRIEVE CURRENT SETTINGS
out   port,al       ; send new setting
```

Although output data rates required for process control are rarely as high as those required for input data, in some cases the microprocessor may be unable to handle the I/O load without limiting its availability for other work. If this occurs, intelligent I/O control boards can be used to handle the low-level details of the I/O operations. Using these boards often reduces the load on the main processor enough to allow the use of high-level languages and popular operating systems such as MS-DOS.

In more complex systems, hardware can be used to off-load the host even further. Software programmable limit switches can be added to certain functions, allowing the hardware rather than the program to make some decisions. Using the motor control example, two latches can be added to the motor speed sensor board with a comparator that causes an interrupt if motor speed either exceeds one limit or drops below the other.

Details of process control hardware vary even more than data acquisition hardware, which makes it difficult to develop many general statements about process control hardware. The application and design goals determine the actual requirements for speed, type of interface, and so forth.

No matter how sophisticated or simple the interface board, it must be able to protect the delicate circuitry of the host computer. This is usually accomplished through the use of opto-isolator circuits, which create an electrical separation between the computer and the equipment being controlled. If the equipment being controlled uses high voltages, the actual switching circuits should be located in a separate enclosure to reduce the possibilities of damage to the computer or excessive noise in the computer's circuits.

Process Monitoring

Because the subject of this chapter is real-time computing in MS-DOS, we limit ourselves to the equipment that is available for MS-DOS machines. For process monitoring, that means video displays that are text only or text and graphics.

If the application requires only display of text information, the rate of the data sent to the display is necessarily low. This limitation is imposed by the simple fact that a human operator can only assimilate data so fast. Any faster and the usefulness of the system drops as the data becomes meaningless.

The other option, graphics displays, is used in different modes of operation, and the choice of a mode makes a large difference in the data rate required and the load presented to the system. Laboratory measurement systems often use graphics display of data for displaying wave forms, etc. If the data is to be presented and held on the screen until the operator requests another test, the data rate is acceptable and no special considerations are required. However, if the equipment is designed to present a continuously updated display, the data rate is very high, and special equipment to drive the display may be required.

Some examples of the special equipment that is available are intelligent graphics boards that handle tasks such as line drawing, freeing the main processor from the task, and DMA controllers that allow high speed transfers of graphics data from memory to the display controller.

Graphics displays are also used extensively in process control and provide the operator with a "schematic" of the process and indicate changes, component status, etc., on the display. In these applications critical information often must preempt other operations, and this requirement extends to the use of the display. The display driver must be capable of quickly switching from one display to another and must be sufficiently fast to allow complete redrawing of the display in reasonable time.

Time Base

The example systems described presented three different uses of time bases: determining the rate of incoming data, determining the time for an action to occur, and determining the sequence of responses. Each of these applications has its own requirements for a time base, and each set of requirements can be met in different ways.

Determining the Rate of Input Data—Internal Timing

Determining the rate of incoming data can be accomplished by the computer system or by the data acquisition board. In the second case, the processor need have nothing to do with timing. However, if the acquisition circuit must be triggered in some way by the main processor, the main processor must be ready when the time comes to issue the trigger. And that implies that the main processor must be able to accurately determine time intervals.

Time intervals can be determined with software timing loops or with external CTCs (counter-timer-clock circuits). CTC circuits, in turn, can be polled or tied to an interrupt. The decision of which type of timing to use is based on the acceptable overhead and maximum rate of data that must be accommodated. Table 4-2 shows maximum resolution that can be obtained with the different approaches. (The resolution can be thought of as a clock with a particular frequency.)

Table 4-2.   Overhead and Timing Rate of High-Speed Timing Options

Timed By:	Clock Cycles	Timing Resolution	Maximum Timing Rate
Software Loop:	17	2.125 μsec	470 kHz
Poll for CTC Ready:	27	3.375 μsec	296 kHz
CTC Interrupt (8086):	83	10.375 μsec	96 kHz
CTC Interrupt (8088):	115	14.375 μsec	69 kHz

All timings are for the 8086/8088 processors running at 8 MHz. Certain instructions run faster on the iAPX188/186 or iAPX286 processors and allow higher data rates.

To time with the LOOP instruction, the CX register is loaded with a particular number of counts, and a tight loop of the form

```
again:    LOOP again
```

is entered. For an 8-MHz 8086 processor, each pass through the loop occupies 2.125 microseconds. If LOOP timing is to be used in conjunction with the IN sequence presented before (label "read"), the "read" sequence must be modified to use an explicit decrement and loop via JNZ because the CX register is required for the timing LOOP.

The CTC polling loop timing is based on reading the status from a port (IN), checking for a ready bit (TEST), and looping if not ready (JNZ). All instruction timings are based on the fastest mode and may run slower if immediate mode source operands are used with the IN or TEST instructions. A sample sequence appears as:

```
again:    IN   ax,dx    ; port specified in DX 2 cycles faster
          TEST ax,bx    ; register/register fastest mode
          JNZ  again     ; loop until ready
```

The times for interrupt handling are taken directly from the Intel *iAPX 86/88, 186/188 User's Manual Programmer's Reference*.

The data acquisition rates are, of course, much lower than the timing rates because of the time required to set up the timers, acquire the data, etc. If faster acquire times are required, the IN loop described previously, padded with NOP instructions, can be used to adjust the timing.

Determining the Rate of Input Data—External Timing

Most data acquisition boards make life easier by providing on-board timing for data sampling. The board contains a clock that can be programmed with the desired sampling rate, which allows data acquisition at set intervals. When the clock "ticks," the board samples the data and stores the value in a latch. If the board has the capability of DMA transfers, the processor is not concerned with acquisition at all because the board is able to transfer transparently data into the processor's memory.

If the board does not have DMA capability, the main processor must either poll the board to see whether the data is ready or have the board interrupt the processor when the data is ready. Table 4-3 shows the times and rates associated with polled versus interrupt acquisition. As before, all timings are based on running the processor at an 8-MHz clock rate.

Table 4-3. Acquire Times and Data Rates for Non-DMA Interfaces

Data Ready Determined By	Timing Cycles	Timing Overhead	Acquire Cycles	Acquire Time	Maximum Acquire Rate
Polling	27	3.375 μsec	43(51)	5.375 μsec 6.375 μsec	114 kHz 102 kHz
Interrupt (8086)	83	10.375 μsec	43	5.375 μsec	63 kHz
Interrupt (8088)	115	14.375 μsec	43(51)	5.375 μsec 6.375 μsec	50 kHz 48 kHz

The number of cycles required to acquire the data is listed as M(N) where M is the number of cycles for the 8086 in all modes and the 8088 in byte mode and N is the number of cycles for the 8088 in word mode. The acquire times include the overhead required to maintain array indices and loop back for the next element. The acquisition rates thus accurately reflect the rate of a real-world program. If only a single acquisition is desired, the number of acquisition clock cycles required to read the data is 26 clock cycles for the 8086 and 8088 byte-mode read and 34 clock cycles for 8088 word-mode read.

Timing for the polling loop is based on reading the status from a port (IN), checking for a ready bit (TEST), and looping if not ready (JNZ). The same conditions and code stated for polling for CTC-based timing apply to polling for a ready bit.

No overhead is included for setting up or clearing the interrupts because the act of servicing the interrupts clears them (what is usually called *automatic end of interrupt mode*).

Determining Absolute Time

If you design a real-time system to water the lawn at certain times, you probably want the actions to take place at those particular times rather than just twenty-four hours since the last watering. Likewise, if you have a real-time system to log phone calls, a log entry reading "call received at 80,286 seconds past system start up" is not likely to thrill you. Both these examples demand a means of determining the time in an absolute sense, which is related to time as understood by humans.

The solution is to implement what is called a *real-time clock,* with *real* meaning *outside world.* This can be accomplished either in software or through the addition of a clock board. Software is cheap, and that is about all that can be said for it. Software clocks have disadvantages: They must be reinitialized every time the system is shut off, they rarely keep accurate time, and if they are interrupt driven, they can interfere with critical timing processes. With any of the 8086 family of processors, a totally software clock is nearly impossible because too many factors affect instruction timing, most notably the pre-fetch queue.

All things considered, if your system requires the capability of determining absolute time, purchase a time-of-day clock board. Usually containing at least a battery backed-up clock, boards are available that also contain other desirable real-time features, such as interrupt controllers, interval timers, space for math chips, and either serial or parallel I/O ports.

Determining Sequence—Interval Time

The last type of time to be determined is interval time, which is required when a sequence of events must be separated by specific amounts of time. Motor controls are common examples of this. If a motor is running at full speed and is suddenly reversed, damage to the motor may occur. The system may need to stop the motor, wait for some interval, then restart the motor in the opposite direction.

Interval time can be determined from software timing loops or from a real-time clock, if the real-time clock has sufficient resolution (you can't time microseconds on a one-second clock). Software timers are adequate if the event does not need to be timed accurately. When higher accuracy is required, hardware interval timers, like the CTC circuit, are a good idea. CTCs operate in many different modes and are useful as delay counters, rate generators, real-time clocks, etc. They also share the advantages of the real-time clock in that because they are implemented in hardware, they relieve the processor from the overhead of timing loops and free it for its decision-making role.

Help for Implementing Real-Time Systems Under MS-DOS

Multitasking

MS-DOS is not currently a multitasking operating system (as of version 3.10). That's the simple truth. MS-DOS also is not reentrant, which means that interrupt routines cannot call MS-DOS without encountering the risk of blowing the system away. Does this mean that real-time systems cannot be designed around MS-DOS? No. It means only that you have to provide some of the missing portions required for your application and work around the other problems. How to do this is the topic for the next section.

The simplest type of real-time program is one that doesn't require any multitasking and does all of its input and output through standard MS-DOS devices. Unfortunately, nothing much can be accomplished under these restrictions. We must extend MS-DOS if we are to be able to implement more advanced systems.

One of many multitasking features that MS-DOS lacks is preemptive scheduling, which is the ability of the operating system to interrupt a currently running routine and start another one. Preemptive scheduling cannot be added to MS-DOS because MS-DOS isn't reentrant. How can we get around this limitation?

The first step is to classify the application so as to identify what operations must be performed. Divide the application into separate tasks, much along the lines used as our evaluation criteria. Then organize the tasks into two groups: those that have critical timing constraints and those that don't. Also decide what types of operations must be performed in the critical sections. Can they be accomplished without calling MS-DOS, or do they require some system services? Finally, decide whether the program will be interrupted by outside events or must it poll for them? Armed with this information, we can begin to design the system.

Methods of Data Acquisition

When interfacing to data acquisition equipment, consider writing an MS-DOS device driver to acquire the data. If you can accomplish this, your program will be that much more portable. Even if you decide against an MS-DOS device driver, in the interests of modular programming you should write a separate routine in your program to handle data acquisition. We call this routine, as part of MS-DOS or not, the device driver.

For a device that must be polled to acquire the data, the device driver is called before the data is acquired. The driver then acquires the data and returns it to the calling program. If the data must be acquired at a certain rate and higher priority events are occurring in the system, this type of driver is not recommended because it is not really interruptable without loss of data elements.

If the device is interrupt driven, the driver has two entry points. One entry point is used as the interrupt vector and starts the section that stores data in a buffer. The other entry point is used by the calling program to obtain the buffered data. This driver is called after the data has been acquired. If this driver is called and the data is not ready, the driver can indicate that it is not ready by returning a status code, or the driver can wait for the buffer to become full.

Critical Timing Sections

Critical timing refers to any event (input, output, or response) that absolutely must occur or be serviced within a set amount of time. If an event can be delayed or is just not that important, it's not critical.

Critical input timing can occur in a sequence of inputs or as unexpected input. If the critical section deals with acquiring a sequence of input data without breaks, the entire sequence should be handled in the same routine, and the routine should not make any CALLs to routines that do not have a guaranteed execution time. (MS-DOS does not have a guaranteed execution time and should not be called either). Once the data has been acquired and timing is not so critical, the program may make any calls it pleases.

Unexpected inputs that must be received or responded to within a set time are usually handled in an interrupt driven routine. If this is not possible, the alternative is to have the routine that scans for critical events be called at specific time intervals, no matter what else is occurring in the system. Because MS-DOS does not guarantee that it returns from a call in a set amount of time (it doesn't even guarantee that it will return at all!), critical timing sections of the program must bypass MS-DOS altogether, even if it means sacrificing compatibility.

Sections involving critical output timing (but not critical response timing) are slightly easier to handle. If the entire sequence of outputs can be done in a single routine, that routine may be implemented in an MS-DOS device driver. Because the program has control over whether to call MS-DOS and "knows" that it must perform critical output, the program can avoid calling the system when it has work to perform.

The greatest difficulty lies in sections that involve critical response timing, where an unexpected input must be responded to within a short length of time. When operating under these constraints MS-DOS must not be called during the critical period, as MS-DOS' response time is not guaranteed.

If the input event that triggers a critical response can be tied to an interrupt, the entire routine to handle the response should be contained in the interrupt service routine. This allows the rest of the system to continue functioning as normal, including making calls to MS-DOS.

Handling Critical Timing without Interrupts

If handling the response in the interrupt routine isn't feasible or if the input event must be scanned for, MS-DOS cannot be called by the main program at all. This is because while MS-DOS is processing a call, the critical event may slip by without receiving service. A proviso to this is that MS-DOS may be called by the program any time that it knows that the input event will not or cannot occur. Unless you are planning to use your system to control a nuclear reactor or a clandestine drug factory (both highly dangerous, illegal, and foolish) the process usually contains logical breaks that allow you to use the resources of MS-DOS.

Systems that attempt to perform real-time processing without interrupts face other problems as well. When a program must scan the I/O for an event at short intervals, the program has difficulty performing other activities in addition to the scan. The problem is that even if the program is able to detect the occurrence of an event, the program cannot easily change its priorities to process the event. Once again MS-DOS's inability to handle multitasking interferes with the goals of a real-time system.

Designing a Scheduler for Real-Time Systems

For systems that must handle a variety of events, the lack of a scheduler is a severe handicap. This applies to both polled and interrupt driven systems. When a scheduler is lacking, you must provide a real-time scheduler for the system. This scheduler must be one that can allow different tasks to run on demand without sacrificing the ability to respond in a timely fashion.

Writing a real-time scheduler is not an easy task and should not be lightly undertaken. Writing it involves building your own operating system that can respond where MS-DOS can't.

A scheduler begins with a list of the routines that need to be executed. The main routine of the scheduler then sequences through this "ready" list, calling each routine in its turn. For polled systems, when each routine returns, the main routine checks to see whether the event has occurred. If the event has not occurred, the main routine calls the next routine in the list. If the event has occurred, the main routine calls the service routine to take care of the event. Because the main routine has the option of calling another routine rather than the next routine on the list, the main routine is described as having the capability of rescheduling the routines on the ready list.

Some routines may not wish to return to the scheduler as often as required to perform the event check, so the routine makes a call, which is called a *checkpoint,* to the scheduler. The main routine then performs whatever checks are necessary, and if nothing more important is pending, immediately returns control to the routine that checkpointed. If something is pending, the scheduler takes care of the event before returning. The process is simpler if all of the routines involved are reentrant. That allows the system to call routines without worrying whether they're already active.

A scheduler in an interrupt driven system is not much different, except that it need not wait for the called routine to return. When an event's interrupt occurs, the scheduler puts the interrupted task on hold and proceeds to schedule the event handler (the routine that handles the event). After the event has been processed, the scheduler returns control to the interrupted task.

By providing a scheduler, we have been able to ensure that the system can respond to events within the required amount of time. What we haven't been able to do is ensure that MS-DOS responds within the same time limit. If the critical timing requirement persists through the entire program, you cannot use calls to MS-DOS and need to duplicate the needed capabilities of MS-DOS in a fashion that allows for quick response. Portability is once again sacrificed for speed.

MS-DOS is still useful for most applications. You don't have to duplicate all of MS-DOS in a real-time system. The most complicated portions of MS-DOS are the disk and file access functions. Since real-time processing is usually incompatible with any disk access, most real-time kernels do not implement disk or file support. Unless you're willing to use some really unusual disk access techniques, these real-time systems can depend on MS-DOS to support their disk access functions. By using MS-DOS's disk support functions, the job of implementing a real-time kernel has been reduced to adding a real-time scheduler and the support for the direct I/O to the real-time devices.

If your application is one that cannot use MS-DOS at all, you should definitely investigate the purchase and use of an off-the-shelf real-time operating system. Should you decide to implement your own complete operating system for real-time processing, some hard work lies ahead.

Summary

Because of the multitude of real-time applications and the complexity of real-time systems, this chapter did not include application-specific programming examples or examples of real-time kernels. Instead, our approach has been to explain the philosophy of real-time programming in real-time systems. We've also provided the information necessary to enable you to analyze the requirements of a real-time system, particularly in the area of I/O transfers. With careful attention you should be able to specify a real-time system to fit your needs. Nevertheless, true real-time response is a difficult thing to achieve, and not much literature has been written on the subject for advanced applications. Should you decide to undertake the creation of a real-time system, maybe you'll be the one to write the next book on the subject!

DEVICES

Part II

Installable Device Drivers

Chapter 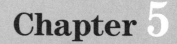5

he primary requirement of any computer system is not only the ability to compute but also the ability to communicate with the outside world through its peripherals. Without communications the computer becomes an expensive paperweight at best. The responsibility of any operating system is to provide communications facilities for application programs and the internal needs of the operating system itself.

An operating system must meet two separate requirements to enable an applications program to communicate with an external device. First, a defined interface between the application program and the operating system must exist and must be flexible enough to allow the program to specify what is desired of the device. Second, the operating system must have the capability of transferring data to and from the device and controlling the device's operation. This system-to-device interface is provided by sections of the operating system called *device drivers.*

Although mainframe and minicomputer operating systems have a tradition of extensive device support, microcomputer operating systems are generally lean in this area. They usually contain support for the primary disk drives, the system's terminal, a printer port, and possibly an auxiliary device. Support beyond that level has been an unexpected plus. In previous operating systems, including MS-DOS version 1.0, adding this support after purchase has been difficult. The operating systems did not contain applications-level function requests for nonstandard devices, and the drivers themselves were embedded deep in the BIOS (basic input/output system). Adding or changing a device driver required editing the BIOS source (if it was available), reassembling it, and copying it to the system disk's boot track (for which task all too often no utility was provided). Computers such as the IBM Personal Computer did not even allow that much. Because its BIOS is in ROM (read-only memory), modifying the BIOS required the use of a PROM programmer (a device that writes to a programmable ROM, which isn't an everyday piece of equipment). After all this effort, no way was available for the applications program to talk via the operating system to the driver.

MS-DOS version 2.0 changed all that. In what is probably the most significant advance in microcomputer operating systems since the inception of CP/M, MS-DOS versions 2.0 and later provide not only the ability to install device drivers without arcane measures but also a standard extensible interface that allows programs to communicate with the drivers. The result has been an explosion in the number of devices that MS-DOS now supports and in virtual devices that supply MS-DOS systems with such features as RAM disks, high-level graphics interfaces, and the like.

The MS-DOS device driver is a subprogram that is called by MS-DOS on one side and communicates with the actual device on the other. The middleman between the system and the hardware, the MS-DOS device driver passes data between the subprogram and the device.

Why Have Device Drivers?

Device drivers serve two purposes. The first is to provide a standard interface to all programs that desire to use a particular device, irrespective of the idiosyncrasies of that device. A program that does text processing or spreadsheet calculations does not really care exactly what type of terminal is connected to the system. The program desires to accomplish functions such as Display Character or Read Keyboard. The terminal device driver takes care of the details of accomplishing the transfers and thus provides the high-level interface desired by the applications program. Change the terminal; change the device driver. No modifications to the application program should be necessary. Device drivers provided for disk drives should present a standard interface for all the different types of disks. A program that performs disk I/O should operate with a floppy disk of any format, a hard disk, and even a RAM disk. It should make no difference to the application program. So we can sum up the first purpose of a device driver as providing a device independent uniform interface.

The second purpose of device drivers is that they serve as a type of RTL (run-time library). Device drivers provide the same measure of support to all programs. Each program is not only relieved of the necessity for supporting multiple device formats but is relieved also of the necessity for supporting any device formats. Support is handled by the device driver. By collecting all the device drivers into the operating system, only one copy of each driver need be maintained. The result is that programs that are written to use the MS-DOS interface don't have to contain any driver code at all.

In the MS-DOS implementation, device drivers may be added to the system to replace the built-in drivers for nondisk devices. If you don't like the way that the system driver handles a certain device, you can write your own driver. The difference is once again transparent to application programs. It's not a trivial matter to write a driver, but at least the option is available.

Given this powerful ability to interface MS-DOS with diverse foreign devices, it is but one more step to conceive of device drivers without physical devices! In other words, device drivers can be written to support devices that don't really exist, such as the ubiquitous RAM disk. These types of devices are called *virtual devices;* and their drivers, *virtual device drivers.*

Virtual devices, or physical devices for that matter, are not limited to strictly input-output functions. Any transformation function that accepts and/or returns data may be placed in a device driver. High speed floating point array processors are only one example of transformation devices. Beyond that, drivers can contain software with no external I/O to emulate the behavior of actual devices that the system does not yet contain, such as a software clock or the floating point processor.

When To Use Device Drivers

At what point should a function be removed from a program and turned into a device driver? The rule of thumb is that a function which performs I/O at a hardware level is a likely candidate for a device driver. Because of the nature of the 8086 processor family, this sort of function is usually an IN or OUT instruction (including the INS or OUTS instructions). If the system uses memory mapped I/O, accesses to absolute memory addresses may also be indicative of hardware level I/O. Reading and writing the interrupt vectors are also absolute memory accesses, but you should really use the MS-DOS functions Get Vector and Set Vector rather than a driver.

Putting the I/O handlers into a device driver accomplishes four things: It makes the main program more transportable, makes the I/O handler available to any other programs that desire to access that device, makes the system slightly larger in terms of memory used, and slows down the access time to the hardware appreciably. A slightly larger system should not be any great concern, but the extended access time can be the critical factor in some applications. Whenever a decision is made to write a device driver, the speed constraints of the application must be weighed against the increase in program compatibility and accessibility of the driver. The increase in access time is more noticeable for a device that transfers data a word or a byte at a time because the overhead penalty is paid on each call of the driver. For device drivers that transfer an entire block of data on each call, the overhead is spread over more transfers and the resultant penalty decreased.

The Limitation of MS-DOS Being Non-Reentrant

Because device drivers are called by MS-DOS, they are subject to the same limitations as memory resident routines. To wit, they may not use MS-DOS to perform any functions. (The single exception to this is that certain MS-DOS function calls may be made during the initialization phase of the driver.) This severely limits the portability of virtual device drivers written to pre-process information that is intended for standard drivers.

For example, a virtual device driver written to provide graphics capability for a dot-matrix printer cannot use the standard MS-DOS print character functions for final output. The virtual device driver must contain all the necessary code to perform the actual output to the printer. (Note that the driver described for this example is considered a virtual device even though it communicates with a physical device. The reason is that the driver provides capabilities not inherent in the device, that is, this driver provides graphics operations on a dumb printer.)

Because MS-DOS is non-reentrant, DEBUG may not be used to debug an installed driver. DEBUG uses MS-DOS to handle its own I/O, and if DEBUG is used inside of a driver, the program destroys the context of the driver call, which leaves it unable to return proper information to MS-DOS. One way to handle this shortcoming is to use any built-in I/O functions (for example, BIOS functions) that your system may contain to perform rudimentary output of debugging information. A more dependable method is to design a test jig to exercise the driver routine. A text jig is a small program that feeds test data to the driver and checks for expected returns. This program is then run by MS-DOS, allowing DEBUG to be used. Of course, if the device is speed dependent, some additional care must be exercised to avoid interfering with the driver's handling of the device.

Installing Device Drivers

As mentioned before, in the days before MS-DOS version 2.0, installing a device driver meant patching the BIOS. Although this method is still possible, the new version 2.0 method installs additional or replacement device drivers during the boot process itself.

The MS-DOS Boot Process

When an 8086 family processor first starts running after power on or a system reset, all registers are cleared with the exception of the code segment register, which is set to FFFF hex. This combination causes code execution to start at absolute address FFFF0 hex. Typically, code is provided at this address in a ROM to perform the primary bootstrap. The primary bootstrap reads the first track of the system disk into memory. If the system that is being booted has a ROM-based BIOS, the first track usually contains only a secondary bootstrap. If the system lacks a ROM BIOS, the first track also contains at least a portion of the BIOS in addition to the secondary bootstrap.

The secondary bootstrap contains code to locate and read two files from the system disk into memory. These files contain the MS-DOS system and the rest of the system's BIOS (or the interface between MS-DOS and the BIOS for systems with a ROM BIOS). The system file is usually named MSDOS.SYS or IBMDOS.COM on IBM PC computers. The other file is usually named IO.SYS or IBMBIO.COM on the IBM PC, although it can have other names as well. (The authors' CompuPro system's file is called PCPRO.SYS). These two files are often marked as *hidden* files in the directory, so they may not appear in directory listings.

The last thing that the secondary bootstrap does before terminating is to inform the MS-DOS system how to communicate with the BIOS. When that has been done, control is passed to MS-DOS, and it takes over the task of bringing up the system. MS-DOS calls the initialization sections of the device drivers contained in the BIOS and finally has complete control over the system. If the system being booted has no installable device drivers, MS-DOS initialization is complete (the system is running), and all that remains is for MS-DOS to load the system's command interpreter (COMMAND.COM) so that any startup batch files may be executed or so that the user can begin entering commands.

The CONFIG.SYS File

After the system is running but before COMMAND.COM is loaded, installable device drivers are loaded. The sequence of events that occurs during system initialization (after the boot process) is shown in Flowchart 5-1. MS-DOS searches the system disk directory for a file called CONFIG.SYS. If this file is found, MS-DOS (not COMMAND.COM) reads the file a line at a time. Each line can contain one of five configuration commands. One of these commands has the format

DEVICE=[*d:*][*path*]*filename*[*.ext*] [*parameters*]

Flowchart 5-1.   MS-DOS initialization process.

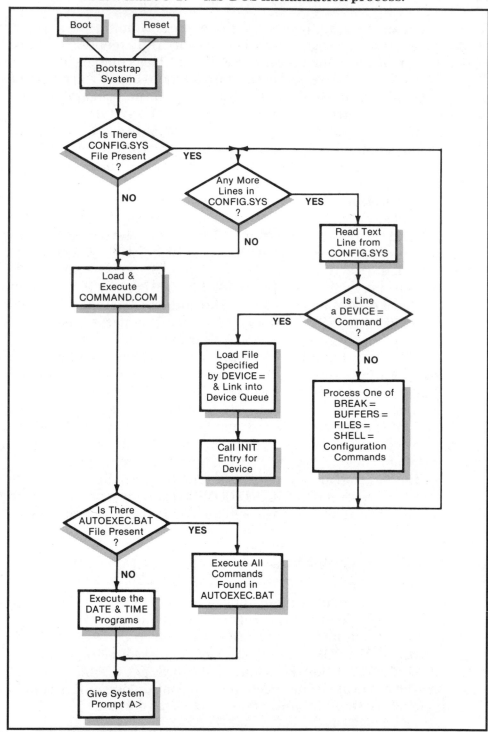

where the items enclosed in brackets are optional portions of the file name. This particular command instructs MS-DOS to install the code contained in the file as a device driver. The file itself is created and structured much like a .COM file, with the exception that the code begins at offset zero instead of offset 0100 (hex) and that the file must begin with a specific header block. For the moment though, our concern is only with how MS-DOS installs this file into the system.

The parameters are passed directly to the device driver by handing the driver a pointer to the command line text buffer during initialization. The driver may then parse the command line to obtain configuration parameters. The pointer actually points to the first character after the " = " in the command line, so the parser should be equipped to skip the driver's file name. We return to this topic in the section on writing device drivers in this chapter.

Device drivers are a special form of a memory resident program. MS-DOS loads the file into memory, reading the header block to obtain information about the type, name, attributes, and entry points of the driver. Once the file has been loaded, MS-DOS calls the driver with an INIT (initialize) command. The driver then performs whatever initialization is required and returns the address of the next free byte of memory located after the driver. This address determines where MS-DOS may load the next driver, if there is one, or where free memory begins after all the drivers are loaded. In this respect the end-of-driver address, as it is called, is similar to the size parameter used by the Keep Process Function. Both inform MS-DOS what memory is reserved and may not be allocated.

MS-DOS organizes the drivers that it loads by stringing them together in a queue. The first double-word of each driver, which is also the first double-word of the header block, contains a pointer to the previous driver loaded by MS-DOS. The end of the chain, which is the first driver loaded, contains the value minus 1 (–1). When MS-DOS wishes to use a device driver, the operating system searches the list of drivers in the reverse order from that in which they were loaded. This allows MS-DOS to install user-supplied drivers with names such as COM, PRN, and AUX. Because they are found before the drivers supplied in the system, they supersede those supplied with the system.

The default device drivers are actually loaded and initialized by MS-DOS before the CONFIG.SYS file is read and parsed. This allows the initialization section of a device driver to use some of the MS-DOS function calls for the purpose of displaying messages or configuring the driver for a particular version of MS-DOS. The calls that may be safely used at this time are functions 01 through 0Ch, which support CON, PRN, and AUX I/O, and function 30h, Get DOS Version Number. Calls related to file I/O or memory management should be avoided as the MS-DOS memory map is not yet stable. However, once the driver has been installed, all MS-DOS function calls are off limits, including MS-DOS interrupts 20h through 27h.

After the CONFIG.SYS file has been processed and the drivers initialized, the standard devices CON, PRN, and AUX are closed and then reopened by MS-DOS so that any replacement drivers for one of these units takes effect. From that point on, the new drivers are used exclusively.

Certain drivers may not be replaced by the user. One of these is the NUL device driver. This limitation results from the fact that MS-DOS uses the NUL device as the head of the device queue. All devices that are added to the system are added after the NUL device. Because the system supplied NUL device is always the first device in the queue, the system supplied device is always the first NUL device found. An example device queue is shown in Figure 5-1. Not all of the labeled areas make sense immediately. They are explained later. The device marked *last device* is actually the first device to be installed, and the device located directly after the NUL device is the last device to be installed.

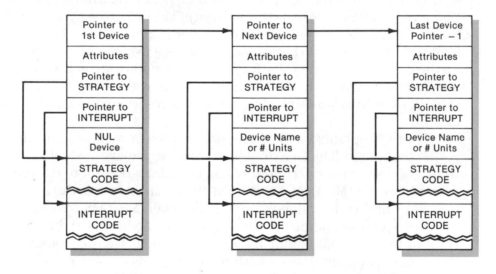

Fig. 5-1.   Example device driver queue.

The NUL device is not the only device that cannot be replaced. Devices that deal with mass storage devices (that is, disks) are also not replaceable. You may add drivers for new disk devices but not remove or replace the old ones. This restriction arises because disk devices have identifying letters assigned by MS-DOS during the boot process (A, B, etc.) rather than unique names (such as CON and PRN). Because you can't name a particular disk device driver, you can't replace it.

Using ASSIGN To Replace Disk Device Drivers

However, don't despair if you don't like your existing disk device drivers. Although they can't be removed, they can be bypassed. After you have written (and tested) the new driver, add it to the CONFIG.SYS file. When MS-DOS is rebooted, the new driver is installed as the next device in the list. For example, if you already have three drives, the new driver is drive D. Now use the MS-DOS command ASSIGN to redirect all accesses of the old drive to the new drive. As an example, let's assume we want to replace the drive A driver. The ASSIGN command for this is

```
ASSIGN A=D
```

MS-DOS redirects all drive A accesses to the new device D driver, including absolute disk access interrupts, 25h and 26h. If you have written the new device driver to access the same physical device as the old one, you have effectively replaced the old device driver. If you decide that you like the old one better, you can restore the original assignments by entering the ASSIGN command without any parameters.

Types of Device Drivers

There are two types of device drivers, named and unnamed, called respectively *character* device drivers and *block* device drivers. The differences between the two types goes much deeper than the issue of names and replaceability. Not only does MS-DOS provide block oriented drivers to support disk devices, it expects a block mode device driver to be controlling one or more disks. The implications of this are that MS-DOS expects the units serviced by block oriented device drivers to support the MS-DOS file structure, with FATs (file allocation tables) and directories.

Truthfully, the names *character* and *block* mode device drivers are somewhat misleading because the character device driver can support block mode transfers just as well as the block mode driver. The actual relationship is something more akin to nondisk and disk drivers. It cannot even be said that character device drivers are sequential and block device drivers random access because character mode drivers can be constructed to perform random access of the devices they support.

Leaving aside for the moment the question of what constitutes a block mode device driver and what constitutes a character mode device driver, let's look at some of the ways that device drivers can be accessed through MS-DOS. This gives us some idea of the type of device driver we wish to write for a particular application.

Accessing Device Drivers from MS-DOS

MS-DOS supports four basic types of device I/O that may be used within an application program. These types can be classified as in the following list. Each of these types is suited for particular applications, and our intention is to present the strengths and weaknesses of each type of I/O so that you can judge which type is suited to your application. We have not presented the details of each of the function calls because that information may be found in the Microsoft *MS-DOS Programmer's Reference Manual* (or your system's equivalent manual).

- CP/M-style dedicated I/O functions for devices such as console, printer, and auxiliary. These are truly character oriented devices. The functions in this group are

  CON: Functions 01, 02, and 06 through 0Ch
  PRN: Function 05
  AUX: Functions 03 and 04

- CP/M-style file access using the FCB (file control block). This method may also be used to access character style devices. FCB access functions are

  Open/Close: Functions 0Fh and 10h
  Device/File Read/Write: Functions 14h and 15h
  File Only Read/Write: Functions 21h,22h, 27h, and 28h

- MS-DOS style file access using file handles. As with the FCB type I/O, character style devices may be accessed as well as disk files. Those functions that are used with file handles are

  Open/Close: Functions 3Dh and 3Eh
  Device/File Read/Write: Functions 3Fh and 40h
  I/O Control for Devices: Function 44h

- Direct disk I/O functions performing absolute disk reads and writes. These are not part of the MS-DOS function call, INT 21h, but are supported instead by interrupts 25h (absolute read) and 26h (absolute write).

CP/M Style Character Device I/O

The CP/M-style functions dedicated to the standard device CON are useful for most terminal I/O and offer the options of buffering, echoing, waiting for a character, and status checking. Support for the PRN and AUX devices is more limited but sufficient for most purposes. However, for nonstandard devices either the FCB (file control block) or file handle methods of access must be used.

Device Access Using the File Control Block (FCB)

The FCB (file control block) method of device access is a mixed blessing. On one hand, FCB is more cumbersome to set up and use than the file handle method, although the use of macros and the STRUC directive can greatly ease the task of setting up the FCB data structure. On the other hand, FCB-type file access allows the programmer to directly specify the record number within a file, making it possible to perform random access I/O on a file. The file handle I/O functions 3Fh (read) and 40h (write) allow only sequential operations. To perform random I/O with file handles, the application program must use function 42h (Move File Pointer). This extra step is not required with FCB-type file accesses.

Using File Handles for Device I/O

Although random access is fine for files, it doesn't do much for nondisk-type devices. When performing I/O to a nondisk device, the file handle method is much simpler to use and doesn't require the programmer to set up an FCB. In addition, the file handle access method supports the IOCTL (I/O control for devices) function call (44h). As we shall soon see, IOCTL can be extremely useful for advanced control of the device.

When using file handles to access nondisk devices, the programmer is not limited to performing I/O one byte at a time. Up to 64K bytes may be transferred to or from the device in a single call of the File/Device I/O functions. As with disk devices, when used by themselves on nondisk devices, these functions perform sequential transfers with each successive block of data following the previous one. However, by using the IOCTL function, additional parameters for the device can be specified. For example, if both the device and device driver are set up to handle random mode transfers, the IOCTL function can be used to control the transfer source or destination within the device.

An example of this last point may help to illustrate the potential of I/O Control for Devices. Suppose that a particular system has associated with it a memory-mapped graphics display device. Using a device driver, data is transferred from system memory to the graphics memory. Because the device is not a mass storage device, its driver must be a character mode device driver. If I/O is performed using only the file handle I/O functions, no way is available to specify where on the display the data is to be sent. However, if the driver supports the IOCTL function, the location of the data in the graphics memory may be specified through the control channel.

The I/O Control for Devices Function—Function 44h

As we have implied, not all device drivers support the IOCTL function call. In those drivers that do support IOCTL, not all of the various features of the call are necessarily supported. However, IOCTL is such a powerful tool for controlling devices that it behooves the MS-DOS programmer to become familiar with its capabilities. The knowledge of what can be done through IOCTL calls surely influences the decisions of what features to incorporate in a device driver.

The I/O Control for Devices function has three basic modes of operation, which are determined by a function code passed in the AL register when the request is made. A list of the function codes supported by IOCTL appears in Table 5-1. The three modes are device configuration (codes 0,1, and 8 and B in version 3.0), control channel I/O (codes 2 through 5), and device status (codes 6 and 7).

Table 5-1.   I/O Control for Devices Function Operation

Code	Description
AL = 0:	*Get device information
AL = 1:	Set device information
AL = 2:	Read from character device control channel
AL = 3:	Write to character device control channel
AL = 4:	Read from block device control channel
AL = 5:	Write to block device control channel
AL = 6:	*Get input status
AL = 7:	*Get output status
AL = 8:	†Does block device support removable media?
AL = B:	†Change sharing retry count

* Function valid for IOCTL on files as well as devices
† Supported only under MS-DOS version 3.0 and later

Examining these modes in reverse order, the device status requests return a simple ready (FFh) or not ready (0) indication. Microsoft includes a warning in the *MS-DOS Programmer's Reference Manual* to the effect that in future versions of MS-DOS, the status code may not be valid by the time the system returns control to the calling program. Presumably the manual is referring to the future possibility of multitasking or multiuser MS-DOS. One can only hope that by that time, Microsoft will have found a way to return the correct information. In any case, until concurrent MS-DOS arrives, the inaccuracy should not be a problem.

We have already mentioned the IOCTL device control channel I/O capability. Simply put, this is a means to transfer a buffer of data to or from an auxiliary channel. The mechanics of the call are identical to the file handle I/O calls (3Fh and 40h), except that the function code specified in the AX register is different. Whether the data is intended for an auxiliary channel on the device or for the driver itself is up to the implementor.

Don't however be misled by the simplicity of the call and dismiss it as just another I/O function. In the proper application, IOCTL can be a real blessing as a secondary channel to communicate with the device driver. Microsoft has provided a "trap door" function to accommodate unforeseen contingencies. They are saying, "You feel our device interface is too limiting? Need more configuration ability? Here, use this." This is a great improvement over the "We don't got it; you don't need it!" attitude taken by systems developers not too long ago.

MS-DOS has also provided for configuration commands with the Get/Set Device Information functions supported by the IOCTL function. Figure 5-2 shows the 16-bit configuration word used by the Get/Set Device Information functions, codes 0 and 1. In current versions of MS-DOS only the lower eight bits of this word may be specified in the Set Device Information word.

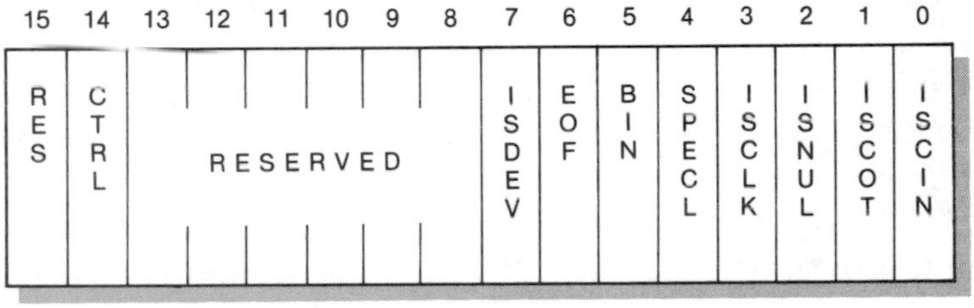

15	14	13	12	11	10	9	8	7	6	5	4	3	2	1	0
R E S	C T R L		RESERVED					I S D E V	E O F	B I N	S P E C L	I S C L K	I S N U L	I S C O T	I S C I N

BIT MEANINGS

CTRL = 1: Supports Control Channel I/O
ISDEV = 1: Channel Is a Device   = 0: Channel Is a File

DEVICE

EOF = 0: END-OF-FILE on Input
BIN = 1: Operating in Binary Mode
SPECL = 1: Device Is SPECIAL
ISCLK = 1: Device Is the CLOCK Device
ISNUL = 1: Device Is the NUL Device
ISCOT = 1: Device Is CONSOLE Output Device
ISCIN = 1: Device Is CONSOLE Input Device

FILE

Channel Has Been Written

BITS 0 through 5
Are
BLOCK DEVICE
NUMBER

Fig. 5-2. IOCTL device configuration word.

The bits of interest in this word regarding device drivers are ISDEV and CTRL. ISDEV is set to one if the channel (handle) is open to a device rather than a file, and CTRL is set to one if the device can process control strings. Note that even if the channel has been opened on a file, the CTRL bit still has meaning because block mode device drivers also can be written to provide a device control channel. If a control channel I/O request is issued on a handle open to a file, the data buffer is still sent directly to the driver for processing, irrespective of the status of the file.

The special bit, SPECL, is related to the special bit contained in the device driver's attribute word in the device header. The exact meaning of this bit is something of a mystery, especially because IBM DOS documentation consistently marks it as *reserved*.

The other bit deserving further scrutiny is the BIN bit, sometimes called the *raw* bit in MS-DOS documentation. This bit doesn't actually affect the operation of the device driver but does indicate whether MS-DOS "cooks" the data or passes raw binary information between the device and the application program. Cooking the data, also called ASCII mode, implies checking for certain control characters, providing tab expansion, echoing characters, etc. More information on this feature is available in the *MS-DOS Programmer's Reference Manual*.

Direct Disk Access with Interrupts 25h & 26h

At the other end of the spectrum from file handle device accesses are the absolute disk access interrupts: Absolute Disk Read (INT 25h) and Absolute Disk Write (INT 26h). As the name implies, the Direct Disk Access interrupts function solely with block mode devices, for instance, disks.

The purpose of absolute disk access is to allow I/O to disks without having to go through the MS-DOS file structure. This is useful in two cases.

In the first case, programmers can read or write selective parts of a standard MS-DOS disk that does contain a file and directory structure. This is often required when part of the disk has gone bad, preventing the FCB or file handle methods from working. Direct disk I/O functions can then be used to "surgically" pick around the disk and recover what may be salvaged. Another use is to allow programs to read and write the FAT or directory on the disk, something not allowed through the other methods. Utilities that sort directories, patch files, etc., require this ability.

The second case for using absolute disk access is where the disk does not contain any FAT entries or directory structure. The disk is to be used purely as a data disk. This can also occur when reading disks written under a different operating system like CP/M or the UCSD pSystem. In such cases, the disk configuration parameters returned to the system by the driver prevent MS-DOS from being able to access the disk in any other way. Any attempts to perform file I/O, including reading the directory, return garbage or the **Non-DOS Disk** error message. (For more information on how MS-DOS determines the format of a disk, refer to the "Build BIOS Parameter Block" driver command described in the Microsoft *MS-DOS Programmer's Reference Manual* (or your system's equivalent manual.))

In return for providing direct access to the drivers, INT 25h and INT 26h do not perform blocking or deblocking for the disk. Blocking and deblocking are required when the physical sector size on the disk is different from the logical record size used within the system. When blocking, the system gathers together enough records to fill a physical sector before issuing a disk write. Deblocking is used when reading from the disk because one physical sector can contain many records. The system reads the entire sector, then extracts the requested record for the calling program. Absolute disk access functions only read and write entire sectors, so the programmer must know the sector size of the disk to determine just how many bytes are transferred.

Because the calling parameters used in these interrupts are passed directly to the device driver without conversion, reads and writes transfer data in units of the physical sector size on the device. This is contrasted with the FCB and file handle access methods where I/O is specified in logical blocks and records and MS-DOS handles the conversion to physical sectors.

One last peculiarity of absolute disk access functions is that they return from the interrupt with a FAR RET rather than an IRET instruction, leaving the flags on the stack. Therefore, after checking to see whether the function completed properly, you must pop the original flags from the stack.

I/O Summary

Now that we have a basic idea of the types of operations that may be requested of a device driver, we are ready to proceed with the actual construction of the driver. To summarize, all device drivers are asked to perform basic I/O. Device drivers may also support an optional separate I/O channel for device control, which is called the I/O Control for Devices channel.

Character-type device drivers may be asked to transfer from one to 64K bytes of data in a single call. Block device drivers are asked to transfer data in units of sectors only because MS-DOS takes care of conversion from sectors to records and back again. As we have hinted, block mode drivers also are asked to return configuration information about the disk that they are currently using.

Writing Device Drivers

Writing device drivers in any operating system has a great advantage over writing standard programs. Device drivers must follow a fairly rigid structure, sort of a "cookbook," and once the structure is understood, the rest follows.

The basic parts of a device driver and a suggested structure are shown in Figure 5-3. The three required sections are the device header, the strategy routine, and the interrupt routine. The interrupt routine is not the same as an interrupt service routine, which can be an optional part of an interrupt driven device driver. Instead, this routine is really the entry point to the driver for processing the request received from MS-DOS. Listing 5-1 shows these three parts as they would occur in a real device driver.

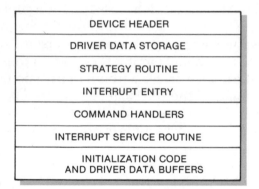

| DEVICE HEADER |
| DRIVER DATA STORAGE |
| STRATEGY ROUTINE |
| INTERRUPT ENTRY |
| COMMAND HANDLERS |
| INTERRUPT SERVICE ROUTINE |
| INITIALIZATION CODE AND DRIVER DATA BUFFERS |

Fig. 5-3.   The parts of an MS-DOS device driver.

Listing 5-1.   Device Header, Strategy, and Interrupt Routines

```
        ORG     0
START   EQU     $                ; start location of driver
;****** DEVICE HEADER **********************************
        dw      -1,-1            ; pointer to next device
        dw      ATTRIBUTE        ; attribute word
        dw      offset STRATEGY  ; strategy entry point
        dw      offset INTERRUPT ; interrupt entry point
        db      8 dup (?)        ; # units/name field
;****** RESIDENT DATA AREA *****************************
req_ptr         dd      ?                ; pointer to request buffer
    :           :       :                        :
    :           :       :                        :
;****** STRATEGY ENTRY POINT FOR DEVICE DRIVER ***********
; Save the request header pointer for INTERRUPT in REQ_PTR.
; Entered with pointer contained in ES:BX registers.
;
stratp proc     far
STRATEGY:
```

Listing 5.1. cont.

```
        mov         cs:word ptr [req_ptr],bx
        mov         cs:word ptr [req_ptr + 2],es
        ret
stratp endp
;****** INTERRUPT ENTRY POINT FOR DEVICE DRIVER ***********
; Process the command contained in the request header.
; The pointer to the request header is located in REQ_PTR
; in the form OFFSET:SEGMENT.
;
interp proc     far
INTERRUPT:
        pusha                       ; save all registers
        lds         bx,cs:[req_ptr] ; get DS & request header
         :          :                   :
```

The Device Header

The device header is an 18-byte block of data that must begin every device driver. This header must be located at origin 0 in the device driver segment. When a device driver is loaded, MS-DOS reads the device header to determine the type of device and the entry points into the device. The header contains four pieces of information critical to MS-DOS' use of the driver: the chain pointer, the attribute word, the entry point vectors, and the unit/name field.

The Device Chain Pointer

The first four bytes of the device header are a double word pointer (offset:segment) to the next device in the device chain. These bytes are normally set to FFFF:FFFF (–1) in the driver code. MS-DOS overwrites them with the address of the next driver when the system loads the new driver. An exception occurs when the device driver file contains more than one device driver, in which case, the first two bytes should contain the offset of the next driver's device header.

The Device Header ATTRIBUTE Word

The next word in the device header is called the *attribute word*. It contains a number of single bit fields that convey the type and capabilities of the device driver to MS-DOS. Figure 5-4 shows the layout and meanings of the bits in the attribute word. Some examples of attribute words for various devices are as follows:

    IBM format disk device—0000
    Standard console terminal driver—8003h
    Standard character device (for example, PRN)—8000h

15	14	13	12	11	10	9	8	7	6	5	4	3	2	1	0
C H R	I O C T L	N O N I B M	N E T W O R K	O C R M			R E S E R V E D				S P E C L	C L O C K	N U L	S T D O U T	S T D I N

BIT MEANINGS

CHR   = 1: Device Is a Character Device
IOCTL   = 1: Driver Supports I/O Control for Devices I/O
* OCRM   = 1: Device Supports OPEN/CLOSE/REMOVABLE MEDIA calls

BLOCK DEVICES

NONIBM = 1: Driver Is for Non-IBM Type Disk.
‡ NETWORK = 1: Driver Is for a Network Device

CHARACTER DEVICES

SPECL   = 1: Device Has SPECIAL Attributes
CLOCK   = 1: Device Is the CLOCK Device
NUL   = 1: Device Is the NUL Device
STDOUT = 1: Device Is the STANDARD OUTPUT Device
STDIN   = 1: Device Is the STANDARD INPUT Device

* = MS-DOS Version 3.00 or later.
‡ = MS-DOS Version 3.10 or later.

Fig. 5-4.   Device driver attribute word.

Because of their importance, three of the bits in the attribute word deserve special attention. The IOCTL bit (bit 14) is used to tell MS-DOS that the driver supports I/O control for devices by reading or writing to the control channel (driver command codes 3 and 12). This implies in turn that the device may be configured or controlled via MS-DOS Function 44h, subcommands 2 and 3 (for character devices) or subcommands 4 and 5 (for block devices). This bit must be set to 0 if the driver does not support I/O on a control channel.

The OCRM (open/close/removable media) bit is used to inform the system that the driver supports the new driver commands introduced with MS-DOS version 3.0: DEVICE OPEN (driver command 13), DEVICE CLOSE (driver command 14), and the check for REMOVABLE MEDIA (driver command 15). If the OCRM bit (bit 11) is set in the driver's attribute word, MS-DOS calls the DEVICE OPEN command each time the device (or file on the device) is opened (for example, using MS-DOS Function 3Dh). Correspondingly, the DEVICE CLOSE command is called each time the device (or file) is closed (for example, MS-DOS Function 3Eh). The REMOVABLE MEDIA driver command is accessed with the I/O control for devices function (MS-DOS Function 44h), using subcommand 8 of the IOCTL function to check whether the device supports removable media.

The third special bit in the device attribute word, bit 12, was introduced in MS-DOS version 3.10. This bit is used to indicate to MS-DOS that the device is a network device. Network devices are marked as block devices in the attribute word. The assumption is made that a network device is a gateway onto the network, allowing entire system calls to be sent to a remote device for processing. However, in order to use the network, some facility for redirection must be provided, such as MS-NET. More detailed information on networking and redirection may be found in Chapter 7.

The SPECL bit tells MS-DOS that the driver has special characteristics. Some sources claim that this bit indicates that a standard I/O driver has installed an Interrupt 29h handler. However, IBM DOS documentation claims that this bit is reserved, so leaving it alone may be best.

The STRATEGY and INTERRUPT Entry Pointers

The next two words in the device header contain the offsets of the strategy routine and interrupt routine, respectively. MS-DOS uses this information together with the segment address of the driver to find the entry points to the routine. MS-DOS knows the segment address, of course, because the system loaded the driver in the first place.

The Number of Units/Name Field

The last eight bytes of the device header is used for two purposes. For character type device drivers, this field contains the ASCII name of the device, padded with blanks. For example, the printer device field would appear as `'PRN    '`.

For block mode device drivers, only the first byte has any meaning. It indicates to MS-DOS how many separate units are supported by this device driver. This is necessary because many disk controllers support more than one physical drive. Because the remaining seven bytes are unused, they may contain the name of the device to assist in finding the device in memory or in identifying the driver. For example, the unit field of the RAM disk driver RDISK (shown in Listing 5-3) is defined as: `1,'RDISK '`.

The STRATEGY Routine

The next required section of the device driver is the strategy routine. This section has the single task of saving the driver request block for later execution by the interrupt routine.

What is the driver request block? Listing 5-2 shows the structure definition for the request header. Every I/O request made to the driver begins with this request header. The request may sometimes require more information than that contained in the request header, which is why the length parameter is included.

Listing 5-2.   Structure for the I/O Driver Request Header Block

```
request  equ     ds:[bx]            ; base addr of request head
reqhdr   struc
length   db      ?                  ; length of request block (bytes)
unit     db      ?                  ; unit #
command  db      ?                  ; driver command code
status   dw      ?                  ; status return
         db      8 dup (?)          ; reserved bytes
reqhdr   ends
```

We will return to the request header, but first we must finish our coverage of the strategy routine.

The reason that the strategy routine must save the request block is because MS-DOS does not make a single call to a driver to perform a function. Instead, the system first calls the driver and tells it what it wants done and then recalls the driver and tells it to actually perform the action.

The reason for the two calls is that when MS-DOS eventually supports a multitasking or concurrent system, multiple driver requests may be outstanding at any given time. By separating the request and execution portions of the driver, multiple requests can be pending, even while the driver is still processing an earlier request.

MS-DOS passes to the strategy routine a pointer to the driver request block in the ES:BX register pair. As the following code fragment demonstrates, most drivers save the driver request block by simply saving the pointer to the block. This is because MS-DOS currently calls the interrupt routine immediately after the strategy routine returns. The data in the request block is still valid.

```
        mov     cs:word ptr [req_ptr],bx
        mov     cs:word ptr [req_ptr + 2],es
```

However, as soon as MS-DOS becomes multitasking, saving the pointer alone no longer suffices. The strategy routine will have to save the contents of the request block. In addition, drivers probably will have to be able to queue multiple request blocks unless MS-DOS handles this function for them. Until the day when MS-DOS becomes multitasking, we can get by with the easier method of saving just the pointer itself.

Both the strategy routine and the interrupt routine must be defined in MASM as FAR procedures and return to MS-DOS with a far RET. Because MS-DOS calls these routines with a far CALL, any other type of return would either return to the wrong location (near RET) or misalign the stack (IRET).

The INTERRUPT Routine

After the strategy routine saves the pointer to the request block and returns, MS-DOS calls the interrupt routine (also called the *request entry point* in IBM DOS documentation). This is the routine that actually performs the requested operation.

The first thing that the interrupt routine must do is save all registers! When a device driver is called, the stack has enough room for about 20 pushes. Pushing all of the registers, including the flags, takes 14 pushes. If the interrupt routine requires more than six words of stack storage for its own use, the interrupt routine should set up its own local stack.

After the state of the machine has been saved, the interrupt routine must retrieve the request block that was saved by the strategy routine. If the pointer to the block was saved, using the code fragment in preceding text, the pointer can be retrieved with an LDS instruction.

```
lds     bx,cs:[req_ptr]   ; get DS & request header
```

Now that the interrupt routine has access to the request block, processing may begin. The first step is to analyze the desired request. Accessing the individual fields of the request header is much simpler if a structure is defined for the header. The structure that we use in the RDISK driver to define the request header was shown in Listing 52.

If the driver supports a block type device, the first element of the header checked should be the unit number, *request.unit*. Once that has been verified, the interrupt routine should fetch the command code, *request.command,* from the header to determine the action to be performed. Character-type device drivers can fetch the command code immediately because each driver supports only one unit.

The easiest way for the driver to parse the command is through the use of a jump table. The RDISK listing at the end of this chapter (Listing 5-3) contains an example of this method. The different command codes that can be supported by the driver are listed in Table 5-2. After determining and executing the command, the driver should set the contents of the status word in the device header, *request.status,* and return to MS-DOS with a far return.

Table 5-2.   Device Driver Command Functions

Command	Block	Char	Function Meaning
0:	X	X	INIT
1:	X		MEDIA CHECK
2:	X		BUILD BIOS parameter block (BPB)
* 3:	X	X	I/O control for devices INPUT
4:	X	X	INPUT (read)
5:		X	Nondestructive INPUT no-wait
6:		X	INPUT STATUS
7:		X	INPUT FLUSH
8:	X	X	OUTPUT (write)
9:	X	X	OUTPUT (write) with VERIFY
10:		X	OUTPUT STATUS
11:		X	OUTPUT FLUSH
*12:	X	X	I/O control for devices OUTPUT
†13:	X	X	DEVICE OPEN
†14:	X	X	DEVICE CLOSE
†15:	X		REMOVABLE MEDIA

* Function valid only if IOCTL defined for the driver
† Supported only under MS-DOS version 3.0 and later, and the function is valid only if OCRM defined for the driver

The status word, shown in Figure 5-5, is used to indicate error conditions for all commands (the error bit) and the status of the device for the Status and Removable Media commands (the busy bit). The error bit is set if an error occurs in processing the command or the command is illegal for that driver. If the error bit is set, the driver must place the proper error code in bits 0 through 7 of the status word. The various error codes that can occur on a device are listed in Table 5-3.

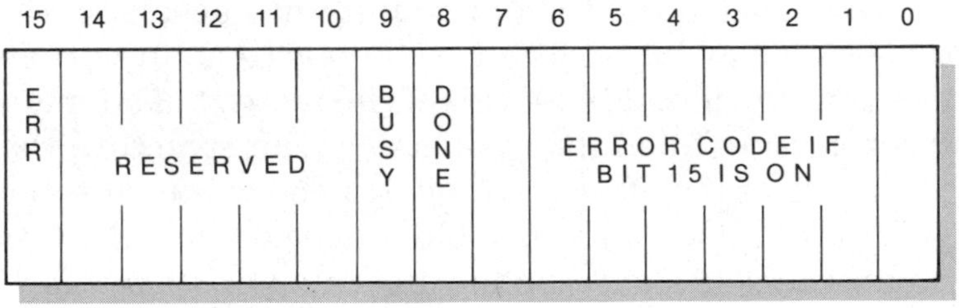

BIT MEANINGS

ERR = 1: Error Has Occurred on Device. Error Code in Bits 0-7.
BUSY = 1: Set by STATUS and REMOVABLE MEDIA Calls.
DONE = 1: Operation Is Complete. Bit Set on Exit.

Fig. 5-5. Device driver status word.

Table 5-3.   Driver Error Codes

Code	Error
0	Write protect violation
1	Unknown unit
2	Device not ready
3	Unknown command
4	CRC error
5	Bad request structure length
6	Seek error
7	Unknown media
8	Sector not found
9	Printer out of paper
A	Write fault
B	Read fault
C	General failure
D	Reserved
E	Reserved
*F	Invalid disk change

All error codes are given as hexadecimal numbers
* Supported only under MS-DOS version 3.0 and later

The done bit must always be set in the status word before the driver returns to MS-DOS.

The Driver Commands

To describe in this chapter all of the driver commands listed in Table 5-2 would be to duplicate the *MS-DOS Programmer's Reference Manual*. Instead, we touch on the highlights of processing driver commands and only cover in depth some of the more complicated commands. Once you have a feel for what's going on, referencing the particular command in the manual will be easy.

For most driver operations, the request header block doesn't contain all the information needed to process the command. Those few commands that do not require additional information are the Status commands, and the Flush, Open, Close, and Removable Media commands. All of the other commands require more information than that contained in the request header. For each of these commands, the additional information required is appended to the request block. The length parameter *request.length* indicates the total size of the request block (in bytes).

Once again, structures can be used to ease the task of accessing the various elements of the request blocks. Listing 5-3, the RDISK listing, shows structure definitions for those commands that RDISK expects to process. Notice that because many of the different requests use similar request blocks, we don't need to define all of the fields in every block. This is convenient because MASM doesn't allow us to use the same name more than once, even in different structures.

The INIT Command

The INIT command is unique because of all the commands used by a driver, INIT operates in an environment closest to that of a standard MS-DOS program. One difference from the other commands is that the INIT command may make use of the INT 21h function calls 01 through 0Ch (the CP/M style I/O commands) and function 30h (Get MS-DOS Version Number).

Another similarity to standard programs is that the INIT function receives a pointer to the command line that appears in the CONFIG.SYS file. This pointer is passed in the BPB parameter field of the INIT command's request block (see *bpbptro* and *bpbptrs* in Listing 2-3, the RDISK program). However, unlike a standard MS-DOS program, this information is not a copy and should only be read, never written to.

Because the INIT command is only called when the driver is first loaded by the system at boot time, the code required to process this command is essentially "throwaway" code. To minimize memory use, the code to handle the INIT command can be co-located with an internal buffer in the driver (having the same origin as the buffer) or located after the break address.

The break address is the address (segment and offset) of the next byte located after the last byte of the program. MS-DOS resumes loading the system at the next memory paragraph following the break address (or the paragraph *of* the break address if the address is on a paragraph boundary). All code vital to the operation of the driver should be located before the break address. The INIT code is vital, but since it is called prior to MS-DOS having the opportunity to overwrite the code (and never called again), it should be located after the break address. (The RDISK routine doesn't locate INIT after the break address because its memory buffer is large enough to accommodate the INIT code. Instead of letting MS-DOS reuse the INIT code's memory, the RDISK driver overwrites this space with "disk" data).

The BIOS Parameter Block and Block-Mode Driver Commands

For block-mode (that is, disk) drivers, two commands return information about the BIOS Parameter Block: the INIT command and the Build BPB (BIOS Parameter Block) command. Both of these commands return information about the format of the disk in the BPB. The layout and contents of the BPB are shown in Figure 5-6.

Looking at Figure 5-6, you can see that the BPB amply describes to the system the format of the disk. This information is not returned directly to the system in the driver request block but rather is returned through a pointer.

The way in which these pointers to the BPB are used is documented and fairly obvious if you read the manual carefully but confus-

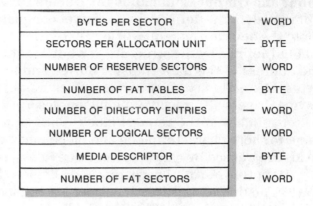

BYTES PER SECTOR	— WORD
SECTORS PER ALLOCATION UNIT	— BYTE
NUMBER OF RESERVED SECTORS	— WORD
NUMBER OF FAT TABLES	— BYTE
NUMBER OF DIRECTORY ENTRIES	— WORD
NUMBER OF LOGICAL SECTORS	— WORD
MEDIA DESCRIPTOR	— BYTE
NUMBER OF FAT SECTORS	— WORD

Fig. 5-6.   Contents of the BIOS parameter block.

ing enough to cause problems if your attention wanders. When a block mode device driver returns the Bios Parameter Blocks (BPBs) to MS-DOS in the INIT command, the driver is returning to the system a pointer to a *table of pointers,* which in turn point to the actual BPBs. If there is only one unit supported by the driver, as in the RDISK routine, the proper parameter to return to the system is a pointer to a pointer to the BPB.

However, when MS-DOS calls a block driver with the Build BPB command, the system expects just a single pointer to the proper BPB. This difference between the address of the BPB and the address of a block of pointers to the BPBs is one that caused the authors unnecessary grief. We hope that forewarned is forearmed for you.

The reason for this difference is that during the INIT command, the driver must inform the system about all the devices the driver is controlling. Thus a table of pointers is returned. However, when the Build BPB command is invoked, MS-DOS is asking for information on only one device, so only a pointer to that device's BPB is required.

Why does MS-DOS have the Build BPB command if the system is already informed by the INIT command of the disk formats? Because a disk may be replaced with another disk of a different format, in which case, MS-DOS needs to informed of the replacement.

The Media Check Command for Disk Devices
The Build BPB command is called whenever MS-DOS thinks that the disk in the drive may have changed. MS-DOS is informed by the Media Check command, which is called before every disk access, that the disk may have changed. When Media Check is called, it returns to MS-DOS a status byte that indicates one of four states: media changed, media not changed, not sure if media changed, or error.

Input and Output Commands for Device Drivers

Nearly half of the defined device driver commands deal with data transfer to the device. The request block extension for input and output commands (defined by the structure "rwhdr" in the RDISK listing) contains the address of the data transfer buffer and a count of the number of bytes (character mode) or sectors (block mode) to transfer. Block mode device drivers also receive the media descriptor byte and the starting sector number in the request block. The request block is actually the same for both character mode and block mode devices, but some of the fields are unused by character mode devices.

Data transfer for character mode devices is relatively straightforward. The driver transfers the specified number of bytes between the buffer and the devices. Block mode devices are only a little more complicated.

When sending I/O commands to the driver, MS-DOS expects sector 0 to be the first physical sector on the disk. (MS-DOS numbers all sectors on a disk starting from 0.) No sectors are hidden from MS-DOS, although it can hide sectors from user programs (number of hidden sectors in the BPB).

The Microsoft *MS-DOS Programmer's Reference Manual* also mentions that a block mode device driver may be asked to write more data to the device than can be addressed by the transfer buffer's segment register, for instance, a write of 64K bytes from a transfer address of XXXX:8000. Attempting to transfer all 64K from that segment address would cause a "wraparound." The manual explains that in this circumstance, it is allowable to transfer only the part of the buffer that can be addressed without changing the segment register.

The IOCTL operations for any type of driver always transfer data in byte increments. This is because IOCTL must be able to process transfers between MS-DOS and the driver as well as between MS-DOS and the device.

The Other Driver Commands

The rest of the driver commands, Status, Flush, Open, Close, and so forth, are more straightforward to implement than the driver commands previously described. These remaining commands don't contain any traps or pitfalls. Their parameter blocks and operations are clearly defined in the manual and shouldn't present any problems for the programmer.

Debugging Device Drivers

Once a driver has been installed in the system, that driver cannot be debugged with MS-DOS (because of the reentrance problem). But there is still a need to be able to debug drivers because (like most things in programming) they cannot be expected to function properly the first time through. Three approaches can help to make simpler the task of debugging the driver.

First, build the driver a block at a time. Get the main routines working first, then move on to the more advanced features. Don't try to do the IOCTL handlers right away. The routines that you need to have operating before the driver loads properly are the strategy and interrupt routines and the INIT command handler. For block mode devices, you also need the MEDIA CHECK command and unless you have specified the NONIBM bit in the attribute word, the BUILD BPB command. You won't be able to perform I/O with just these command handlers, but MS-DOS should at least be able to load your driver successfully.

Another approach that can help in debugging drivers is to use the BIOS functions to handle simple output that can inform you of the current state of the driver. It is helpful to know just how far the driver got before it crashed. If you don't have a ROM BIOS to rely on, you can "kludge" some sort of output routine together and include it in the driver source. For example, when debugging the RDISK driver at the end of this chapter, the authors had the driver display a single character for each command that it processed (*I* for interrupt, *S* for strategy, *i* for init, and so forth). That was a real help when the driver loaded and could be accessed with the Absolute Disk Access functions but crashed the system when an attempt was made to read the device's directory. The interaction between the driver and the system can be one of the most complex problems to solve and unfortunately usually can only be debugged with the driver in place in the system.

If you decide to add debugging statements to your driver, be aware that such actions most likely will increase the depth of the stack required, and you may need to change your driver to use a local stack if the driver doesn't do so already.

When testing the individual pieces of the driver, you don't need to debug it in place. If you are willing to spend the time to write a simple test program that creates request blocks and passes them to the driver for processing, you will be able to use DEBUG to debug that test program and the driver, too. This enables you to get the driver at least to a state where it probably should boot. After that, you can continue with other types of debugging to flush out the final bugs.

When developing drivers *always* use a copy of your system disk, not the original system disk. An error in the driver code can prevent the system from booting. An error in a disk driver may destroy valuable data on the disk. For these reasons, you should always have a copy of your system disk to return to in case of failures.

The Ubiquitous RAM Disk

As noted in the program comments, the RAM disk program that is presented here is intentionally simplified. It is still 100 percent functional and may be used on any MS-DOS system running MS-DOS version 2.0 or higher. You need at least 192K of memory in your system to use this driver because the RAM disk occupies 64K, and you should really leave at least 128K of memory for MS-DOS and your programs.

Once the program has been assembled and linked, rename the file to RDISK.SYS. Now create the file CONFIG.SYS if it does not already exist and put in the following command line.

```
DEVICE=RDISK.SYS
```

The next time you reboot your system, the 64K RAM disk will be installed as the next drive in your system (probably drive C if you don't have a hard disk). No additional operations are required to install the driver.

The RAM disk can be accessed with any MS-DOS function calls or programs with the exception of the DISKCOPY and DISKCOMP commands. Both of those programs expect a particular type of disk and don't work with RAM disks.

Now that we have thoroughly discussed Listing 5-3, you can study it.

Listing 5-3.   The RDISK Ram Disk Driver

```
        page    60,132
;****************************************************************;
;                                                              ;
;                       R D I S K                              ;
;                                                              ;
; RDISK is a block-mode installable device driver that         ;
; uses system RAM memory to simulate a 64K disk drive.         ;
;                                                              ;
; The purpose of this program is to demonstrate the            ;
; components of an MS-DOS device driver. For this reason,       ;
; RDISK does not contain as many features as are possible       ;
; in a RAM disk program. Once you understand this program       ;
; you may wish to add some of these possible enhancements       ;
;       1) Extend the buffer beyond the 64K limit.             ;
;       2) Allow specifying the disk configuration on the       ;
;          command line in the CONFIG.SYS program and          ;
;          alter the buffer allocation and BPB tables to       ;
;          use the new parameters.                             ;
;       3) CRC (cyclical redundancy check) type memory         ;
;          error detection/correction for the "disk".          ;
```

Listing 5.3. cont.

```
;                                                                 ;
;************************************************************* ;
;****** GENERAL & DEVICE DRIVER EQUATES ********************
FALSE   equ     0
TRUE    equ     OFFFFh
; Status bits defined in the request header status word
error_bit       equ     8000h   ; error status
busy_bit        equ     0200h   ; busy status
done_bit        equ     0100h   ; done status
; Error codes defined for the request header status word
err_unit_bad    equ     1       ; unit number error
err_command     equ     3       ; command error
err_CRC         equ     4       ; CRC error
err_sector      equ     8       ; sector error
err_general     equ     OCh     ; general failure
; Return codes for the MEDIA_CHECK command function
is_changed      equ     -1      ; media changed
dont_know       equ     0       ; unsure
not_changed     equ     1       ; media not changed
;****** ASCII EQUATES ************************************
CR      equ     13
LF      equ     10
;************* STRUCTURE DEFINITIONS ***************************
; Note: ALL pointers passed as parameters are in the form:
; OFFSET followed by SEGMENT
request equ     ds:[bx]         ; base addr of request head
; REQUEST HEADER (Common Section)
reqhdr struc
        db      ?               ; length
        db      ?               ; unit #
command db      ?               ; command code
status  dw      ?               ; status return
        db      8 dup (?)       ; reserved bytes
reqhdr ends
; INIT COMMAND HEADER
inithdr struc
        db      (type reqhdr) dup (?)
units   db      ?               ; number of units
endadro dw      ?               ; ending address offset
endadrs dw      ?               ; ending address segment
bpbptro dw      ?               ; BIOS parameter block ptr
bpbptrs dw      ?               ; BIOS parameter block ptr
inithdr ends
; MEDIA CHECK COMMAND HEADER
medhdr struc
        db      (type reqhdr) dup (?)
media   db      ?               ; media descriptor
change  db      ?               ; change status
medhdr  ends
; BUILD BIOS PARAMETER BLOCK COMMAND HEADER
bpbhdr struc
        db      (type reqhdr) dup (?)
        db      ?               ; media descriptor
xfradro dw      ?               ; transfer address offset
xfradrs dw      ?               ; transfer address segment
```

Listing 5.3. cont.

```
        dw        ?                    ; BIOS parameter block ptr
        dw        ?                    ; BIOS parameter block ptr
bpbhdr ends
; READ/WRITE COMMAND HEADER
rwhdr   struc
        db        (type reqhdr) dup (?)
        db        ?                    ; media descriptor
        dw        ?                    ; transfer address offset
        dw        ?                    ; transfer address segment
count   dw        ?                    ; sector count
strtsec dw        ?                    ; starting sector
rwhdr   ends
transfer equ    dword ptr xfradro       ; transfer address
;**************************************************************
;
;   B E G I N    R E S I D E N T   C O D E   S E C T I O N
;
;**************************************************************
RDRIVE SEGMENT PARA
        ASSUME   CS:RDRIVE,DS:NOTHING,ES:NOTHING
        ORG      0
START   EQU      $                   ; start location of driver
;====== DEVICE HEADER ====================================
        dw       -1,-1               ; pointer to next device
        dw       0                   ; block IBM format device
        dw       offset STRATEGY     ; strategy entry point
        dw       offset INTERRUPT    ; interrupt entry point
        db       1,'RDISK  '         ; 1 unit RAM disk
;====== RESIDENT DATA AREA AND TABLE STORAGE =============
jumptab         label   word             ; command routing table
        dw       offset INIT              ; 0--INITialization
        dw       offset MEDIA_CHECK       ; 1--MEDIA check
        dw       offset BUILD_BPB         ; 2--build BIOS param block
        dw       offset IOCTL_INPUT       ; 3--IO control input
        dw       offset READ              ; 4--input from device
        dw       offset READ_NOWAIT       ; 5--nondest input no-wait
        dw       offset INPUT_STATUS      ; 6--input status
        dw       offset INPUT_FLUSH       ; 7--flush input queue
        dw       offset WRITE             ; 8--output to device
        dw       offset WRITE_VERIFY      ; 9--output with verify
        dw       offset OUTPUT_STATUS     ; A--output status
        dw       offset OUTPUT_FLUSH      ; B--flush output queue
        dw       offset IOCTL_OUTPUT      ; C--IO control output
req_ptr         dd       ?               ; pointer to request buffer
;====== STRATEGY ENTRY POINT FOR DEVICE DRIVER ============
; Save the pointer to the request header for INTERRUPT.
; Saved in REQ_PTR data area.
; Entered with pointer contained in ES:BX registers.
stratp proc     far
STRATEGY:
        mov      cs:word ptr [req_ptr],bx
        mov      cs:word ptr [req_ptr + 2],es
        ret
stratp endp
;====== INTERRUPT ENTRY POINT FOR DEVICE DRIVER ============
```

Listing 5.3. cont.

```
; Process the command contained in the request header.
; The pointer to the request header is located in REQ_PTR
; in the form OFFSET:SEGMENT.
;
; Maximum stack depth achieved is 14 words in INIT
; (10 registers + 1 call + 1 INT )
interp proc      far
INTERRUPT:
        push     ax                 ; save all registers
        push     bx
        push     cx
        push     dx
        push     bp
        push     si
        push     di
        push     ds
        push     es
        pushf
        lds      bx,cs:[req_ptr] ; get DS & request header
        mov      al,request.command      ; get command
; Check for command in range of 0 through 12 (decimal)
        cbw
        cmp      al,0Ch             ; check for command range
        jae      cmd_error          ; too high--abort
; Command in range--build the index into the command table
        shl      ax,1               ; two words per table entry
        mov      si,ax
; Set up status (AX => 0) & return address--then JUMP
        mov      ax,offset exit  ; set return address
        push     ax                 ; return to EXIT location
        xor      ax,ax              ; clear status indicator
        jmp      cs:jumptab[si]  ; execute function
;=========================================================
; Unsupported Commands--Flag Command Error in Status Word
;
IOCTL_INPUT:    ; 3--IO control input
READ_NOWAIT:    ; 5--nondest input no-wait
INPUT_STATUS:   ; 6--input status
INPUT_FLUSH:    ; 7--flush input queue
OUTPUT_STATUS:  ; A--output status
OUTPUT_FLUSH:   ; B--flush output queue
IOCTL_OUTPUT:   ; C--IO control output
        pop      ax                 ; clear return address
cmd_error:
        mov      ax,err_command  ; command error occurred
        or       ax,error_bit    ; add error bit to status word
;=========================================================
; Collected Exits
;
; At this point, we assume that AX contains the status return
; or the value zero (which indicates a valid return).
EXIT:
        lds      bx,cs:[req_ptr] ; get DS & request header
        or       ax,done_bit     ; set status done
        mov      request.status,ax
```

Listing 5.3. cont.

```
        popf                      ; restore all registers
        pop     es
        pop     ds
        pop     di
        pop     si
        pop     bp
        pop     dx
        pop     cx
        pop     bx
        pop     ax
        ret
interp endp
;====== COMMAND HANDLERS ==================================
; The INIT handler occupies the same space as the first
; "sector" of the RAM disk, allowing it to be reused.
;------ MEDIA_CHECK ---------------------------------------
mediap proc     near
MEDIA_CHECK:    ; 1--MEDIA check--always "not changed"
        mov     request.change,not_changed
        ret
mediap endp
;------ BUILD BIOS PARAMETER BLOCK ------------------------
; NOTE: Unlike the INIT code, which expects a POINTER TO A
; TABLE OF POINTERS to the BPBs, the BUILD_BPB command
; expects only a POINTER TO THE BPB. Do not confuse the two
; returns.
;
bbpbp proc      near
BUILD_BPB:      ; 2--build BIOS param block--return ptr.
        mov     request.bpbptro,offset bpb
        mov     request.bpbptrs,cs
        ret
bbpbp endp
;------ READ ----------------------------------------------
; READ transfers data from the RAM "disk" to the DTA
; (All registers except BX destroyed)
readp proc      near
READ:           ; 4--Input from device
        call    verify              ; verify & setup xfer params
        mov     ax,es               ; source segment
        mov     si,di               ; source offset
        les     di,request.transfer
        mov     ds,ax               ; source segment established
        rep     movsw               ; do transfer
        xor     ax,ax               ; no errors
        ret
readp endp
;------ WRITE ---------------------------------------------
; WRITE transfers data from the DTA to the RAM "disk"
; (All registers except BX destroyed)
writep proc     near
WRITE:          ; 8--output to device
WRITE_VERIFY:   ; 9--output with verify
        call    verify                ; verify & setup parameters
        lds     si,request.transfer
```

Listing 5.3. cont.

```
        rep     movsw               ; do transfer
        xor     ax,ax               ; no errors
        ret
writep endp
;------ VERIFY -------------------------------------------
; VERIFY performs the following tasks:
;       Verify that "disk" sectors are within bounds
;       Calculate "disk" segment & offset for transfer
;       Clip count to prevent wraparound of DTA
;
; Entered w/ DS:BX pointer to request_block
; Return w/ "disk" address in ES:DI
;          Word count in CX
;
; AX & DX registers destroyed--DS:BX pointer preserved
;
verify proc    near
; verify starting & ending sectors
        mov     cx,request.strtsec
        cmp     cx,cs:disk_size          ; starting sector
        jae     out_of_range             ; (0...n) < # sectors
        add     cx,request.count
        dec     cx                       ; back off 1 sector
        cmp     cx,cs:disk_size          ; strt + len + 1 = end
        jb      in_range                 ; ending sector
                                         ; (0...n) < # sectors
out_of_range:
        pop     ax               ; clear ret. adr. in READ/WRITE
        mov     ax,err_sector    ; sector not found
        or      ax,error_bit     ; indicate error
        mov     request.count,0 ; no sectors transferred
        ret                      ; return to EXIT
in_range:
; Calculate segment:offset of "disk" address
        mov     ax,cs:sector_size
        mov     cl,4             ; divide bytes/sector by
        shr     ax,cl           ; ... 16 to get paragraphs
        mul     request.strtsec ; start para relative RDISK
        add     ax,RPARA        ; start para relative CS
        mov     dx,cs           ; start para relative Oh
        add     ax,dx
        mov     es,ax           ; set start segment in ES
        xor     di,di           ; offset 0 (64K max move)
; Calculate transfer count & check for excessive size
        mov     ax,cs:sector_size    ; convert # bytes
        shr     ax,1            ; /sector to words/sector
        mov     cx,request.count     ; convert # sectors
        mul     cx              ; /xfer to words /xfer
        cmp     dx,0            ; over 128K byte xfer (high)
        jne     out_of_range    ; excessive size
        cmp     ax,8000h        ; 64K or more xfer (low)
        ja      out_of_range    ; excess size
; Clip the transfer size to the amount of room in the DTA
; Compare CX (buffer size) to AX (requested size) & adjust
; Store the result in CX & calculate # sectors in AX
```

Listing 5.3. cont.

```
        shl     ax,1                ; convert back to bytes
        mov     cx,request.xfradro      ; get DTA offset
        cmp     cx,0                ; offset 0 passes
        je      set_size
        neg     cx                  ; 64K -offset = buffer
        cmp     cx,ax               ; buffer larger than req?
        jae     set_size
        mov     ax,cx               ; clip ax to size in cx
; Set number of sectors transferred
set_size:
        mov     cx,ax               ; set transfer count ...
        shr     cx,1                ; ... in words to transfer
        div     cs:sector_size      ; get # sectors to transfer
        mov     request.count,ax        ; store xfer count
; Set forward direction & exit
        cld                         ; increment move string
        ret
verify endp
;====== BIOS PARAMETER BLOCK & POINTER ====================
; The BIOS parameter block is presented here as if it were
; part of the standard IBM boot sector. The format is:
        jmp     near ptr boot       ; 3 byte JUMP
        db      'OEM NAME'          ; 8 bytes OEM name & vers.
BPB     label   word                ; BIOS parameter block
sector_size     label   word
        dw      512                 ; # bytes/sector
        db      1                   ; # sectors/alloc unit
        dw      0                   ; # reserved sectors
        db      2                   ; # FATs
        dw      32                  ; # root direct. entries
disk_size       label   word
        dw      128                 ; # sectors on disk
        db      0F8h                ; media descriptor byte
        dw      1                   ; # of sectors/FAT
; This section added for compatibility
        dw      8                   ; # sectors/track
        dw      1                   ; # of heads
        dw      0                   ; # of hidden sectors
boot:
BPB_TAB         dw      offset BPB      ; pointer to BPB
;====== DISK AREA =========================================
; Note that the Media-Descriptor byte as defined by
; IBM (and used by most other MS-DOS systems) for a RAM
; disk is F8, which means ''not 2-sided, not 8-sectored,
; and not removable.'' This descriptor is also used to
; indicate a hard disk, which meets the same criteria.
; Paragraph align on segment boundaries
        if      ($-start) mod 16
        org     ($-start) + 16 - (($-start) mod 16)
        endif
RDISK label   byte                  ; start of the ram disk
RPARA equ     ($-START) / 16        ; code size in segments
;====== RAM DISK BUFFER ===================================
FAT_1 db      0F8h,0FFh,0FFh        ; 1st two FAT entries
        db      509 dup (0)         ; zero remained of FAT
```

Listing 5.3. cont.

```
FAT_2   db       0F8h,0FFh,0FFh   ; 1st two FAT entries
        db       509 dup (0)      ; zero remained of FAT
DIREC   db       'RAM_DISK '
        db       08h              ; volume name
        db       10 dup (?)       ; reserved
        dw       06000h           ; time 12:0:0 noon
        dw       021h             ; date Jan 1, 1980
        dw       0                ; starting cluster 0
        dd       0                ; file size 0
        db       992 dup (0)      ; remainder of 2 sectors ...
                                  ; comprising total of 32 directory entries
BUFFER  label    byte
;===== INITIALIZATION SECTION ===============================
; This code is overwritten the first time that the RAM disk
; is written to. The INIT section for this RAM disk simply
; returns the necessary parameters: # of units, offset to
; the BIOS Parameter Block, and the Ending address. The
; ending address is calculated by getting the address of
; the beginning of the RAM disk (RDISK) and incrementing
; the segment register by 1000 (hex), resulting in 64K of
; memory being reserved. (1 extra paragraph of buffer is
; also reserved).
;
; AX, DX, & DS registers destroyed.
initp   proc     near
INIT:                            ; 0--INITialization
        mov      request.units,1           ; only 1 unit
        mov      request.bpbptro,offset bpb_tab
        mov      request.bpbptrs,cs
        mov      request.endadro,offset rdisk
        mov      request.endadrs,cs
        add      request.endadrs,01000h
; get original data segment for message display
        push     cs
        pop      ds
        mov      dx,offset sign_on
        mov      ah,9                      ; display string
        int      21h                       ; call MS-DOS
        xor      ax,ax                     ; no errors
        ret
sign_on db       '64K RAM Disk Installed',cr,lf,'$'
initp   endp
rdrive  ends
        end
```

Summary

You're now ready to write and install device drivers on your own. Follow our guidelines and the information in the *DOS Programmer's Reference*

Manual when you are presented with technical questions. You should have very few problems.

Some ideas for device drivers that may be useful are a driver for a dot matrix printer that accepts graphics commands (such as *draw line*) and converts them to the format required by the printer driver or a terminal driver (see Fig. 5-7) that supports virtual screens. The terminal driver can have a number of memory buffers that contain copies of screen information. By sending commands to the driver's IOCTL channel, the driver can be told which memory buffer to update and which to display on the screen. Programs that use this driver have a type of "windowing" capability. Initially, care must be taken not to use the standard MS-DOS console I/O functions, which know nothing of the virtual "windowed" device. If the driver is successful, you can use it to replace the existing console driver.

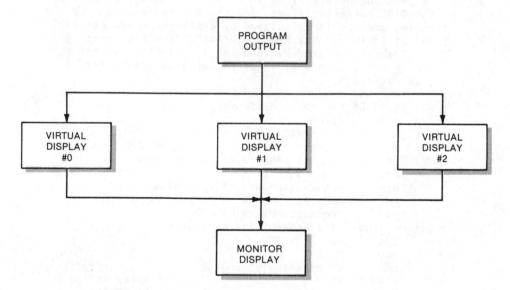

Fig. 5-7.   Virtual screen device driver.

The list of ideas for device drivers is endless. You have probably already thought of a few of your own that you would like to implement. With a little patience and care, there's no reason why you can't, so go to it!

Writing Programs for the Intel 8087/80287 Math Coprocessor

Chapter 6

A Programmer's View of the 8087
Using MS-DOS Tools with the 8087
Programming Examples for the 8087 with MASM
Summary

The MS-DOS world belongs exclusively to Intel. That fact provides users of MS-DOS with two benefits. One, programs written for MS-DOS systems are generally portable even at the object code level. Two, most MS-DOS systems have the capability of using the Intel 8087 math coprocessor chip.

The 8087's purpose is to provide 8086 systems with the ability to perform *fast* floating point calculations. The 8087 supplies the system with instructions for number conversions, basic mathematics, and even some transcendental functions, such as sine, cosine, and log.

The benefits of the 8087 are not limited to speed alone. By supplying what amounts to a library of floating point math routines, the 8087 spares the programmer the burden of writing those routines, thus speeding the programming job. In addition, because these routines are contained in the 8087 chip rather than in program memory, use of the 8087 can result in a smaller program, which can mean a cost savings in some developments.

Unlike earlier math processors, such as the Intel 8231A and 8232, the 8087 is accessed with escape sequences that appear to the assembly language programmer as machine language instructions. The 8087 does not require the installation of any additional software or hardware (as long as the 8088 or 8086 chip is configured in "max mode"), nor does the 8087 require programmed I/O or DMA transfers for access.

Because the 8087 is fully compatible with the proposed IEEE (Institute of Electrical & Electronics Engineers) standards for floating point computations, a large and expanding base of advanced numerical calculation software is available. This base conforms with the 8087's way of processing numbers. For a programmer who doesn't have the time to write complicated numerical routines, this software base represents a great savings in time and money.

Throughout this chapter, we have been using, and will continue to use, 8087 and 8086 to refer to the numeric coprocessor and the main

CPU. However, use of the 8087 is not limited to just the iAPX 8086 and iAPX 8088 processors. The 8087 can also be used with the iAPX 186 and iAPX 188 processors. For users of the iAPX 286 processor, Intel has provided the 80287 numeric processor. The information presented in this chapter is valid for all of these combinations.

A Programmer's View of the 8087

The Data Registers in the 8087

Although it's true that 8087 instructions appear as part of the main processor's instruction set, the 8087 has no means of accessing the main CPU's registers. Instead, the 8087 has its own set of registers and communicates with the main CPU through common memory. That really isn't much of a limitation because the main CPU's registers aren't well suited to real numbers. Instead of the 16-bit registers used in the main CPU, the 8087 has eight 80-bit registers and can therefore hold much more information. These registers are shown in Figure 6-1.

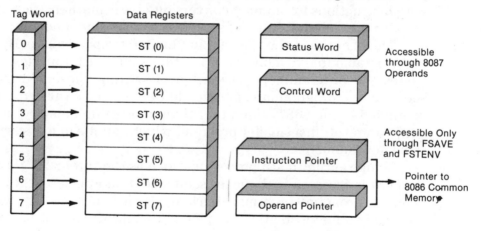

Fig. 6-1.   Register layout in the 8087.

You should notice that unlike the main CPU, the 8087's data registers don't have unique names but are indexed entries in a stack (for example, ST (1)). Values are loaded into the 8087 by pushing them onto this stack, and some values (but not all) are retrieved by popping them from the stack. Many of the 8087's instructions operate only on the top of the stack, and most of the other instructions default to operating on the stack's top.

The fact that the 8087 addresses its registers as a stack is very important because all register addresses are relative to the top of the stack! For example, a value contained in register i is contained in register $i-1$ if the stack is popped and register $i+1$ if a new entry is pushed on the stack.

When programming for the 8087, pay close attention to the behavior of the stack. You can't stuff a value into a register and assume that value will be in the same place later.

Floating Point Real Number Representation in the 8087

These registers also differ from the main CPU's registers in that they may hold only one type of number, a floating point real number (called a *temporary real* in Intel parlance). The topmost format in Figure 6-2 shows what this floating real number looks like in an 8087 register. From the picture, you can see that the register is divided into three fields: the sign bit, the biased exponent (15 bits), and the significand (64 bits). Each of these numbers taken by itself is an unsigned binary integer, but when combined they can represent a very large number!

Let's take a closer look at the individual parts of this floating point real number. The leftmost part (bit 79) is the sign bit. When this bit is a 0, the number is positive. When it's a 1, the number is negative. Simple, but there are two effects to note. Unlike two's complement binary integers (as used in the 8086 CPU), this floating point real number has exactly as many positive numbers as negative numbers (you'll see why later). The other, more important effect is that this numbering system has two types of 0! This means that 0 can be a positive or negative number and that 0 doesn't necessarily equal 0. The 8087 takes care of this effect, but it's something to be remembered if you attempt to compare real numbers with the 8086 (you shouldn't ever need to because the 8087 compares numbers just fine).

Skipping to the right hand side of the number, we see the significand (bits 0 through 63). This is where the significant digits part of the number is represented. Because each entry can be either positive or negative, the range is exactly the same size for each. You'll also note that bit 63 (the most significant bit of the significand) is shown as a 1. This is because the 8087 usually stores numbers in a *normalized* format, which means that the 8087 finds the leftmost 1 in a binary number and shifts it up or down until that 1 is in bit 63. (A number with no 1 is 0, and its representation is *all* 0's.) Let's do a short example with the number 10.

```
Decimal:                                                      10
Hexadecimal:                                                   A
Binary 64 bit integer:    000000000000000...000000000001010
8087 64 bit real:         101000000000000...000000000000000
```

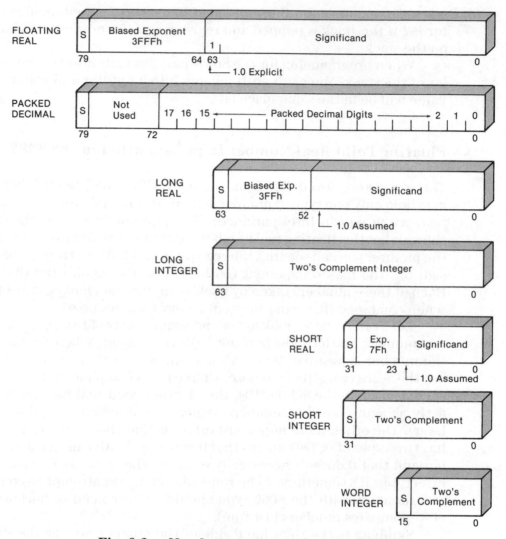

Fig. 6-2.   Number representations in the 8087.

See how the 8087 slid the number to the left? This allows much more room for other digits to be represented, such as 10.1, 10.12, etc. The only problem is that the number shown for the 8087 is no longer 10. It's now 10×2^{60}. How does the 8087 know that it's really just 10? It uses something called the exponent field (bits 64 through 78).

The 8087 always assumes that the number in the significand is between 1 and 2. By itself the number shown above would be 1.01 binary or 1.25 decimal. (Each binary digit in a fraction is $\frac{1}{2}$ the previous binary digit, so the positions to the right of the decimal point in binary are $\frac{1}{2}$, $\frac{1}{4}$, $\frac{1}{8}$, $\frac{1}{16}$, etc.) The 8087 remembers in the exponent field how many positions it shifted the original number. For the case of 10, the 8087 shifted the decimal point three positions from 1010.0 (binary) to 1.0100 (binary). The value 3 is stored in the exponent field. There is one more trick to the 8087's storage of numbers. Because the exponent is stored as an unsigned integer, if the 8087 just put the true exponent in the field, there would be no way to store numbers less than 1 (no negative exponents means no number less than 2^0 or one). So the 8087 biases (it adds a bias to) the exponent. The bias used in the 8087 is 3FFFh or 16,383 decimal. For the example of storing the number 10, the biased exponent is 3 plus 3FFFh or 4002h.

We're all done, so let's look at Figure 6-3 to see what the number 10 looks like inside the 8087.

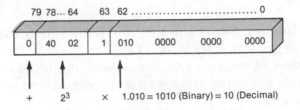

Fig. 6-3.   8087 representation of the number 10.

Why must we understand how the 8087 stores numbers? Because there are times when you'll want to inspect the contents of 8087 registers during debugging and in order to understand the uses and limitations of some of the more advanced 8087 instructions, you must first know the types of data being manipulated.

Other Data Formats Used with the 8087

Figure 6-2 contains six other data formats in addition to the 80-bit floating-point real number format used internally. What are these representations used for? In addition to the 80-bit real, these forms are those that the 8087 can use to read data from or write data to memory. If the data is in one of these formats, it can be understood by the 8087. Otherwise all bets are off.

Three basic types are shown in Figure 6-2. These types are real, integer, and packed decimal.

Short Real and Long Real Data Formats
The short real (32 bits) and long real (64 bits) formats are very similar to the 80-bit floating-point real just discussed.

These numbers are also capable of representing floating-point real numbers but with less range and accuracy. The differences can be summed up as shown in Table 6-1.

Table 6-1.   Differences Among Real Data Formats

Data Type	# Bits Significand	# Bits Exponent	Exponent Bias	Leftmost One
80 bit real	64	15	3FFF (16383)	Explicit
64 bit real	52	11	3FF (1023)	Assumed
32 bit real	23	8	7F (127)	Assumed

In addition to their size, the short and long real forms also differ from the 80-bit real in that the most significant one bit does not actually appear! Because of their limited space, these forms always assume a 1 at the leftmost position but don't store the 1 and thus gain another digit position.

Word Integer, Short Integer, and Long Integer Data Formats
The integer forms should be familiar by now. These forms are used by the 8086 CPU to store two's complement integer numbers (although the 8086 can't use the 8-byte long integer format). These numbers have ranges as follows:

    64 bit: –9,223,372,036,854,775,808 to 9,223,372,036,854,775,807
    32 bit: –2,147,483,648 to 2,147,483,647
    16 bit: –32,768 to 32,767

These numbers differ from the real numbers in that any value loaded from this form is an exact representation of the number. Also remember that although these are signed numbers and the most significant bit reflects the sign of the number, these are still two's complement numbers.

Packed Binary Coded Decimal (BCD) Formats
The last form of the 8087 is called packed BCD (binary coded decimal). What is packed BCD? In binary coded decimal notation, each 4-bit nibble is a separate digit that can have a value between 0 and 9. The entire number has no real meaning other than as a string of digits. In this way, the number is more like an ASCII string. In Figure 6-4, we've taken the number 256 and shown its forms in normal binary and binary coded decimal. The little calculation attached is shown in decimal base.

From Figure 6-4, you can see that in binary coded decimal we write the number as if it were hexadecimal (one digit every 4-bit nibble) but interpret it as decimal. But why is the data form so important? Because it's a snap to convert between ASCII and packed BCD. Figure 6-5 shows that to convert from BCD to ASCII, you need only unpack the digits (one per nibble) into bytes and add 30 hex to form the ASCII characters 0 through 9 (hex 30 through 39). To convert the other way, subtract 30h from each character and pack them down, two per byte.

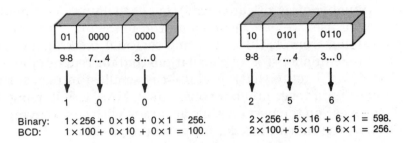

Binary: $1 \times 256 + 0 \times 16 + 0 \times 1 = 256.$ $2 \times 256 + 5 \times 16 + 6 \times 1 = 598.$
BCD: $1 \times 100 + 0 \times 10 + 0 \times 1 = 100.$ $2 \times 100 + 5 \times 10 + 6 \times 1 = 256.$

Fig. 6-4.   Binary coded decimal number representation.

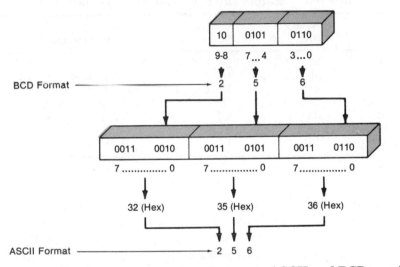

Fig. 6-5.   Conversions between ASCII and BCD numbers.

This data form is used by the 8087 only for loading and storing numbers. None of the arithmetic instructions can use packed BCD form. Even with this limitation, the packed BCD load and store instructions of the 8087 are two of the most useful instructions that it possesses. This is because the ability to calculate is worthless without the means to communicate results to the user, and most people use standard decimal notation for floating-point numbers.

The 8087 provides for conversion from base 10 to base 2 and back again. The programmer need only take care of the conversions between ASCII strings and packed BCD and of locating the decimal point correctly (we'll see that in the section on converting between decimal and binary floating point numbers). The 8087 takes care of the rest.

Summary of Data Types

In Table 6-2, we've summarized the size of the numbers that can be represented by each data type along with the approximate decimal resolution (number of significant digits) that each data type supports. In terms of actual use, we can recommend the following: Use packed BCD for converting from ASCII to floating real and back again. Use floating-point real numbers for all calculations and for real number constants in MASM (we'll get to that). And use the smallest integer form that fits a number for integer number constants in MASM. Following these guidelines gives you the best possible accuracy with some savings in memory by using the shorter integer forms where possible.

Table 6-2.   Range and Precision of 8087 Data Types

Data Type	Binary Bits	Decimal Digits	Approximate Range
Floating real	80	19	$3.4 \times 10^{-4932} \leq N \leq 1.2 \times 10^{4932}$
Packed decimal	80	18	$-10^{18} -1 \leq N \leq 10^{18} -1$
Long real	64	15-16	$4.19 \times 10^{-307} \leq N \leq 1.67 \times 10^{308}$
Long integer	64	18	$-9 \times 10^{18} \leq N \leq +9 \times 10^{18}$
Short real	32	6-7	$8.43 \times 10^{-37} \leq N \leq 3.37 \times 10^{38}$
Short integer	32	9	$-2 \times 10^{9} \leq N \leq +2 \times 10^{9}$
Word integer	16	4	$-32,768 \leq N \leq +32,767$

Figure 6-6 shows the range of number representation in the 8087. Note that the 8087 stores numbers with greater accuracy internally (80-bit real) than is normally used when loading or storing the 8087's registers (long real). This allows an extra margin of accuracy for calculations. Note also that the spacing between unique representable numbers (the distance between two adjacent numbers that the 8087 may represent exactly) decreases towards zero (from either direction), and increases towards infinity (plus or minus). This *density* of number representation implies that the 8087 has more accuracy processing extremely small numbers than large numbers.

The Instruction Set of the 8087

The 8087 has what is known in the industry as a *rich* instruction set. This doesn't necessarily mean that there are a lot of instructions (although it does have 69 different instructions) but that the instruction set is well suited for the types of operations desired from the 8087. There is an instruction for nearly every purpose, greatly reducing the number of steps (and associated programming difficulties) that might be encountered with a lesser numerical coprocessor.

The list of the 69 instructions appears in Table 6-3. This table is organized by classes of operations rather than alphabetically because you

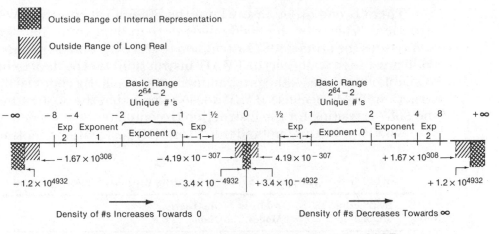

Fig. 6-6.   Representational range of the 8087.

are most likely to want to look up an instruction by type rather than by name. Two designations in Table 6-3 need to be explained. First is the (P) mark appearing next to some instructions. This signifies that the associated instruction may be used in a POP form, F*op*P. The POP form tells the 8087 to increment the stack pointer and tag the old stack top register as empty, which essentially throws away the stack top. This is all made clearer in following text, so "hang in there."

The FWAIT Prefix

The second designation in Table 6-3 is the (N) mark. The (N) mark means that the associated instruction may be used in a no wait form, as in FN*op*. Normally the MASM assembler generates an FWAIT prefix for every 8087 instruction. The "no wait" form tells the MASM assembler not to generate an FWAIT prefix. Now, just what is an FWAIT prefix?

Normally the 8087 must wait to finish the current instruction before it can accept a new one. This is accomplished by the FWAIT opcode prefix (9B hex), which is really an 8086 opcode! When the 8086 executes this instruction, the 8086 CPU waits until the TEST pin on the 8086/8087 interface becomes active. This occurs when the 8087 has finished executing and is ready for the next instruction. The 8086 CPU starts executing again and the next 8087 instruction is fetched starting the cycle over again.

The reason that FWAIT is used as a prefix is so that the 8086 only waits when it wants to send the 8087 another instruction. Once an 8087 instruction has been sent, the 8086 and 8087 can both be processing simultaneously, and when the 8086 needs the 8087 again, the 8086 must check to ensure that the 8087 is ready.

There is one other case where the 8086 must use the FWAIT instruction. Whenever the 8086 needs to read data from the 8087, the 8086 issues the proper 8087 instruction to store the data in memory. The 8086 must then wait (via the FWAIT instruction) for the data to become available. In this case, the programmer must explicitly code the 8087 instruction FWAIT because MASM doesn't know that the 8086 rather than the 8087 is waiting for the instruction to complete.

Now that you understand the (P) and (N) designations, look at Table 6.3.

Table 6-3.   List of 8087 Instructions and Addressing Forms

Notes	Instruction Mnemonic	Address Modes	Instruction Name
Data Transfer Instructions (9)			
	FXCH	//d	Exchange Registers
	FLD	s	Load Real
(P)	FST	d	Store Real
	FILD	s	Load Integer
(P)	FIST	d	Store Integer
	FBLD	s	Load Packed BCD
	FBSTP	d	Store Packed BCD
Constant Instructions (7)			
	FLDZ		Load $+0.0$
	FLD1		Load $+1.0$
	FLDPI		Load Pi
	FLDL2T		Load $\log_2 10$
	FLDL2E		Load $\log_2 e$
	FLDLG2		Load $\log_{10} 2$
	FLDLN2		Load $\log_e 2$
Transcendental Instructions (5)			
	FPTAN		Partial Tangent
	FPATAN		Partial arctangent
	F2XM1		$2^x - 1$
	FYL2X		$Y \times \log_2 X$
	FYL2XP1		$Y \times \log_2(X + 1)$
Comparison Instructions (7)			
(P)	FCOM	//s	Compare Real
(P)	FICOM	s	Compare Integer
	FCOMPP		Compare and POP Twice
	FTST		Test Stack Top
	FXAM		Examine Stack Top
Arithmetic Instructions (25)			
(P)	FADD	*	Add Real
	FIADD	s	Add Integer

Table 6-3. cont.

Notes	Instruction Mnemonic	Address Modes	Instruction Name

Arithmetic Instructions (25)

Notes	Instruction Mnemonic	Address Modes	Instruction Name
(P)	FSUB	*	Subtract Real
	FISUB	s	Subtract Integer
(P)	FSUBR	*	Subtract Real (reversed)
	FISUBR	s	Subtract Integer (reversed)
(P)	FMUL	*	Multiply Real
	FIMUL	s	Multiply Integer
(P)	FDIV	*	Divide Real
	FIDIV	s	Divide Integer
(P)	FDIVR	*	Divide Real (reversed)
	FIDIVR	s	Divide Integer (reversed)
	FSQRT		Square Root
	FSCALE		Scale
	FPREM		Partial Remainder
	FRNDINT		Round to Integer
	FXTRACT		Extract Exponent and Significand
	FABS		Absolute Value
	FCHS		Change Sign

Process Control Instructions (16)

Notes	Instruction Mnemonic	Address Modes	Instruction Name
(N)	FINIT		Initialize Processor
	FLDCW	s	Load Control Word
(N)	FSTCW	d	Store Control Word
(N)	FSTSW	d	Store Status Word
†(N)	FSTENV	d	Store Environment
	FLDENV	s	Load Environment
†(N)	FSAVE	d	Save State
	FRSTOR	s	Restore State
	FINCSTP		Increment SP
	FDECSTP		Decrement SP
	FFREE	d	Free Register
	FNOP		No Operation
	FWAIT		CPU Wait
(N)	FDISI		Disable Interrupts
(N)	FENI		Enable Interrupts
(N)	FCLEX		Clear Exceptions

*Instruction operand forms for FADD, FSUB, FSUBR, FMUL, FDIV, FDIVR

    : F<op>   . . . generates F<op>P ST(1),ST
    : F<op>s   . . . generates F<op> ST,<memory>
    : F<op>d,s . . . d,s registers only
    : F<op>P d,s . . . d,s registers only

(P) F<op> or F<op>P forms
(N) F<op> or FN<op> forms
 s source
 d destination
//s none or source
//d none or destination
 † Instruction not self-synchronizing

Addressing Modes of the 8087

Addressing modes in the 8087 reflect the stack architecture of the processor. All of the 8087's numeric opcodes, as distinguished from control opcodes, use the top of the stack as at least one operand. Some instructions operate only on the top of the stack, for example, FSQRT and FABS. Others operate on both the top of the stack and the next stack register, for example, FSCALE and F2XM1. The remaining double operand instructions vary according to type. Some take their second operand from another stack register. Others can take their second operand from memory.

Table 6-4 shows the various allowed combinations of operand addressing and 8087 instructions. Note that although some math and comparison instructions may use a memory operand as the source, memory operands may never be used as a destination except by the store instructions (FST<P>, FIST<P>, and FBSTP). Note also that the source operand for any integer instruction (FI*op*) must be a memory operand because the 8087's registers always contain real numbers.

Table 6-4. Allowed Types for 8087 Numeric Instructions

Example 8087 Instructions	Word	SECOND OPERANDS Double Word	Quad Word	Ten Bytes	8087 Reg.	Math Compare Inst.
FLD source		YES	YES	FLD	YES	REAL
FST dest		YES	YES	FSTP		none
FILD source	YES	YES	YES			INT
FIST dest	YES	YES	YES			none
FBLD source				YES		none
FBSTP dest				YES		none

Some confusion still may exist about how the 8087 addresses its operands. A short example should help to clear the fog, so let's take a look at the operation of three 8087 opcodes.

```
FLD       <arg1>      ; load 1st argument from memory
FLD       <arg2>      ; load 2nd argument from memory
FADD                  ; encodes as FADDP ST(1),ST
FSTP      <result>    ; store result into memory
```

This operation uses FLD to read two memory operands into the 8087 register stack, adds them using the "classical" form of FADD, and stores the result using FSTP. Remember that when one of the basic arithmetic instructions (FADD, FSUB, FMUL, and FDIV) is coded by itself, MASM generates the "classical" stack operation with a pop, using the stack top, ST, as the source and the next stack element, ST(1), as the destination.

The operation of the four instructions above is graphically displayed in Figure 6-7. We've separated the two parts of the FADD instruction so that you can better see the effects of the pop. Looking at the operation, you can see that the 8087 conceptually completes the arithmetic part of the operation (storing the result in ST(1)), then pops the stack, moving the result to the stack top, ST or ST(0).

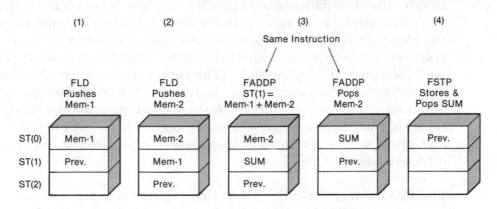

Fig. 6-7.   Example of 8087 stack operations.

At the end of our little demonstration, the stack is left exactly as it was when we arrived. Or is it? It is if there was room on the stack for additional arguments. If, however, the stack doesn't have enough room to accommodate the new data, the 8087 declares an **invalid operation exception** due to stack overflow. (We'll get to exceptions in following text.) Therefore, before we can do even our tiny example, we must be sure that the 8087 can accept the data. Two ways are available to accomplish this.

The FINIT and FFREE Instructions

The easiest way to prepare the 8087 for operations is through the FINIT instruction. This is the first instruction that should be given to the 8087 whenever a new program is run. FINIT initializes the 8087 as if a hardware reset had occurred, which means that the instruction clears all registers and exceptions and provides a clean slate for the programmer to work with.

The other method of ensuring that the 8087 has free registers is with the FFREE instruction. FFREE tags the designated register as empty and allows the programmer to use that register for subsequent calculations. Note that it isn't necessary to clear the registers at the top of the stack. If the bottom of the stack, (ST(7), has enough free room, the upper registers are pushed down into the stack when a new value is loaded.

Controlling the 8087

The Control Word and the Status Word

Besides the eight data registers the 8087 has four other registers that are accessible to the programmer. In Figure 6-1, we can see that these are the *status* word, the *control* word, and the *operand* and *instruction* pointers. The 8087 also has another register, called the *tag* word, but it is only used internally by the 8087. (The tag word is where the 8087 marks its registers as empty, zero, or not-a-number). The two pointers, operand and instruction, are only useful during external exception handling, a topic that we'll discuss in forthcoming text. What's left are the control and status words. You need to understand these two registers to make effective use of the 8087.

The 8087 Control Word   The first register that we'll look at is the control word. This 16-bit word defines the way that the 8087 treats the different exception conditions and how it views the numbering system that it uses. We've diagrammed the control word in Figure 6-8, showing the various fields and their effects. Basically, the control word contains three control fields and seven flags for use with exceptions. Let's describe the exception flags first.

At this stage in the game, we want to use as much of the built-in facilities of the 8087 as is possible. Part of this means availing ourselves of the built-in exception handling capabilities of the 8087. You see, the 8087, all by itself, can take care of most of the errors that could occur, either fixing up the number as best it can or returning a special value called *not-a-number*. Because handling these errors ourselves is not easy, we let the 8087 do it for us. We do this by masking the exceptions, and we do that by setting the exception masks in the control word. All the exception masks, along with the master interrupt enable mask, are contained in the lower byte of the control word.

To set up the 8087 to use its internal error handlers, we set the lower byte to BF (hex), using the load control word instruction FLDCW. We simply define a word in 8086 memory with a lower byte that has the value BF (hex), then load it as follows:

```
     :        :        :                    :
  cw87       dw      03BFh                  ; 8087 control word value
     :        :                             :
           FLDCW    cw87                    ; load 8087 control word
     :        :                             :
```

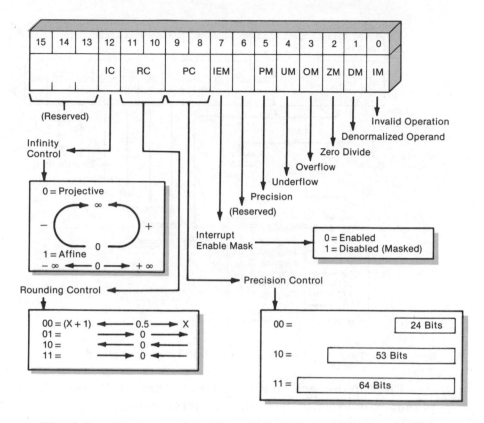

Fig. 6-8.   The control word and its effect on 8087 operations.

Why did we use the value 3 for the upper byte of the control word? The upper byte contains three fields for determining what number model the 8087 uses. These three fields are also shown in the insets in Figure 6-8. Comparing the diagram with our value of 3, you can see that we've chosen 64-bit precision, round to the nearest integer, and projective infinity. These values are the ones that Intel recommends and also the ones that the 8087 uses as defaults. If you want to change these settings, Figure 6-8 tells you what values to use.

The 8087 Status Word   The 8087's status word contains four types of information: 1) a busy indicator, 2) a top-of-stack pointer, 3) condition codes reflecting the results of the FCOM, FTST, and FXAM instructions, and 4) the exception indicators, which signal any errors that may occur. Figure 6-9 gives the positions of the different indicators within the status word.

The busy indicator signals whether the 8087 is currently processing an instruction. This indicator really isn't of much use to us because the contents of the status word can't be used until the 8087 signals that it is finished storing the status word. At that point, you know that the 8087 is idle because the FWAIT instruction finishes.

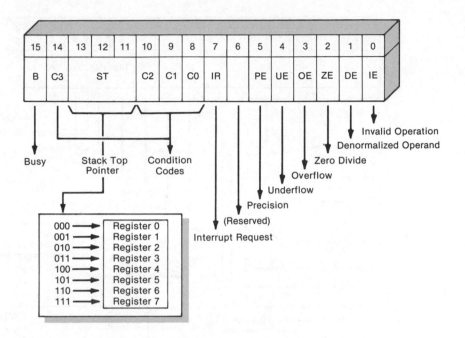

Fig. 6-9.   The 8087's status word.

The top-of-stack pointer, in bits 11 through 13, is useful to the programmer who writes complicated 8087 routines that perform successive operations in sequence and store many values on the 8087 stack. In these cases, to ensure that enough room is available for the next operation, check the stack depth before proceding with a routine. If the stack has insufficient room to support the operation, some or all of the registers must be saved in memory to allow the routine to safely execute.

The stack pointer is initialized by FINIT to point to 000 (0), and each successive load operation decrements the stack pointer, wrapping around past 111 (7) until it finally reaches 001 (1). The stack pointer may also be manipulated by the FINCSTP (increment stack pointer) and FDECSTP (decrement stack pointer) instructions. However, because these operations do not mark the registers *empty*, using FDECSTP or FINCSTP could invalidate using the top-of-stack indicator to check for free registers.

The condition codes are needed most often to decide what action to take at a decision point in the program. We'll see in the *Programming Examples* section some examples of using the condition codes. Briefly, to check the condition codes, store the status word in memory by using the FSTSW instruction, then check the codes with the 8086. When storing 8087 status information for the 8086 to check, remember to add an FWAIT instruction after the store instruction is issued. The following code fragment shows how a comparison sequence might appear.

```
      :       :       :                     :
sw87  dw      ?                     ; 8087 status word space
              :                     :
      FCOM    ST(1)                 ; check relationship of ST & ST(1)
      FSTSW   sw87                  ; store 8087 status word
      FWAIT                         ; wait for 8087 to complete
      test    sw87,4000h            ; are operands equal?
      je      are_equal             ; yes ...
      :                             :
```

The meanings assigned to these codes by the various compare instructions are given in Table 6-5. Note that the condition codes do not occur in one group but are split by the stack pointer and that the codes returned by the FCOM and FTST instructions are also split by condition bit C1, which is not used. Note also that NAN means "not a number."

Table 6-5. Status Conditions Set by the FCOM, FTST, and FXAM Instructions

	Condition Codes				
	C3	C2	C1	C0	Result
F	0	0	D	0	ST > source
C	0	0	O	1	ST < source
O	1	0	N	0	ST = source
M	1	1	'T	1	ST ? source
F	0	0	C	0	ST > 0.0
T	0	0	A	1	ST < 0.0
S	1	0	R	0	ST = 0.0
T	1	1	E	1	ST ? 0.0
F	0	0	0	0	+ Unnormal
X	0	0	0	1	+ NAN
A	0	0	1	0	– Unnormal
M	0	0	1	1	– NAN
	0	1	0	0	+ Normal
	0	1	0	1	+ Infinity
	0	1	1	1	– Infinity
	1	0	0	0	+ Zero
	1	0	0	1	Empty
	1	0	1	0	– Zero
	1	0	1	1	Empty
	1	1	0	0	+ Denormal
	1	1	0	1	Empty
	1	1	1	0	– Denormal
	1	1	1	1	Empty

Exception Handling in the 8087

The lower byte of the status word contains the exception flags. These flags correspond to the exception masks in the control word. When an exception occurs, the 8087 sets the proper flag, then checks to see whether that exception is masked or not. Because most operations use the masked response (the 8087's internal error handlers), we summarize their operation in Table 6-6. You should still remember to check for exceptions periodically to ensure the accuracy of the results. If an exception occurs, the proper flag is set and stays set until cleared by initializing the 8087 (FINIT) or with the clear exceptions instruction, FCLEX. Because the flags stay set, they provide a cumulative record of any errors that occur during processing.

Table 6-6.   The 8087's Default Exception Response
(Exceptions Masked)

Exception	Masked Response
Precision	Return rounded result
Underflow	Denormalize result
Overflow	Return signed infinity
Zero-divide	Return infinity signed with exclusive-or of operand signs
Denormal operand	If memory operand, ignore. If register operand, convert to "unnormal" and reevaluate.
Invalid operation	If one operand NAN, return it. If both are NANs, return one with larger absolute value. If neither is NAN, return *indefinite*.

The other method of handling exceptions involves unmasking one or more of the exceptions and enabling interrupts in the 8087's control word. In this mode, if the 8087 detects an exception, it signals an interrupt and requests the 8086 to process the exception. The 8087, however, is not necessarily tied into the 8086's interrupt request line! An external interrupt handler circuit is required to field interrupt requests from the 8087. Do not enable the 8087 external interrupts unless your system supports them!

If your system supports external interrupts and you enable them, you must provide an exception handler when the 8087 interrupts the 8086. The 8086 routine should read the 8087's status word to determine the nature of the problem. If you desire, your exception handler can also determine the instruction and operand that caused the problem by examining the 8087's instruction and operand pointers. To obtain this information, the exception handler must issue one of the 8087 instructions FSTENV or FSAVE. These instructions write into 8086 memory at least the contents of the five 8087 control registers (status word, control word, tag word, instruction pointer, and operand pointer). The exception handler can retrieve this information from memory and process it. If you would like a more detailed picture of these registers, Listing 6-1 in the section on *Programming Examples* contains a sample program that dumps, then decodes this information.

Using MS-DOS Tools with the 8087

The only difference between writing programs for the 8087 and writing them without is that with the coprocessor, there are more instructions to use for numeric operations. Because the difference is visible only at the instruction level, the MS-DOS tools that need to know about the 8087 are MASM and DEBUG. All of the other tools, LINK, LIB, and CREF remain ignorant of the 8087's presence.

Using MASM and the 8087

When using MASM with the 8087, the programmer simply enters 8087 instructions in the same manner as 8086 instructions. Instructions for the 8087 have the same fields as 8086 instructions: labels, opcodes, operands, and comments. The only difference in encoding instructions is that 8087 operands may be only 8087 registers or memory, and 8086 operands may be only 8086 registers or memory. In the case of memory operands, the two forms are not different. 8087 instructions may use any of the five basic memory forms shown below.

```
-Displacement Only              FSTSW     mem_word
-Base or Index Only             FIADD     word ptr [bx]
-Displacement + Base or Index   FSTP      base[di]
-Base + Index                   FLDCW     [bp][si]
-Displacement + Base + Index    FILD      [bp]table[di]
```

CAUTION

MASM version 1.25 has an error that causes it to exchange the opcodes FSUB with FSUBR or FDIV with FDIVR and vice versa if any of these are used in "classic" form (without specifying the operands). If you are using an older version of MASM, explicitly specify the operands and type for these instructions, as in:

```
FSUBP     ST(1),ST
FDIVRP    ST(1),ST
```

Remember that the classic form always uses the pop form of the instruction.

MASM's 8087 Switches—/r and /e

Once the program has been entered into a file, MASM must be used to assemble the program. If the standard MASM command line is used, every 8087 instruction encountered produces a **Syntax Error.** This is because in the normal mode of operation MASM doesn't know anything about the 8087. To actually assemble 8087 instructions, tell MASM on the command line that the source file contains 8087 instructions by using the command line switch "/r" (real mode), as in the command:

```
A:>masm test.asm test.obj test.lst test.crf/r
```

This lets MASM know that the program being assembled is intended for execution on a real 8087. MASM then generates the proper 8087 opcodes, prefixed with the FWAIT opcode unless one of the FN<*op*> instructions is used. (Note, however, that although the 8087's no-operation instruction, FNOP, begins with FN, it generates an FWAIT prefix).

MASM has yet another switch that instructs it to assemble 8087 instructions. This is the "/e" (emulation mode) switch. The /e mode switch functions nearly identically to the real mode switch, except that "no-wait" instructions (FN<*op*>) are not assembled. The purpose of this switch is for users who have emulation libraries that can replace the 8087 opcodes with 8086 CALLs to emulation subroutines. Because MASM does not provide such an emulation library and because there is no point to using the library if you have a real 8087, we don't provide further information on this topic.

8087 Data Types in MASM

You now know that the 8087 supports seven different data types: word; short and long integer, short and long real; packed binary coded decimal; and the floating-point real. To use these types, the proper storage locations must be defined in memory. Table 6-7 shows the correspondence between the 8087's data types and the methods used in MASM to define and reference them.

Storage locations are allocated by using the define data (dw, dd, dq, or dt) MASM directives, followed by a question mark (?). This format tells MASM to reserve the space but not initialize it. In order to initialize the reserved location to a particular real number value, MASM provides three different forms: the scientific notation without an exponent, the scientific notation with an exponent, and the real (R) form. Each of these forms may be used with any of the larger "define data" directives, as follows.

```
double  dd 3.14159              ; scientific without exponent
quad    dq 1.23456E + 03        ; scientific with exponent
tenbyte dt 0123456789ABCDEF0123R ; real
```

Table 6-7.   A Comparison of Data Types for the 8087 and MASM

8087 Data Type	8086 Data Type	Size Bytes	MASM Directive	Operand Name	8087 Compatible
Word integer	word	2	dw	word ptr	Yes
Short integer	double word	4	dd	dword ptr	Yes
Short real	double word	4	dd	dword ptr	No
Long integer	quad word	8	dq	qword ptr	Yes
Long real	quad word	8	dq	qword ptr	No
Packed BCD	ten byte	10	dt	tbyte ptr	"R" form
Floating real	ten byte	10	dt	tbyte ptr	Yes

Defining real numbers with the define byte (db) or define word (dw) directives isn't possible. Real numbers may only be initialized to integer values.

The scientific notations are evaluated into a floating point format (sign, exponent, and significand), whereas the real notation is used on a digit-per-nibble basis so that the real notation's hexadecimal representation exactly corresponds to its definition.

Note that although MASM has the ability to define real numbers in both 4- and 8-byte lengths, the format used to initialize these numbers is not compatible with the 8087! Figure 6-10 shows how Microsoft implemented real numbers for these sizes. By comparing them with Figure 6-2, you can see that they are quite different. If you must use these formats (for compatibility with existing software, for example), you can write conversion routines to change from one format to the other.

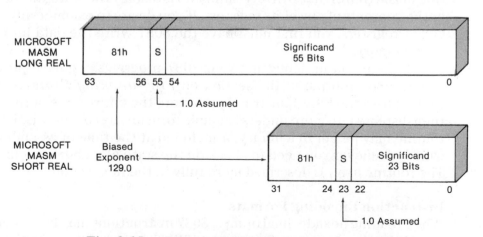

Fig. 6-10.   Microsoft MASM real number formats.

Using DEBUG with the 8087

DEBUG always knows about 8087 instructions. This explains why when you sometimes attempt to "unassemble" memory, DEBUG lists strange instructions. (One common technique used in debugging is to fill unused memory with the hex word DEAD. This distinctive pattern allows the programmer to quickly see what memory is being altered. However, DEBUG disassembles this as FISUBR WORD PTR [DI + ADDE].)

Even though DEBUG is always in 8087 mode, so to speak, DEBUG doesn't recognize all the 8087 instructions. It doesn't display, nor allow you to assemble, any of the FN <op> form instructions. The rationale behind this is that DEBUG recognizes the FWAIT as a separate instruction from the 8087 opcode, which it really is. So, DEBUG decodes an FN <op> instruction as a standard instruction that doesn't happen to be prefixed by FWAIT.

The reverse is that unlike MASM, DEBUG does not automatically insert the FWAIT prefix on standard 8087 instructions. You must remember to manually assemble the FWAIT when entering 8087 instructions in DEBUG.

You should remember also that when specifying memory operands in DEBUG, you must always tell DEBUG what size the operand is, as in the form:

```
FLD   TBYTE PTR [200]
```

The brackets are required to inform DEBUG that the number is an address rather than an immediate value.

Debugging the 8087's Registers

One of the things that DEBUG cannot do is display the status of the 8087 or the contents of any of its registers. If you desire to examine any of the 8087's registers, you first must have the 8087 write the data into common memory.

To help you in debugging your 8087 programs, we have provided the *dump87* routine in the section on *Programming Examples*. This routine uses the FSAVE instruction to store the entire state of the 8087, then displays it in more understandable form on the console display. The routine may be put in a library or included at the time of assembly and called whenever you need to check on the state of an 8087 calculation. The routine itself is described more fully in the next section.

Instruction Encoding Formats

When reading hexadecimal dumps, 8087 instructions may be recognized in code by the presence of either the FWAIT opcode (9B) or by their distinctive escape codes, D8 through DF (hex). Figure 6-11 shows the different forms that an 8087 instruction may take, but all instructions start with the 11011 bit pattern.

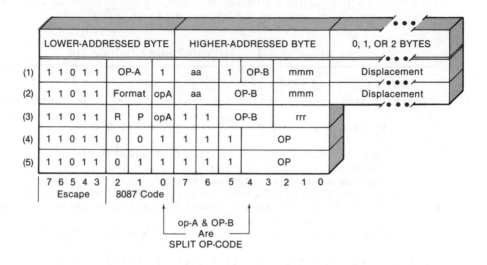

Fig. 6-11.   Instruction-encoding formats.

Programming Examples for the 8087 with MASM

Even with a good technical knowledge of the 8087 and a copy of the Intel instruction reference (which is a must for serious programming of the 8087), it's hard to understand the 8087 without some "hands-on" experience. Because we can't give you an actual computer and 8087, we do the next best thing. We present here a number of nontrivial programming examples that should give you a better understanding of the 8087's mode of operation and provide a starting place for building your own library of 8087 routines.

The FWAIT and FINIT Instructions

Let's stress once again that if the 8086 CPU intends to use results from the 8087, it must first ensure that the 8087 is finished by issuing an FWAIT.

Another point that must be understood is that the 8087 must be initialized with the FINIT instruction at the start of the program. It is very important to force the 8087 into a known state before proceeding with operations.

DUMP87 Routine

We previously pointed out that the DEBUG program is unable to examine the contents or state of the 8087, and we promised to help in that situation by providing a routine to dump the contents of the 8087 and examine them. That routine is shown in Listing 6-1.

Listing 6-1.   DUMP87 8087 Debug Aid

```
        page    60,132
;****************************************************************
;
;       L I B R A R Y   I M P L E M E N T A T I O N
;
        public  dump87          ; DEFINED LIBRARY ROUTINE
code    segment para public 'code'
        assume cs:code,ds:code,es:code,ss:code
        extrn   bin2hex:near    ; CALLED LIBRARY ROUTINE
;****************************************************************
;
;    D U M P 8 7 -- 8 0 8 7   D E B U G G I N G   T O O L
;
; This procedure dumps the entire state of the 8087 onto the
; stack, then formats and outputs said state to the terminal.
;
; Setup Requirements: NONE
; Stack Requirements: 108 bytes free on the stack
;
; ... wd--Word Defines for bit fields within various words.
; The defined structures take advantage of the fact that the
;     SW and CW interrupt structures match.
;
;****************************************************************
;
;          M A C R O   D E F I N I T I O N S
;
;; Display a character (from DL)
dis_chr macro   char
        push    ax
        push    dx
        mov     dl,&char
        mov     ah,02h
        int     21h
        pop     dx
        pop     ax
        endm
;; Display a String by Label
dis_str macro   string
        push    ax
        push    dx
        mov     dx,offset &string
        mov     ah,09h
        int     21h
        pop     dx
```

Listing 6.1. cont.

```
        pop     ax
        endm
;; Display a String (from DS:DX)
display macro
        mov     ah,09h
        int     21h
        endm
;****************************************************************
;
;       S T R U C T U R E   D E F I N I T I O N S
;
intrpt  record  master:1,nul0:1,pr:1,un:1,ov:1,zd:1,de:1,inv_op:1
control record  infc:1,rndc:2,prec:2
status  record  busy:1,c3:1,stp:3,c2:1,c1:1,c0:1
tag     record  onetag:2
ipwd    record  ipseg:4,nul2:1,opcode:11; opcode & instruction pointer
opwd    record  opseg:4,nul3:12         ; operand pointer segment
expwd   record  sign:1,exp:15           ; sign & exponent
; Basic Environment Structure
enviro  struc
cw87    dw      ?                       ; control word
sw87    dw      ?                       ; status word
tw87    dw      ?                       ; tag word
ipo87   dw      ?                       ; instruction pointer offset
ips87   dw      ?                       ; IP segment & opcode
opo87   dw      ?                       ; operand pointer offset
ops87   dw      ?                       ; OP segment
enviro  ends
; Register Structure
fltreg  struc
man87   dq      ?                       ; mantissa (significand)
exp87   dw      ?                       ; exponent & sign
fltreg  ends
; Entire State Save Structure
state87 struc
        db      size enviro dup (?)     ; environment header
reg87   db      size fltreg * 8 dup (?) ; 8 data registers
state87 ends
dump87s struc                     ; stack format for dump 87
rec87   db      size state87 dup (?)    ; space for 8087 state
;oldbp  dw      ?                       ; entry base pointer
dump87s ends
base    equ     [bp - size dump87s]     ; structure index
;****************************************************************
;
;       B E G I N   P R O G R A M   C O D E
;
dump87  proc    near
        push    bp                      ; save entry BP
        pushf                           ; save caller's flags
        push    ds                      ; save caller's data segment
        mov     bp,sp                   ; and set up index
        sub     sp,size dump87s         ; allocate space for local store
        push    ax                      ; save caller's registers
        push    bx
```

Listing 6.1. cont.

```
        push    cx
        push    dx
        push    di
        push    si
        mov     ax,cs           ; set DS to point to this routine's
        mov     ds,ax           ; ... data area.
; Get copy of the 8087's internal state
        pushf                   ; save caller's interrupt state
        cli                     ; don't allow interrupts while
                                ; saving
        FSAVE   base.rec87      ; save state of 8087
        FRSTOR  base.rec87      ; restore state that was just saved
        FWAIT                   ; wait to complete restore
        popf                    ; reenable interrupts ?
; Now that we have a copy of the 8087's state, decode it and present
; it to the user on the terminal.
;
;       Presentation consists of the following items:
;
;       ==================== 8087 DUMP ========================
;       Infinity: Affine    Round....... near     Precision: 64
;       Inst Addr: x:xxxx    Oper Addr: x:xxxx    Opcode:  Dxxx
;
;               INT PRE UND OVR ZER DEN IOP         C3 C2 C1 CO
;       Enable: x   x   x   x   x   x   x           x  x  x  x
;       Signal: x   x   x   x   x   x   x   x means unmasked
;                                               or signaled
;               exponent        significand
;       ST(x)   + xxxx   xxxx xxxx xxxx xxxx #0 tag
;          :       :       :    :    :    :    : :
;       --------------------------------------------------------
;
; Infinity, Rounding, and Precision Control
        dis_str line_1          ; start display
        mov     al,byte ptr base.cw87+1 ; get control word
        and     al,mask infc    ;           infinity control
        mov     cl,infc
        shr     al,cl           ;           condition #
        mul     inf_siz         ;           condition offset
        add     ax,offset inf_cnd ;         condition address
        mov     dx,ax
        display
        dis_str rnd_lab
        mov     al,byte ptr base.cw87+1 ; get control word
        and     al,mask rndc    ;           rounding control
        mov     cl,rndc
        shr     al,cl           ;           condition #
        mul     rnd_siz         ;           condition offset
        add     ax,offset rnd_cnd ;         condition address
        mov     dx,ax
        display
        dis_str pre_lab
        mov     al,byte ptr base.cw87+1 ; get control word
        and     al,mask prec    ;           precision control
        mov     cl,prec
```

Listing 6.1. cont.

```
        shr     al,cl                       ;           condition #
        mul     pre_siz                     ;           condition offset
        add     ax,offset pre_cnd           ;           condition address
        mov     dx,ax
        display
; Instruction & Operand Pointers, and Opcode
        dis_str line_2                      ; next line
        mov     ax,base.ips87               ;           instruction pntr.
        and     ax,mask ipseg               ;               segment
        mov     cl,ipseg
        shr     ax,cl                       ;               digit
        mov     ch,1                        ;               display 1
        call    bin2hex
        dis_chr ':'
        mov     ax,base.ipo87               ;           instruction pntr.
        mov     ch,4                        ;               offset
        call    bin2hex
        dis_str opadr                       ; operand pointer
        mov     ax,base.ops87               ;               segment
        and     ax,mask opseg
        mov     cl,opseg
        shr     ax,cl                       ;               digit
        mov     ch,1                        ;               display 1
        call    bin2hex
        dis_chr ':'
        mov     ax,base.opo87               ;           operand pntr.
        mov     ch,4                        ;               offset
        call    bin2hex
        dis_str ocode                       ; opcode
        mov     ax,base.ips87
        and     ax,mask opcode
        or      ax,0800h                    ; add OPCODE assumed bit
        mov     ch,3                        ;               3 digits
        call    bin2hex                     ;               display
; Interrupt/Exception--Enable Flags
        dis_str line_3                      ; next line
        mov     al,byte ptr base.cw87       ; exception enable flags
        call    exception_flags             ; show status
; Condition Codes
        dis_str space10
        mov     ah,byte ptr base.sw87+1     ; condition codes
        push    ax                          ;           (save codes)
        mov     al,30h                      ;           (ASCII "0")
        and     ah,mask c3                  ;           C3
        sub     ah,mask c3                  ;           0 -> CY, 1 -> NC
        cmc                                 ;           0 -> NC, 1 -> CY
        adc     al,0                        ;           0 -> "0", 1-> "1"
        dis_chr al                          ;           display
        pop     ax                          ;           (save codes)
        mov     ch,c2 + 1                   ; # of codes to display
next_cc:
        dis_str space2
        mov     al,30h                      ;           (ASCII "0")
        and     ah,mask c2 + mask c1 + mask c0
        sub     ah,mask c2                  ;           0 -> CY, 1 -> NC
```

Listing 6.1. cont.

```
        cmc                             ;       0 -> NC, 1 -> CY
        adc     al,0                    ;       0 -> "0", 1-> "1"
        dis_chr al                      ;       display
        shl     ah,1                    ; next code
        dec     ch                      ; 1 less to go ...
        jnz     next_cc                 ; ... until all done
; Interrupt/Exception--Status Flags
        dis_str line_6
        mov     al,byte ptr base.sw87   ; exception signal flags
        call    exception_flags         ; show status
; Data Register Display
        dis_str crlf
        mov     dh,8                    ; # of reg. to display
        mov     si,0                    ; start with reg #0
register_display:
        dis_str line_8                  ; registers status
        push    dx                      ; save count
        mov     al,8                    ; calculate register #
        sub     al,dh
        add     al,30h                  ;       convert to ASCII
        dis_chr al                      ;       and display
        pop     dx
; Sign of Data Register
        dis_str paren                   ; sign comes next
        mov     ax,word ptr base.reg87[si].exp87
        test    ax,mask sign            ; what is it?
        jnz     sign_minus
        dis_str plus
        jmp     show_exponent
sign_minus:
        dis_str minus
; Exponent Portion of Data Register
show_exponent:
        and     ax,mask exp             ; obtain exponent
        xor     cx,cx                   ;       four characters
        call    bin2hex                 ;       and display
        dis_str space3
        mov     di,si                   ; base of register
        add     di,offset exp87         ; location of mantissa
        mov     dl,4                    ; 4 words per register
; Display Significand Portion of Data Register
show_significand:
        sub     di,2                    ; point at word start
        mov     ax,word ptr base.reg87[di]
        call    bin2hex                 ;       and display
        dis_str space1
        dec     dl                      ; another word gone
        jnz     show_significand
; True Register Number
        dis_str truenum
        mov     al,byte ptr base.sw87+1 ; get stack pointer
        and     al,mask stp
        mov     cl,stp
        shr     al,cl                   ; have stack pointer
        mov     cl,8                    ; convert counter to ...
```

Listing 6.1. cont.

```
             sub     cl,dh                   ; ... 0 through 7
             add     al,cl                   ; current reg. #
             and     al,07H
             push    ax                      ; save register number
             add     al,30h                  ;      convert to ASCII
             dis_chr al                      ;        and display
             dis_str space2                  ; now for the TAG field
; Tag Word Status
             mov     ax,base.tw87            ; get tag word
             pop     cx                      ; get register number in CL
             shl     cl,1                    ; multiply by 2
             shr     ax,cl                   ; and get proper tag word
             and     ax,mask tag
             push    dx
             mul     tag_siz                 ;      condition offset
             add     ax,offset tag_cnd       ;      condition address
             mov     dx,ax
             display                         ;      show tag status
             pop     dx
; All Done for That Register!
             add     si,size fltreg          ; next register
             dec     dh                      ; 1 less
             jz      finished
             jmp     register_display        ; until all gone
; All Done for All Registers!
finished:
             dis_str line_9                  ; all done!
; Restore the 8086 to the way it was and return
; Start w/ saved registers
             pop     si                      ; restore caller's registers
             pop     di
             pop     dx
             pop     cx
             pop     bx
             pop     ax
             mov     sp,bp                   ; restore stack
             pop     ds                      ; restore data segment
             popf                            ; restore caller's flags
             pop     bp                      ; restore entry BP
             ret                             ; return when finished
;****************************************************************
; Display subroutine for displaying MASK & SIGNAL status of
; exceptions.
; Test byte in AL for bits corresponding to exception flags
;
exception_flags           proc     near
             test    al,mask master          ;      master control
             call    mark_it
             mov     cl,pr                   ; next is PR flag
             ror     al,cl                   ; move to 1's position
             inc     cl                      ; count 1 > than bit #
test_exception:
             test    al,1                    ; is flag set?
             call    mark_it
             rol     al,1                    ; next flag
```

Listing 6.1. cont.

```
        dec     cl                              ; keep track of count
        jnz     test_exception                  ; continue until done.
        ret
;**********************************************
; Mark result according to flags set on entry
;
mark_it         proc    near
        jz      mark_space
        dis_str marky
        ret
mark_space:
        dis_str markn
        ret
mark_it         endp
exception_flags         endp
;******************************************************************
;
; D U M P 8 7   L O C A L   C O N S T A N T   S T O R A G E
;
;          ----- this section read only -----
;
; "_lab"--label for section
; "_cnd"--condition for label
; "_siz"--number of bytes in condition
cret    macro                                   ;; new line macro
        db      0Dh,0Ah
        endm
line_1  equ     $
        cret
        db '==================== 8087 DUMP ======================='
        cret
        db          'Infinity:  $'
rnd_lab db          '    Round:....... $'    ; Label
pre_lab db          '    Precision: $'       ; Label
inf_siz db          7
inf_cnd db          'Proj. $'                ;            infinity state
        db          'Affine$'                ;            infinity state
rnd_siz db          5
rnd_cnd db          'near$'                  ;            round state
        db          'down$'                  ;            round state
        db          'up  $'                  ;            round state
        db          'chop$'                  ;            round state
pre_siz db          3
pre_cnd db          '24$'                    ; "ret" precision state
        db          '**$'                    ; "ret" precision state
        db          '53$'                    ; "ret" precision state
        db          '64$'                    ; "ret" precision state
line_2  equ     $
        cret
        db          'Inst Addr: $'           ; "x:xxxx"
opadr   db          '    Oper Addr: $'       ; "x:xxxx"
ocode   db          '    Opcode:  D$'        ; "xxx","ret","ret"
line_3  equ     $
        cret
        cret
```

Listing 6.1. cont.

```
        db      '    INT PRE UND OVR ZER DEN IOP'
        db      '        C3 C2 C1 CO'
        cret
        db      'Masked:$'
;               condition codes                    "ret"
line_6  equ     $
        cret
        db      'Signal:$'                        ; "ret"
marky   db      ' x  $'
markn   db      '    $'
line_8  equ     $
        cret
        db      'ST($'                            ; "x"
paren   db      ')  $'
plus    db      '+ $'
minus   db      '- $'                             ; "xxxx"
space10 db      '          '                      ; 10 space
space2  equ     $ + 1                             ; 2 space
space1  equ     $ + 2                             ; 1 space
space3  db      '   $'                            ; 3 space
                                                  ; "xxxx " 4 times
truenum db      ' #$'                             ; " #x", then " "tag
tag_siz db      6
tag_cnd db      'Valid$'                          ;           tag state
        db      'Zero $'                          ;           tag state
        db      'Spec.$'                          ;           tag state
        db      'Empty$'                          ;           tag state
line_9  equ     $
        cret
        db '-----------------------------------------------------'
crlf    equ     $
        cret
        db      '$'
dump87  endp
;******************************************************************
code    ends
        end
```

DUMP87 obtains the information to display by using the 8087 FSAVE instruction. This instruction saves the entire state of the 8087 in 94 bytes in the format shown in Figure 6-12. However, FSAVE also initializes the 8087 as if an FINIT had been performed. This allows a numeric subroutine to save the state of the 8087, then initialize it in one instruction, which is analogous to pushing the registers and clearing them on entry to an 8086 subroutine. Because we wish to continue processing without disruptions, we must follow the FSAVE with the FRSTOR instruction, which reloads the 8087 from the saved information.

From Figure 6-12, you can also see that the first 14 bytes of the saved information are identical to that saved by the FSTENV (store environment) instruction. FSTENV does not reinitialize the 8087 but is intended to allow the programmer access to that information which is required in exception handling: the status word and instruction and operand pointers. Like FSAVE, FSTENV has a corollary instruction called FLDENV that can reload the environment from stored information.

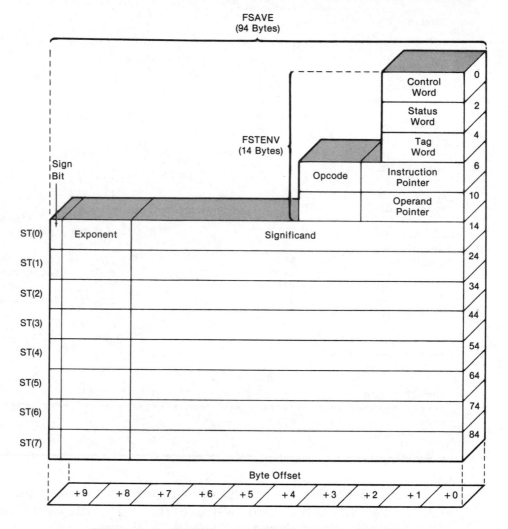

Fig. 6-12.   **FSAVE & FSTENV memory structure.**

Using the DUMP87 Routine

The remainder of the program has nothing to do with the 8087. Instead, the rest of the program uses MASM structure and record definitions to break down the information returned by FSAVE and present it to the user. The format used to present the information is documented in the routine's header section. The listing as presented is suitable for assembly and inclusion in a library file. If you follow this procedure, DUMP87 may be included in any other file by matching DUMP87's segment and class names, by declaring it external, and by providing the external routine BIN2HEX. One variation for using DUMP87 is as follows:

```
code      segment para public 'code'        ; library segment
          assume  cs:code,ds:code,es:code,ss:code
          extrn   dump87:near                ; LIBRARY ROUTINE
          ORG     0100h                      ; .COM FORMAT
main      proc    far
start:
          FINIT                              ; initialize 8087
          :       :                          :
          call    dump87                     ; analyze 8087
          :       :                          :
```

DUMP87 requires in excess of 120 bytes on the CPU stack. In return, the program does not use any data storage, which allows greater freedom of placement and use. As mentioned, DUMP87 requires a routine called BIN2HEX. BIN2HEX appears in Appendix A.

Using the 8087 To Do Binary to Decimal to Binary Conversions

Now that we are equipped to check what the 8087 is up to, we can turn to some more serious programming. The first necessity for using the 8087 is to provide some means to get data into and out of the 8087 in a form that humans can understand. And that means decimal representation.

Integer Operations

Performing integer to binary conversions on the 8087 is a snap, thanks to the FBLD and FBSTP packed BCD load and store instructions. All that is needed is a simple 8086 routine to pack and unpack the BCD digits from and to ASCII strings. To convert from decimal to binary, load the decimal number with FBLD and store it as a binary integer with FIST. To convert in the other direction requires an FILD followed by the decimal store instruction, FBSTP.

Note that as long as the numbers being converted are small enough to fit within a 16-bit register, it is not worth using the 8087 to convert from decimal to binary. The overhead associated with packing the digits and executing an FBLD-FIST sequence is greater than that which is involved with the standard "shift-multiply" conversion routine as follows:

```
; Assume number being accumulated is in AX and the new digit is
; in the CL register.
          shr     ax,1              ; existing number × 2
          mov     bx,ax             ; save
          shr     ax,1              ; number × 4
          shr     ax,1              ; number × 8
          add     ax,bx             ; (# × 8) + (# × 2) = # × 10
          xor     ch,ch             ; prepare for 16-bit add
          add     ax,cx             ; next digit added in
```

For small numbers (one to three decimal digits), the 8087 takes about twice as long to convert from decimal to binary, including the time necessary to create the packed BCD vector from an ASCII string.

When numbers get larger than 16 binary bits, the 8086 begins to slow down because it must continuously check for carries, possible overflows or underflows, etc. In the range of 16 to 64 binary bits, the 8087 really makes the conversions fly!

As long as the numbers are no longer than 18 decimal digits (which is hard to exceed!), no 8087 operations beyond the load and store instructions are required. Once numbers begin to exceed 18 digits, they must be scaled, and we enter the realm of floating-point real numbers.

Floating Point Operations

Handling conversions between decimal and binary numbers in the floating point world is mainly a matter of scaling. That is, we can use the FBLD and FBSTP instructions to get the basic numbers in and out of the 8087, but then we need to adjust the numbers by some power of ten. To understand how these operations take place, let's review some basic mathematical identities of number conversions.

1. $10^X = 2^{X * \log_2 10}$

2. $E^X = 2^{X * \log_2 E}$

3. $Y^X = 2^{X * \log_2 Y}$

4. $\log_{10}X = \log_{10}2 * \log_2 X$

5. $\log_E X = \log_E 2 * \log_2 X$

Fortunately, the 8087 knows how to calculate some of these operations and can provide constants for others. The pertinent instructions that we need to accomplish our conversions are

A. F2XM1 calculates $2^x - 1$ D. FYL2X calculates $Y * \log_2 X$
B. FLDL2T constant $\log_2 10$ E. FLDLG2 constant $\log_{10}2$
C. FLDL2E constant $\log_2 E$ F. FLDLN2 constant $\log_E 2$

We know that once an integer number has been loaded, we must either multiply it by a power of ten for a number with a positive base ten exponent or divide it by a power of ten for a number with a negative base ten exponent. From rule number 1, we can see that the first step toward obtaining a power of 10 is calculating 2 to some power X.

The 2^X Calculation

Generally, 2 can be raised to a power through a simple shift, and this is indeed what the 8087 accomplishes with its FSCALE instruction. Unfortunately, that is not the entire solution because integer powers of 10 don't correspond to integer powers of 2. Some fractional part of the power of 2 needs to be calculated. This is where the 8087 instruction F2XM1 applies (see rule A).

F2XM1 has the capability of calculating 2 to the Xth power for a value of X from 0.0 through 0.5, inclusive. Given an arbitrary number X, we can separate it into its factional and integer parts by evaluating the expressions:

$$\text{integer}(X) = \text{FRNDINT}(X)$$
$$\text{fractional}(X) = \text{FSUB } X - \text{integer}(X)$$

The integer portion of X is used in FSCALE to raise 2 to an integer power, and the fractional portion becomes the input for F2XM1. We can use two successive operations because we know that for any Y and Z the following holds true:

$$2^{(Y+Z)} = 2^Y * 2^Z$$

The absolute value of the fractional part of X is held within the range of 0.0 to 0.5 by ensuring that the 8087's rounding control is set to nearest, which ensures a maximum fraction of 0.5.

We may then calculate the total result by applying F2XM1, adding 1 back to the result and using FSCALE on that. Of course, we must watch to see that if the factional part is negative, we use its absolute value and use the identity

$$2^{(Y-Z)} = 2^Y/2^Z$$

for the correct result. This is essentially the sequence of events that takes place in the routine EXP2, which appears near the end of Listing 6-2.

The 10^X Calculation

Now that we have determined how to calculate 2 to the Xth, we have accomplished the major part of calculating 10 to the Xth. From rule number 1, we know that

$$10^X = 2^{X*\log_2 10}$$

which means that all we need to find is the value

$$X * \log_2 10$$

in order to be able to use the 2 to the Xth routine just developed. From looking at rule B, we see that the 8087 can supply us with the value for the base 2 log of 10. Calculating 10 to the Xth then becomes the operation FLDL2T, followed by the multiplication FMUL and finishing with a call to EXP2. These are the instructions that appear in the routine EXP10, also contained in Listing 6-2.

By changing identities from base 2 log of 10 to base 2 log of *e* to base 2 log of X, we can calculate the values of 10 to the Xth, *e* to the Xth, and Y to the Xth, all with the EXP2 routine.

The Decimal to Real Scaling Function

Once we have the value of 10 to the Xth, what do we do with it? We wanted this number so that we could use scientific notation in the 8087. Given a packed BCD number and a word integer X for the exponent, we can convert the parts to a floating-point real number by loading the packed BCD significand with FBLD, calculate 10 to the absolute value of X, then either multiply the result by the significand for positive X (FMUL) or divide the significand by the resulting 10 to the Xth for negative exponents (FDIV). As you've probably guessed, that's what the routine DEC2FLT does in Listing 6-2. This routine looks larger than it is because we needed to keep track of and adjust for the sign of the exponent.

The resulting package of routines, EXP2, EXP10, and DEC2FLT can take a two-part number (packed BCD significand and integer exponent), which the 8086 can generate, and turn it into a floating-point real number inside of the 8087.

The Real to Decimal Scaling Function

Once we have numbers inside the 8087, we can calculate with them to our hearts content. If we run out of room, we can always store them in common memory as temporary reals (the FSTP instruction does that). But what about when its time to see the results? How do we go about turning a floating-point real number into a two-part integer number.

The answer is that we must play with the 8087's biased exponent so that the 8087 can give us an integer significand.

You see, when storing a number as a packed BCD string, the FBSTP instruction first rounds the number to the nearest integer. If the number is too large to be represented by a packed BCD string, the 8087 is unable to store that number. If the number is too small, significant precision is lost when the number is rounded. In order to use the FBSTP instruction, we must first make sure that the number stored in the register is in the proper range.

We can tell that a number is in the proper range because its biased exponent (a sort of binary decimal point) has a value less than 64 (otherwise, the number is too large) and greater than the number of significant binary digits (otherwise, we lose precision). Typically, we choose a number that we know gives us good precision. For a number that we wish to be accurate to 10 decimal digits, a true exponent of 32 is a good number. That means that the binary decimal point is on bit 32, about halfway through the floating point. Not too large and not too small.

Now what if the number has an exponent that's not in that range? We have to change the exponent. The first step is to determine what the exponent really is. We use the FXTRACT instruction, which splits an 8087 data register into two, one holding the significand with an exponent of zero (ST) and the other holding the original number's true exponent as a real number (ST(1)). The part that we're interested in is ST(1).

The first step of this calculation is to determine how many binary decimal places we're off. Another way of saying this is that we wish to determine the distance between the desired exponent and the existing exponent. FSUB can tell us that pretty quickly.

Once we have the distance, can't we just apply it as a scaling factor (with FSCALE) to the original exponent? No, because when we display the number, we're going to tell the user what the exponent is in scientific notation, as in:

$$+1.2345600000E+00$$

and we won't be able to do that if the exponent is a power of two. The idea of this exercise is to have the 8087 produce an integer number and then know how many powers of 10 that number was shifted to make it an integer. Straight-up scientific notation.

What we have to do is convert somehow the distance, which is currently in powers of two, into a distance of integer powers of ten. As it turns out, the relationship between the two values is expressed by the rule

$$2^X = 10^{X*\log_{10} 2}$$

or

$$2^X = 10^{X/\log_2 10}$$

The second relationship results from the identity that states that

$$\log_a b = 1/\log_b a$$

Either way we calculate, we have determined the value of X (for the expression 10 to the Xth) required to create the proper scaling factor. Creating the factor can be accomplished through the FLDLG2 (load base 10 log of 2) followed by an FMUL or through FLDL2T (load base 2 log of 10) followed by an FDIV. However, these methods give us an exact number of X for 10 to the Xth, and we need the closest integer. So we apply FRNDINT to round the number, and we have our base 10 exponent.

Given the exponent, we have but a moment's work to calculate 10 to the Xth (with EXP10), and we have the scaling factor to turn the real number into an integer (with FMUL). We return the exponent of 10 via FIST (store integer) and the significand portion with FBSTP (store packed BCD). Everything except the BCD store is contained in FLT2DEC in Listing 6-2.

Another useful trick is that once the packed BCD number is stored in memory, we can use a binary to hexadecimal display routine (such as BIN2HEX) to display the digits because they look exactly like a hexadecimal number.

We've been talking about Listing 6-2, and it finally follows. Notice that as with the DUMP87 listing, this one is formatted to be used as a library also. In addition, all operations take place on the 8086 stack or in locations specified by the caller, so there should be no problem with portability.

Listing 6-2. DE2FLT, FLT2DEC and the Exponent Routines EXP2, EXP10, EXPE, and EXPY

```
        page    60,132          ; wide listing
        public  dec2flt         ; DECLARE LIBRARY ROUTINE
        public  flt2dec         ; DECLARE LIBRARY ROUTINE
        public  exp10           ; DECLARE LIBRARY ROUTINE 10**x
        public  expE            ; DECLARE LIBRARY ROUTINE e**x
        public  expY            ; DECLARE LIBRARY ROUTINE y**x
        public  exp2            ; DECLARE LIBRARY ROUTINE 2**x
;===============================================================
;
```

Listing 6-2. cont.

```
;       I M P L E M E N T A T I O N
;
code    segment para public 'code'
        assume cs:code,ds:code,es:code,ss:code
;****************************************************************
;
; DEC2FLT--Convert decimal integer with exponent to floating
;          point real number. Accept exponent and pointer to
;          packed BCD string on stack. Return result in ST(0)
;
; Use:        push        offset (tbyte ptr packed_BCD)
;             push        exponent
;             call        dec2flt
;
; Requirements:       3 stack locations
; Notation:    N ...... exponent for 10**N
;              S ...... significand portion of loading real
;
d2fltd  struc
d2fltbp dw      ?                       ; old base pointer
        dw      ?                       ; return address
d2fltex dw      ?                       ; exponent
d2fltpd dw      ?                       ; pointer to packed BCD
d2fltd  ends
dec2flt proc    near
        push    bp
        mov     bp,sp                   ; address parameters
        cmp     word ptr [bp].d2fltex,0 ; check sign of exponent
        jz      d2flt_nxp               ; if zero, no 10**N needed
        pushf                           ; save sign of exponent
        jg      d2flt_pos               ; if positive, start 10**N
        neg     word ptr [bp].d2fltex   ; ... else make exp positive
d2flt_pos:
        FILD    word ptr [bp].d2fltex   ; get exponent of 10
        call    exp10                   ; calculate 10**N
d2flt_nxp:                              ; enter here if exp is 0
        push    si
        mov     si,[bp].d2fltpd         ; get pointer to packed BCD
        FBLD    tbyte ptr [si]          ; ST => S; ST(1) = 10**N
        pop     si
        popf                            ; restore exponent's sign
        jz      d2flt_end               ; done if exp is 0
        jl      d2flt_neg               ; if negative, do divide
        FMUL                            ; ST => significand * 10**N
        jmp     d2flt_end               ; and done
d2flt_neg:
        FDIVR                           ; ST =>
d2flt_end:
        pop     bp                      ; restore bp
        ret     4
dec2flt endp
;****************************************************************
;
; FLT2DEC--Convert floating real to decimal integer with exponent.
;          ST(0) contains number to be converted. Stack contains
```

Listing 6-2. cont.

```
;               number of binary digits desired and pointer to 10's
;               exponent location.
;               Returns with ST(0) converted to an integer and writes
;               the 10's exponent to the designated location.
;
; Use:      push        sig_digits
;           push        offset (word ptr to exponent)
;           call        flt2dec
;
; Requirements:        4 stack locations
; Notation:    R ...... Real number to display
;              N ...... Exponent of 10 to convert R to integer
;              I ...... Integer portion of resultant number
;              n(N) ... nearest integer of N
;
f2decd  struc
f2deccw dw        ?                  ; original control word
f2decbp dw        ?                  ; old base pointer
        dw        ?                  ; return address
f2decex dw        ?                  ; pointer to exponent
f2decsd dw        ?                  ; number of significant binary digits
f2decd  ends
; *** check rounding control at this point--use other ?? ***
f2decct equ       03BFh              ; new control word--round nearest
flt2dec proc      near
;           Set up the 87's control word and open storage on the stack
;
        push      bp                 ; save old base pointer
        sub       sp,(f2decbp-f2decd)    ; make storage on the stack
        mov       bp,sp              ; address new structure
        push      ax                 ; save AX
        mov       ax,f2decct         ; push new control word on stack
        push      ax
        FSTCW     word ptr [bp].f2deccw
        FLDCW     word ptr [bp-4] ; set to round to nearest INT
        pop       ax                 ; clean up stack
        pop       ax                 ; restore AX
;           Find N for 10**N to convert to integer
;
        FLD       ST(0)              ; duplicate R (preserve until end)
        FXTRACT                      ; ST(1) => exponent portion of R
        FSTP      ST(0)              ; ST => exponent portion of R
        FISUBR    word ptr [bp].f2decsd ;sigdig - exp=# of scale digits
        FLDL2T                       ; ST => log2 (10), ST(1)=>scale
        FDIV                         ; ST => scale/log2 (10)=N
        FRNDINT                      ; ST => n(N)
;           Store nint (N) as exponent & calculate 10**nint(N)
        push      si
        mov       si,[bp].f2decex    ; get pointer to exponent
        FIST      word ptr [si]      ; store base 10 scale
        FWAIT
        neg       word ptr [si]      ; direction to move dec. point
        pop       si
        call      exp10              ; calculate 10**N (scale)
;           ST(1) now has R (the original real #)--scale it
```

Listing 6-2. cont.

```
;
        FMUL                                ; ST => R*10**N=Integer
        FLDCW    word ptr [bp].f2deccw      ; restore control word
        add      sp,(f2decbp-f2decd)        ; resize stack to original
        pop      bp                         ; restore BP
        ret      4                          ; clear stack on return
flt2dec endp
;***************************************************************
;
; EXP10--Calculate 10 to the power of ST(0)
;        Return result in ST(0)
;
; Uses formula: 10**N = 2**(N*log2(10))
;
; CALLS:        EXP2
;
; Requirements:       3 stack locations
; Notation:     N ...... exponent for 10**N
;               X ...... equivalent exponent for 2**X
;               n(x) ... nearest integer of X
;               f(x) ... fractional part of X
;
exp10  proc    near
        FLDL2T                              ; ST > log2 (10); ST(1) => N
        FMUL                                ; ST => N * log2 (10) => X
        call     exp2                       ; raise 2 to ST power ...
        ret                                 ; for 10 ** N
exp10  endp
;***************************************************************
;
; EXPE--Calculate E to the power of ST(0)
;        Return result in ST(0)
;
; Uses formula: E**N = 2**(N*log2(E))
;
; CALLS:        EXP2
;
; Requirements:       3 stack locations
; Notation:     N ...... exponent for E**N
;               X ...... equivalent exponent for 2**X
;               n(x) ... nearest integer of X
;               f(x) ... fractional part of X
;
expe   proc    near
        FLDL2E                              ; ST > log2 (e); ST(1) => N
        FMUL                                ; ST => N * log2 (e) => X
        call     exp2                       ; raise 2 to ST power ...
        ret                                 ; for E ** N
expe   endp
;***************************************************************
;
; EXPY--Calculate Y [ST(0)] to the power of N [ST(1)]
;        Return result in ST(0)
;        ST(1) (value of N) is lost!
;
```

Listing 6-2. cont.

```
; Uses formula: Y**N = 2**(N*log2(Y))
;
;       **** Y MUST BE POSITIVE ****
;
; CALLS:         EXP2
;
; Requirements:      3 stack locations
; Notation:    N ...... exponent for Y**N
;              X ...... equivalent exponent for 2**X
;              n(x) ... nearest integer of X
;              f(x) ... fractional part of X
;
expy    proc    near
        FYL2X                       ; ST => N * log2 (Y) => X
        call    exp2                ; raise 2 to ST power ...
        ret                         ; for Y**N
expy    endp
;****************************************************************
;
; EXP2--Calculate 2 to the power of ST(0)
;        Return result in ST(0)
;
; Requirements:         3 stack locations
; Notation:    X ...... exponent for 2**X
;              n(x) ... nearest integer of X
;              f(x) ... fractional part of X
;
exp2d   struc
exp2cc  dw      ?                   ; condition codes
exp2cw  dw      ?                   ; original control word
exp2bp  dw      ?                   ; old base pointer
        dw      ?                   ; return address
exp2d   ends
exp2ct  equ     03BFh               ; new control word--round nearest
exp2    proc    near
;       Set up the 87's control word and open storage on the stack
;
        push    bp                  ; save old base pointer
        sub     sp,(exp2bp-exp2d)       ; make storage on the stack
        mov     bp,sp               ; address new structure
        push    ax                  ; save AX
        mov     ax,exp2ct           ; push new control word on stack
        push    ax
        FSTCW   word ptr [bp].exp2cw
        FLDCW   word ptr [bp - 4]   ; set to round to nearest INT
        pop     ax                  ; clean up stack
        pop     ax                  ; restore AX
;       Start processing the number now.
        FLD     ST(0)               ; ST => ST(1) => X for 2**X
        FRNDINT                     ; ST => n(X); ST(1) => X
        FXCH                        ; ST => X; ST(1) => n(X)
        FSUB    ST,ST(1)            ; ST => f(X); ST(1) = n(X)
        FTST                        ; set condition codes
        FSTSW   word ptr [bp].exp2cc        ; store CC's
        FWAIT
        and     byte ptr [bp + 1].exp2cc,45h        ; mask all but CC's
```

Listing 6-2. cont.

```
        cmp     byte ptr [bp + 1].exp2cc,1        ; test for negative
        ja      exp2_err                   ; NAN or infinity => error
        je      exp2_neg                   ; fractional part is minus
;
        F2XM1           ; ST => (2**f(X)) - 1; ST(1)=n(X)
        FLD1            ; ST => 1; ST(1) => (2**f(X)) - 1; ST(2)=n(X)
        FADD            ; ST => 2**f(X); ST(1)=>n(x)
        FLD1            ; ST => 1; ST(1) => (2**f(X)) - 1; ST(2)=n(X)
        FADD            ; ST => 2**f(X); ST(1) => n(X)
        FSCALE          ; ST => 2**(X) => 2**(N*log2(?)) => ?**N
        FSTP    ST(1) ; ST => ?**N; ST(1) => restored
        jmp     exp2_mer ; merge
;
exp2 neg:
        FABS            ; ST => 1 - f(x); ST(1)=n(X) + 1
        F2XM1           ; ST => (2**(1 - f(x))) - 1; ST(1)=n(X) + 1
        FLD1            ; ST => 1; ST(1) => (2**(1 - f(x))) - 1
        FADD            ; ST => 2**(1 - f(x)); ST(1) => n(X) + 1
        FXCH            ; ST => n(X) + 1; ST(1) => 2**(1 - f(x))
        FLD1            ; ST => 1; ST(1)=n(X) + 1
        FSCALE          ; ST => 2**(n(x) + 1); ST(2) => 2**(1 - (f(x))
        FDIVRP ST(2),ST; ST(1) => 2**(n(X) + 1)/2**(1 - f(x))
        FSTP    ST(0) ; ST => 2**(n(x) + 1 - 1 + f(x) => 2**(X)
;
exp2_mer:
        clc                             ; no errors
exp2_out:
        FLDCW   word ptr [bp].exp2cw    ; restore control word
        add     sp,(exp2bp-exp2d)       ; resize stack to original
        pop     bp                      ; restore BP
        ret
exp2_err:
        stc                             ; errors occurred
        jmp     exp2_out
exp2    endp
;***********************************************************
code    ends                            ; end code segment
        end
```

Summary

By providing as examples these routines for debugging and I/O, we hope that we have not only given you an understanding of how the 8087 works and what is possible with it but also that we have made it more possible for you to develop applications for the 8087. Equipped with this boost, you should be able to branch out on your own into whatever field interests you. Trigonometric analysis, Fourier transforms—all are much easier when the power of the 8087 can be brought to bear. Good luck and happy numeric coprocessing!

LANs and MS-DOS 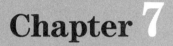 Chapter 7

L ocal Area Networks (LANs) are fast becoming the most important market segment for business related software. Although personal computers boost the individual's computing power, LANs increase the communication power between computer systems, thus giving people access to a wider range of information and cutting the costs of data processing. Software that is written to take advantage of a LAN's distributed processing power and resource sharing will have a competitive edge on single-user PC software in the years to come.

Our goal for this chapter is to give you an overview of the types of LANs on the market and how they function. We also explore the basics of writing software that takes advantage of the many resources offered by Local Area Networks. We focus primarily on MS-NET and PC-Net, but you should note that other (proprietary) operating systems are equally as important and may be better for specific applications.

Local Area Networks

Local Area Networks increase the functionality of applications software by making a whole range of resources and devices available to the programmer and the end user. All the expensive and redundant hardware, such as hard disk storage, printers, modems, and larger processors, can be accessed by microcomputer users on a network through well integrated LAN software. It's no wonder that the growth of LAN software in businesses has been so explosive.

The very purpose of LANs, resource and information sharing, necessitates rethinking the way in which applications software is written. A single-user program can operate very well on a network if only one user wishes to use it on a private storage device. But this defeats or at least cripples the very power and usefulness of a network. To take advantage of a LAN, single-user software must become multiuser and integrate the networking features that the end user is looking for.

A major problem for network applications writers is that the variety of microcomputers which can be linked together on a network make it difficult for one program to run on all nodes. A possible solution to this dilemma may be in the standardization of network software. If the network protocols take care of data communications between dissimilar computers, the application program has half the problem solved. One method for this standardization is the layering concept.

Layered Network Software

Network software is written so that each layer communicates only with the layer immediately above and below it. This allows the division of network tasks into independent layers and makes it possible for one layer to change without affecting any other layers or the applications.

These different layers interact to transport data across a physical medium, send and receive data between stations, interface with the operating system and application programs, and provide disk access with file security. Taken together, all this seems like an enormous data handling task. This is especially true when the network links dissimilar computers and communication devices. Network developers spend a great deal of time developing these interactive software layers.

Fortunately for applications developers, good networks make it relatively easy to make the network protocols transparent to the application software. Ideally, the programmer should only have to integrate a set of function calls to make a program work on a network. Other considerations, however, must be addressed if an application is to take full advantage of all the network's features and be able to run cooperatively with other software.

Standards are being written to define the network layers and make the task of adapting software to various networks even easier. Not all the present LANs, however, adhere to the standards and some use only certain layers defined in the standards. (True uniform compliance to the standards may never be workable in the heavily competitive network market.)

Currently two independent organizations have developed network Protocol and Layering standards. The ISO/OSI (International Standards Organization/Open Systems Interconnection) standards outline a seven layer model for network software. The IEEE (Institute of Electrical and Electronic Engineers) has developed another model. Some of the layers in these standards are the same but not all layers have been defined as of this writing. As an introduction to network models, let's see how the ISO/OSI model is structured and how it affects the applications programmer.

ISO/OSI Seven Layer Network Model

The Open Systems Interconnection seven layer model is one of the most widely followed standards among the major networking companies. The layers are organized from the physical transmission methods through the application layer. Not all layers are defined completely as yet, however.

The network layers in the OSI model are structured so that each layer represents a task in the communications and data handling chain. Each layer communicates with the layers directly above and below it and indirectly with its "sister" layers in other nodes. An instruction that originates with the host or application running on the host computer passes the data to the top layer. The data is formatted as it is passed down through the layers, each layer adding its own control parameters. These parameters may add error control (CRC), links with other nodes (addresses) or protocols for communication (packet formats).

Figure 7-1 represents the layers in the OSI model.

Fig. 7-1.   OSI model layers.

Physical Layer

Data transmission is regulated at the physical layer. In the OSI standard, this layer is called X.21. Its purpose is to activate, maintain, and deactivate the physical connections between computers (and other types of communication nodes). This layer is analogous to the RS-232 and RS-422 standards for cabling. The physical layer can be considered as hardware devices which convert the digital information presented by the computer into a format that is compatible with the network medium, for instance, analog signals for broadband networks. The physical layer is defined to assist interfacing the network hardware correctly. In a good network environment, the applications program should not even be aware of this layer.

Data Link Layer

The next layer may be more important for some types of systems programmers. The data link layer is known as HDLC (high-level data link control). If you are familiar with IBM's SDLC (synchronous data link control), you know part of HDLC. HDLC is a superset of SDLC and supports station to station send and receive codes. SDLC supports only master-slave communication. Systems programmers need access to this layer to develop interface calls to various host computers. Normally this is not at all necessary for the applications programmer. Most networks in fact discourage any communication with the HLDC by applications. Unless you know what you are doing, severe problems can result. Let the network engineers worry about the data link layer inteface.

Network Layer

The third layer in the OSI model is the network layer. This is called X.25 by the ISO committee. The network layer controls the manner in which data is packaged and transmitted through the data link and across the physical bus. Data integrity and error handling, that is, CRC, is also controlled in the network layer. Again, this layer is generally for systems programmers.

Transport Layer

The fourth layer in the OSI Model is not yet fully defined by the ISO committee. The functions of the transport layer are mostly concerned with data transfer between other network layers independent of specific hardware and with error correction services. Several levels of error correction and recovery are being written into the standards.

Two important distinctions in the transport layer are datagram and reliable frame protocol services. Sending information by datagram services does not guarantee error correction or retransmit protocols. The actual send/receive protocols are left up to the two interacting entities. Reliable frame services (a generic term) processes the data that is to be passed between entities into error corrected frames. The protocols are well established and guarantee reliable data transmission. (Frames and frame construction are discussed later.)

Programmers should evaluate the error handling services of a network by examining the final specifications when they are released.

Session Layer

The session layer adds a fifth level of software to a network. The ISO committee is still defining this layer. Its predominant functions are to coordinate data transfer between the other layers and specific nodes on the network. These protocols are system dependent as opposed to the transport layer, which is meant to be hardware independent.

Presentation Layer

The presentation layer is the first layer that may have a direct interface with an application program. This layer is responsible for encoding data that is presented to the end-user on the screen. Three protocols are being written to allow

- different terminals (screen formats) to support different applications

- code conversions in files, file communication, and file formatting

- control of jobs and records for transfer and manipulation

These protocols are very valuable for applications programmers who want to make their programs portable among not only networks but terminals and file formats.

Application Layer

The top level of networking protocols reside in the application layer. This is where the services reside that support user and application tasks and network management, such as database access, remote job entry and bulk data transmission. This top layer is the most undefined of the seven. It provides routine protocols for applications to access the lower layers directly.

As an applications programmer, you may be wondering whether the ISO model really does you much good if the upper layers are still undefined. The answer is yes. Standards are always slow to develop, slow to be accepted, and slow to be implemented. You are not likely to be faced with a command to "Adhere to the ISO model or else." However you will benefit from studying the standards and using them in your programs whenever possible. Following the standards can help to make your applications viable and transportable in the years to come.

Although ISO/OSI has gained a lot of acceptance since it was introduced, the IEEE 802 project is another standard that needs consideration. Several volumes, however, would be required to describe its complete structure. You should be aware of it as an important evolving standard that undoubtedly will influence software development. Let's look at the IEEE 802 project.

IEEE 802 Standards Project

The IEEE has developed a LAN model that differs in many respects from the ISO model, mostly because IEEE has decided to concentrate on the lower levels of data communication and has recommended the standardization of three specific LAN topologies. (LAN topology refers to the physical layout and data transfer methods of a LAN. We discuss these in more detail in following sections of this chapter.) IEEE believes that no single LAN topology can be the solution to all applications. This approach has lead to a more defined physical layer, which in fact has been split into two layers for more control.

As you might expect from the Institute of Electrical and Electronic Engineers, the 802 model is more concerned (so far) with hardware than software specifications. The model is very complete in its lower (physical) layers and therefore offers a good beginning for understanding LAN topologies. Because the 802 documents contain over 500 pages of specifications, let's use it as an introduction to the three most popular LAN architectures.

Network Architectures and Topologies

The IEEE 802 Project recommends three LAN topologies as standards.

802.3:   Ethernet-like systems using CSMA/CD protocols (carrier sense multiple access/collision detection)
802.4:   Token bus
802.5:   Token ring

These three present different methods of packaging and passing information on a network. In the 802 Project (see Fig. 7-2), these three standards represent the bottom two layers of the model: physical and link.

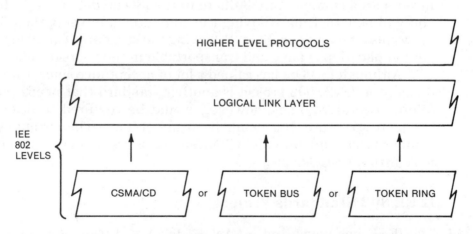

Fig. 7-2.   802 project model layers.

This demonstrates the value of layered standards. Even though the bottom layer of physical interfaces is different, the top layers remain unaffected. Thus software controlling transport, for example, works the same with Token Bus, token ring or CSMA/CD networks. Applications that interface with the upper layers don't care what the physical layers are as long as they are compatible with the standard model.

Although the actual physical layer may indeed not affect an applications programmer, a software engineer who is thinking about LAN applications is wise to understand some of the principles involved in the three network standards.

The two basic communication methods that can be applied to either of the three LAN architectures are baseband and broadband transmission. Baseband uses a digital bit-by-bit transmission sequence over various types of cable, for example, flat ribbon, coax, or twisted pair. The main problem is that the speed and bandwidth are limited in baseband installations. Only one "channel" is operable for all network communications. Therefore, baseband is too limited for complex data transmissions. It is, however, a proven and reliable system for LANs that need an inexpensive, reliable medium which doesn't exceed a mile in total length.

Broadband uses RF (radio-frequency) modems to transmit data over two channels, which leaves plenty of capacity for voice, video, and other types of transmissions over the same CATV coax cable. Broadband networks use one of the two channels to carry data transmitted from stations. A remodulator converts the data to a higher frequency and retransmits the converted data over the network coax cable. Stations listen to the higher frequency channel for data with their address or "name" attached to it.

Broadband is more expensive than baseband because of the price of the cable and the specialized RF modems and related circuitry. However, for LANs with complex data/voice/video requirements and transmission distances greater than a mile, broadband is a must.

Packets and Frames

Each of these two transmission methods contains the basic building blocks for communication between network nodes. The packet or frame is the structure within which all data is passed through the network. The packet contains not only the core data but also the address of the receiving node, the origin address, length of the frame, error correction codes, and start and stop indicators. These parameters define the data transmission sequence. Each of the three networks have different packet structures. Let's look at two of the packets before we describe the protocols.

The CSMA/CD packet defines a transmission in terms of destination and source addresses; the length count of the packet; the network destination and source information up to 12K bits of data, padding bits to make up a minimum packet length; CRC bits for error correction; and start and stop delimiters. An Ethernet data packet might look like the one shown in Figure 7-3.

Preamble, Begin Frame Delimiter	Destination & Source Address 16-48 Bits Each	Length Count	Network Destination & Source	Data 368 - 12K Bits	Padding Bits	CRC Checking	End Frame Delimiter

Fig. 7-3.   Ethernet CSMA/CD packet.

When a station receives a packet with the station's address, it checks the CRC to see whether the packet was corrupted by a collision with another packet while being transmitted. If everything is correct, the length count is used to determine how much padding must be stripped out along with all other nondata information. This leaves just the data sequence for processing.

Token passing packets are similar in some respects to CSMA/CD packets, but they do not need a length count or padding bits. They do, however, use an idle pattern after the packet to make up the minimum transmission time for the station. In structure, a token passing packet for a token bus network might look like the one shown in Figure 7-4.

Start Frame Delimiter	Network Access Information	Destination & Source Addresses	Network Destination & Source Info	Data 0-32,792 Bits	Frame Checking Sequence	End Frame Delimiter	Idle Pattern

Fig. 7-4.   Token bus packet.

Notice that more data can be transmitted in the token passing frame. The idle pattern also helps keep the receiving modems tuned to the proper receiving channel. This cuts down on problems caused by noise on the network.

From our discussions on the network software layers, you can see that specific sections of the packet are defined by different layers. As the data is passed from the application layer down to the physical layer where transmission over the network bus takes place, control information is added to ensure correct delivery. For example, the data link layer adds the destination and source address to the packet, and the network layer adds the network source and destination addresses.

Now let's see how the three protocols handle these packets on the network.

CSMA/CD (IEEE 802.3)

CSMA/CD and CSMA/CA (carrier sense multiple access/collision avoidance) are techniques for controlling data flow on baseband and broadband networks. Ethernet is a well known network that combines both detection and avoidance techniques (CSMA/CD/CA).

Essentially, CSMA/CD/CA allows every station equal access to the network. Any station that wants to transmit a message (which is a strictly defined packet) first listens to the network to see whether any other station is transmitting. If not, the station can send a packet. After the packet is transmitted, it listens again to see whether another station might have transmitted at the same time and garbled its packet. As the network gets busier, that is, more stations are trying to transmit, the chances of a collision increase. If the packet comes back garbled, the sending station knows that it has to transmit it again. So do the other stations that transmitted at the same time and collided with the packet. Therefore, all sending stations "back off" for a random period of time before retransmitting.

As you can see, a heavily loaded network has more collisions and each transmission takes longer and longer to get through. The major drawback is that no definite amount of time can be guaranteed for a transmission or reception. For applications requiring time sensitive responses, CSMA/CD/CA networks can be crippling.

Token Bus (IEEE 802.4) and Token Ring (IEEE 802.5)

One answer to the problem of running time-sensitive programs on a network is to give each station on the network an allotted amount of time to send messages. This can be controlled in several ways but the evolving standards are pointing to token passing control.

Token passing is based on the simple rule that a station can only transmit on the network when it possesses a logical token. This token is a special packet that is transmitted from station to station in a predetermined sequence. When a station receives the token packet, that station may transmit data packets to other addresses on the network for a defined amount of time. When the station is finished transmitting or the allotted time has been reached, the token is passed to the next station (called the successor station).

In a token ring topology, successor stations are the next physical station in the ring. The addresses of the stations are predefined by their physical placement. In a token bus, the token is passed to a logical successor. This successor station can be anywhere on the network bus rather than just the next station physically. The token bus allows flexibility according to statistical use or priority in determining who gets the token next.

In both configurations, the time that passes before a station can transmit again can be precisely determined by multiplying the number of stations on the network by the amount of time a station can hold the token. An application knows how long to wait for a reply or permission to transmit before timing out.

Token passing networks are more complex than most other kinds, but they have been given the blessing of the standards committees as well as IBM (token ring), General Motors (MAP [Manufacturing Automation Protocol] token bus) and network manufacturers such as Ungermann-Bass (both ring and bus). The token passing protocols, furthermore, are being put on chips, which will bring the cost of hardware down over the next years. Intel already makes an Ethernet chip that incorporates the CSMA/CD/CA protocols, dramatically reducing per station connection costs. Industrial Networking, Inc., has developed the first MAP token bus network chips for factory automation. These chips not only decrease costs but improve efficiency and transmission speed.

As previously stated, the physical and data link layers of network protocols usually should not concern an applications programmer beyond knowing the capabilities of a particular network. Now that you have an idea of how data is handled in different network architectures, you may be wondering how your application interfaces with the network.

Similar to single-user software which uses the native operating system and BIOS calls to handle I/O, applications accessing networks can still use the station's DOS to read and write files. However, to make the network as transparent to the user as possible and to utilize the power of the network, an application must access the *network's* MS-DOS and BIOS calls. These calls let the program use the network's distributed resources and shared data without loss of data integrity or security. Our next section deals with the network operating system and the real substance as related to MS-DOS.

Network Operating Systems

Network operating systems perform functions similar to standard single-user MS-DOS except that they have many more resources and, of course, added complications. Want to open a file? Sure. Where? Which hard disk? Which directory? Shared or private file? Lock a record for updating or just read it? Print a file? Whose printer do you want to use? Here comes an electronic mail message. Do you want to interrupt screen display or alert on status line? Erase a file. Who owns it? Is it shared? And so on and on . . .

This may appear overwhelming at first and although you must be aware of the potential problems of network I/O and what resources are available, the primary responsibility of the network OS (operating system) is to make life easy for you. One problem is that every network vendor has its own idea of how your application should behave on the network because the standards previously discussed have not thoroughly defined the upper application layers for networks.

Networks divide MS-DOS into two groups, one of which is a subset of the other. On a simpler level, networks intercept application MS-DOS calls and translate them into network calls. A superset of the network OS calls then deals with the problems of shared files and resources. For example, an MS-DOS write call to a station's local disk must be handled through the local MS-DOS, whereas a write to a file on a server's remote disk requires the network OS to redirect a call and pass it to the network's OS.

MS-NET and PC-NET use a set of interrupts, in addition to the standard single user MS-DOS calls, that provides network services to applications. Before discussing the specific interrupts, let's see how the network software interacts with MS-DOS and the application program.

A fundamental part of the MS-Net OS is the redirector. This function intercepts the application's MS-DOS calls and passes them to the network BIOS or back to the local MS-DOS for the appropriate processing. All disk I/O must go through MS-DOS, but because the network OS actually executes as an MS-DOS application, the redirector is always aware of the user's application requests.

Some network designers, such as Novell (Netware) have redesigned the network OS to act more as a network management system than as an MS-DOS application. The result is a network shell that runs over MS-DOS and processes requests before MS-DOS sees them. This increases the efficiency of the network OS and adds control over requests such as file sharing and remote resource management. The additional functionality provided by Novell has gained the attention of IBM. As a result, Netware has been endorsed by IBM as an enhanced version of PC-Net.

Novell's Netware is a good example of a network file server OS as opposed to a network disk server OS. Disk servers typically take I/O requests at the MS-DOS level, translating local MS-DOS read/write requests into special format commands that control the actual disk-level functions on remote shared hard disks. These systems are somewhat limited in providing file sharing and locking. The application has to provide MS-DOS with clumsy arguments, such as lock strings for file locking.

File servers are complete operating systems in their own right. These take MS-DOS requests for file service and translate them into I/O requests that are completely different from what the local MS-DOS understands. The file requests are carried out in an enhanced multiuser environment that specializes in file sharing, locking, and remote resource management—capabilities far beyond the local MS-DOS. The returned data is translated back to a format that the local MS-DOS understands (including error codes) and finally goes to the application.

Figure 7-5 shows how an application might interact with a network operating system—in this case MS-NET.

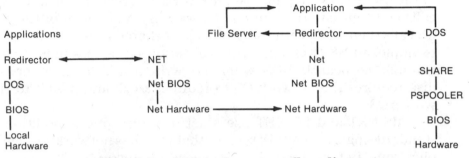

Fig. 7-5.   Network request flow diagram.

In Figure 7-5, you can see that an application's request for service passes through the redirector before the local MS-DOS. The local MS-DOS sees only the calls that have to deal with local I/O. The redirector sees the functions that have to do with the network and passes them to a server.

What network services are usually available for applications? The list varies from network to network but generally you can count on the following basic services:

    File sharing
    Record locking
    Create new file
    Create temporary unique file
    Get network information
    Direct file to shared printer
    Read file from remote device
    Write to a file on a remote device

These common services form the basis of network I/O. Depending on how sophisticated the network OS is, there are many combinations and variations of these basic services. Naturally, the more services that are available, the more your application can take advantage of the network's resources.

Let's take a closer look at some of the network services available under MS-NET. Remember that implementations probably differ between vendors.

INT 21h accesses many of the network services under MS-NET. These services are listed in Table 7-1.

Table 7-1.   MS-NET Network Services

Registers		Function
AH	**AL**	
3D	—	Open file for sharing
44	09	IOCTL—is device redirected?
44	0A	IOCTL—is handle local or remote?
44	0B	IOCTL—Change sharing retry count
59	—	Get extended error
5A	—	Create temporary file with unique name
5B	—	Create new file
5C	00	Lock byte range
5C	01	Unlock byte range
5E	00	Get machine name
5E	02	Setup printer control string
5F	02	Get assign list entry
5F	03	Redirect device to network
5F	04	Cancel redirection

Let's look at some of the network service functions to see how they are used on the network.

File Sharing

The most valuable network service is the ability to share files among multiple users. Generally this means that more than one user can read a file and can also add and update it. The two kinds of file sharing implementations involve either locking the whole file while it is updated or locking specific records (blocks) of a file.

File locking is a less sophisticated method of sharing files. When an application opens a file for reading and potentially for writing, the application must issue a lock file command. This secures the file from being updated by any other user on the network. This may be fine for a word processing program that is not normally a multiuser application. However, for a network database where records may be changed by different users, this method is inefficient.

Record (or block) locking is a fine-tuned method of protecting data against multiple writes. An application requests that specific blocks of a file be locked while the application updates them. This allows other users to update other blocks in the file at the same time.

Some networks go even further in their record locking calls by letting an application request an entire string of blocks to lock before implementing the lock function. This avoids the dreaded deadlock (or deadly-embrace) problem. Deadlock occurs when two processes wait for blocks to be released by the other process before updating and releasing their own blocks. The processes wait, theoretically forever, for the other to release the required data. By requesting the entire number of blocks and waiting for confirmation of ownership before actually locking the records, the potential for deadlock is eliminated.

MS-NET uses two classifications for a file when it is opened for read/write: deny-all and deny-none. If an application uses record locking, the file can be opened as deny-none. This allows other users to lock and update other records in the file. If the entire file must be protected or the application cannot do record locking, the deny-all attribute must be used. Locks can also be shared so that one application has exclusive write permission, whereas other processes can only read the records.

Under MS-NET, INT 21h, function 5Ch locks and unlocks regions of a file. If AL is 00h, the specified region is locked. If AL is set to 01h, the region is unlocked. The region is defined by giving the file handle, the high and low offset, and high and low length. If an error occurs—for example, the region or part of the file is already locked—the error flag is set in AX. The extended error call 59h can be used to get more information on why the error occurred.

Semaphores are another locking technique used on networks that specialize in multiuser and shared resources. Semaphores are labels for records, files, disks, printers, etc. Almost any physical or logical device on the network can potentially be locked for temporary write ownership. Semaphores work like gates; when one is closed by an application, no other processes can get through the gate to access the device or file. When an application is done with the device or file, the application unlocks the gate by opening the semaphore.

Novell's Netware incorporates semaphores into INT 21h, along with record locking. Table 7-2 shows the five semaphore functions available under Netware.

Table 7-2.   Netware's Five Semaphore Functions

Registers		Function
AH	AL	
C5	00	Open a semaphore
C5	01	Examine a semaphore
C5	02	Wait for a semaphore
C5	03	Signal a semaphore
C5	04	Close a semaphore

These functions allow even more control in multiuser situations than record locking.

Temporary Work Files

A single-user application often opens temporary files to work on while leaving the original file untouched. Usually a standard name is given to these temporary files. This works fine for single-user systems where no one else accesses the same disk space. However, if another user uses the same application to open another file in a shared directory area, the temporary files with the common name continuously overwrite each other.

A solution to this problem in a shared environment is to create temporary files with unique names. The application should leave this naming function up to the network OS. The MS-NET function call 5Ah (Create Unique File) creates unique temporary file names that an application can use. The call is made by placing 5Ah in register AH and a pointer in DS:DX to an ASCIZ string that describes the path to a directory where the file is to be placed. On return, DS:DX has the temporary unique file name appended to the pathname. The file handle is returned in AX. The temporary file is not automatically removed when the program terminates. You must delete the file before restoring the OS environment.

Create New File

Another example of file-name conflict in shared environments arises out of the practice of an application program creating a file in two separate steps. Normally, an application requests that MS-DOS check whether a file name already exists. If it doesn't, the application requests MS-DOS to create a new file. This may cause problems if another application opens a file by the same name between the check for existence and the file creation.

MS-NET solves this problem by supplying a function called Create New File (function 5Bh). This procedure combines the file-name search with a file creation in one uninterrupted sequence. If the file name exists, an indicator is returned to the application and the file creation process is aborted. If no duplicate file names are found, the file is created in read/write mode.

Network Information Calls

Most networks supply BIOS calls for getting information about the network, such as disk space, record locks, system time and date, spool and printer status, number of users, and user and machine addresses.

The MS-NET function call INT 2Ah, 0500h returns network resource information to the calling application. This information includes the number of network names, the number of network commands available, and the number of network sessions available. Invoke INT 2Ah, 0500h before using any network commands. You need to keep track of the returned information to avoid calling more resources than are configured in the network. If the application needs more resources than are available, an error should be generated to the user indicating that the network should be reconfigured before running the application. Be specific about what needs to be changed, for example, more sessions may be needed.

These calls permit an application to have direct knowledge of changeable network parameters. An application that takes advantage of this information can more readily adapt to network resources and conditions.

Redirect Devices

Part of the power of a network lies in the ability of a program to receive input from and direct output to other devices. Some networks have this ability. For example, an application may be able to send output to a specific printer attached to another microcomputer or to a hard disk on a remote server. Network services must supply methods of naming these devices and directing commands to those devices.

MS-NET uses the MS-DOS Redirect Device function (number 5F03h) for directing output through the network. This function permits sending files to remote printers (BL = 03) or to remote disk drives (BL = 04). DS:SI defines the source ASCIZ device name and ES:DI defines the destination network path. A password may be necessary to set redirection for certain devices. The method for defining the destination network path is as follows:

- Printers are defined by the name of the attached computer, and a short name for the printer itself. These values are predefined by the network configuration program and the network manager.

- Files are sent to remote disk drives by defining the source of the file (the local drive letter) and the network path to the destination resource (that is, the directory on a remote disk).

Once the redirection is made, all files or print jobs sent to the local drive or print device (that is, PRN, LPT1, etc.) are sent instead to the associated name. The Get Redirection List function call (5F02h) is used to get the names of local devices that have been redirected, along with their destination network path.

Redirection can be canceled with function 5F04h—Cancel Redirection. DS:SI holds the device name or pathname that is to be removed. All further commands to that local device act on that device instead of the previously associated device.

File Control Blocks and the MS-NET HANDLE Functions

If you are familiar with MS-DOS, you know about FCBs (file control blocks). These are descriptions of the files that are used when reading and writing files. However, when writing for the MS-NET environment, FCBs SHOULD NOT be used. FCBs do not have any of the file sharing or locking functions needed for files in a network. Microsoft has added a file descriptor called HANDLE to describe files in the network environment.

The HANDLE function calls allow an application to describe access privileges for other users and to specify files in other directories. Handles employ a different method for creating and opening files than with FCBs. An application uses a pointer to an ASCIZ string that describes the drive letter, directory path and file name of the file that the applications wants to open. When creating a file, the read/write privileges are also specified in the string. The network OS returns a value that is called the file handle. Any I/O to that file which is performed by the application uses the handle value instead of the entire string as specified earlier. This frees the application from having to be in the same directory as the opened file. (Handle has its own sequential I/O functions for reading (3Fh) and writing (40h) to the file.)

Network Control Blocks

MS-NET (and PC-NET) use NCBs (network control blocks) to pass commands from an application to the local network hardware (for example, the network adapter board.) The network hardware translates these NCB formatted requests by passing them through the layers of network software. Each layer adds its own control functions as required by the protocols. The NCB stays resident in local memory until the process is finished. Results of the NCB command are returned in a special NCB return code field or in a register (usually AL).

NCBs have 13 fields that must be filled in by the application (and one reserved field for the BIOS). The NCB fields are summarized below.

NCB_COMMAND—the command number issued to the local network hardware. Examples: Reset, Cancel, Status, Net Errors, Add Names (addresses of other nodes and processes), session commands, datagram support commands

NCB_RETCODE—the error codes returned on command success or failure. Examples: 00h—success, 03h—invalid command, 21h—interface busy

NCB_LSN—a number identifying the session link with another process on the network

NCB_NUM—a number indicating another name on the network. Used to send datagrams

NCB_BUFFER ADDRESS—a 4-byte pointer to a buffer used along with an NCB_COMMAND

NCB_LENGTH—the length of the data to be transferred

NCB_CALLNAME—the name of the receiver of the command or data, local network hardware addresses or remote nodes

NCB_NAME—the name of the local process that issued the NCB, that is, you

NCB_RTO—a field defining the local session time-out for receive commands

NCB_STO—a field defining the local session time-out for send commands

NCB_POST ADDRESS—a field pointing to the address of a routine to be executed after an NCB_COMMAND has been completed

NCB_LANA NUM—the values 00h or 01h select which of two network hardware boards the NCB is directed to

NCB_CMD_CPLT—the command status, for instance, pending, completed, completed with error

NCB_RESERVE—reserved for the BIOS

Some of these NCB fields have default values that relieve programmers from having to consider each value when simple local procedures are being done.

A great deal of flexibility is built into the NCB system of network communication. For example, interstation communication is supported through the use of the session control features of the NCB. This opens up a wide range of possibilities, such as communication between applications.

Using Networks with Non-MS-DOS Computers

Another network option is the use of a non-MS-DOS computer as a file or device server on the network. Because of the popularity of MS-DOS computers and their prevalence in the workplace, many manufacturers of larger computers are providing support for networking their non-MS-DOS computers with the IBM PC series (and compatibles). One example is the DECNET network offered by Digital Equipment Corportation for use with their VAX series of super-minicomputers.

This support usually consists of a program that runs on the larger computer (usually called the *host* in this context) and another program that runs on the MS-DOS machine. These programs allow the MS-DOS user to access the larger file storage capacity of the host (usually hundreds of megabytes) as well as printers and other serial devices connected to the host.

Unlike standard MS-DOS networks, these host-based networks support true "shared" access in that each of the network's MS-DOS nodes thinks that it has ownership of the host's resources. For example, the host's printer is always available to the MS-DOS node. This is made possible only through the extensive multiuser systems support built into the host's operating system.

Because of the large market in this area, many manufacturers of both MS-DOS computers and host computers are developing almost daily new products for this type of network. Look forward to versions of MS-DOS in the near future that support the entire network interaction in the system, totally transparent to the user or application program! You can also expect to see support for all popular protocols and transmission media at a resonable cost, including serial (RS-232), Ethernet, MAP, and so forth.

Software Licensing for Networks

One issue about multiaccess software on networks may directly affect you, the application programmer, in the pocket. As with any software for personal computers, the problem of illegal copying and distribution can be a sore spot for all parties involved. You, of course, would like to be paid for your software by every person who uses it. The end user would like to be able to buy a single copy and have everyone on the network access it without elaborate copy protection tricks making it troublesome to use. Both are legitimate points of view.

No matter what trick you come up with, there is sure to be someone who finds a way to get around it and who probably makes money doing it. A really complex copying or distribution trap annoys the end user and decreases your referral sales. No single method prevents the overuse of your software on a network. Trying to sell the software as a *system* is a solution for multiuser network environments. If customers believe that the product is really good and works with all the network's resources, they may be more willing to pay a higher price for a network version than a single-user version. Common sense can prevail over a tight budget.

Summary

This chapter has introduced you to the general concepts of networks and presented some examples of programming in networks' shared resource environment. It would be impossible to cover all of the available networks and their operating systems. MS-NET alone would require an entire book just to acquaint you with all of the programming requirements.

We hope that the important point of writing and adapting software for networks has been made. The future of business software belongs to multiuser (multiaccess) distributed processing systems. To think in these terms when conceiving and creating your applications is to participate in the next generation of tools for the computer work place.

RECOVERY

Disk Layout and File Recovery Information   Chapter 8

If you've been using MS-DOS for a while, you probably have inadvertently deleted or accidentally lost a file that you later realized you needed. The ERASE (or DEL) command in MS-DOS is very useful and powerful and, by its very nature, is a destructive command. Its destructiveness, of course, is essential for it to accomplish its task, but when we're careless, it can become more destructive than we want it to be.

The only safeguard against inadvertently deleting files with the ERASE or DEL command is displayed when you specify that all files on a disk be deleted by entering ERASE *.*. A prompt asks whether you're sure you want the operation executed. If you enter N (for no), the command's execution is stopped. But when you use the command to delete a particular file or group of files, the only other safeguard is to discipline yourself to freeze your fingers before pressing the RETURN (or ENTER) key and to carefully examine the file-delete command sequence you've just typed. Even then, no matter how certain we may be that the file or files we've specified for deletion are the ones we ultimately want deleted, at some point we'll make a mistake. Because computers are designed to obey your commands to the letter, your request for deleting files is executed immediately after you've pressed the RETURN or ENTER key following the command sequence.

So what does one do when a file that hasn't been backed up is accidentally deleted? Fortunately, the MS-DOS file system was designed so that, under certain conditions, restoring a file isn't difficult. As a result of this design, several utilities have been developed to recover erased files. Some of these are in the public domain. Others are commercially available products. One utility which you've probably heard of is called UE (UnErase), which is included in the set of utilities for MS-DOS called the Norton Utilities. Another similar product is called Ultra Utilities, which consists of a set of utilities in the "freeware" category currently available through various channels of public domain software distribution. (A donation is requested for user registration with the originators of the programs.)

In this chapter, we discuss how to use Norton Utilities and Ultra Utilities for recovering erased files and how to use the MS-DOS utilities CHKDSK and RECOVER for recovering damaged files. First, you must understand how the MS-DOS file system works so that you understand the limitations of these file-recovery utilities. Note that both Norton Utilities and Ultra Utilities operate only on IBM Personal Computers or close compatibles. Both Norton Utilities and Ultra Utilities work with standard 5¼-inch floppy disks. Starting with version 2.01, Norton Utilities also supports the recovery of files on hard disks (10-megabyte hard disks on the IBM PC or compatible environment), and Norton Utilities version 3.0 includes support for both the IBM AT's 20-megabyte hard disk and extended-capacity floppy format (under MS-DOS version 3.0 or later).

Although both these utility packages are extremely useful in the environments for which they were designed, they may not work properly in your particular MS-DOS environment, especially if your system is not an IBM PC or not sufficiently compatible with the IBM PC. For this reason, this chapter includes a program that you can try if the other utilities fail or if you decide they are not appropriate for your machine. The program called RESCUE is simple in design so that it can be expanded and customized as the environment of your system changes with the addition of different types of disk drives. RESCUE is designed to support 5¼-inch disks that adhere to the standard formats of MS-DOS versions 1.0 through 2.1 but can be easily enhanced to include higher-capacity 5¼-inch and 8-inch disks. Before we show you how to use Norton and Ultra Utilities and the alternate program RESCUE presented in this chapter let's begin with the basics of the MS-DOS floppy disk storage system and file recovery.

Principles of File Recovery

You probably are wondering how it is possible to restore a file that's been erased. It would seem, initially, that if a file is erased, it must have been wiped off the face of the disk forever. This initial assumption is partially correct because after a file is erased it is no longer visible or accessible by any of the standard MS-DOS commands.

Each file stored by MS-DOS on a disk, however, consists of the following three parts:

1. The file's directory entry,
2. The file's space allocation, and
3. The data sectors containing the data of the file itself.

When a file is erased, only the first two parts of the file, the directory entry and the space allocation, are affected. These two parts act as control points for MS-DOS to reference the file's data sectors. The data sectors of the file, however, are not erased, which is why it is possible to recover a file if we know something about the first two parts of the file. We'll talk about the space allocation and directory sections in more detail a little further on, but first we'll cover the layout of disks that have been formatted in various ways under MS-DOS.

Layouts of 5¼-Inch, 40-Track, Single-Sided Floppy Disks

Figure 8-1 shows the basic layout of a 5¼-inch, 40-track, single-sided disk. It shows the tracks and sectors and provides an example of how file data can be arranged on a disk. The first part shows the layout of a disk formatted to eight sectors per track. The portion to the right shows the difference on Track 0 of a disk formatted to nine sectors per track.

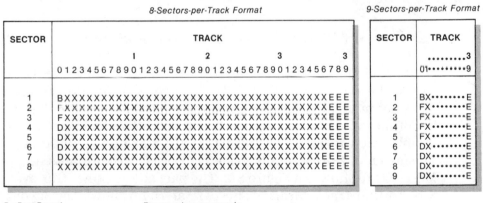

B = Boot Record
D = Directory Entry
F = File Allocation Table

For example purposes only:
X = Sectors containing file data
E = Empty sectors

Fig. 8-1.   Information layout on a single-sided, 40-track, 5¼-inch floppy disk.

The left part of Figure 8-1 shows the simplest disk format under MS-DOS. Because all standard disk formats under MS-DOS support a sector size of 512 bytes, we can easily verify the information in Figure 8-1 by calculating the total capacity of the disk as follows:

40 tracks × 8 sectors × 512 bytes = 163,840 bytes (160Kb) total capacity

The total disk capacity value shown above can be checked against the results displayed when the FORMAT or CHKDSK command is used.

A disk formatted to nine sectors per track (MS-DOS version 2.0 and above only) is similar to an 8-sector-per-track disk (as shown on the right of Fig. 8-1), except that a ninth sector is added at the end of each track, thereby increasing total disk space. This can be verified with the following formula and checked against the results displayed by the FORMAT or CHKDSK command:

$$40 \text{ tracks} \times 9 \text{ sectors} \times 512 \text{ bytes} = 184{,}320 \text{ bytes (180Kb) total capacity}$$

Another difference between 8- and 9-sector-per-track disks is the number of FAT (file allocation table) sectors. Although both formats have one boot sector and four directory sectors, the number of FAT sectors is greater in the 9-sector-per-track format. Eight-sector-per-track disks have two FAT sectors (Sectors 2 and 3 of Track 0). Nine-sector-per-track disks have four FAT sectors (Sectors 2 through 5 of Track 0). The extra number of FAT sectors in 9-sector-per-track disks is necessary for the extra file space permitted by the 40 extra sectors (one per track).

Layouts of 5¼-Inch, 40-Track, Double-Sided Floppy Disks

Double-sided, 40-track, floppy disks formatted under MS-DOS are assigned the same number of FAT sectors (proportionally) as single-sided disks but more directory sectors are provided to increase the total number of files that can be stored on a disk. In both 8- and 9-sector-per-track double-sided formats, seven sectors are assigned as directory sectors. The layout of the two double-sided, 40-track, disk formats supported by MS-DOS are shown in Figure 8-2. The part at left shows the layout in the 8-sector-per-track format. The part at right shows the layout in the 9-sector-per-track format.

The layout of the disk in Figure 8-2 is very similar to the one in Figure 8-1. Notice, however, that on all double-sided floppy disks formatted under MS-DOS, storage information on a track always begins at Side 0, Sector 1; moves to the last sector of the track; continues from Side 1, Sector 1 to the last sector of the track; then reverts back to Side 0, starting with the first sector on the next track; and so on until the last sector on the last track of Side 1 is reached. Also note that the arrangement of directory sectors and FAT sectors differs from that of single-sided disks. Both double-sided formats have one boot track and have proportionally the same number of FAT sectors as single-sided disks. However, the number of directory sectors for both double-sided formats is increased to seven. Again, by comparing the results of the following calculations with the results of the CHKDSK program, we can verify the total capacity of the two 40-track, double-sided floppy disk formats.

40 tracks × 8 sectors × 512 bytes × 2 sides = 327,680 bytes (320Kb) total capacity

40 tracks × 9 sectors × 512 bytes × 2 sides = 368,640 bytes (360Kb) total capacity

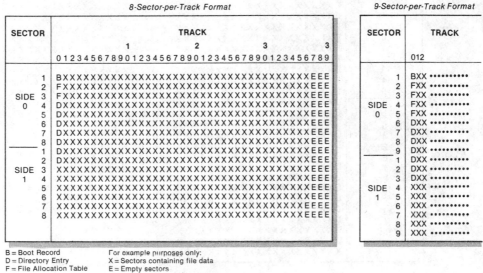

Fig. 8-2. **Information layout on a double-sided, 40-track, 5¼-inch floppy disk.**

Layouts of 5¼-Inch, 80-Track, Double-Sided Floppy Disks

MS-DOS version 3.0 supports a new floppy disk format, commonly known as the "extended-capacity" format, which provides a data storage capacity of 1.2 million bytes. The structure of this format is very similar to the older formats we've just described. The format's higher capacity depends on the use of floppy disks with double the number of tracks (80) and the formatting of more sectors (15) per track. Figure 8-3 illustrates the layout of this format and shows the higher number of directory and FAT sectors needed to support the extended capacity.

The following formula can be used to verify the results displayed by the CHKDSK program when it is used with an 80-track 5¼-inch floppy disk.

80 tracks × 15 sectors × 512 bytes × 2 sides = 1,228,800 bytes (1,200Kb or 1.2Mb) total capacity

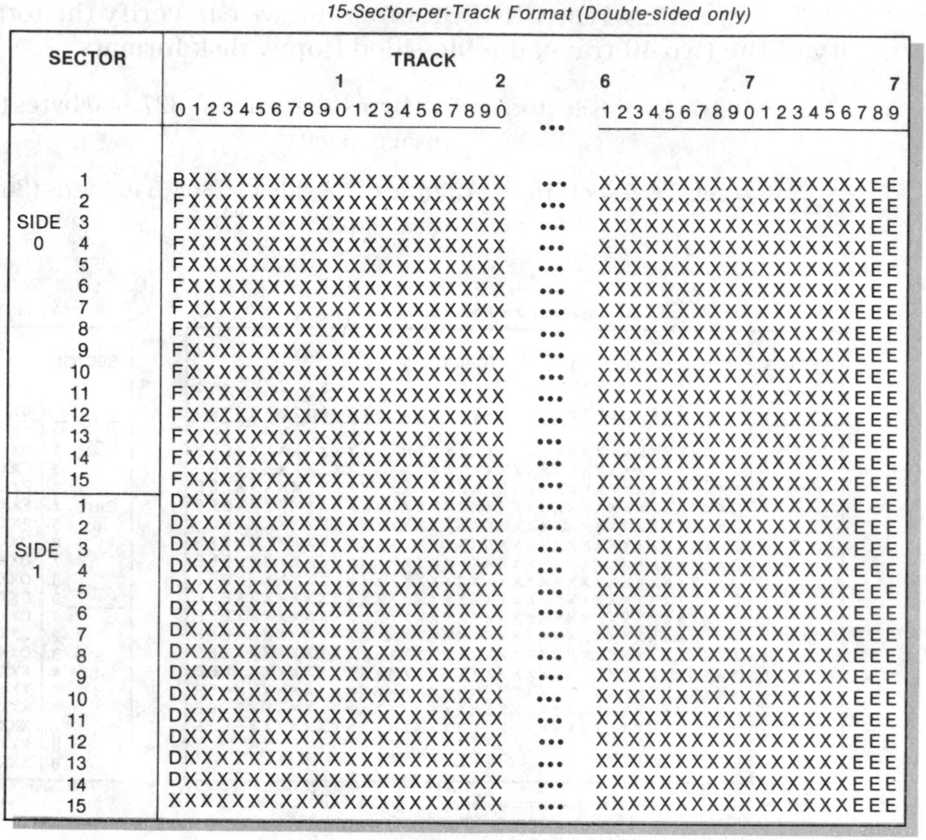

```
                        15-Sector-per-Track Format (Double-sided only)

    SECTOR                      TRACK
                        1               2        6         7               7
                        0 1 2 3 4 5 6 7 8 9 0 1 2 3 4 5 6 7 8 9 0    1 2 3 4 5 6 7 8 9 0 1 2 3 4 5 6 7 8 9

            1       B X X X X X X X X X X X X X X X X X X X X   ...  X X X X X X X X X X X X X X X X X X E E
            2       F X X X X X X X X X X X X X X X X X X X X   ...  X X X X X X X X X X X X X X X X X X E E
  SIDE   3       F X X X X X X X X X X X X X X X X X X X X   ...  X X X X X X X X X X X X X X X X X X E E
   0     4       F X X X X X X X X X X X X X X X X X X X X   ...  X X X X X X X X X X X X X X X X X X E E
            5       F X X X X X X X X X X X X X X X X X X X X   ...  X X X X X X X X X X X X X X X X X X E E
            6       F X X X X X X X X X X X X X X X X X X X X   ...  X X X X X X X X X X X X X X X X X X E E
            7       F X X X X X X X X X X X X X X X X X X X X   ...  X X X X X X X X X X X X X X X X X E E E
            8       F X X X X X X X X X X X X X X X X X X X X   ...  X X X X X X X X X X X X X X X X X E E E
            9       F X X X X X X X X X X X X X X X X X X X X   ...  X X X X X X X X X X X X X X X X X E E E
           10       F X X X X X X X X X X X X X X X X X X X X   ...  X X X X X X X X X X X X X X X X X E E E
           11       F X X X X X X X X X X X X X X X X X X X X   ...  X X X X X X X X X X X X X X X X X E E E
           12       F X X X X X X X X X X X X X X X X X X X X   ...  X X X X X X X X X X X X X X X X X E E E
           13       F X X X X X X X X X X X X X X X X X X X X   ...  X X X X X X X X X X X X X X X X X E E E
           14       F X X X X X X X X X X X X X X X X X X X X   ...  X X X X X X X X X X X X X X X X X E E E
           15       F X X X X X X X X X X X X X X X X X X X X   ...  X X X X X X X X X X X X X X X X X E E E

            1       D X X X X X X X X X X X X X X X X X X X X   ...  X X X X X X X X X X X X X X X X X E E E
            2       D X X X X X X X X X X X X X X X X X X X X   ...  X X X X X X X X X X X X X X X X X E E E
  SIDE   3       D X X X X X X X X X X X X X X X X X X X X   ...  X X X X X X X X X X X X X X X X X E E E
   1     4       D X X X X X X X X X X X X X X X X X X X X   ...  X X X X X X X X X X X X X X X X X E E E
            5       D X X X X X X X X X X X X X X X X X X X X   ...  X X X X X X X X X X X X X X X X X E E E
            6       D X X X X X X X X X X X X X X X X X X X X   ...  X X X X X X X X X X X X X X X X X E E E
            7       D X X X X X X X X X X X X X X X X X X X X   ...  X X X X X X X X X X X X X X X X X E E E
            8       D X X X X X X X X X X X X X X X X X X X X   ...  X X X X X X X X X X X X X X X X X E E E
            9       D X X X X X X X X X X X X X X X X X X X X   ...  X X X X X X X X X X X X X X X X X E E E
           10       D X X X X X X X X X X X X X X X X X X X X   ...  X X X X X X X X X X X X X X X X X E E E
           11       D X X X X X X X X X X X X X X X X X X X X   ...  X X X X X X X X X X X X X X X X X E E E
           12       D X X X X X X X X X X X X X X X X X X X X   ...  X X X X X X X X X X X X X X X X X E E E
           13       D X X X X X X X X X X X X X X X X X X X X   ...  X X X X X X X X X X X X X X X X X E E E
           14       D X X X X X X X X X X X X X X X X X X X X   ...  X X X X X X X X X X X X X X X X X E E E
           15       X X X X X X X X X X X X X X X X X X X X X   ...  X X X X X X X X X X X X X X X X X E E E
```

B = Boot Record   For example purposes only:
D = Directory Entry   X = Sectors containing file data
F = File Allocation Table   E = Empty sectors

**Fig. 8-3.   Information layout on an ''extended-capacity,''
double-sided, 80-track, 5¼-inch floppy disk.**

Now that we're armed with the basic information we need about the definitions of sectors in the five main 5¼-inch floppy disk formats, we're ready to tackle the information that's actually inside the boot sector, each directory sector, and the FAT sectors. Although all sectors on a disk are potentially important when recovering files, we normally need concern ourselves only with the directory sectors, the FAT sectors, and the data sectors. The boot sector is of little importance in recovering files, but a description of what this sector contains is presented next to complement the definitions of the other sectors.

The Boot Sector

The very first sector on a disk formatted under MS-DOS is always defined as the boot record. It always contains a short program that is automatically loaded into memory when the disk is used to load the MS-DOS operating system after system power-up or reset. This program then instructs the computer where to look for the files on the disk that contain the MS-DOS operating system. Once the files are found, the boot program loads the files into memory and transfers control to MS-DOS. Because the number of MS-DOS files and the way in which they are stored may differ according to the type of implementation (IBM PC, Compaq, CompuPro, for example), the contents of the boot record may vary. For the sake of consistency, the boot sector is always defined first on a formatted disk, regardless of whether you intend to make the disk a "boot" disk or a "data-only" disk. Even though the boot sector is of little value when recovering files, you need to know that the first sector of the disk is always stored with the boot record and is never used for anything else.

Although the FAT sectors are next in the sequence of sectors on the disk, we're going to talk about the directory sectors next because you must understand what the directory sectors contain in order to understand what is stored on the rest of the disk.

The Directory Sectors

The directory sectors store the directory information for all files on the disk. When you issue the DIR command, the information displayed is obtained directly from the directory sectors and nowhere else on the disk. Regardless of the MS-DOS disk format, each directory sector contains space for 16 directory entries. Because a sector is always 512 bytes long, we can easily deduce that each directory entry is 32 bytes in length. The total number of directory entries permitted for the entire disk depends on how many directory sectors are defined. For example, single-sided disks have a total of 64 directory entries, whereas double-sided 40-track disks have a total of 112 directory entries and double-sided 80-track disks have a total of 224 directory entries. In most hard disks, the total number of directory entries depends on how the disk is formatted. In the case of the IBM PC and some compatible systems, the total number of directory entries depends on the size of the MS-DOS partition created when the disk is first formatted. The total number of directory entries determines the maximum number of files that can be stored on the disk.

The information contained in a directory entry is divided into six components, four of which are directly or indirectly relevant to recovering erased files. Figure 8-4 shows the components of a directory entry, the length of each component, and how each is defined.

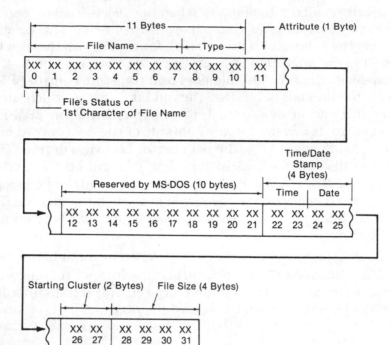

Fig. 8-4.   Components of a directory entry.

The four parts of a directory entry with which we need to be concerned, as shown in Figure 8-4, are the file name and type, the attribute(s), the starting cluster, and the file size.

File Name, File Type, and File Status
The file name and type consist of 11 bytes, each byte containing an ASCII character, and represent the name of the file to which the directory entry corresponds. In MS-DOS versions 2.0 and above, the file name in a directory entry always refers to a file in the root directory. Because subdirectory names are treated as files by MS-DOS, they also have their own entries in the directory sectors. A subdirectory name, however, contains information in its directory entry that is slightly different from normal files. We'll cover these differences in following sections of this chapter.

Note also that under MS-DOS versions 2.0 and above, the maximum number of files or directory entries that a floppy disk can accommodate (64, 112, and 224) correspond only to the root directory. Because all files stored in a subdirectory have directory entries in the subdirectory "file" itself, there is effectively no limit to the number of files that can be stored on a disk within the space provided by the particular type of disk and format. We'll talk about subdirectories and file recovery in more detail later in this chapter.

When a file is erased, two things happen to the disk. The first item affected is the first character of the file name in the directory entry. As shown in Figure 8-4, the first byte in a directory entry can either indicate the file's status or represent the first ASCII character of the file's name. If a directory entry has not been used since the disk was last formatted, this first byte is always set to 00. In this way, MS-DOS only needs to read the first byte of a directory entry to determine whether it can be used. When a file is created, the first byte is changed to represent the first character of the file's name. When the file is later erased, the first byte is changed to a hexadecimal value of E5. The rest of the information in the erased file's directory entry is left intact. When you examine the disk's sectors for the information on the erased file's directory entry, this value is your first clue that the desired directory entry has been found.

The second clue, of course, is the presentation of the rest of the file's name and type in ASCII format. But the first character of hex value E5 tells you that the directory entry represents an erased file. The byte is set to this value so that MS-DOS knows that the directory entry is free to be overwritten with new file information should the space be needed. Thankfully, the designers of MS-DOS saw fit to implement file deletion in this manner. Because they did, we are able (most of the time) to restore a file that has just been erased.

Attribute

The attribute byte contains information about the file's storage attributes. Attributes indicate how MS-DOS treats the file. Table 8-1 shows the definitions of each attribute and the respective hexadecimal values that can be stored in the attribute byte. Each bit in the byte defines a specific attribute and is set to 1 when the attribute is assigned to the file.

Table 8-1.   File Attribute Definitions

Bit	Hex Value	Attribute
1st	80	Not defined (in MS-DOS version 3.0 and below)
2nd	40	Not defined (in MS-DOS version 3.0 and below)
3rd	20	ARCHIVE STATUS: set when the file has been opened and closed and is used by some hard disk backup and restore utilities
4th	10	SUBDIRECTORY ENTRY: indicates that the directory entry pertains to a subdirectory "file"

Table 8-1. cont.

Bit	Hex Value	Attribute
5th	08	VOLUME LABEL: indicates that directory entry contains a volume label (DOS 2.0 and above only); rest of entry contains no useful information
6th	04	SYSTEM STATUS: serves no useful purpose but functions in same manner as hidden status
7th	02	HIDDEN STATUS: file is excluded from normal directory searches
8th	01	READ-ONLY STATUS: file cannot be erased

Notice that a file can have more than one attribute. For example, if a file is assigned the read-only (hex 01) and hidden (hex 02) attributes, the resulting value in the attribute byte is the sum of both attribute values—hex 03. Information contained in the attribute byte may or may not be useful when recovering a file. For example, we wouldn't very likely try to recover a file that is assigned the read-only attribute unless we were trying to recover a damaged disk. We normally won't care what the file's attributes are, but if we're recovering a file with the hidden attribute assigned to it, we want to change the attribute because otherwise we won't be able to see the file listed when we use the DIR command to verify that the file was recovered. Another reason we may want to reference the file's attribute byte is if we try to recover a subdirectory name.

Starting Cluster

A starting cluster is a 2-byte, 16-digit binary number that represents the first section of the disk occupied by the file. This section of the disk is referred to as a *cluster*. Although we've shown a disk formatted by MS-DOS mapped out in terms of tracks and sectors, MS-DOS actually views the disk in terms of clusters of sectors rather than individual sectors. The starting cluster is the initial "pointer" to the file's first data sector as well as to subsequent pointers in the FAT sectors. Having read this initial pointer in the directory entry, MS-DOS proceeds to read the rest of the pointers to the file's data sectors in the FAT sectors. We talk about FAT sectors next, but for now note that referencing the starting cluster is one of the most important first stages in the restoration of an erased or damaged file.

File Size

A file's size is represented by a 4-byte binary number, the first byte of which represents the least significant part of the file's size. The fourth byte is the most significant part of the file size and we use that value to determine the exact length of a file and thus determine the number of sectors that an erased file occupies or is supposed to occupy.

Now that the essential portions of the directory entry have been defined, we move on to the FAT sectors. The information in these sectors provides additional clues about how an erased or damaged file can be recovered.

File Allocation Table (FAT) Sectors

The sectors containing the FAT are used by MS-DOS to determine the locations on the disk of each part of every file. Unlike some operating systems which always store files consecutively and utilize sectors in a contiguous manner, MS-DOS is capable of storing files and parts of each file in a random manner. A system that always stores files contiguously keeps track of files more easily and can thus access the files more quickly. To recover a file that is stored contiguously, we need only locate the beginning and end of the file. All the data in between pertains to the file.

But contiguous file storage is less efficient when a file that is stored between several files is deleted and replaced by a larger file. For if the free space made available by the deleted file is not large enough to accommodate the new file, sufficient contiguous space for the new file must be allocated toward the end of the string of files. If the disk doesn't contain sufficient space for the file, the disk is considered full. This can pose a real problem when using floppy disks with fairly low storage capacity because a lot of storage space can go to waste. MS-DOS and similar disk-based microcomputer operating systems were designed to allow random storage as well as contiguous or sequential storage. The information in the FAT sectors permits MS-DOS to accomplish this feat.

When a disk is first formatted under MS-DOS and several files are copied to that disk, information stored in the FAT sectors is used by MS-DOS to determine the location of each part of a file. Files are referenced by the FAT in terms of clusters. A file always occupies at least one cluster and, if it is large enough, is divided into several clusters. A cluster is really a section of allocation and consists of one data sector in single-sided floppy disks and two data sectors in double-sided floppy disks. The entire data storage area of a disk (except for the boot, FAT, and directory sectors) is divided equally into clusters, and the entire range of clusters is mapped out by the FAT. Figures 8-5 and 8-6 show how single- and double-sided, 40-track, floppy disks, in both the 8- and 9-sector formats, are mapped in terms of clusters. Figure 8-7 shows how the 80-track "extended capacity" floppy disk is mapped out.

8-Sector-per-Track Format

SECTOR	TRACK				
	0	1	2		39
1	Boot	3	11	········	•
2	FAT#1	4	12	········	•
3	FAT#2	5	13	········	309
4	Dir	6	14	········	310
5	Dir	7	15	········	311
6	Dir	8	16	········	312
7	Dir	9	•	········	313
8	2	10	•	········	314

9-Sector-per-Track Format

SECTOR	TRACK				
	0	1	2		39
1	Boot	2	11	········	•
2	FAT#1	3	12	········	•
3	FAT#1	4	13	········	346
4	FAT#2	5	14	········	347
5	FAT#2	6	15	········	348
6	Dir	7	16	········	349
7	Dir	8	17	········	350
8	Dir	9	•	········	351
9	Dir	10	•	········	352

Fig. 8-5.   Cluster numbers in single-sided, 40-track, floppy disks.

Notice that in the previous three figures the FAT sectors are either numbered one or two. They're shown this way because the designers of the MS-DOS file system reserved twice as many FAT sectors as are actually necessary to map out the disk. A possible reason for this design was to allow room for the FAT to grow with larger capacity floppy disks. In versions 1.0 through 3.1 of MS-DOS, however, the extra set of sectors is used to store an exact copy of the FAT. Having redundant sets of the FAT can prove to be convenient if the first set is damaged for some reason. Repairing a damaged FAT can be very tedious and complicated. When recovering files, however, you normally only need to reference the first FAT.

Each cluster on the disk has a corresponding FAT entry. The FAT entry that corresponds to the first cluster of a file contains the number of the next cluster occupied by that file. By looking in the FAT entry corresponding to this "next" cluster, we either find that the end of the file has been reached or the entry contains the number of yet another cluster occupied by the file. Thus, the FAT entries effectively contain

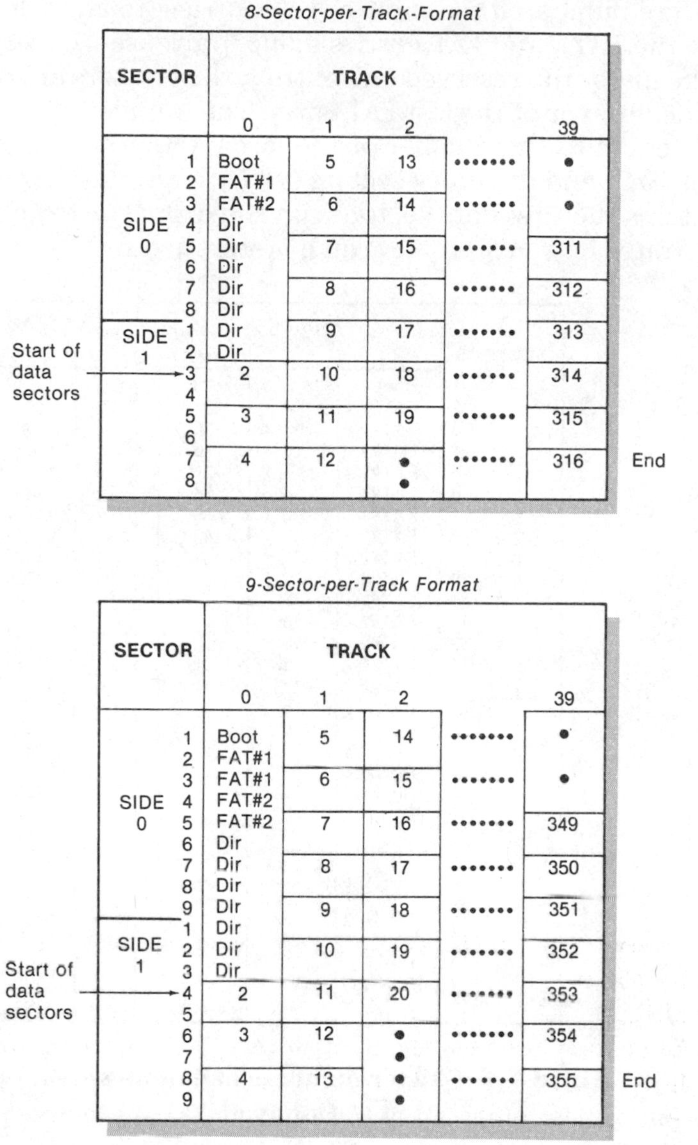

8-Sector-per-Track-Format

SIDE	SECTOR	TRACK 0	1	2		39	
SIDE 0	1	Boot	5	13	....	•	
	2	FAT#1					
	3	FAT#2	6	14	....	•	
	4	Dir					
	5	Dir	7	15	....	311	
	6	Dir					
	7	Dir	8	16	....	312	
	8	Dir					
SIDE 1	1	Dir	9	17	....	313	
	2	Dir					
	3	2	10	18	....	314	
	4						
	5	3	11	19	....	315	
	6						
	7	4	12	•	....	316	End
	8			•			

Start of data sectors → (SIDE 1, sector 3)

9-Sector-per-Track Format

SIDE	SECTOR	TRACK 0	1	2		39	
SIDE 0	1	Boot	5	14	....	•	
	2	FAT#1					
	3	FAT#1	6	15	....	•	
	4	FAT#2					
	5	FAT#2	7	16	....	349	
	6	Dir					
	7	Dir	8	17	....	350	
	8	Dir					
	9	Dir	9	18	....	351	
SIDE 1	1	Dir					
	2	Dir	10	19	....	352	
	3	Dir					
	4	2	11	20	....	353	
	5						
	6	3	12	•	....	354	
	7			•			
	8	4	13	•	....	355	End
	9			•			

Start of data sectors → (SIDE 1, sector 4)

Fig. 8-6. Cluster numbers in double-sided, 40-track, floppy disks.

pointers both to the clusters occupied by the file and to subsequent FAT entries that correspond to additional clusters occupied by the file. Because the total number of entries in the FAT sectors exceeds the total number of clusters on the disk, the entire disk can be easily mapped even when it has reached maximum storage capacity. In Figures 8-5, 8-6, and 8-7, the numbering of clusters begins with 2. This is because clusters are numbered the same as FAT entries (to allow for quick indexing into the FAT), and FAT entries 0 and 1 are used for other purposes. To make up for the reserved FAT entries, the clusters are numbered from 2 to the number of the last FAT entry. The number of clusters on a disk is thus equal to the number of the last FAT entry minus 1. Because the boot, FAT, and directory sectors do not have cluster numbers, cluster 2 contains the first data sector(s) on the disk. The example in Figure 8-8 illustrates how FAT entries can be referenced.

| | | TRACKS | | | | TRACK |
SECTORS		0	1	2		79
	1	Boot	3	33		•
	2	FAT#1	4	34		•
	3	FAT#1	5	35		1166
	4	FAT#1	6	36		1167
	5	FAT#1	7	37		1168
	6	FAT#1	8	38		1169
	7	FAT#1	9	39		1170
SIDE 0	8	FAT#1	10	40		1171
	9	FAT#2	11	•		1172
	10	FAT#2	12	•		1173
	11	FAT#2	13	•		1174
	12	FAT#2	14	•		1175
	13	FAT#2	15	•		1176
	14	FAT#2	16	•		1177
	15	FAT#2	17	•		1178
	1	Dir	18	•		1179
	2	Dir	19	•		1180
	3	Dir	20	•		1181
	4	Dir	21	•		1182
	5	Dir	22	•		1183
	6	Dir	23	•		1184
SIDE 1	7	Dir	24	•		1185
	8	Dir	25	•		1186
	9	Dir	26	•		1187
	10	Dir	27	•		1188
	11	Dir	28	•		1189
	12	Dir	29	•		1191
	13	Dir	30	•		1192
Start of data sectors →	14	Dir	31	•		1193
	15	2	32	•		1194

Fig. 8-7. Cluster numbers in double-sided, 80-track, floppy disks.

Decoding the FAT Entries

The value in FAT entry 0 always indicates the format of the disk. Entry 1 is always set to FFF to act as a barrier or filler between entry 0 and entry

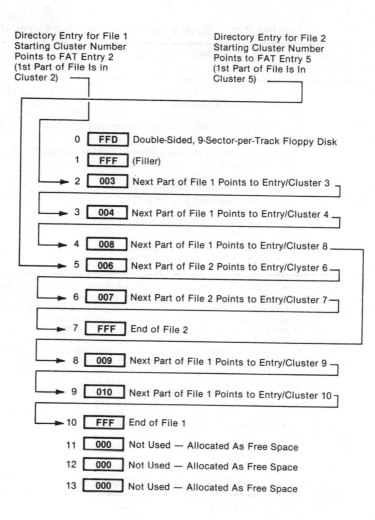

Fig. 8-8.   Sample FAT.

2. Table 8-2 shows the different values for each format supported under MS-DOS versions 1.0 through 3.1.

All subsequent FAT entries are used for mapping the disk. Each of these entries contains one of four types of information: 1) the next cluster number of a file, 2) the end-of-file marker, 3) an unused cluster, or 4) a cluster that is marked as reserved or bad. Table 8-3 lists the values that can exist in FAT entries.

Table 8-2.   Disk Type Values in FAT Entry 0

FAT Entry 0 (Hex value)	Type of Disk and Format
FF8	Hard disk (fixed) (IBM PC, XT, and AT with MS-DOS 2.0 and higher versions)
FF9	Floppy Disk: 2 sides, 15 sectors per track (MS-DOS 3.0 and higher versions) 9-sector-per-track format under MS-DOS 2.0 and higher versions)
FFC	Single-sided floppy disk
*FFD	Double-sided floppy disk
	8-sector-per-track format under MS-DOS 1.0 and higher versions)
*FFE	Single-sided floppy disk
FFF	Double-sided floppy disk

* Some implementations of MS-DOS support 8-inch, soft-sectored floppy disks. Although custom device drivers must be written for the particular type of 8-inch disk drives used in the system, "generic" MS-DOS supports three standard 8-inch disk formats: two single-density (128 bytes per sector) formats and one double density (1,024 bytes per sector) format. The only difference between the two single-density formats is that one has a single reversed sector and the other has four reversed sectors.

The disk format definition value in FAT entry 0 is FFE for both the single-density format with one reversed sector and the double-density format. For the single-density format with four reversed sectors, the value is FFD. Sharing the same value with 5¼-inch disks is no problem because MS-DOS, through its device driver, knows when it is accessing 8-inch disks. However, in order for MS-DOS to distinguish 8-inch formats when it encounters FFE in FAT entry 0, the system first reads the disk assuming it is single-density and subsequently tries to read the single density address mark in the first sector. If no error occurs, MS-DOS continues reading the disk, knowing that it is in single-density format. If an error occurs, MS-DOS assumes the disk is formatted to double density and, expecting a double-density format, returns to the beginning to read the data. If your system is equipped with 8-inch floppy disk drives, the MS-DOS manual accompanying the particular implementation of MS-DOS you are using should have the technical information about 8-inch disk formats.

Table 8-3.   FAT Entry Values Controlling File Allocation

FAT Entry Hex Value	Meaning
000	Cluster is unused and is available for new file storage
FF0 thru FF6	Reserved cluster (not available for normal file storage)
FF7	Cluster is marked as bad by MS-DOS and is not used for file storage
FF8 thru FFF	Last cluster occupied by a file
XXX	Any other value indicates a cluster number in the chain defining how a file is stored

As shown in Tables 8-2 and 8-3, all floppy disk FAT entries contain a 3-digit hexadecimal number. At first glance, we might assume that a fourth digit is present but not used because we normally think of data as stored in whole bytes or pairs of whole bytes. We know that one byte is too small to contain the highest cluster number on the disk because there are more than 255 (decimal) clusters mapped out on the disk. And yet, a 512-byte sector isn't big enough to accommodate all the FAT entries necessary to map out the disk if each FAT entry is two-bytes long. (On floppy disks there are fewer clusters than the maximum number that can be stored in two bytes anyway.) The designers of MS-DOS wanted to keep the space used by the FAT entries on floppy disks to a minimum, so they developed an ingenious but complicated system in which each FAT entry contains 1½ bytes or three hexadecimal digits. Systems, such as the IBM XT, IBM AT, and most other compatible systems, using hard disks, however, use 2 whole bytes for each FAT entry because a much greater number of clusters need mapping out when dealing with 10 or 20 megabytes of storage space.

The MS-DOS scheme of storing numbers that are 1½-bytes wide in FAT entries on floppy disks may seem strange. But MS-DOS is designed to be able to decode these bytes easily. The way MS-DOS stores FAT information is to scramble FAT entries into pairs in which two 1½-byte entries are interweaved into a tidy 3-byte pair. If we want to determine the cluster number in FAT entry 2, we also need to look at FAT entry 3. If we want to look at the cluster number in FAT entry 3, we have to look back to FAT entry 2. FAT entries 4 and 5 would be paired together in the same manner as well as entries 6 and 7, 8 and 9, and so on.

Figure 8-9 illustrates how two cluster numbers can be encoded into a pair of FAT entries.

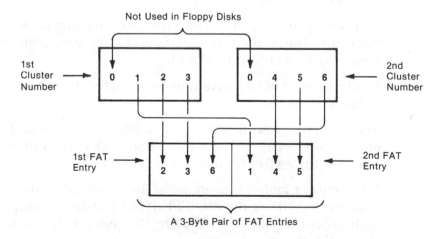

Fig. 8-9.   Encoding two cluster numbers into a pair of FAT entries.

Figure 8-10 shows how two cluster numbers can be decoded from a pair of FAT entries.

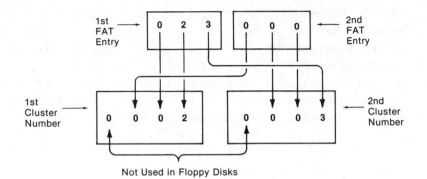

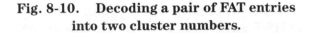

Fig. 8-10. Decoding a pair of FAT entries into two cluster numbers.

If only three digits are extracted from the cluster number, why is the second most significant digit of the first cluster number swapped with the least significant digit of the second cluster? The swapping scheme operates faster in terms of how the machine itself decodes bytes and extracts information. The digits *appear* swapped only when humans read the FAT in DEBUG.

To decode the information in FAT entries on paper or in a program, use the following formula.

1. Multiply FAT entry or cluster number by 1½ bytes. (Multiply the number by 3, then divide by 2.)

2. Use the result as an offset into the FAT, pointing to the entry that maps the cluster just used. That entry contains the number of the next cluster occupied by the file.

3. Load the word (a two-byte number) located at that offset into a register.

4. There are now four hexadecimal digits in the register. Because we only need three digits for a three-digit FAT entry, determine whether the FAT entry number is even or odd.

5. If the entry number is even, keep the low-order three digits in the register by ANDing it with 0FFF. If the number is odd, keep the high-order three digits by shifting the register right four bits with the SHR instruction.

6. If the resulting three digits represent a number from FF8 through FFF, you have reached the end of the file. Otherwise, the three

digits represent the number of the next cluster occupied by the file.

If you write a program that accesses the data storage area of disks, you find that MS-DOS facilities such as interrupts INT 25h (Absolute Disk Read) and INT 26h (Absolute Disk Write) as well as the DEBUG program require that you specify logical sector numbers. Although the disk layout illustrations (see Figs. 8-2 and 8-3) identify the first sector of a disk as Side 0, Track 0, Sector 1, the first sector actually equates to logical sector 0. All subsequent logical sectors are sequential offsets of 0. Thus, logical sector 1 would be Side 0, Track 0, Sector 2, and logical sector 2 would be Side 0, Track 0, Sector 3. Because each FAT entry, according to the results in the above formula, always produces a cluster number, the following formula shows you how to convert a cluster number to a logical sector number.

1. Subtract 2 from the cluster number.

2. Multiply the result by the number of sectors used in a cluster, as follows:

    a. For all single-sided floppy disk formats or for the double-sided 80-track 5¼-inch (extended capacity) format, multiply by 1.

    b. For all double-sided 40-track 5¼-inch floppy disks, multiply by 2.

    c. For double-sided, double-density 8-inch floppy disks, multiply by 4.

    d. For hard disks, use one of the above values or another number depending on the disk format.

3. Add the result to the logical sector number of the beginning of the data storage area.

By applying the proper formulas in the right order you can go now from a directory entry to a FAT entry to the cluster number to the logical sector number. Given this, who needs MS-DOS? You could read the files yourself, a sector at a time!

An Overview of Recovery Procedures

When a file on a disk has been damaged in some way, three basic approaches to correcting the problem are possible. The first approach is to use one of MS-DOS's built-in facilities, such as CHKDSK or RECOVER. These programs can isolate damaged areas of the disk so that you can recover some or all of a damaged file.

The second approach is to use DEBUG, which allows you to do anything that you want in attempting to recover a damaged or erased file. Unfortunately, DEBUG offers little intelligence to aid you in this goal and is often the "court of last resort." Similar in approach is to write your own recovery program, such as the RESCUE program presented later in these chapter. The information presented in the preceding section on decoding the disk's directory and FAT is essential to writing your own recovery programs.

The last approach, and a more comfortable one if your pocketbook can stand it, is to use one of the available off-the-shelf utilities, such as Norton Utilities or Ultra Utilities. These utilities are like a toolbox, providing all the capabilities of the above methods, including decoding the FAT, inspecting individual sectors on the disk, repairing damaged files, and restoring erased files.

Recovering Damaged Files Using CHKDSK and RECOVER

Understanding how a disk is laid out under MS-DOS can be very useful if a file or a part of a disk appears to be damaged. Fortunately, the operating system contains several functions which not only call attention to damaged parts of a disk, but also allow you to recover data that is otherwise not accessible. When faced with file storage problems or defective disks, MS-DOS automatically isolates the problem part of the disk when the system attempts to access it. Although MS-DOS doesn't necessarily tell you exactly what has happened, you probably get an error message indicating that the part of the disk you wanted to read from cannot be accessed properly. If this happens, use the DIR command to examine the directory of the disk. If the DIR command shows the directory as normal, the recovery of the file(s) should be more or less straightforward: use the RECOVER command on the file or files.

If the directory entries are not in the directory, use the CHKDSK command, initially without any parameters. You probably get a message stating that a certain number of clusters are lost on the disk, which is a good sign, because it indicates that you can again use the CHKDSK command, this time accompanied by the /F parameter. This causes CHKDSK to read all "lost" clusters and store them in one file. Sometimes CHKDSK cannot recover all the lost data in one pass. Use CHKDSK as many times as is necessary until the **lost clusters** message disappears. CHKDSK creates a new file each time the command is used to recover lost data. Once the new file(s) are created, copy the file(s) to a new disk, then look at the contents of the file(s) just created by CHKDSK.

If the recovered data corresponds to text files, you can open the file with a text editor or word processor and sort out the information. If, however, the recovered data corresponds to files that are not in a readable text format (such as object code or machine code), you have to use DEBUG or some other utility to look at the information and sort it out. In either case, do not be surprised if a small part of the data is missing. The part of the disk on which the data was stored may have been so badly damaged that it can't be read. Most of the time, data that isn't recoverable consists of increments of 512 or 1,024 bytes, depending on the format of the disk (one 512-byte sector in one cluster for single-sided floppies or two 512-byte sectors in one cluster for double-sided floppies). The reason MS-DOS can't recover this data is that the cluster(s) in question already have been isolated in the corresponding FAT entries and each entry contains a value of FF7, indicating the clusters are bad and that no program is to use them under any circumstances. You could try to read these clusters with DEBUG, but they may be so badly damaged that even DEBUG won't be able to read them.

The following section shows how to use DEBUG to read portions of a disk on a sector-by-sector basis.

Recovering Erased Files

Fortunately, when a file is erased under MS-DOS, only part of the file's directory entry is modified: the first character of the file name is changed to a hexadecimal E5. This value is used as a flag. When MS-DOS scans the directory sectors for a free spot to store a new file's directory information, the system finds and uses the first entry that begins either with hex E5 (erased file) or 00 (directory entry hasn't been used yet). The rest of the information in the directory entry is left intact. If all we had to do was change E5 to the value of the first character of the erased file name, recovering erased files would be very easy. Unfortunately, however, MS-DOS is much more efficient in erasing the information stored in the FAT sectors. Although MS-DOS doesn't touch the information stored in the data sectors or clusters occupied by a file, the system sets to 000 all FAT entries corresponding to these clusters. MS-DOS does this because that's the only way the system can quickly scan the disk for blank space when it wants to store new files. Thus, our task of recovering an erased file is a little more involved than it might seem at first. Some basic guidelines to recovering erased files are described next.

The Basics

You might lose a file by inadvertently using the ERASE or DEL command. Maybe your hardware malfunctioned or power was lost during an edit session. After scanning the disk, you discovered that the file you were editing could not be found.

Generally, a file is only truly "erased" (with the first character in the file's directory entry equaling hex E5) if it is erased with the ERASE or DEL command or by another program that performs the same function. If you lose a file due to a hardware malfunction or power loss, the file probably isn't truly erased. It's simply lost on the disk if the program you are using didn't have time to close the file properly. In such a case, you can use the MS-DOS disk recovery programs RECOVER and CHKDSK to recover the lost data.

CAUTION

When recovering files, the first thing you should do is make an exact duplicate of the disk using the disk copy program. Do not store any new files on the disk until you've made an attempt to recover the lost or erased files.

The above caution is very important because storing new data to the disk probably makes file recovery difficult if not impossible. And by first making an exact copy of the disk you avoid the possibility of corrupting certain parts of the disk (thereby guaranteeing permanent data loss) due to improper file recovery. Thus, if things don't go right the first time, you still have the original disk from which you can copy the data and the file recovery process can begin again.

The best way to determine whether a file is truly erased or is merely lost is to use the CHKDSK program without any parameters. If the file is lost, the CHKDSK program displays a message, **Lost clusters found.** This message is displayed if CHKDSK finds a break in the chain of clusters described in the FAT—if, for example the last cluster in the chain doesn't point to a FAT entry that contains an end of file marker (FF8 through FFF). When this happens, you should reenter CHKDSK with the /F parameter to recover all lost clusters and store the data into a file that is created by CHKDSK.

This is where the initial step of making an entire copy of the original disk may prove to be a blessing. For if you also had other files that were truly erased on the disk, the CHKDSK/F command sequence quite likely stores the file containing the recovered data *over* the area containing the erased files! File recovery, no matter what the circumstances, should be approached in a methodical and careful manner.

Once it is clear that a file has been truly erased, and if no additional files have been stored on the disk since the file was erased, you know three things with certainty: First, the file's directory entry is intact, except for the first character, which is hex E5. Second, the clusters or sectors in the data area of the disk originally used by the file still contain the file's data. Third (sadly), the FAT entries originally used to map out the clusters occupied by the file each contain 000.

To recover an erased file, the following steps should be taken.

1. Search through the directory entries until you find an entry that begins with hexadecimal E5 at byte 00. Look at the characters of the rest of the file name in bytes 1 through 10 and verify that it's the file you want to recover.

2. Look at the starting cluster number (bytes 26 and 27). Use the starting cluster number as a pointer to the first cluster in the data area of the disk occupied by the file as well as to the first FAT entry originally used.

3. Look at the file's size (bytes 28 through 31, the last four bytes in the directory entry). Knowing the file's size is important if the file takes up more than one cluster in the data area of the disk and especially important if parts of the file are scattered at different parts of the disk.

4. Having determined the cluster number occupied by the beginning of the file, examine the contents of that cluster. Search for an ASCII <**CONTROL-Z**> character (hex 1A) in the cluster. If you know that the file contains text (ASCII) and one or more <**CONTROL-Z**> characters are found, recover the file as follows. (Otherwise, proceed to Step 5.)

   a. If one or more <**CONTROL-Z**> characters were found, you know that the file occupies only one cluster. Begin recovering the file by storing any number from FF8 through FFF in the FAT entry corresponding to the cluster.

   b. Change the hex E5 in the directory entry to whatever you think the first character of the file's name should be.

c. Back at the MS-DOS prompt, use the DIR command to verify that the file is listed. Open the file with a text editor or word processor to verify that the contents are intact. You're done! Stop here and ignore the following steps.

5. If the end of the file wasn't found, search through the subsequent FAT entries (sequentially) until one containing 000 is found. Look at the contents of the cluster numbered the same as the FAT entry. If the contents appear to be part of the erased file, make note of the cluster number and continue the search through the FAT entries and the equivalent clusters until you think the end of the file has been reached. The amount of searching you do depends on several things, as described in the next step.

6. Determine from the size of the file extracted from the directory entry how many clusters the file *should* occupy. Also keep in mind that if you're recovering an ASCII text file, the presence of a <**CONTROL-Z**> character (hex 1A) in a cluster indicates the end of the file. Therefore, loop back to step 5 until you reach the maximum number of clusters occupied by the file. Make note of each cluster number that contains data you think is part of the erased file. If you find a <**CONTROL-Z**> in a cluster but haven't yet examined a sufficient number of clusters matching the file's size, be careful: The cluster with the <**CONTROL-Z**> on it could mark the end of another erased file. Search through subsequent directory entries for erased files and make note of their starting clusters as well as their file sizes. It's possible that two or more erased files have interweaving paths for any given sequence of clusters.

7. Once you're reasonably certain about the clusters occupied by the file and how they're chained together and you're fairly certain you've found the end of the file, reconstruct the FAT. Beginning with the first cluster, go to the equivalent FAT entry and store the number of the next cluster occupied by the file. Then go to this next FAT entry and store the number of the subsequent cluster. Continue this operation until the last cluster is reached, storing in the corresponding FAT entry any number from FF8 through FFF to mark the end of the file. Next, go to the file's directory entry, and change the first character of hex E5 to the ASCII equivalent (in hexadecimal) of whatever you think the first character of the file should be.

8. That's it! When you're back at the MS-DOS prompt, use the DIR command to verify that the file is listed. If the recovered file is a

text file, open the file with a text editor or word processor to verify its contents. If it's some other type of file, such as a .EXE or .COM file, load the file as a program to verify that it works correctly.

The previous steps might suggest that the procedure for recovering a file is fairly straightforward. Depending on the tools you have at your disposal, however, actually looking at the data on the disk and writing information to the disk can be a bit cumbersome. Notice also that Steps 6 and 7 provide cautions about the possibility that several erased files might be interwoven through a sequence of clusters. Recovering data that is interwoven in this way can be very tedious and at times rather mind-boggling. But with patience (possibly quite a bit) and by forcing yourself to be methodical, you can untangle the files.

Now that you have a good idea of the effort that it takes to recover erased files, this is a good time to point out that the fastest way to recover erased files is to copy them off your backup disk. You should try to get into the habit of backing up your work frequently, and always use a copy of your purchased or private software, never the original disk(s).

Recovering Erased Files the Hard Way

If all you have at your disposal is the DEBUG program for recovering files, and you don't have the time or the patience to type and assemble the program RESCUE described in this chapter, the following tips may prove useful to you. The four DEBUG functions or commands of interest are L (Load), D (Display), E (Enter), and W (Write). Once you make a copy of the disk with the erased file on it, load DEBUG. At the DEBUG's prompt, enter the L command to load data from the part of the disk you're interested in looking at.

```
L <address> <drive> <start sector> <end sector>
```

In this case, <address> represents the beginning address in memory where the data is to be loaded, <drive> is the drive number (for example, 0 for A, 1 for B, 2 for C), and <start sector> and <end sector> indicate the range of logical sectors (hexadecimal numbers only) you want to load. To load the contents of all the directory sectors on a double-sided, 40-track, 5¼-inch diskette formatted to nine sectors per track and that is inserted in drive B, enter the following:

```
A>DEBUG
-L 0 1 5 B
```

When the information is loaded, you can use the D command to display the contents in memory and the E command to change individual bytes as needed. Once you note the information you need and make any changes, the data can be written back to the disk using the W command. The W command uses the exact same syntax as the L command. Make sure that you specify the same parameters as you did with the L command. This ensures that only the correct part of the disk is overwritten.

The only time you need to write information to the disk is when you change the first character of an erased file name in its directory entry or when you modify the contents of the FAT entries that correspond to the file. When examining the contents of the clusters occupied by the actual file, you don't have to write the information back to the disk unless you're doing some tricky repair work that could otherwise not be accomplished. Refer to the *MS-DOS User's Manual* (or your system's equivalent manual) for more information on how to use DEBUG and its commands.

Using the RESCUE Program

The program described in the following listing is very straightforward and easy to use. The command RESCUE is typed, followed by the file specification of the erased file. If the name of the file is found in the directory, an attempt is made to recover the file by analyzing and writing information to the FAT. If the file was not found or was found to be not deleted, a message is displayed to that effect. As explained earlier, the allocation path taken through the FAT for a given file can be complex sometimes. If RESCUE cannot resolve the allocation path of a file (maybe it was interwoven with a path of another file), the program terminates and no information is written to the disk. An important factor in the way the program works is that it won't write any information to the disk until all aspects of the file have been resolved. It accomplishes this by reading all directory and FAT sectors into memory where all of the modifications to the file's directory entry and its FAT entries are made. When all modifications have been made, RESCUE writes the entire directory and FAT back to the disk. If difficulties are encountered in analyzing the data and making the modifications, RESCUE terminates and the disk is left untouched.

As noted earlier, RESCUE has been designed so that it can be easily modified to support future disk formats. The program makes extensive use of macros and subroutines, so many of the modifications that could conceivably be made would affect only parts of the program. The program can be assembled as is, although it does make use of two external library routines. These two routines are included in the listing for the BIN2CON library file in Appendix A. In order to create RESCUE.COM, the library file BIN2CON.LIB must be created and must be linked with RESCUE.OBJ using LINK.

Listing 8-1. RESCUE Program

```
        page 60,132
        .SALL            ; suppress macro expansion listing
;********************************************************************
;** RESCUE Version 1.00
;**
;** This program searches for a specified file that has been
;** erased and if found, attempts to "unerase" it. The file is
;** unerased by patching all FAT entries containing 000 in sequence
;** after the first offset into the FAT until the file's size is
;** matched. The selection of the FAT entries is made on a "best
;** guess" basis--the program has to be enhanced if more
;** sophistication is required in the recovery of erased files.
;**
;** FORMATS SUPPORTED:
;**     40-track floppy disks:  8- and 9-sectors-per-track formats,
;**                             single and double sided
;**     80-track floppy disks:  15-sectors-per-track format, double
;**                             sided
;**
;** NOT SUPPORTED:
;**     Subdirectories and subdirectory files
;**     3-1/2-inch disks
;**     96TPI (80-track) 5-1/4-inch floppy disks (other than 15-sector
;**     format)
;**     8-inch floppy disks
;**     Hard disks
;**
;**     CAUTION: Do not attempt to use this program with a RAM-disk
;**     that doesn't emulate EXACTLY one of the standard floppy
;**     formats!
;********************************************************************
;
;****** MACRO DEFINITIONS ******************************************
;
doscall         macro
        int     21h              ; call an MS-DOS function
        endm
;
disk_read macro
        int     25h              ; read a logical sector of a disk
        endm
;
```

Listing 8-1. cont.

```
disk_write macro
        int     26h                 ; write to a logical sector of a disk
        endm
;
dis_chr         macro   character       ; display a character
        push    dx
        mov     dl,character
        mov     ah,02h
        doscall
        pop     dx
        endm
;
dis_str         macro   string          ; display a string
        push    dx
        mov     dx,offset string
        mov     ah,09h
        doscall
        pop     dx
        endm
;
newline         macro       ; display carriage return and line feed
        dis_str cret
        endm
;
push_all macro              ; save all registers onto the stack
        push    ax
        push    bx
        push    cx
        push    dx
        push    bp
        push    di
        push    si
        endm
;
pop_all         macro       ; restore all registers off of the stack
        pop     si
        pop     di
        pop     bp
        pop     dx
        pop     cx
        pop     bx
        pop     ax
        endm
;
;***** INITIALIZATION ********************************************
;
code    segment para public 'code'
;
        extrn bin2hex:near ; library routine to output hex digits
        extrn bin2dec:near ; library routine to output decimal digits
;
        assume  cs:code,ds:code,ss:code,es:code
;
        org     0100h               ; make this a .COM file
;
```

Listing 8-1. cont.

```
main    proc    far
entry:  jmp     start                   ; bypass data area and go to program
;
;***** STANDARD EQUATES ***********************************
;
lf              equ     0Ah     ; ASCII linefeed
cr              equ     0Dh     ; ASCII carriage return
file_fcb        equ     5Ch     ; location of FCB in the PSP
deleted_mark    equ     0E5h    ; deleted file mark (in directory)
;
base            equ     [bp]    ; base structure for stack addressing
dfmt            equ     [si]    ; pointer to disk format parameter block
files           equ     [di]    ; pointer to directory file entries
;
none            equ     -1
;
read            equ     0
write           equ     1
dir             equ     0
FAT             equ     1
;
;**** STRUCTURE DEFINITIONS ******************************
;
file_entry      struc           ; template for file descriptor
file_name       db      8 dup (?)       ; file name
file_ext        db      3 dup (?)       ; extension
attribute       db      ?               ; file attribute
                db      10 dup (?)      ; reserved
create_time     dw      ?               ; creation time
create_date     dw      ?               ; creation date
file_start      dw      ?               ; starting cluster of file
file_length     dd      ?               ; number of bytes in file
file_entry      ends
;
                format struc    ; template for disk format data
media           dw      ?               ; disk media word
bytes_sector    dw      ?
cluster_size    dw      ?               ; ... in bytes
fat_sectors     dw      ?               ; # sectors per FAT
fat_entries     dw      ?               ; # entries in a FAT
dir_sectors     dw      ?               ; # sectors per directory
dir_entries     dw      ?               ; # entries in a directory
                format ends
;
;**** DATA AREA *****************************************
;
; Variable storage:
;
temp_data       db 1024 dup(?)  ; space for temporary data storage
fat_data        db 3584 dup(?)  ; space for FAT
dir_data        db 7168 dup(?)  ; space for directory
;
disk_drive      db 0            ; drive of deleted file
disk_format     dw ?            ; disk format (pointer)
;
```

Listing 8-1. cont.

```
start_cluster   dw    ?                   ; beginning cluster of deleted file
cluster_bytes   dw    ?                   ; number of bytes in a cluster
file_bytes      dd    ?                   ; file size in bytes (4 bytes)
file_clusters   dw    ?                   ; file size in clusters (sectors)
;
previous_index dw    ?                    ; back-link in chained FATS
;
; The following disk format parameters table easily can have new
; formats added to because its size is self-adjusting.
;
; Parameters are defined and arranged in following order:
;       format ID
;       size of a cluster in bytes
;       number of sectors in a cluster
;       number FAT sectors
;       total number of clusters on disk
;       number of directory sectors
;       number of root directory entries
;
format_table    equ     $                         ; disk format parameters
        format <OFFEh,512,1,1,314,4,64>   ; ss sd: 8 sec/track 1 sided
        format <OFFFh,512,2,1,316,7,112>  ; ds sd: 8 sec/track 2 sided
        format <OFFCh,512,1,2,352,5,64>   ; ss dd: 9 sec/track 1 sided
        format <OFFDh,512,2,2,355,7,112>  ; ds dd: 9 sec/track 2 sided
        format <OFF9h,512,1,7,1194,14,224>; ds ed: 15 sec/track 2 sided
format_entries equ     ($-format_table)/size format
;
;**** TEXT MESSAGES ******************************************************
;
welcum1 db      'Welcome to RESCUE version 1.0 ( MS-DOS version $'
welcum2 db      ' )'
CRET    db      cr,lf,'$'
ver1xx db       '1.XX$'
msg_bad_drv     equ     $
        db      'The drive specified is not allowed. Please try again.'
        db      CR,LF,'$'
msg_not_support equ     $
        db      'This program presently does not support'
        db      'hard disks with format code FF8h.',CR,LF,'$'
msg_not_known equ      $
        db      'The disk format is not recognizable.',CR,LF
        db      'The format code is: $'
msg_not_fnd     equ     $
        db      'File was not found deleted.',CR,LF,'$'
msg_nofree      equ     $
        db      'Not enough free clusters to rescue the'
        db      'file--aborting.'
        db      CR,LF,'$'
msg_file_gone equ      $
        db      'The original clusters associated with the file'
        db      'have',CR,LF
        db      'been allocated to another file--the erased file'
        db      'has',CR,LF
        db      'been written over.',CR,LF,'$'
msg_rescued     equ     $
```

Listing 8-1. cont.

```
        db         'The erased file has been RESCUED!',CR,LF,'$'
;
;**** MAIN PROGRAM *********************************************
;
start:
;
; Display start-up message
;
        dis_str welcum1                  ; start up message ...
        call    disp_dos_ver             ; ... MS-DOS version number ...
        dis_str welcum2                  ; ... and new line.
;
; Get disk drive number/name:
;
get_disk_drive:
        mov     al,byte ptr cs:file_fcb ; get the specified drive
        cmp     al,0             ; was drive specified? (0 if not)
        jbe     get_default_drive ; no, get default drive
        dec     al                ; decrement drive number by 1
                                  ; (0 = A:, 1 = B:, 2 = C:, 3 = D:,
                                  ; etc.)
        cmp     al,15             ; is it equal to or less than 15 (P:)?
        jbe     drive_used        ; yes, jump to store drive number
        dis_str msg_bad_drv       ; no, display error message
        jmp     terminate         ; exit to MS-DOS
get_default_drive:
        mov     ah,19h            ; get default drive
        doscall
drive_used:
        mov     disk_drive,al    ; store drive
;
; -----------------------------------------------------------
; Read 1st FAT sector & determine identity of disk format
; -----------------------------------------------------------
;
get_disk_format:
        mov     cx,1             ; specify 1 sector
        mov     dx,1             ; specify logical sector 1
                                 ; (Side 0, Track 0, Sector 2)
        lea     di,temp_data     ; point to temp_data
        mov     ax,none          ; set dir/FAT flag to none
        push    ax
        mov     ax,read          ; set up for read operation
        push    ax
        call    abs_disk_i_o     ; read the disk
        xor     ax,ax            ; clear ax
        push    ax               ; want FAT entry # 0
        push    di               ; address of FAT table
        call    decode_fat       ; extract FAT entry
        pop     ax               ; value of FAT # 0 = media word
;
; Establish disk format parameters
;
        lea     si,format_table          ; start of disk formats table
        mov     cx,format_entries        ; number of formats supported
```

Listing 8-1. cont.

```
chk_fmt:
        cmp     dfmt.media,ax           ; does media word match?
        je      set_cluster_len         ; yes, use that format
        add     si,size format          ; no, check next one
        loop    chk_fmt
;
; Handle unsupported and unrecognizable formats with error messages
;
        cmp     ax,0FF8h        ; is it a hard disk?
        jne     fmt_not_known   ; no, format is not known
        dis_str msg_not_support ; yes, display not-supported message
        jmp     terminate
fmt_not_known:
        push    ax                      ; save unknown format
        dis_str msg_not_known
        pop     ax
        mov     ch,3            ; 3 digits
        call    bin2hex         ; output the format code
        newline
        jmp     terminate
;
; Format is found--now calculate cluster length (bytes) from
; parameters
;
set_cluster_len:
        mov disk_format,si      ; save pointer to disk parameters
        mov ax,dfmt.bytes_sector ; multiply # of bytes in a sector
        mul dfmt.cluster_size    ;   by # of sectors in a cluster
        mov cluster_bytes,ax     ; save # of bytes in a cluster
;
; ------------------------------------------------------------
; Read in the directory & search for matched file name
; ------------------------------------------------------------
;
get_disk_info:
        mov     ax,dir          ; set dir/FAT flag to DIRECTORY
        push ax
        mov     ax,read         ; set up for read operation
        push ax
        call abs_disk_i_o        ; read the disk
;
; Search for directory entry of erased file
;       --Search for E5h--possible 1st byte of erased file entry
;         BX = loop counter, DI = pointer to directory entries
;
read_dir_entry:
        lea di,dir_data         ; point to directory information
        mov bx,dfmt.dir_entries ; count = # entries in directory
find_erase_flag:
        cmp     files.file_name,deleted_mark
        je      check_rest
find_erase_2:
        add     di,size file_entry      ; next entry
        dec     bx                      ; one less entry to go
        jnz     find_erase_flag         ; keep searching
```

Listing 8-1. cont.

```
        jmp     file_not_found          ; no more entries to check
;
;     --E5h found--check rest of file name for possible match
;       Compare entry (SI) and deleted file name (DI)
;       CX = loop counter, DI, SI = pointers, AX = temp
;
check_rest:
        push    di                  ; save possible base point
        inc     di                  ; point to name + 1
        cld                         ; (increment SI & DI compare)
        mov     si,file_fcb + 2     ; point to 2nd char of file name
        mov     cx,10               ; compare remaining characters
        repe    cmpsb               ; compare until stopped ...
        pop     di                  ; (restore pointer to dir entry)
        jnz     find_erase_2        ; ... if mismatch, try again
;
; Found the file entry! Names match!
;
        mov     al,byte ptr cs:file_fcb + 1 ; restore 1st character ...
        mov     files.file_name,al         ; ... into deleted entry
                                           ; (was E5h)
        jmp     get_start_cluster          ; get file's starting cluster
;
;     --Didn't find match file name--give up
;
file_not_found:
        dis_str msg_not_fnd
        jmp     terminate
;
; ----------------------------------------------------------
; Get starting cluster to use as a pointer into the FAT
; and determine the file's size.
; ----------------------------------------------------------
;
get_start_cluster:
        mov     si,disk_format
        mov     ax,files.file_start     ; get start cluster
        mov     start_cluster,ax        ; and store it
;
; Get file's size & store in file_bytes
;
        mov     ax,word ptr files.file_length
        mov     dx,word ptr files.file_length + 2
        mov     word ptr file_bytes,ax
        mov     word ptr file_bytes + 2,dx
;
; Determine the number of clusters occupied by the file
;
        div     cluster_bytes       ; divide by num. of bytes in a cluster
        cmp     dx,0                ; is there a remainder?
        je      store_file_clusters ; no, save the number of clusters
        inc     ax                  ; yes, add 1 cluster to quotient
;
store_file_clusters:
        mov     file_clusters,ax    ; save the number of clusters in file
;
```

Listing 8-1. cont.

```
;
;-------------------------------------------------------------------
; Search for starting FAT entry and other entries containing 000
;-------------------------------------------------------------------
;
; Read in the FAT
        mov   ax,FAT              ; set dir/FAT flag to FAT
        push  ax
        mov   ax,read            ; set up for read operation
        push  ax
        call  abs_disk_i_o        ; read the disk
;
        lea   di,fat_data        ; set index to FAT table
        mov   bx,start_cluster    ; (and set FAT number entry)
        mov   cx,dfmt.fat_entries ; set number of FATS to test
        sub   cx,start_cluster    ; ... from where we start
        mov   dx,file_clusters    ; total number of clusters to recover
        mov   previous_index,none ; haven't found one yet
;
; Search for zero FAT entry (starting with the one we just got)
;       AX = FAT contents (for test)
;       BX = FAT # (index)
;       CX = max # of FATS that can be checked
;       DX = # of clusters that make up the file
;       DI = base address of FAT table
;
search_for_fat:
        push    bx                   ; get FAT # ...
        push    di                   ; ... from table
        call    decode_fat           ; get fat entries from [DI]
        pop     ax                   ; ... & retrieve FAT content
        and     ax,ax                ; is this a zero FAT?
        jnz     get_next_fat         ; no, check next
;
; FAT is 000--use it in the chain
;
        cmp     previous_index,none ; is there a back-link yet?
        jne     save_back_link       ; yes, save this index in previous
        cmp     bx,start_cluster     ; no, is this the starting cluster?
        je      save_previous_index ; yes, so remember its index only
        dis_str msg_file_gone        ; file was overwritten
        jmp     terminate
save_back_link:
        push    bx                   ; save current index ...
        push    previous_index       ; ... in back_link ...
        push    di                   ; in table
        call    encode_fat
save_previous_index:
        mov     previous_index,bx    ; this index is now previous
;
; Check if all done
;
        dec     dx                   ; 1 less FAT to find
        jnz     get_next_fat         ; ... but still not done
        mov     ax,0FF8h             ; (EOF)
```

Listing 8-1. cont.

```
        push    ax                          ; set end-of-file ...
        push    bx                          ; ... on this FAT ...
        push    di                          ; ... in this table
        call    encode_fat                  ; stuff it away
        jmp     rescued                     ; and we're done
get_next_fat:
        inc     bx                          ; bump FAT index
        dec     cx                          ; dec. max # to check
        jnz     search_for_fat              ; continue if more left
no_free_FAT:
        dis_str msg_nofree                  ; tell user ran out of FATs
        jmp     terminate
;
; ---------------------------------------------------------
; Write the FAT and directory out to the disk
; ---------------------------------------------------------
;
rescued:
                        ; DIRECTORY
        mov     ax,dir                      ; set dir/FAT flag to dir
        push    ax
        mov     ax,write                    ; set up for write operation
        push    ax
        call    abs_disk_i_o                ; write directory the disk
                        ; FIRST FAT
        mov     ax,FAT                      ; set dir/FAT flag to FAT
        push    ax
        mov     ax,write                    ; set up for write operation
        push    ax
        call    abs_disk_i_o                ; write directory the disk
                        ; SECOND FAT
        mov     cx,1                        ; specify 1 sector
        mov     dx,1                        ; specify logical sector 1
        add     dx,dfmt.fat_sectors         ; + 1st FAT = 2nd FAT
        lea     di,fat_data                 ; point to fat_data
        mov     ax,FAT                      ; set dir/FAT flag to none
        push    ax
        mov     ax,write                    ; set up for write operation
        push    ax
        call    abs_disk_i_o                ; write directory the disk
        dis_str msg_rescued                 ; tell user, file recovered.
;
terminate:
        mov     ax,04C00h ; terminate program and return to MS-DOS
        doscall
;
main    endp
;
;****************************************************************
; ROUTINES CALLED BY MAIN PROGRAM
;****************************************************************
;
;=== ROUTINE TO READ OR WRITE A SECTOR ==========================
;
```

Listing 8-1. cont.

```
; NOTE: On entry, R_W_FLAG = 0 for read or 1 for write,
; D_F_FLAG = -1 for anything, 0 for directory or 1 for FAT
; Data are copied into or out of the DIR_DATA if directory,
; FAT_DATA if FAT, or a predefined area if something else.
;
; (Note: If D_F_FLAG = -1 (read/write anything), on entry the
; following must be set up: DX = first logical sector, CX = num. of
; sectors)
;
abs_dio_stk     struc
                dw      ?               ; old bp
                dw      ?               ; return address
rw_flg          dw      ?               ; read/write flag
dfr_flg         dw      ?               ; directory/FAT/random flag
abs_dio_stk     ends
;
abs_disk_i_o    proc    near
        push    bp                      ; save old bp
        mov     bp,sp                   ; access parameters
        push_all                        ; save the registers
        mov     bx,di                   ; set default transfer address
        mov     al,disk_drive           ; specify disk drive
        cmp     base.dfr_flg,none       ; read/write anything?
        je      do_disk_i_o             ; yes
        cmp     base.dfr_flg,FAT        ; no, read/write the FAT?
        je      process_fat             ; yes
; process directory:
        mov     dx,dfmt.fat_sectors     ; get # of fat sectors
        mov     dh,0                    ; ... to word ...
        shl     dx,1                    ; multiply by two
        inc     dx                      ; and add 1
        mov     cx,dfmt.dir_sectors     ; specify num. sectors for
directory
        lea     bx,dir_data             ; point to dir_data area
        jmp     do_disk_i_o
process_fat:
        mov     cx,dfmt.fat_sectors     ; specify num. sectors for FAT
        mov     dx,1                    ; specify logical sector 1
                                        ; (Side 0, Track 0, Sector 1)
        lea     bx,fat_data             ; point to fat_data area
do_disk_i_o:
        cmp     base.rw_flg,write       ; is sector to be written?
        je      write_sector            ; yes
        disk_read                       ; no, execute disk read interrupt
        jmp     done_disk_i_o           ; finished
write_sector:
        disk_write                      ; execute disk-write interrupt
done_disk_i_o:
        popf                            ; restore flags (originally PUSHed
                                        ; by INT 25h or INT 26h)
        pop_all                         ; ... and restore the registers
        pop     bp                      ; restore bp
        ret     4                       ; return
abs_disk_i_o    endp
;
```

Listing 8-1. cont.

```
;=== ROUTINE TO DECODE A FAT ENTRY PAIR ===============================
;
fat_stack       struc           ; stack for calls to DECODE/ENCODE
                dw      ?       ; BP
                dw      ?       ; return address
fat_table       dw      ?       ; pointer to FAT table
fat_index       dw      ?       ; FAT (cluster) # to Get/Put
                                ; replaced by FAT contents during get
fat_value       dw      ?       ; FAT contents during ENCODE (put) only
fat_stack       ends
;
decode_fat      proc    near
        push    bp
        mov     bp,sp                   ; address parameters
        push    ax                      ; save AX for transfers ...
        push    cx                      ; ... CX for rotates ...
        push    di                      ; ... DI for table access.
;
        mov     di,base.fat_table       ; get table address ...
        mov     ax,base.fat_index       ; ... & FAT index #
        add     di,ax                   ; convert FAT index # ...
        shr     ax,1                    ; ... into the physical ...
        add     di,ax                   ; ... address.
;
        mov     ax,[di]                 ; get FAT word
        test    base.fat_index,1        ; even or odd index # ?
        jz      decode_done             ; all done if even
;
        mov     cl,4                    ; Set up for 4-bit shift
        shr     ax,cl                   ; Make upper 4 bits the lower ones
decode_done:
        and     ax,0FFFh                ; (only lower 12 bits)
        mov     base.fat_index,ax       ; save result
        pop     di                      ; restore user's registers
        pop     cx
        pop     ax
        pop     bp                      ; restore old BP
        ret     2                       ; clear stack of other param
decode_fat      endp
;
;
;=== ROUTINE TO ENCODE A FAT ENTRY PAIR ==============================
;
encode_fat      proc    near
        push    bp
        mov     bp,sp                   ; address parameters
        push    ax                      ; save AX for transfers ...
        push    cx                      ; ... CX for rotates ...
        push    di                      ; ... DI for table access
;
        mov     di,base.fat_table       ; get table address ...
        mov     ax,base.fat_index       ; ... & FAT index #
        add     di,ax                   ; convert FAT index # ...
        shr     ax,1                    ; ... into the physical ...
        add     di,ax                   ; ... address
```

Listing 8-1. cont.

```
;
        mov     ax,base.fat_value       ; get FAT word to store
        and     ax,0FFFh                ; (only lower 12 bits)
        test    base.fat_index,1        ; even or odd index # ?
        jnz     encode_odd
; encode even
        and     byte ptr [di + 1],0F0h  ; mask unused portion
        or      ah,[di + 1]             ; combine with other entry
        mov     [di],ax                 ; and save both
        jmp     encode_done
encode_odd:
        mov     cl,4                    ; prepare for shift-left by 4
        shl     ax,cl                   ; align odd entry (0 low 4)
        and     byte ptr [di],0Fh       ; mask unused portion
        or      al,[di]                 ; combine with other entry
        mov     [di],ax                 ; and save both
encode_done:
        pop     di                      ; restore user's registers
        pop     cx
        pop     ax
        pop     bp                      ; restore old BP
        ret     6                       ; clear stack of other param
encode_fat      endp
;
;
;=== ROUTINE TO DISPLAY MS-DOS VERSION ===============================
;
;       AX destroyed, CX saved, other registers unused
;
disp_dos_ver    proc    near
;
; Get MS-DOS version
;
        push    cx
        mov     ah,30h                  ; get DOS version function call
        doscall
        cmp     al,0                    ; is it pre-version 2.00
        jnz     dos2plus                ; no, it's 2.00 or above
        dis_str ver1xx                  ; yes, output 1.XX (could be 1.00 or 1.10)
        jmp     end_ver                 ; ... and terminate routine
dos2plus:
        push    ax                      ; save (minor version number)
;
; Display DOS Version
;
        xor     ah,ah                   ; clear upper to print major version
        mov     ch,1                    ; display at least 1 digit
        call    bin2dec
        dis_chr '.'                     ; separator digit
        pop     ax                      ; restore (minor version number)
        xchg    ah,al                   ; minor in AL
        xor     ah,ah                   ; clear upper
        mov     ch,2                    ; display at least two digits
        call    bin2dec
end_ver:
```

Listing 8-1. cont.

```
        pop     cx
        ret                             ; return
;
disp_dos_ver    endp
;
;********************************************************************
; End of routines
;********************************************************************
;
code    ends
;
        end     entry                   ; set the starting address to ENTRY
```

Using Norton Utilities

Norton Utilities arc very easy to use, especially when you know something about how MS-DOS disks are laid out. In versions of Norton Utilities prior to 3.0, the DL (DiskLook) and UE (UnErase) programs are the most useful for file recovery. DiskLook examines sector by sector any part of the disk, showing hexadecimal data on the left side of the screen and the ASCII equivalent on the right side. Smart enough to recognize the disk format as well as the type of sectors being read (such as boot, FAT, directory, or data area), the program displays this information on the screen. The program is also capable of displaying a simple map of the disk, similar to the disk layout illustrations in this chapter, showing what each sector or cluster is used for on a per-track basis. It also shows what parts of the disk contain files and which are empty.

The UnErase program is similar to DiskLook. However, UnErase has difficulties if it encounters the types of problems discussed in this chapter, problems such as incomplete files that have been overwritten with new information or several files with complex interwoven chains.

To some extent, the value of Norton Utilities depends on how well you understand how MS-DOS disks are laid out and what you know about FAT sectors and directory sectors, and where they begin and end. Even so, you may find using the programs very educational because of the clear and detailed manner in which they display disk data. Another advantage is that safeguards are built into the programs to prevent you from doing any damage to disks.

In version 3.0 of Norton Utilities, the functions of both DiskLook and UnErase are combined in the program NU (Norton Utilities). The functions in this implementation have been improved and include more detailed text interpretations of what is on the disk instead of relying mostly on cryptic hexadecimal data. Only version 3.0 is capable of working with the 80-track, double-sided, 5¼-inch (extended capacity) floppy disks as well as with the 20-megabyte hard disk in the IBM PC AT and compatibles. None of the versions (including 3.0) are capable of working with 8-inch floppy disks formatted under MS-DOS nor can they work with hard disks that have formats that are different than those used in IBM XT and IBM AT systems. Additionally, because of the fancy way in which these programs display information on the screen, they only operate with display equipment compatible or closely compatible with equipment used in IBM systems. However, if you use an IBM PC or compatible system, you'll find Norton Utilities are effective and entertaining because they deal very well with the topics described in this chapter.

Using Ultra Utilities

Ultra Utilities are a set of file recovery programs similar to Norton Utilities. Ultra Utilities are "user-supported" programs, also sometimes known as "freeware," and can be obtained through various channels of public domain software distribution. Ultra Utilities include a notice to the user that if the programs are found to be useful, a suggested fee be paid to the originators, in return for which the user becomes a registered user and is eligible for future software updates.

Three programs are provided on the main Ultra Utilities disk: U-ZAP, U-FORMAT, and U-FILE. U-ZAP is similar to the Norton Utilities DiskLook program and provides extensive capabilities for modifying any of the contents of a disk. U-FORMAT is a very special program because it provides the capability of formatting individual tracks on a disk. U-FORMAT can even reformat a track without destroying any MS-DOS data stored on it. This can prove very useful on troublesome disks with formatting problems so severe that even MS-DOS can't recover inaccessible data. The U-FILE program has many capabilities of displaying and modifying files on the disk, including recovering erased files.

Ultra Utilities are a fine alternative to Norton Utilities if you are cost-conscious. And don't be dissuaded by the semi-free aspect of this package—Ultra Utilities are very fine programs designed by professionals who use low-cost methods of distribution.

Summary

This chapter has focused on disk layout and file recovery under MS-DOS. The information in this chapter has shown that, if equipped with the necessary information, you can recover erased, damaged, and lost files. Even though the various tools mentioned for recovering files provide varying degrees of simplicity and disk file accessibility in their use, the basic sequence of file recovery outlined in this chapter remains the same.

This knowledge can also be applied to subdirectories and subdirectory files. The only difference between files in the root directory and files in subdirectories is that subdirectory entries are contained in *files* rather than the directory sectors in the root. Once you have obtained the entry, the rest of the process (with FATs, clusters, and sectors) is exactly the same. An excellent project would be to enhance the RESCUE program to include rescuing files from subdirectories and to support the FAT entries used in hard disks. You will truly be a master of MS-DOS file allocation once you complete the program.

The next chapter presents a similar topic: recovering data lost in memory. Understanding disk layouts and file storage helps you understand the information in the next chapter.

Recovering Data Lost in Memory

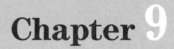
Chapter 9

lmost every computer user has at some point lost valuable data in RAM (random access memory). Losing data that's currently in memory can be caused by operator error, hardware malfunction, an elusive bug in a program, or a power failure. In many cases, some if not all of the data lost in memory can be recovered and stored safely to a disk if you're willing to do some patient investigating. Before taking any drastic measures, like resetting the system, any problem short of a power failure or an automatic system reset is worth investigating.

Of course, it's a good idea to experiment with data recovery and explore the memory of your system before something goes wrong. Word processing programs and BASIC interpreters are good starting points in experimenting with data recovery. Note that the procedures for recovering lost data are only appropriate if the malfunction was not severe enough to lock up the entire system. If, however, the MS-DOS prompt returns and you're able to enter commands, you can start searching for the lost data.

Recovering from Word Processing/Text Editing Failures

Probably the easiest way to explore your system memory is to simulate a problem. Load your favorite word processor or text editor, create a short, simple text file, then exit normally to MS-DOS. Immediately afterwards, load the DEBUG program and, using the D (Display) command, start scanning the contents of memory. DEBUG always assumes memory offset 0100h as the beginning point. Don't worry about setting the segment address (DEBUG defaults to one anyway) but make note of what that address is in case you need to return to it later.

For this exercise, we used the WordStar word processing program on an IBM Personal Computer. If you use a different word processor or a different system, don't worry. Although no two word processing programs utilize memory in exactly the same way (there are even differences between WordStar versions 2.0 and 3.0), the very nature of the way MS-DOS loads programs aids us in our endeavor. Nearly all word processors or text editors load the program first and use the memory *above* the program to store the text. When we load DEBUG into the system, more often than not, DEBUG will overlay the program portion of the word processor or text editor, allowing us to scan upward in memory looking for our lost text. If by chance your favorite text editor is smaller than DEBUG (in terms of code space used), some data may be lost, but on average sized files the majority of the data will still be there, above DEBUG.

The following examples begin with a sample text file, followed by a description of the contents of memory after loading WordStar, the text file, then exiting back to MS-DOS.

Load WordStar and create the following TEST.TXT file:

```
xxxx1xxxx2xxxx3xxxx4xxxx5xxxx6xxxx7xxxx8xxxx9x10
xxx11xxx12xxx13xxx14xxx15xxx16xxx17xxx18xxx19x20
xxx21xxx22xxx23xxx24xxx25xxx26xxx27xxx28xxx29x30
xxx31xxx32xxx33xxx34xxx35xxx36xxx37xxx38xxx39x40
xxx41xxx42xxx43xxx44xxx45xxx46xxx47xxx48xxx49x50
xxx51xxx52xxx53xxx54xxx55xxx56xxx57xxx58xxx59x60
xxx61xxx62xxx63xxx64xxx65xxx66xxx67xxx68xxx69x70
xxx71xxx72xxx73xxx74xxx75xxx76xxx77xxx78xxx79x80
xxx81xxx82xxx83xxx84xxx85xxx86xxx87xxx88xxx89x90
xxx91xxx92xxx93xxx94xxx95xxx96xxx97xxx98xxx99100
```

The contents of the file TEST.TXT may look a little strange at first, but the purpose of the text arrangement becomes clear when you see it (or part of it) in memory. This file consists of 100 5-character or 5-byte words. Each word is numbered 1 through 100, which enables us to count the number of portions or words of text we actually see in memory. Note that the last "words" on each line (x10, x20, . . . 100) consist of only three characters. Because we have to accommodate the carriage return and line feed characters at the end of each line, these three-character words become five-character words. Note that some word processor and text editor programs insert only a carriage return character when the RETURN or ENTER key is pressed. Such programs execute the line feed function automatically without actually inserting it in the text. In such cases, expand the last words on each line to four characters (xx10, xx20, . . . x100).

Now exit WordStar by saving the file using the <**CONTROL-KX**> command (or <**CONTROL-KD**>, then <**X**>). Immediately load DEBUG and start searching through memory for the lost text. Use the "d" (Display) command to dump the contents of memory on the screen until you see the sought-after text on the right side of the display. The following screen shows what our sample file looked like when we finally found it on our system. (Note that the actual addresses will quite likely be different on your system.)

```
A>debug
-d 7e10
68F8:7E10  00 00 00 00 00 00 00 00-B9 00 78 78 78 78 31 78   ........9.xxxx1x
68F8:7E20  78 78 78 32 78 78 78 78-33 78 78 78 78 34 78 78   xxx2xxxx3xxxx4xx
68F8:7E30  78 78 35 78 78 78 78 36-78 78 78 78 37 78 78 78   xx5xxxx6xxxx7xxx
68F8:7E40  78 38 78 78 78 78 39 78-31 30 0D 0A 78 78 78 31   x8xxxx9x10..xxx1
68F8:7E50  31 78 78 78 31 32 78 78-78 31 33 78 78 78 31 34   1xxx12xxx13xxx14
68F8:7E60  78 78 78 31 35 78 78 78-31 36 78 78 78 31 37 78   xxx15xxx16xxx17x
68F8:7E70  78 78 31 38 78 78 78 31-39 78 32 30 0D 0A 78 78   xx18xxx19x20..xx
68F8:7E80  78 32 31 78 78 78 32 32-78 78 78 32 33 78 78 78   x21xxx22xxx23xxx
-d
68F8:7E90  32 34 78 78 78 32 35 78-78 78 32 36 78 78 78 32   24xxx25xxx26xxx2
68F8:7EA0  37 78 78 78 32 38 78 78-78 32 39 78 33 30 0D 0A   7xxx28xxx29x30..
68F8:7EB0  78 78 78 33 31 78 78 78-33 32 78 78 78 33 33 78   xxx31xxx32xxx33x
68F8:7EC0  78 78 33 34 78 78 78 33-35 78 78 78 33 36 78 78   xx34xxx35xxx36xx
68F8:7ED0  78 33 37 78 78 78 33 38-78 78 78 33 39 78 34 30   x37xxx38xxx39x40
68F8:7EE0  0D 0A 78 78 78 34 31 78-78 78 34 32 78 78 78 34   ..xxx41xxx42xxx4
68F8:7EF0  33 78 78 78 34 34 78 78-78 34 35 78 78 78 34 36   3xxx44xxx45xxx46
68F8:7F00  78 78 78 34 37 78 78 78-34 38 78 78 78 34 39 78   xxx47xxx48xxx49x
-d
68F8:7F10  35 30 0D 0A 78 78 78 35-31 78 78 78 35 32 78 78   50..xxx51xxx52xx
68F8:7F20  78 35 33 78 78 78 35 34-78 78 78 35 35 78 78 78   x53xxx54xxx55xxx
68F8:7F30  35 36 78 78 78 35 37 78-78 78 35 38 78 78 78 35   56xxx57xxx58xxx5
68F8:7F40  39 78 36 30 0D 0A 78 78-78 36 31 78 78 78 36 32   9x60..xxx61xxx62
68F8:7F50  78 78 78 36 33 78 78 78-36 34 78 78 78 36 35 78   xxx63xxx64xxx65x
68F8:7F60  78 78 36 36 78 78 78 36-37 78 78 78 36 38 78 78   xx66xxx67xxx68xx
68F8:7F70  78 36 39 78 37 30 0D 0A-78 78 78 37 31 78 78 78   x69x70..xxx71xxx
68F8:7F80  37 32 78 78 78 37 33 78-78 78 37 34 78 78 78 37   72xxx73xxx74xxx7
-d
68F8:7F90  35 78 78 78 37 36 78 78-78 37 37 78 78 78 37 38   5xxx76xxx77xxx78
68F8:7FA0  78 78 78 37 39 78 38 30-0D 0A 78 78 78 38 31 78   xxx79x80..xxx81x
68F8:7FB0  78 78 38 32 78 78 78 38-33 78 78 78 38 34 78 78   xx82xxx83xxx84xx
68F8:7FC0  78 38 35 78 78 78 38 36-78 78 78 38 37 78 78 78   x85xxx86xxx87xxx
68F8:7FD0  38 38 78 78 78 38 39 78-39 30 0D 0A 78 78 78 39   88xxx89x90..xxx9
68F8:7FE0  31 78 78 78 39 32 78 78-78 39 33 78 78 78 39 34   1xxx92xxx93xxx94
68F8:7FF0  78 78 78 39 35 78 78 78-39 36 78 78 78 39 37 78   xxx95xxx96xxx97x
68F8:8000  78 78 39 38 78 78 78 39-39 31 30 30 0D 0A 1A 1A   xx98xxx99100....
-d
68F8:8010  1A 1A 1A 1A 1A 1A 1A 1A-1A 1A 00 E8 EC 01 E8 C2   ..........hl.hB
68F8:8020  ......
```

Write down the address where you found the text. In our case this was 68F8:7E10 (hex). Now, continue scanning memory until you no longer see the text you wish to recover and write down the last address (68F8:8019 in our example).

We see in the preceding screen that the entire file is still resident in memory. If we have created a file that is larger than the available memory, only the part of the file last edited is resident in memory. By scanning the memory beyond the limits shown in the preceding screen, we found that on our system, 19,449 bytes of text may be retained in memory. If we could recover that many bytes of text from memory, we could avoid a lot of retyping! In the previous example, however, we know we've reached the end of text at location 8019 because that's where the string of <**CONTROL-Z**> (ASCII 1A hex) values end. These values are required by WordStar as end-of-file markers, so these values are written to the disk when the file is saved.

The following screen shows how text stranded in memory can be saved to the disk while you are still in DEBUG.

```
-n test.sav
-h 8019 7e1a
FE33  01FF
-r bx
BX 0000
:
-r cx
CX 0000
:1ff
-r
AX = 0000 BX = 0000 CX = 01FF DX = 0000 SP = FFEE BP = 0000 SI = 0000 DI = 0000
DS = 68F8 ES = 68F8 SS = 68F8 CS = 68F8 IP = 0100    NV UP DI PL NZ NA PO NC
68F8:0100 C9            DB      C9
-w 7e1a
Writing 01FF bytes
-q
A>dir test.sav
 Volume in drive A has no label
 Directory of A:\
TEST     SAV        522   4-09-85 11:03a
         1 File(s)      188416 bytes free
 A>
```

The first step in this example is to specify a file name that DEBUG uses for disk read and write operations by using the N (Name) command. A new file name should be used, such as TEST.SAV. Next, use the offset address of the beginning of text (7E1A) and the ending address (8019) to calculate how many bytes should be written to the disk. DEBUG's built-in H ("hexarithmetic") command is a useful tool for calculating the result we need. When specifying the address values after the H command, make sure you specify the ending address before the starting address because the difference must be a positive integer. In the preceding screen, the result on the left is the sum of the two hexadecimal address values. The difference between the two address values (on the right) represents the number of bytes that we want to write to the disk. Load this value into the CX register in preparation for the W (Write) command. Note that the BX register is also used along with CX for values greater than FFFF (otherwise it should contain zero). We then "write" the data to the disk specifying the starting address.

When the file is saved and you've returned to MS-DOS, type the file to the screen to verify its contents. You can later combine this file with other parts of the recovered file using your word processor.

But what do we do when not all of the lost text can be found in RAM memory? WordStar, like most other word processing programs, constantly shuffles text in and out of memory as you move around in the text being edited. If you've been editing an existing file, say TEST.TXT, WordStar creates a file called TEST.$$$, which is used to store the new edited text. When you finish editing and save the edit session to disk, the program renames TEST.TXT to TEXT.BAK (overwriting the old TEST.BAK if it exists) and renames TEST.$$$ to TEST.TXT. Thus, in normal operation, TEST.$$$ is never seen in the directory when you return to MS-DOS. However, if the program fails abnormally, you find TEST.$$$ listed in the directory. If not all the text can be found in memory using DEBUG, check the contents of the $$$ file for the rest of the text. If the status of your file is not immediately obvious by looking at the directory listing, you may have to resort to a disk utility (such as Norton Utilities or Ultra Utilities described in the previous chapter) that shows hidden information on the disk. Before doing so, however, check the status of the disk with the CHKDSK program. This lets you know whether there are any stranded clusters on the disk. If stranded clusters are introduced to the disk after the failed edit session, part of the lost text may be in these lost clusters. You can recover them by specifying the /F parameter with CHKDSK but do so only after you've examined the contents of RAM memory and have saved stranded text to the disk.

As mentioned previously, the ways in which various word processing and text editing programs utilize memory differ greatly. All have different locations in memory for their work space. Some have larger work spaces than others. Some programs have multiple areas of memory for text manipulation, sometimes called buffers, which can complicate things even further. However, if you've never before tried to recover stranded data from memory, the previous examples illustrate some useful tools and techniques.

Recovering BASIC Programs from Memory

Have you ever done extensive work on a program using a BASIC interpreter only to discover that, after testing the program, a Return to MS-DOS command imbedded in the program terminated the interpreter before you had a chance to save the program to the disk? If the program is short (20 lines or less), this is a minor frustration. If the program is long, unexpected termination of the interpreter is disastrous.

Just as we were able to recover lost text from memory, we also should be able to recover "lost" BASIC programs because they must reside in memory in their entirety for the convenience of the interpreter. And for those interpreters which always deal with normal ASCII program text, the techniques described previously for recovering text from memory can be applied. But this is not the case with interpreters that deal with programs in "protected" mode or programs which are tokenized. A tokenized program, as seen by the interpreter, is a series of hexadecimal instruction values and absolute integer values. An ASCII program, on the other hand, consists of a series of two-digit ASCII values for each character or number, thus increasing the size of the file considerably.

Microsoft BASIC and IBM BASIC are the most popular examples of interpreters that deal with tokenized programs. Although these interpreters can read programs in standard ASCII format, they default to the tokenized state. They convert an ASCII program to its tokenized equivalent when it's loaded by the interpreter. The problem with trying to recover a lost tokenized BASIC program in memory is that it is virtually impossible to decipher with DEBUG's D (Display) command. So a slightly different approach must be taken.

The following example shows how to recover a program using Microsoft/IBM BASIC on the IBM Personal Computer. A variation of this procedure is required for other BASIC interpreters or different machines, but the following example provides some tips on how to approach the problem of program recovery on other machines.

Immediately after losing the program, the first step is to load DEBUG. According to the technical manual for the system, the address of the BASIC segment (where the beginning of our program is) can be found by examining location 0050:0010. Use the D command to display the first two values at this location. These values vary depending on the version of MS-DOS, the version of the BASIC interpreter, and the amount of memory installed in your system. Study the following screen and explanation.

```
A>debug
-d 0050:0010 l2
0050:0010 73 6B        BASIC segment address
-d 6b73:30 l2
6B73:0030 EF 11        This is the beginning address of the lost program
-f 6b73:11ee l1 ff     Enter an FF at the beginning address of the lost program at offset -1 (again,
                       reverse the two beginning-address bytes)
-d 6b73:358 l2         Locate the ending address of the lost program at offset 0358
6B73:0358 88 12        This is the ending address
```

The descriptive text beside the debug lines reads:

- `-d 0050:0010 l2` / `0050:0010 73 6B` — BASIC segment address
- `-d 6b73:30 l2` — Examine the segment (reverse the bytes) at offset 0030
- `6B73:0030 EF 11` — This is the beginning address of the lost program
- `-f 6b73:11ee l1 ff` — Enter an FF at the beginning address of the lost program at offset –1 (again, reverse the two beginning-address bytes)
- `-d 6b73:358 l2` — Locate the ending address of the lost program at offset 0358
- `6B73:0358 88 12` — This is the ending address

```
-h 1288 11ee          Calculate the number of bytes used by the program (reverse the 2-byte ending
                      address as well)
2476 009A             The second number is the difference, and therefore the program's length
-r cx                 Load the program's length into the
CX000                 CX register
-n %test.bas          Establish the file specification in which the program is to be stored
-w 6b73:11ee          Write the bytes starting at the program's beginning address
Writing 009A bytes
-q                    Return to MS-DOS
A>
```

When you return to the MS-DOS prompt, check the recovered file by loading it in the BASIC interpreter and listing it to the screen. The contents of the file are tokenized, so it can't be read any other way. The contents of the file should be intact.

Summary

This chapter shows some of the techniques that can be used to recover data stranded in memory. The two types of programs covered, Word Processors/Text Editors and BASIC Interpreters, are the most likely to be involved when data is lost in memory. Similar problems with other programs, such as database managers, for example, or communications programs, can often be approached using these techniques. If you lose important data in memory due to any circumstance short of a power failure or system reset, spending your time to investigate what can be done is well worth the effort.

COMPATIBILITY

Part

Differences Between
MS-DOS Versions

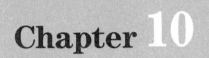

Chapter 10

ince the introduction of the first version of MS-DOS in 1981, the operating system has been enhanced to accommodate new hardware environments, fix problems, and generally improve its operation. Although many of these enhancements resulted in more powerful capabilities, they have also caused a few headaches because the new functions are not compatible with older versions of MS-DOS. In order to keep the value of these enhancements in proper perspective, this chapter includes information that helps you determine the compatibility among the different versions of MS-DOS when developing application programs using a particular version. The information in this chapter is especially useful if you're using assembly language to develop your programs.

Except for those commands which are, by design, tools for programmers, such as the debugger (DEBUG) and linker (LINK), new and enhanced MS-DOS commands are of relatively little use to programmers. Changes that are of special interest to a programmer include MS-DOS interrupts, function calls, error codes, floppy and hard disk formats, and file manipulation. These areas can be dealt with fairly easily because topics such as function calls exist in all implementations of a given MS-DOS version.

Other areas, such as memory mapping, cannot be dealt with generically because they often vary according to the hardware environment for which an implementation of MS-DOS is targeted. This is the case with the IBM Personal Computer and close compatibles. Systems with radically different hardware architectures have different memory mapping schemes specific to the implementation of MS-DOS. Even among some of the more "standard" areas, such as interrupts, critical differences exist.

Therefore, a programmer needs to know the dos and don'ts when developing an application program. The differences are especially important if you're developing a program that is intended to have as wide a distribution as possible. Remember that there are different machine-specific versions of MS-DOS and that there are also lots of machines with different hardware architectures and implementations of MS-DOS. Simply following the *MS-DOS Technical Manual* can be very misleading if you're developing a program that is intended to run under *all* implementations of MS-DOS.

This chapter is not meant to replace the *MS-DOS Technical Manual,* but by presenting an overview of the differences between the versions of MS-DOS, is intended to complement the technical manuals of all versions of MS-DOS. The information is divided into topics by which the differences between all the versions of MS-DOS (beginning with 1.0 and through 3.1) are presented. Where appropriate, this chapter includes for programmers specific technical information and tips about suggested procedures and things to avoid, depending on the nature of the application program you're developing.

General Compatibility Recommendations

Various degrees of compatibility are available to a programmer. In most cases, you want to achieve total compatibility. However, because we generally like to design "slick" programs, we often take advantage of the "new and improved" functions built into our implementation of MS-DOS, such as fancy screen functions or special-purpose interrupts, and frequently forget the consequences of noncompatibility. Choosing a degree of compatibility is often the compromise we make. If we must achieve total compatibility, the following rules are useful.

1. Do not under any circumstances use any 8086-family INT (interrupt) instruction, except those that are designated as *MS-DOS Interrupts.*

2. Never write data to any absolute memory location. Let MS-DOS handle memory usage.

3. Never use the 8086-family IN and OUT instructions.

4. Avoid using instructions that are only provided by the 80188, 80186, and 80286 microprocessors, as follows:

   PUSH *immediate* (push immediate)
   PUSHA (push all registers)
   POPA (pop all registers)
   SHR *>1* (shift right with immediate value greater than 1)
   SHL *>1* (shift left with immediate value greater than 1)
   IMUL *dest.-reg.,source,immediate* (multiply immediate signed integer)

INS *source-string,port* (in string)
OUTS *port,dest.-string* (out string)
ENTER (enter procedure)
LEAVE (leave procedure)
BOUND (detect value out of range)

Avoid using the instruction POP CS because it functions properly only with the 8088 and 8086 microprocessors. Be aware of all the other differences in operation between the different processors in the 8086 family.

5. If the machine you're using to develop a program has routines stored in ROM, never call these routines. Don't even attempt to read them.

6. Never use an MS-DOS function call that is supported only in MS-DOS versions above version 1.0.

7. Always make sure that information written to the screen consists only of standard ASCII characters (00 through to 7F hexadecimal). Avoid using any other characters, such as those in the extended character set of IBM PCs and compatibles. Avoid bit-mapped graphics.

If you find that you must break any of the rules from number 1 through 5, you might as well break rule number 6 because your first option would be to write a device driver targeted for a machine that would otherwise be incompatible. And because installable device drivers are supported only under MS-DOS version 2.0 and above, you'll find yourself using function calls not supported by MS-DOS versions 1.0 and 1.1. If you need (or want) to break rule number 7, write a device driver for the target machine or a "universal" installation program that can be used to customize the application program for a variety of terminals and monitors. The installation program must, of course, at least follow rule number 7.

Because one solution to incompatibility might be a device driver, we find ourselves already breaking rule number 6, which introduces another level of compatibility that needs to be considered. In many cases, you want to break rule number 6 intentionally because not all versions of MS-DOS provide a particular function call that you like or need to use. For example, if your application program made extensive use of tree-structured directories, you probably would want to use function calls 39 through 3B, in which case the level of compatibility would be restricted to MS-DOS version 2.0 and higher versions and would exclude versions 1.0 and 1.1. Similarly, if your program needs to make use of the networking functions supported by MS-DOS 3.1, the program would not be compatible with MS-DOS versions 1.0 through 2.1.

Never forget to state plainly the compatibility restrictions of your program, either in the source code or the documentation (preferably both). If your program is to be made commercially available, make sure that compatibility restrictions (or the lack of restrictions!) are clearly stated both in the packaging and in advertisements.

If you develop a program designed to operate under any version of MS-DOS but which contains some routines that can be optionally executed if a particular version of MS-DOS is being used, use Function 30h (Get DOS Version Number) to control whether or not certain routines are executed. Although this function is provided only in MS-DOS version 2.0 and higher versions, it can be executed using versions 1.0 and 1.1 without ill effects as long as the precautionary steps described under *Invoking DOS Functions* in your MS-DOS manual are followed.

To use this function, load 30h into the AH register. When INT 21h is executed, the major version number is returned in register AL and the minor version in register AH. If AL contains 00, you can assume that the version of MS-DOS is either 1.0 or 1.1. Any other number in AL indicates the version number. For example, if you are using MS-DOS version 2.00, 02 is found in AL and 00 is found in AH. If you are using MS-DOS version 3.10, you find 03 in AL and 10 in AH. Even if you don't need to control the optional execution of certain routines, this function allows you to control the display of a friendly message if a user attempts to run the program under an incompatible version of MS-DOS. The routine in Listing 10-1 can be implemented in your programs to accomplish this function.

Listing 10-1. Routine To Determine the MS-DOS Version

```
; ROUTINE TO DETERMINE THE VERSION OF MS-DOS UNDER WHICH
; THE PROGRAM CONTAINING THIS ROUTINE IS RUNNING
;
; NOTE: Make sure that the following statements are defined
; either in the data segment or in the data area of the
; code segment in your program:
;
;       majver db ?     ; major version number (hex)
;       minver db ?     ; minor version number (hex)
;
;
getdosver       proc    near    ; change to far if needed
;
        push    ax              ; save registers
        push    bx
        push    cx
;
        mov     ah,30h          ; get the function number ready
        int     21h             ; execute the MS-DOS function call
```

Listing 10-1. cont.

```
;
        cmp     al,0            ; see whether it's pre-version 2.0
        jnz     dos2plus        ; if not, it's version 2.00 or above
        mov     al,1            ; major version is 1.00 (because we
        mov     ah,0            ; know AH still contains the function
                                ; number (30h), we won't be able
                                ; to find out what the minor version
                                ; is, so we assume the worst case:
                                ; version 1.00)
;
dos2plus:
        mov     majver,al       ; save major version
        mov     minver,ah       ; save minor version
;
        pop     cx              ; restore registers
        pop     bx
        pop     ax
;
        ret                     ; return
;
getdosver       endp
```

In the previous subroutine, you can do several things with the version number stored in the two variables "majver" and "minver." Each number can be converted to decimal ASCII for output to the screen with a message, or you can use these variables to control whether or not certain parts of the program are to be executed.

High-Level Language Considerations

If you're writing a program with a high-level language, be aware of the specifications of the particular compiler or interpreter being used. If the product specifications state that your compiler or interpreter only runs under a particular version of MS-DOS, your compiled or interpreted programs probably don't function under an earlier version. This is especially true for BASIC interpreters, such as Microsoft/IBM BASIC and GWBASIC because new versions of these interpreters are often released to complement new versions of MS-DOS.

MS-DOS Interrupts

The software interrupts defined for use by MS-DOS are consistent among all versions except interrupt 2Fh, which has been added to version 3.0. Table 10-1 lists the interrupts.

Table 10-1.   MS-DOS Interrupts

| Interrupt | | MS-DOS Version | | | | | |
INT	Description	1.0	1.1	2.0	2.1	3.0	3.1
20	Program terminate						
21	Function request						
22	Terminate address						
23	<**CONTROL-BREAK**> exit address						
24	Critical error handler vector			yes			
25	Absolute disk read						
26	Absolute disk write						
27	Terminate but stay resident						
28	Not usable			(Used internally by MS-DOS)			
29				(reserved)			
2A	MS-NET access*			no			yes
2B thru 2E	Not usable			(reserved)			
2F	Printer					yes	///
2F	Multiplex interrupt			no		///	yes
30 thru 3F	Not usable			(reserved)			

* Not part of the MS-DOS Operating System.

Many machines have several interrupts not listed in Table 10-1. These interrupts are defined for special uses, such as accessing the BIOS (basic input/output system) routines or communicating with serial communications ports. Don't confuse these interrupts with those defined for use with MS-DOS. Only those interrupts described in your *MS-DOS Technical Manual* are true MS-DOS interrupts. In order to maintain compatibility with all implementations of MS-DOS, avoid using any interrupts that are not true *MS-DOS interrupts*.

Function Calls

The use of function calls is probably the most important factor of compatibility when programming in assembly language. Because almost all operations that you normally need performed by MS-DOS can be initiated by function calls, you can avoid the use of interrupts (except INT 21) and BIOS calls. By using MS-DOS function calls, you also eliminate any need to include in your programs certain types of routines, such as those that manipulate files. If blindingly fast execution of your programs is not crucial, it's worthwhile to let MS-DOS perform all standard operations by means of function calls. MS-DOS performs function calls fast enough for most situations.

Performing Function Calls the Standard Way

When the first version of MS-DOS was introduced, two methods were provided to perform function calls. The first is recommended for use with all versions of MS-DOS and the procedure is as follows.

1. Save the contents of the AX, BX, CX, and DX registers as appropriate by pushing them onto the stack.

2. Place the function number in the AH register.

3. Place other data in the registers specified for the particular function to be executed if and when appropriate.

4. Execute the INT 21h instruction.

5. Depending on the function executed, variable data is returned in specified registers that can be later read and used by your program. Some functions don't return anything.

6. Perform the desired operation, if needed, based on the returned data from the function just executed.

7. Restore the original contents of the registers.

The previous procedure is recommended for all versions of MS-DOS. The second method is described in the following section.

Performing Function Calls in Compatibility Mode

The second method that MS-DOS provides for compatibility with other operating systems applies specifically to CP/M-80 and CP/M-86. This method doesn't really provide the capability of running CP/M programs under MS-DOS. It only simplifies the conversion of CP/M programs to MS-DOS by not always requiring the redefinition of the function call process. You will, however, probably have to change many of the function numbers. This method only works with MS-DOS functions 0 through 24h. You might also encounter difficulties with register usage of some function calls, so this method should be avoided unless you want to test a program before it has been fully converted. MS-DOS requires that function calls using this second method be made using the following procedure.

1. Save the contents of the AX, BX, CX, and DX registers as appropriate by pushing them onto the stack.

2. Place the function number in the CL register. (Only function numbers 0 through 24h may be used.)

3. Place other data in the registers specified for the particular function to be executed as desired.

4. Make an intrasegment call to location 5 in the current code segment. This location contains a long call to the MS-DOS function dispatcher.

5. Depending on the function executed, variable data is returned in specified registers that can be later read and used by your program. Some functions don't return anything.

   NOTE: This procedure always wipes out the contents of the AX register. All other registers, however, are affected in the same manner as when the standard function call procedure is followed.

6. Restore the original contents of the registers.

And Yet Another Method (MS-DOS 2.00 and Higher Versions Only)

A third method for making function calls was introduced in MS-DOS version 2.00. This method can be used with higher versions as well but doesn't operate correctly with any previous versions. The third method is accomplished in the following manner.

1. Save the contents of the AX, BX, CX, and DX registers as appropriate by pushing them onto the stack.

2. Place the function number in the AH register.

3. Place other data in the registers specified for the particular function to be executed.

4. Make a long call to offset hex 50 in the program segment prefix.

5. Depending on the function executed, variable data is returned in specified registers that can be later read and used by your program. Some functions don't return anything.

6. Restore the original contents of the registers by POPing the stack.

As of the release of MS-DOS version 3.10, both Microsoft and IBM recommend that this method not be used. Why then was it introduced? One possible use of the method may explain why it was introduced. Offset 50 hex in the PSP (program segment prefix) usually contains an INT 21h instruction. By using the method described previously, the programmer has channeled all MS-DOS function code accesses (excluding other interrupts) through one location. By altering the instruction located at offset 50 hex, you can redirect all of the program's MS-DOS accesses. Was this an abandoned attempt of Microsoft's to implement multitasking? Only Microsoft knows for sure.

Functions Supported in Different Versions

Table 10-2 lists all the MS-DOS functions supported in versions 1.0 through 3.1 and indicates which functions are new for certain versions.

Table 10-2. MS-DOS Functions

Function		MS-DOS Version					
Num (Hex)	Description	1.0	1.1	2.0	2.1	3.0	3.1
0	Program terminate						
1	Keyboard input						
2	Display output						
3	Auxiliary input			yes			
4	Auxiliary output						
5	Printer output						
6	Direct console I/O						
7	Direct console input without echo						

Table 10-2. cont.

Function		MS-DOS Version					
Num (Hex)	Description	1.0	1.1	2.0	2.1	3.0	3.1
8	Console input without echo						
9	Print string						
A	Buffered keyboard input						
B	Check standard input status						
C	Clear keyboard buffer and invoke keyboard function						
D	Disk reset						
E	Select disk						
F	Open file			yes			
10	Close file						
11	Search for first entry						
12	Search for next entry						
13	Delete file						
14	Sequential read						
15	Sequential write						
16	Create file						
17	Rename file						
18	(reserved)	///					
19	Current disk						
1A	Set disk transfer address						
1B	Allocation Table information			yes			
1C	Allocation Table information for specific device						
1D thru 20	(reserved)	///					
21	Random read						
22	Random write			yes			
23	File size						

Table 10-2. cont.

Num (Hex)	Description		1.0	1.1	2.0	2.1	3.0	3.1
Function			**MS-DOS Version**					
24	Set relative record field		yes	yes	yes	yes	yes	yes
25	Set interrupt vector		yes	yes	yes	yes	yes	yes
26	Create new program segment		yes	yes	yes	yes	yes	yes
27	Random block read		yes	yes	yes	yes	yes	yes
28	Random block write		yes	yes	yes	yes	yes	yes
29	Parse file name		yes	yes	yes	yes	yes	yes
2A	Get date		yes	yes	yes	yes	yes	yes
2B	Set date		yes	yes	yes	yes	yes	yes
2C	Get time		yes	yes	yes	yes	yes	yes
2D	Set time		yes	yes	yes	yes	yes	yes
2E	Set/reset verify switch		yes	yes	yes	yes	yes	yes
2F	Get disk transfer address		no	no	yes	yes	yes	yes
30	Get DOS version number		no	no	yes	yes	yes	yes
31	Terminate process and remain resident		no	no	yes	yes	yes	yes
32	(reserved)		/////	/////	/////	/////	/////	/////
33	<CONTROL-BREAK> check		no	no	yes	yes	yes	yes
34	(reserved)		/////	/////	/////	/////	/////	/////
35	Get vector		no	no	yes	yes	yes	yes
36	Get disk free space		no	no	yes	yes	yes	yes
37	(reserved)		/////	/////	/////	/////	/////	/////
38	Country dependent information	Get only	no	no	no	yes	yes	/////
		Get/Set	no	no	no	no	no	yes
39	Create subdirectory (MKDIR)		no	no	no	yes	yes	yes
3A	Remove subdirectory (RMDIR)		no	no	no	yes	yes	yes
3B	Change current directory (CHDIR)		no	no	no	yes	yes	yes

Table 10-2. cont.

Function		MS-DOS Version					
Num (Hex)	Description	1.0	1.1	2.0	2.1	3.0	3.1
3C	Create a file (CREAT)						
3D	Open a file						
3E	Close a file handle						
3F	Read from a file or device						
40	Write to a file or device						
41	Delete a file from a specified directory (UNLINK)	no		yes			
42	Move file read/write pointer (LSEEK)						
43	Change file mode (CHMOD)						
44	I/O control for devices (IOCTL)						
45	Duplicate a file handle (DUP)						
46	Force a duplicate of a handle (CDUP)						
47	Get current directory						
48	Allocate memory						
49	Free allocated memory						
4A	Modify allocated memory blocks (SETBLOCK)						
4B	Load or execute a program (EXEC)						
4C	Terminate a process (EXIT)	no		yes			
4D	Get return code of a subprocess (WAIT)						
4E	Find first matching file (FIND FIRST)						
4F	Find next matching file						
50 thru 53	(reserved)	///////////////////////////////////////					
54	Get verify setting	no		yes			

Table 10-2. cont.

Num (Hex)	Description	1.0	1.1	2.0	2.1	3.0	3.1
Function		MS-DOS Version					
55	(reserved)	//////////////////////////////////////					
56	Rename a file	no			yes		
57	Get/set a file's date and time						
58	(reserved)	//////////////////////////////////////					
59	Get extended error	no				yes	
5A	Create temporary file						
5B	Create new file						
5C	Lock/unlock file access						
5D	(reserved)	//////////////////////////////////////					
5E00	Get machine name	no				yes	
5E03	Printer setup						
5F02	Get redirection list entry						
5F03	Redirect a device						
5F04	Cancel redirection						
60 & 61	(reserved)	//////////////////////////////////////					
62	Get program segment prefix address (PSP)	no				yes	

In view of how MS-DOS functions are defined in the various versions as shown in Table 10-2, the range of functions can be divided into "functional" groups, which, incidentally, tend to define boundaries between different versions of MS-DOS, but not always. These groups are described in the following paragraphs.

Program Terminate Group

The only function in this group is Function 0. This function is almost identical to the INT 20h interrupt. Although INT 20h is defined as Program Terminate in almost all implementations of MS-DOS, you should use Function 0 instead so that the use of the INT instruction is avoided. Another thing to watch out for is that the manuals of MS-DOS version 2.0 and higher versions recommend that Function 4Ch (Terminate a Process, also known as EXIT) be used as the "preferred" method to terminate a program. However, Function 4Ch doesn't exist in versions prior to 2.00.

Following the manual's advice for terminating a program is a good idea. We highly recommend that you always use Function 4Ch to terminate your programs for MS-DOS version 2.00 and higher. If you want your programs to run under all versions, use the Get DOS Version function (30h) to determine which program terminate code to use: Use Function 0 for MS-DOS versions 1.0 and 1.1, and use Function 4Ch for all other versions.

Standard Character Device Input/Output Group (01h-0Ch)

This group includes Functions 01 through 0Ch. They're used for input from the keyboard, output to the console display, output to the printer, and as input and output to and from the auxiliary (logical) devices. These functions operate the same way throughout all versions of MS-DOS and are similar in nature to the equivalent range of functions in CP/M.

Standard File Management Group (0Dh-24h, 27h-29h)

This group includes functions 0Dh through 24h and 27h through 29h. Using these functions to manipulate files allows compatibility with all versions of MS-DOS. Some of these functions are similar to the equivalent range of functions used in CP/M. Although some fancier functions for file manipulation were introduced in MS-DOS 2.00 (described next), carefully consider the compatibility implications when using them. The section on file manipulation towards the end of this chapter also contains some important information that you should know about when deciding which group of functions to use.

Standard Non-Device Functions (25h, 26h, 2Ah-2Eh)

This group includes functions 25h, 26h, and 2Ah through 2Eh. Note that Function 2Eh is the highest function supported in MS-DOS versions prior to 2.00. These functions perform a variety of different tasks that aren't related to devices: retrieving and setting the current time and date, setting the interrupt vector, creating a new program segment, and setting or resetting the verify switch. All of these functions are specific to MS-DOS, and equivalents are not found in CP/M. All of these functions perform well in all versions of MS-DOS, but special attention should be given to Function 25h (Set Interrupt Vector). This function requires two things before it is executed: the address of the interrupt handling routine must be loaded into the DX register and the data segment (DS:DX), and the interrupt number must be loaded into the AL register. Because this function deals with interrupts, be careful with its use because it may make your program incompatible with other implementations of MS-DOS and hardware environments.

Extended (General) Function Group (2Fh-38h, 4Ch-4Fh, 54h-57h, 59h-5Fh, 62h)

This group of functions crosses the boundaries of MS-DOS versions 2.00 through 3.10. Functions 59h through 5Ch and 62h exist only in versions 3.00 and higher and functions 5Eh and 5Fh exist only in versions 3.10 and higher. None of these functions are available under MS-DOS versions below 2.00. Additionally, as of MS-DOS version 3.10, functions 32h, 34h, 37h, 50h through 53h, 55h, 58h, 5Dh, 60h, and 61h are reserved (not defined for use). Functions existing in all versions also work consistently among them, with the following exceptions.

1. Function 38h (Country Dependent Information). Under MS-DOS version 3.00 and higher versions, this function can be used to set country-dependent information as well as to retrieve the information. However, in versions starting with 2.00 up to (but not including) 3.00, the function can only be used to retrieve information.

2. Function 44h (I/O Control for Devices [IOCTRL]) has two new additional parameters in MS-DOS version 3.00 to support device drivers (AL = 08h to check for removable media and AL = 0Bh to change the sharing retry count on a block device). In MS-DOS 3.10, two more parameters were added to check for redirection on a network (AL = 09h checks devices, whereas AL = 0Ah checks file or device handles).

3. Functions 5Eh and 5Fh are supported only under versions 3.1 and higher and are used only in network environments. Each is subdivided into several subfunctions: they are loaded into the AX register as 4-digit hexadecimal (16-bit) function numbers, with the last two digits representing the specific function (or

subfunction). Function 5E00h is used to retrieve the name of a machine connected to the same network as the machine making the function call. Function 5E02h is used to initialize a printer connected to a network that is shared by several computers. Functions 5F02h through 5F04h are used to control redirection of data throughout a network: 5F03h redirects a device, 5F02h retrieves redirection information, and 5F04h cancels redirection.

Directory Group (39h-3Bh, 47h)

This group consists of Functions 39h through 3Bh and 47h, provided under MS-DOS versions 2.00 and higher. They each complement the sub-directory commands: 39h creates a subdirectory (MKDIR or MD), 3Ah removes a directory (RMDIR or RD), and 3Bh changes the current directory (CHDIR or CD). Function 47h is used to retrieve the current-directory information (as if the CD command were entered without any parameters).

Memory/Process Management Group (48h-4Bh)

Several functions added to MS-DOS version 2.00 can be used for the management of processes and memory. Most of the functions in this group deal with controlling memory allocation. The last function, 4Bh, is useful for programs that call and load other programs or overlays. Note that Function 4Ch (Terminate a Process [EXIT]) should always be used in programs that are called and loaded by function 4Bh.

Clearly maintaining a total or reasonable degree of compatibility can be complex and rather frustrating. It's always good practice to decide beforehand what level of compatibility you want to achieve, then make note of the MS-DOS functions you can use.

Error Codes

The errors generated by MS-DOS, their types, and the way they're handled have changed considerably from earlier versions of MS-DOS. Not only have new error codes been introduced in later versions, but new mechanisms of error reporting have been introduced as well. The following paragraphs describe the differences in error handling among the versions of MS-DOS.

Critical or Hard Error Codes (via INT 24h)

In MS-DOS version 1.0, the process of returning error codes is handled exclusively by the INT 24h interrupt vector. All of these error codes represent errors that are hardware-related and are considered serious or critical in nature. These same codes and their reporting mechanism are supported in all later versions, although some new error codes were introduced in MS-DOS version 2.0.

For an application program to respond to this error reporting mechanism, the program's initialization code should save the INT 24h vector and replace the vector with one pointing to the program's custom error routine. Before the program terminates, the original INT 24h vector should be restored to its original state. Up to seven codes can be returned through this mechanism under MS-DOS version 1.0, up to 13 codes under MS-DOS version 2.0, and up to 16 codes under MS-DOS version 3.0 and higher.

Table 10-3 lists the codes and indicates which are supported only in MS-DOS Version 2.00 and above. The critical error codes shown in Table 10-3 can also be retrieved through another error reporting mechanism introduced in MS-DOS version 2.0. Under this version, certain function calls return error codes when an error condition occurs. This mechanism is described in the paragraph following the table.

Function Call Error-Return Codes (MS-DOS Version 2.0 and Above Only)

Beginning with version 2.0, in all versions of MS-DOS, some function calls return error codes in certain registers if an error results after the function executes. If an error occurs, the carry flag is set, and the appropriate register can be examined (if supported by the function) for the error code. If the carry flag is clear, you can assume no error occurred. The critical or hard errors described previously (determined via the INT 24h mechanism) are also presented through this mechanism, although different code values are used. Under all versions of MS-DOS from 2.0 to 3.1, the following functions return an error code in the AX register if the carry flag is set after execution: 38h through 4Bh, 4Eh, 4Fh, 56h, 57h, 5Ah through 5Ch, and 5E00h through 5E04h. The AL half of AX should always be examined for the error code because some functions return other information in AH. For all of these functions, the presence of 0 in AL indicates that no error occurred.

Table 10-4 lists all of the error codes that can be returned after a function call is made. The version(s) of MS-DOS under which each code is supported is indicated. Note also that error codes 19 through 31 correspond on a one-to-one basis to INT 24h type error codes 0 through Ch, and error code 34 corresponds to INT 24h type error code Fh.

Table 10-3.   Critical Error Codes (via INT 24h)

Error Code	Description	MS-DOS Version 1.XX	2.XX	3.XX
0	Write attempt on write-protected disk	yes		
1	Unknown unit	no		
2	Drive not ready	yes		
3	Unknown command	no		
4	Data error (CRC)	yes		
5	Bad request structure length	no		
6	Seek error	yes		
7	Unknown media type	no	yes	
8	Sector not found	yes		
9	Printer out of paper	no		
A	Write fault	yes		
B	Read fault	no		
C	General failure	yes		
D	Not defined	///////	///////	///////
E	Not defined	///////	///////	///////
F	Invalid disk change	no		yes

Table 10-4.   Function Call Error Codes
(MS-DOS Versions 2.0 through 3.1 only)

Error Code	Description	MS-DOS Version 2.0	2.1	3.0	3.1
1	Invalid function number				
2	File not found				
3	Path not found		yes		
4	Too many open files				
5	Access denied				

Table 10-4. cont.

Error Code	Description	MS-DOS Version			
		2.0	2.1	3.0	3.1
6	Invalid handle				
7	Memory control blocks destroyed				
8	Insufficient memory				
9	Invalid memory block address				
10	Invalid environment				
11	Invalid format				
12	Invalid access code				
13	Invalid data				
14	(reserved)				
15	Invalid drive specified				
16	Remove attempt of current dir.				
17	Not the same device				
18	No more files		yes		
19	INT 24h error 0 (Table 10-3)				
20	INT 24h error 1 (Table 10-3)				
21	INT 24h error 2 (Table 10-3)				
22	INT 24h error 3 (Table 10-3)				
23	INT 24h error 4 (Table 10-3)				
24	INT 24h error 5 (Table 10-3)				
25	INT 24h error 6 (Table 10-3)				
26	INT 24h error 7 (Table 10-3)				
27	INT 24h error 8 (Table 10-3)				
28	INT 24h error 9 (Table 10-3)				
29	INT 24h error A (Table 10-3)				
30	INT 24h error B (Table 10-3)				
31	INT 24h error C (Table 10-3)				
32	Sharing violation				
33	Lock violation	no		yes	
34	INT 24h error F (Table 10-3)				

Table 10-4. cont.

Error Code	Description	MS-DOS Version			
		2.0	2.1	3.0	3.1
35	FCB unavailable	no		yes	
36 thru 49	(reserved)	/ / / / / / / / / / / / / / /	/ / / / / / / / / / / / / / /	/ / / / / / / / / / / / / / /	/ / / / / / / / / / / / / / /
50	Network request not supported	no		yes	
51	Remote computer not listening				
52	Duplicate name on network				
53	Network name not found				
54	Network busy				
55	Network device no longer exists				
56	Net. BIOS command limit exceeded				
57	Network adapter hardware error				
58	Incorrect response from network.				
59	Unexpected network error				
60	Incompatible remote adapter				
61	Print queue full				
62	Queue not full				
63	Not enough space to print file				
64	Network name was deleted				
65	Access denied				
66	Network device type incorrect	no		yes	
67	Network name not found				
68	Network name limit exceeded				
69	Net. BIOS session limit exceeded				
70	Temporarily paused				
71	Network request not accepted				
72	Print/disk redirection paused				
73 thru 79	(reserved)	/ / / / / / / / / / / / / / /	/ / / / / / / / / / / / / / /	/ / / / / / / / / / / / / / /	/ / / / / / / / / / / / / / /

Table 10-4. cont.

Error Code	Description	MS-DOS Version			
		2.0	2.1	3.0	3.1
80	File exists	no		yes	
81	(reserved)	/////	/////	/////	/////
82	Cannot make <function>	no		yes	
83	Failure on INT 24h				

Function Call Extended Error Information (MS-DOS Version 3.0 and Above Only)

Because of concerns about compatibility between all versions of MS-DOS, it wasn't possible to add error-return information handling to all new and existing function calls in later versions. Therefore, in order to enhance MS-DOS' error handling capabilities, a new mechanism called the Extended Error Code was introduced under MS-DOS version 3.0. Under 3.0 and all subsequent versions, when a function executes and either the carry flag is set or the AL register contains FFh, additional detailed error information can be retrieved by immediately loading 0 into the BX register, then issuing Function Call 59h (Get Extended Error). The information returns as shown in Table 10-5.

Table 10-5.   Extended Error Return Information

Register	Contents
AX	Error code (see Table 10-4)
BH	Error class
BL	Suggested action
CH	Locus

Error Code
The error code returned in the AX register can be any one of those listed in Table 10-4, depending on the version of MS-DOS.

Error Class
One of the values in Table 10-6 is returned in the BH register and indicates the general category of the error. This can help determine the actual cause of the error because the same error code could occur twice because of different causes.

Table 10-6.   Error Classes

Value	Definition
1	Out of resource (no more space, channels, etc.)
2	Temporary situation (problem may go away, such as a locked file)
3	Authorization (denied access)
4	Internal (MS-DOS determined that error was caused by an internal bug, not by the user or the system)
5	Hardware failure (problem not caused by user program)
6	System failure (Serious failure of system software, although may not be directly the fault of the user program—such as missing or faulty configuration files)
7	Application program error (such as, inconsistent requests)
8	Not found (file or other item not found)
9	Bad format (file or item of incorrect format)
10	Locked (file or item is interlocked)
11	Media (media failure such as incorrect disk, CRC error, incorrect disk in drive, or damaged media surface)
12	Already exists (collision with existing item such as a file name or machine name)
13	Unknown (error not categorized or is inappropriate)

Suggested Action

One of the values in Table 10-7 is returned in the BL register and suggests a course of action to recover from the error condition.

Table 10-7.   Suggested Error-Recovery Actions

Value	Definition
1	Retry (retry a few times and if failure persists, prompt user to determine whether program should continue or be aborted)
2	Delay retry (same as retry but pause first to determine whether error recovers itself)
3	User (prompt user to reenter input—incorrect text may have been typed)
4	Abort (terminate the program normally after cleanup)
5	Immediate exit (terminate the program abnormally skipping cleanup)
6	Ignore (the error can be ignored)
7	Retry after user intervention (continue operation after user interaction, such as replacing a disk)

Locus

The values in Table 10-8 are returned in the CH register and provide additional information as to where the problem is located.

Table 10-8.   Locus of Error

Value	Definition
1	Unknown (nonspecific or not appropriate)
2	Block device (related to disk storage media)
3	Network (MS-DOS version 3.1 only [error is related to the network])
4	Serial device (error is related to a serial link or device)
5	Memory (error is related to RAM memory)

Because of the changes made in error handling in newer versions of MS-DOS, programmers face difficult choices. The new "extended error" information technique is obviously the most useful for designing error trapping routines in your programs. But its price is noncompatibility. If you must include this technique in your programs and also must maintain some form of downward compatibility with older versions of MS-DOS, the Get MS-DOS Version routine (described earlier in this chapter) could prove useful. For MS-DOS versions below 2.0, you would check only for those error codes supported by the version. For versions 2.0 and 2.1, you would expand the error-handling capability and provide for the detection of more error codes. And for versions 3.0 and higher, you could expand error-handling even further with the Get Extended Error information function call.

Disk Formats

As pointed out in Chapter 8, *Disk Layout and File Recovery Information,* several disk formats are supported by the various versions of MS-DOS. Table 10-9 provides a summary of the specifications of all the 5¼-inch and 8-inch floppy disk formats supported under MS-DOS up to version 3.1. For more detailed information, however, refer to Chapter 8.

Although other formats and types of disks, such as 3½-inch disks, are supported under some implementations of MS-DOS, Table 10-9 only shows those formats which are officially supported by MS-DOS as of the printing of this book. Similarly, specifications of hard disks are not covered because many variations are product or system specific and therefore not officially supported under "generic" MS-DOS. The only hard disk formats that can be considered standard are those used in the IBM XT (10Mb) and the IBM AT (20Mb). Many other hard disks designed to be

Table 10-9. MS-DOS Floppy Disk Formats

	5¼-Inch					8-Inch		
MS-DOS version	1.00	1.10	2.00	2.00	3.00	*		
Format descriptor byte	FFE	FFF	FFC	FFD	FF9	FFE	FFD	FFE
Sides	1	2	1	2	2	1	1	2
Tracks per side	40	40	40	40	80	77	77	77
Sectors per track	8	8	9	9	15	26	26	8
Bytes per sector	512	512	512	512	512	128	128	1024
Sectors per cluster	1	2	1	2	1	4	4	1
Reserved sectors	1	1	1	1	1	1	4	1
Sectors per FAT	1	1	2	2	7	6	6	2
Num. of FATs	2	2	2	2	2	2	2	2
Root directory sectors	4	7	4	7	14	17	17	6
Root directory entries	64	112	64	112	224	68	68	192
Total number of sectors	320	640	360	720	2400	2002	2002	1232
Total number of usable sectors	313	630	351	708	2371	1972	1968	1221
Total number of clusters	313	315	351	354	2371	493	492	1221
Total capacity	160 Kbytes	320 Kbytes	180 Kbytes	360 Kbytes	1.2 Mbytes	250.25 Kbytes	250.25 Kbytes	1.232 Mbytes
Total usable capacity	156.5 Kbytes	315 Kbytes	175.5 Kbytes	354 Kbytes	1.1855 Mbytes	246.5 Kbytes	246 Kbytes	1.221 Mbytes

* The format descriptor byte values used to identify the format of 8-inch disks are the same as those used for some of the 5¼-inch disks. The distinction is handled either within the BIOS of the particular implementation of MS-DOS or within a device driver. Most implementations of MS-DOS, especially in those systems that have the BIOS stored in ROM, do not have the necessary routines within the BIOS for 8-inch disks. Thus, support is usually handled with a special device driver. Because the first single-density 8-inch format has the same descriptor byte value (FFE) as the last (double-density) format, MS-DOS makes the distinction when it tries to read the disk: The system first assumes that the disk is formatted to single density. If no error occurs after reading the first sector, MS-DOS continues treating the disk as a single-density disk. If an error occurs after first reading the disk, MS-DOS assumes that the disk is formatted to double density and tries to read the first sector again. Note also that some systems support a double-density format for single-sided 8-inch disks, which yields a total disk capacity approximately half that of double-sided disks (610Kb).

added to the IBM PC series have similar if not identical formats. However, trying to come up with a common denominator for hard disk formats can be challenging. With the simple addition of a device driver or a new ROM BIOS, much higher capacity hard disks can be made to work with a machine running MS-DOS. And then arises the problem of different sizes and types of hard disks—3½-inch, 5¼-inch, or 8-inch Winchester disks, removable 3½- or 5¼-inch rigid disks, and 8-inch Bernoulli cartridges—all of which require the addition of a device driver or a modified BIOS when they're added to virtually any machine running MS-DOS.

File Manipulation

When dealing with different MS-DOS versions, consider the way in which files are handled in your programs. When MS-DOS was first released, it provided file handling capabilities similar to those used under the CP/M (control program for microcomputers) operating system. This similarity was intentional because it provided programmers with a relatively painless method to convert both 8-bit and 16-bit programs from CP/M to MS-DOS. In order to maintain compatibility, all versions of MS-DOS up to version 3.1 have the same file handling capabilities. A new method, however, was introduced under version 2.0 that represents a major departure from CP/M-style file handling. This method is very similar to the file handling method used in the Xenix operating system. Although much easier to use, the new method is not, however, compatible with the older method and therefore requires cautious attention. The following paragraphs describe the differences between these two methods.

Using File Control Blocks (FCBs)

Function calls 0Fh through 29h, introduced in the first version of MS-DOS, are used in conjunction with what is called an FCB (file control block) to create, modify, and delete a file. An FCB is a segment of code written to memory that defines the parameters of a program-manipulated file. MS-DOS and the application program use the FCB parameters to ascertain the file's location, name, size, and other pertinent information. However, because no function call was provided to actually create an entire FCB, the FCB must already be defined before any of the file-related function calls are used in a program. In all cases, each of the file-related function calls (0Fh through 29h) requires that the location of the FCB in memory be loaded into the DS:DX register pair prior to executing the function. This means that the application program must first create an FCB and load it to a known location in either the data segment or the data area of the code segment of memory (whichever is initially defined by the program).

When MS-DOS loads a program the system creates and formats two FCBs in the program's PSP (program segment prefix). The location of these FCBs in the PSP, as well as the means of accessing the PSP, are described in Chapter 3. The file name fields are filled in from information typed on the command line when the program is entered (as with "A>MUNG infile outfile"). However, if a file specification contains a path name, only the drive number in the FCB is valid. Additionally, no redirection directives appear in the FCB. Finally, note that if the program opens the first FCB in the PSP, the second FCB is overwritten.

Table 10-10 shows the structure of an FCB and indicates both the size and the offset location in memory for each parameter within the FCB. Notice that not all parameters within an FCB are controlled by the application program. Some are modified only by MS-DOS itself, and others can be modified by both the program and MS-DOS. In either case, space must be allotted for all parameters when an FCB is created.

Table 10-10.   MS-DOS FCB Format

Offset Byte	Size	Description	Modified By
–7	1	0FF hex	Program
–6	6	Reserved (must be zero)	Program
–1	1	File attribute	Program/MS-DOS
0	1	Drive number (0 through 16)	Program/MS-DOS
1	8	File or device name	Program
9	3	File extension or type	Program
12	2	Current block	Program
14	2	Record size in bytes	Program
16	4	File size in bytes	MS-DOS
20	2	Date	MS-DOS
22	10	Reserved	MS-DOS
32	1	Current record	Program/MS-DOS
33	4	Random record number	Program/MS-DOS

Both offset and size values are in decimal

In Table 10-10, fields with negative offsets are used under MS-DOS versions 2.0 or higher to turn the FCB into what is called an *extended FCB*, which allows the use of the file attribute parameter in offset –1. 0FFh must be at offset –7 to denote the FCB as an extended FCB.

MS-DOS File Handles

MS-DOS version 2.0 provided a much easier method for the manipulation of files. Instead of painstakingly defining and creating an FCB whenever a file is created or opened, several function calls can be used that require only that you specify a single ASCII string describing the entire file specification and terminated by a zero. Called an ASCIZ string, it can be as long as 64 bytes to accommodate long path names and follows the same syntax as a normal file specification.

```
drive:\path\filename.extension
```

When either function call 3Ch (Create a File) or function 3Dh (Open a File) is executed, MS-DOS creates what is called a *file handle* based on the information contained in the ASCIZ string. Function calls 3Ch through 57h are all file-related functions that involve the use of file handles. These include three new functions (5Ah through 5Ch) introduced in MS-DOS version 3.0.

Because MS-DOS creates and controls file handles, the application program no longer needs to keep track of where the file information is located in memory. Simply referencing the ASCIZ string is sufficient to inform MS-DOS as to what the program is doing according to the functions being used. This built-in facility also has another benefit: Several file handles can exist at one time because MS-DOS always keeps track of where they're located in memory.

The only disadvantage with file handles is that they're not supported by versions of MS-DOS prior to 2.0. So if a program must be compatible with all versions of MS-DOS, avoid the use of file handles. Note, however, that with the introduction of file handles, as well as many other features, MS-DOS versions 2.0 through 3.1 have proven to be stepping stones of sorts between older operating systems (such as CP/M) and the more advanced Xenix operating system.

Almost all of the new MS-DOS file-related function calls are directly compatible with those under Xenix, as are other features such as pathnames, tree-structured directories, and redirection. Thus upward compatibility should also be considered, especially when one realizes that current versions of Xenix do not support the old FCB method of file handling. With more advanced future versions of MS-DOS, the traditional FCB method of handling files may be removed from the operating system entirely.

MS-DOS and the IBM Personal Computer Series

The IBM Personal Computer (IBM PC) undoubtedly has been the most popular of all the computers installed with MS-DOS. Indeed, the high popularity of MS-DOS has been due to the unprecedented success of the IBM Personal Computer series and compatible machines. How does MS-DOS, as it is implemented on the IBM PC, compare with the implementations described in this chapter and in this book? When reading the MS-DOS manual for the IBM PC (in which MS-DOS is called DOS or IBM PC DOS) and the MS-DOS manual published by Microsoft, you notice both similarities and significant differences. The similarities involve parts of MS-DOS that are standard or "generic" to all implementations of MS-DOS. The differences represent features of MS-DOS that are often unique to particular implementations. The goal of this book is to cover programming in the MS-DOS environment from the "generic" point of view and the focus is thus on items of programming that are applicable to all implementations of MS-DOS. However, because MS-DOS on the IBM PC is the most popular implementation, the similarities and differences must be made clear. Having this information helps you make crucial compatibility design decisions for your programs.

Similarities

The following generic aspects of MS-DOS are the same throughout all implementations of MS-DOS for any version.

- **DOS (disk operating system) program.** This program *is* MS-DOS and is stored in a hidden file on the boot disk. On the IBM PC, this file is called IBMDOS.COM. Although it may be called something else on other machines, this file is always the same for a given version and can be broken down into the following parts.

   1. Operating system executive

   2. Function calls

   3. Memory management (not memory layout) up to 640K

   4. BIOS interface (not the BIOS itself)

- **The BIOS interface program.** The BIOS (basic input/output system) interface program acts as an interface or translator between MS-DOS and the BIOS. In the IBM PC, this interface is stored on the boot disk in a hidden file called IBMBIO.COM. The input part of the program is the same for any version of MS-DOS, but the output depends on the particular machine (IBM PC, IBM

PC*jr,* IBM PC Portable, IBM PC XT, or IBM PC AT). DOS for IBM PC-compatible machines has a similar file, but it is called something else. In some implementations of MS-DOS, such as MS-PRO and PC-PRO for the CompuPro (Viasyn) computers, this file is replaced by the entire BIOS itself.

- **Command interpreter (COMMAND.COM).** This non-hidden file exists on all boot disks. It is normally the same for all implementations, but you occasionally encounter some differences. It provides the "interface" between MS-DOS and the user of the computer, displays prompts, and provides built-in commands and functions, such as DIR, COPY, RENAME, ERASE, and redirection.

- **External commands.** A set of external commands is standard throughout all implementations of MS-DOS. However, some external commands unique to particular implementations of MS-DOS are often added. For example, the commands COMP and DISKCOMP are unique to the IBM PC series. Most other implementations of MS-DOS have equivalent commands, but they're slightly different and normally called something else.

Differences

The following parts of MS-DOS are implementation specific:

- **BIOS.** On the IBM PC series, as well as almost all IBM PC-compatible machines, the BIOS is stored in ROM. The BIOS contains routines that function as extensions of MS-DOS to control the hardware. Because the hardware is always based on the proprietary design of the computer's manufacturer, the design of the BIOS must also be proprietary unless it is purchased from another manufacturer. The following general aspects of the BIOS are often machine specific:

  1. Hardware and software interrupt handlers

  2. Routines for disk controllers and disk drivers

  3. Routines for the console, printer, and communications ports

  4. Other miscellaneous functions, such graphic controllers and game adapters

- **BIOS interface program.** On all machines containing a BIOS interface file (such as IBMBIO.COM on the IBM PC series), the input part of the program is the same so that it can accept "generic" data from the MS-DOS operating system. The output part of this file, however, is different because it has to be able to communicate with the proprietary BIOS.

- **Device drivers.** In order to control certain unique aspects of the system's hardware, many systems now include device drivers as part of MS-DOS. In the IBM PC series, the device driver called ANSI.SYS adds extended functions to the monitor system. A similar file is provided with some IBM PC-compatible machines but is rarely provided for non-IBM PC-compatible machines.

- **External commands.** Special nonstandard external commands are often included in implementations of MS-DOS.

Generally, the most important difference between implementations of MS-DOS involves the BIOS itself because the BIOS contains the routines required by the unique hardware (such as disk controllers, monitors or terminals, and keyboards) of the machine. Thus, when making design decisions about a program, the intended level of program compatibility should be carefully considered. If you want your program to be compatible with all implementations of MS-DOS, never access the BIOS directly and never use system-specific functions, such as interrupts. If system specific functions are necessary but across-the-board compatibility is still required, such functions should be handled either in device drivers or if accompanied by an installation program that can make machine-specific modifications, in the program itself.

Even within the series of IBM PCs, compatibility issues arise. For example, the capabilities of BIOS programs stored in ROM vary among the IBM PC, IBM PC XT, and IBM PC AT. Although the BIOS functions in the IBM PC also exist in the IBM PC XT, the XT provides additional functions. Comparable differences exist between the IBM PC XT and the IBM PC AT. If you're unsure about the differences, refer to the *IBM Technical Reference* (hardware) manuals for each machine. The entire listing of the BIOS is provided in each manual.

Compatibility with Other Operating Systems

As mentioned earlier in this chapter, MS-DOS is in various ways similar to other operating systems. The first version of MS-DOS, from both the programmer's and the user's standpoints, is similar to the CP/M operating system. Although many features of MS-DOS do not exist in CP/M, the basic structure and command usage (such as the DOS **A**> prompt and .COM command files) are virtually identical. MS-DOS version 2.00, however, introduced several features and functions derived from a much more advanced operating system called Xenix, also from Micro-soft. (Xenix is a variation of the popular minicomputer and mainframe operating system called UNIX.) Functions such as file and device redi-rection, pipes, device drivers, and file handles are derivations of similar functions provided by Xenix. With several versions of MS-DOS now available, some of the newer operating systems offer MS-DOS compati-bility. Probably the best known examples are Concurrent PC DOS and Concurrent DOS286 from Digital Research, Inc. (the original designers of CP/M). The following paragraphs overview the similarities and differ-ences among MS-DOS and these compatible and pseudo-compatible op-erating systems.

CP/M-80

After examining the architecture and capabilities of MS-DOS, you will know that the designers got their ideas from the CP/M operating system for 8080, 8085, and Z80 microprocessor-based machines. Before the in-troduction of the IBM PC with MS-DOS, CP/M was considered the *de facto* standard operating system for microcomputers. CP/M still remains the most popular operating system for 8-bit machines. When computer manufacturers began to entertain plans for designing 16-bit computers using the then recently introduced 8086 microprocessor from Intel, many of them had to wait because a 16-bit version of CP/M (now called CP/M-86) was not available. A company called Seattle Computer Prod-ucts went ahead and designed their own operating system, which they called QDOS (Quick 'n Dirty Operating System) and which, after several improvements, they later renamed 86-DOS.

The architecture of 86-DOS was very similar to that of CP/M, but Seattle Computer Products improved on many functions and added some new ones. 86-DOS was then sold to Microsoft and was renamed MS-DOS. This first version of MS-DOS (which was essentially an un-changed 86-DOS) was adopted for use by IBM on their newly released personal computer, the IBM PC. Microsoft then made several enhance-ments to MS-DOS, which resulted in MS-DOS version 2.00. MS-DOS 2.0 retained most of the functions of the first version. Thus, the similarity to CP/M was maintained, which was of great benefit to programmers be-cause most CP/M programs can be easily converted to MS-DOS. From the programmer's point of view, the following similarities are impor-tant:

- **Function calls.** Most of the function calls in the first version of MS-DOS, especially those related to file functions, are very similar to those provided by CP/M versions 2.2 and 3.0. Although register usage differs considerably between the 8-bit 8080/Z80 and the 16-bit 8086 family of microprocessors, the way in which the functions are set up and return information is very similar. Even some of the function call numbers themselves are the same. MS-DOS functions which are virtually identical to those of CP/M include functions 0 through 24 hex. These functions and their operation have been retained in later versions of MS-DOS up to version 3.1.

- **FCBs.** The only way the first version of MS-DOS could create, open, change, or delete a file was through the use of an FCB. The format of an FCB under MS-DOS and the way in which it is set up is almost identical to FCB usage under CP/M. Because file handling is crucial in most any DOS-based operating system, the similarities between FCB usage in CP/M and in MS-DOS are invaluable to programmers. Although a new file handling mechanism was introduced in MS-DOS version 2.00, all versions up to version 3.1 still retain, for compatibility purposes, the "old" FCB method.

- **Commands.** The use of built-in commands and external program commands is very similar in both operating systems. CP/M has its built-in commands in what is called the CCP (console command processor), which is part of the operating system when loaded into memory. MS-DOS handles built-in commands in much the same way, except that its command processor exists in a disk file called COMMAND.COM. MS-DOS also has an 8-bit compatibility mode for external commands and thus handles .COM files in a manner almost identical to the way they are handled by CP/M. Under MS-DOS, .COM files use only a 64Kb segment of memory, thereby emulating the memory usage of an 8080 or Z80 microprocessor based system. The .EXE command format under MS-DOS, however, is only used in machines with 8086-family microprocessors and therefore is not compatible with CP/M.

CP/M-86 and Concurrent CP/M-86

The CP/M-86 operating system is the 16-bit counterpart of the original CP/M for the 8086-family of microprocessors. Many of its features, carried over from the 8-bit CP/M version, are similar to MS-DOS. For example, FCBs and file-related function calls (excluding file handles) are referenced in CP/M-86 much like the methods that are used in MS-DOS.

Shortly after the introduction of CP/M-86, a new version was introduced called Concurrent CP/M-86, which added multitasking and windowing features to CP/M-86. Special versions of both operating systems were released for the IBM PC, which made special use of these features. Most of the functions of CP/M-86 were carried over to Concurrent CP/M-86, but many of them were further complicated by the multitasking features of the newer operating system.

Concurrent PC-DOS and Concurrent DOS-286

With the emergence of MS-DOS as the *de facto* standard operating system for 16-bit 8086-family based microcomputers (especially the IBM PC and compatible machines), the makers of CP/M realized that they would have to provide some form of compatibility with MS-DOS due to the large user-base of MS-DOS systems. Digital Research, Inc., released an enhanced version of Concurrent CP/M-86 called Concurrent PC DOS, which, in its initial release, provided MS-DOS version 1.0 compatibility. Version 3 of Concurrent PC DOS was enhanced yet again to include MS-DOS version 2.00 compatibility. This operating system is capable of running both CP/M-86 and MS-DOS programs concurrently and accepts all of the function calls supported under the equivalent versions of MS-DOS.

Another variation of Concurrent PC DOS called Concurrent DOS286 is planned for machines with the Intel 80286 microprocessor. This operating system is designed for use with the 80286 processor in "virtual" (also called "protected") mode, providing a memory addressable range of 16 megabytes. This operating system is also capable of running in the "real" mode (8086-compatibility mode) concurrently with the virtual mode so that both MS-DOS and CP/M-86 programs can be run. Concurrent DOS286 provides the same MS-DOS compatible features as Concurrent PC DOS. As of the publication of this book, we know that Concurrent DOS286 has some difficulties running on some versions of the 80286 processor. Caution should be exercised when dealing with the compatibility of this operating system because its correct operation depends heavily on the version of the 80286 processor used in the system (earlier versions of the processor had problems switching and communicating between the virtual and real modes).

Xenix and UNIX

As indicated previously, later versions of MS-DOS (beginning with version 2.0) incorporated some features found in Xenix, another Microsoft operating system. Most of the features introduced in MS-DOS version 2.0, such as device drivers, redirection, piping, and file handles, are features based on those found in Xenix, which in turn is based on the UNIX operating system from AT&T. Thus, although you should pay attention to downward compatibility issues (MS-DOS and CP/M), upward compatibility should also be a consideration because the Xenix-like features of MS-DOS represent an indication of what's in store for future versions of MS-DOS.

Summary

Many things—more than can be covered in one chapter—must be considered when you develop programs intended to be compatible with all or most versions and implementations of MS-DOS. The information presented here should provide a good basis for starting to investigate the many compatibility issues you're likely to encounter. Most manufacturers of computers that run MS-DOS have published technical information about how MS-DOS is implemented on their machines. If you're writing a program that's targeted for a particular machine (or is intended to be compatible with a particular machine), these manuals can help you considerably.

PRODUCTS

Part

High-Level Languages

Chapter 11

TURBO PASCAL COMPILER
LATTICE/MICROSOFT C COMPILER
Summary

f all programming languages, assembly language offers the greatest programming flexibility and can produce the fastest and most compact programs. Assembly language is often used when developing application programs for 8086-family-based machines running MS-DOS. However, assembly language can be cumbersome when used for very large, complex applications and can be a disadvantage if you intend to port your applications over to machines using different processors, such as the Motorola 68000 series, Zilog Z8000 series, National 16000 series, as well as the many 8-bit processors. Assembly language can also pose problems if an application is intended to operate under other operating systems such as CP/M and CP/M-86, UCSD-p System, or one of the many versions of UNIX.

Because of these problems, programmers often turn to high-level languages, such as Pascal, C, COBOL, FORTRAN, or BASIC. One of the most important advantages of some high-level languages is their ability to compile or interpret programs that can then be recompiled or reinterpreted on other machines (using different processors and operating systems) with little or no changes to the source code. Another advantage of high-level languages is that they often make writing programs easier in the first place. Most high-level languages provide functions, which when compared to the equivalent assembly language statements, require fewer words or characters in the source code. Also, most high-level languages do not require the programmer to meticulously manipulate registers as is required in assembly language. Standard functions, such as Output Text on Screen or Read the Disk, generally require less source code text when a high-level language is used. Compare the examples in Listings 11-1 and 11-2.

Listing 11-1 shows how text is output to the console using assembly language.

Listing 11-1. Outputting Text to the Console Using Assembly Language

```
code_seg segment para public 'code'
        assume  cs:code_seg,ds:code_seg,ss:code_seg,es:code_seg
        org     0100h
entry:  jmp     start
;
msg1    db      'This is a test.',0Dh,0Ah,'$'
;
start:
main    proc    near
        push    ax              ; save AX
        push    dx              ; and DX
        mov     dx,offset msg1  ; point to data
        mov     ah,09h          ; set up MS-DOS Func. Call 09h
        int     21h             ; execute function
        pop     dx              ; restore DX
        pop     ax              ; restore AX
;
        mov     ax,04C00h       ; terminate program function call
        int     21h             ; execute function
;
main    endp
code_seg ends
end     entry                   ; set starting address to ENTRY
```

Listing 11-2 shows how the program in Listing 11-1 could be written in Pascal.

Listing 11-2. Outputting Text to the Console Using Pascal

```
program Test1;
begin
    WriteLn('This is a test.')
end.                                    { End of program Test1 }
```

The dramatic difference in source code length between Listings 11-1 and 11-2 shows why programmers often use a high-level language to write application programs. The amount of planning and typing involved in high-level languages and the length of the source code is considerably less than if assembly language is used.

The object code produced by a high-level language almost always is longer than that produced by assembly language because the high-level language compiler will often require significant overhead to produce a correctly formatted program. The authors found that the size of the object code produced by the Microsoft Macroassembler after assembling the program in Listing 11-1 was 37 bytes long. The object code produced by Turbo Pascal after it compiled the program in Listing 11-2 was 11,461 bytes, almost 310 times the size of the assembly language program! The execution times of the programs, however, were comparable, although the assembly language program was marginally faster. If the two programs had been more complex, the greater execution speed of the assembly language program would have been more noticeable.

Another problem that programmers often encounter when using high-level languages, especially Pascal, BASIC, and FORTRAN, is that high-level languages lack inherent functions that would permit the detailed manipulation of the processor's operation and are unable to access MS-DOS function calls. Thus, depending on your requirements, the disadvantages of using a high-level language can often be as great as the advantages.

Because programmers encounter such limitations in high-level languages, they often resort to assembly language or pure machine code to accomplish the needed results. Some high-level languages provide the ability to call external programs or functions within an external program that can be written in assembly language. Other languages provide the ability to accept in-line assembly language object code. Determining a language's capabilities of interfacing with assembly language often is a deciding factor in the selection of a language to develop a significant application program project.

Some of the so-called "high-level" languages (such as C and PL/M) tend to have relatively low-level capabilities as well as high-level capabilities and therefore often are categorized as "medium-level" languages. Some variations of certain types of high-level languages (such as Pascal) contain capabilities that allow a programmer to perform "low-level" operations if required. One such variation is the very popular Turbo Pascal compiler available for MS-DOS and CP/M. In addition to being able to handle the standard external function calls, this compiler is capable of accepting in-line machine code produced previously by an assembler.

This chapter focuses on two of the most popular development languages for MS-DOS in use today: Turbo Pascal and Lattice/Microsoft C. This does not mean that the authors recommend them above all others. But if you are going to use Pascal, no MS-DOS system is complete without Turbo Pascal due to its reasonable price and its outstanding capabilities as a compiler. Most of the C compilers on the market today have generally comparable capabilities. However, Lattice/Microsoft C has become the most widely used C compiler in the MS-DOS microcomputer community.

The remainder of this chapter examines the capabilities of both Turbo Pascal and Lattice/Microsoft C for interfacing with assembly language and external programs. If you've been using other languages or are considering doing so, the following sections can still help you determine the assembly language interfacing and external function capabilities of those languages.

TURBO PASCAL COMPILER

Turbo Pascal offers several advantages over all other Pascal compilers and almost all other languages. The advantage which has probably most contributed to its unprecedented popularity is its low cost. But Turbo Pascal is also an excellent compiler: It compiles quickly, produces relatively compact object code, and compiled programs generally have fast execution times. Turbo Pascal also provides features useful to programmers who do extensive applications development or require unusual capabilities normally not provided by a typical Pascal compiler. These capabilities are discussed in more detail in the following paragraphs.

Inline Assembly Language Coding

Turbo Pascal is capable of accepting assembled machine code within a source program. This is accomplished by using the reserved word *inline* followed by the appropriate machine code instruction values in hexadecimal. The entire machine code section is enclosed within parentheses and is terminated by a semicolon. Machine code values are each prefixed by a dollar sign ($) and separated from each other by a forward slant (/). Other than these standard modifications, the entire machine code procedure is generally the same as you would see it on the left side of an assembly language listing.

Machine code values and other statements can be mixed throughout the statement part of an inline block. This ability can allow you to refer to data variables (equivalent to data labels in assembly language) elsewhere in the program without having to define them in their entirety using machine code statements. This mechanism allows you to pass data between the machine code section and the main part of the program.

Listing 11-3 shows a modified implementation of the *Get MS-DOS Version* assembly language routine described in Chapter 10.

Listing 11-3.   Using Inline Machine Code in Turbo Pascal

```
procedure GetDosVer (var Strg: version);
{Str is type String[255]}
```

Listing 11-3 cont.

```
begin
  inline
    ($B4/$30/           {       mov     ah,30h          }
     $CD/$21/           {       int     21h             }
     $3C/$00/           {       cmp     al,0            }
     $75/$04/           {       jnz     L1              }
     $B0/$01/           {       mov     al,1            }
     $B4/$00/           {       mov     ah,0            }
     $C4/$BE/version/   { L1:   les     di,version[bp]  }
     $88/$05/           {       mov     [di],al         }
     $88/$65/$08);      {       mov     [di + 8],ah     }
  WriteLn('The version of MS-DOS is ',version);
end;
```

Producing the machine code shown in Listing 11-3 can be a bit cumbersome because the code must first be written in assembly language, then assembled to produce the machine code in the listing file. Apart from this inconvenience, however, the inline statement can be a very useful tool to implement functions which ordinarily could not be handled by the compiler.

Restrictions

Several restrictions apply to the use of registers when using inline machine code. Although all registers can be used, the contents of the BP (base pointer), SP (stack pointer), DS (data segment), and SS (stack segment) must be the same on exit as on entry. Additionally, segment registers are used when pointing to data labels that are defined in the main program, and the choice of register depends on the location of the data label in the program. If the data label is located in the main program block, the DS is used. If the variables are located within the current subprogram, the SS is used and the variable offset is relative to the BP register (the use of which automatically selects the SS). The base segment of typed constants is the CS (code segment). Inline machine code should never attempt to access variables that are not declared in the main program or in the current subprogram.

Options

You can make several other optional modifications to inline machine code. Normally, Turbo Pascal sizes each machine code element to 8 bits on output if the value is an integer within the range or 0 through 255. Any other type of value generates a word (16 bits) with the least significant byte first. This size selection can be overridden with the use of the "<" and ">" characters. If a code element starts with "<," only the least significant byte of the value is coded, even if it's a 16-bit value. If ">" is used, a word is always coded and the most significant byte is 0 if the code element was an 8-bit value.

Calling MS-DOS Functions

Under Turbo Pascal version 3.0, a new function was introduced called *MsDos* which is used to make MS-DOS function calls within Turbo Pascal without using inline statements. The use of this function can often considerably simplify programs that have extensive inline machine code statements. Before Turbo Pascal makes an MS-DOS function call, the registers AX, BX, CX, DX, BP, SI, DI, DS, and ES are loaded with the values specified in the record parameter. These record parameter values can be expressed the following two ways:

```
record
  AX,BX,CX,DX,BP,SI,DI,DS,ES,Flags: Integer;
end;
```

or

```
record case Integer of
  1: (AX,BX,CX,DX,BP,SI,DI,DS,ES,Flags: Integer);
  2: (AL,AH,BL,BH,CL,CH,DL,DH          : Byte);
end;
```

When MS-DOS is finished executing the function call, the *MsDos* procedure restores all registers to the record, thereby making available any results from MS-DOS. The example in Listing 11-4 shows a much simplified version of the program in Listing 11-3.

Listing 11-4.   Using the *MsDos* Procedure in Turbo Pascal

```
procedure GetDosVer (var MajVer,MinVer: Integer);
type
  RegStorage = record
                 AX,BX,CX,DX,BP,SI,DI,DS,ES,Flags: Integer;
               end;
var
  Regs:        RegStorage;
begin
  with Regs do
  begin
    AX := $3000               { load function 30h into AH    }
    MsDos(Regs);              { execute MS-DOS function call }
    MajVer := lo(AX);         { and save the result          }
    MinVer := hi(AX);
  end;
  ;
end; { end procedure }
```

Although unfortunately unavailable in versions of Turbo Pascal before 3.0, the *MsDos* procedure is worth using because it eliminates the need to produce the machine code that would otherwise be required.

Using MS-DOS Interrupts and Machine-Specific Interrupts

Turbo Pascal supports interrupts from both sides: "inline" statements can form an interrupt service routine, whereas the "Intr" procedure allows the programmer direct access to the 8086 INT machine instruction.

When an interrupt handler is written in an inline machine code block, all registers must be saved on entering the interrupt handler, and then restored before exiting the procedure. The following line should be the first statement in the interrupt handler procedure:

```
inline ($50/$53/$51/$52/$56/$57/$1E/$06/$FB);
```

The previous statement PUSHes all required registers on the stack. The last byte ($FB) is an optional STI instruction which enables further interrupts. The following must be the last statement in the procedure:

```
inline ($07/$1F/$5F/$5E/$5A/$59/$5B/$58/$8B/$E5/$5D/$CF);
```

This statement POPs the registers off of the stack and restores the SP and the BP. The last byte ($CF) is an IRET instruction which overrides the RET instruction generated by the compiler.

An interrupt service routine should not use any input/output operations involving the standard procedures and functions of Turbo Pascal because MS-DOS is non-reentrant. The interrupt vector used to activate the interrupt service routine must be initialized separately.

Using the *Intr* Procedure

The *Intr* procedure can be used as an alternative to inline statements. The *Intr* procedure is expressed in the following manner:

```
Intr(InterruptNo, Result)
```

"InterruptNo" is an integer constant representing the interrupt number, and "Result" contains any values returned after the interrupt was executed.

The *Intr* procedure is advantageous because it initializes the registers and flags as specified in the parameter "Result":

```
Result = record
            AX,BX,CX,DX,BP,SI,DI,DS,ES,Flags: Integer;
         end;
```

Calling Functions and Procedures Contained in External Programs

Turbo Pascal reserves the word *external* for use with external functions and procedures. External functions and procedures are contained in another file and are generally in machine code format. The use of the external function makes up for Turbo Pascal's lack of compatibility with the Microsoft linker and librarian utilities.

When an external function is used, its first occurrence in the program specifies the name of the file that contains all the external functions and procedures. Once the external file has been established, all subsequent occurrences of "external" within the procedure refer to the parts of the external file that are to be accessed. When the file containing the word *external* is compiled, Turbo Pascal locates the external file and includes it in the target object code. The external file must therefore contain machine code. And because the location of the external code in the target object code file cannot be predicted, the external machine code *must be relocatable,* and no references may be made to the data segment. More than one external reference may be made to an external file by specifying offsets into the file. However, each section of code in the file that is referenced must end with the RET instruction so that control can be returned to the main program. Additionally, each referenced external machine code section that is terminated by a RET instruction must contain instructions to save and restore the BP, CS, DS, and SS registers *before* the RET instruction is executed.

Listing 11-5 shows how various sections of an external file can be accessed and executed. Note that the offsets into the external file are enclosed in square brackets and represent byte offsets from the beginning of the file.

**Listing 11-5.   Example of Accessing External Files
and Functions**

```
procedure AbsDiskRead; external 'DISKREAD.BIN';
function DiskFormat: boolean; external AbsDiskRead[5];
procedure FATsectors: Char; external AbsDiskRead[20];
procedure DIRsectors: Char; external AbsDiskRead[30];
```

Although Turbo Pascal does not produce linkable object code compatible with the Microsoft LINK linker, Pascal does offer many powerful ancillary assembly language interfacing capabilities. Combining the ease of writing programs in Pascal and the flexibility of assembly language, Turbo Pascal can be a very powerful tool for developing MS-DOS application programs.

LATTICE/MICROSOFT C COMPILER

Lattice C was one of the first C compilers for the 8086-series of processors. Because it contained many features which made it compatible with MS-DOS and the Microsoft LINK linker, Lattice C was adopted by Microsoft as part of their language product line. Lattice C quickly became the most popular C compiler for use with MS-DOS systems because of its early introduction and compatibility with MS-DOS. Although the C language has many intrinsic functions which are often low-level enough for them to replace the need for an assembly language, Lattice/Microsoft C is capable of interfacing with assembly language. The following paragraphs describe how Lattice/Microsoft C can be interfaced with assembly language and how MS-DOS function calls can be performed.

Interfacing to Assembly Language

Because Lattice/Microsoft C provides excellent facilities for manipulating registers in the 8086-series of processors, interfacing the main program with assembly language routines is relatively easy as long as certain conventions are adhered to. The main difference between Lattice/Microsoft C and other languages and compilers is that assembly language routines must be assembled separately and the object code must be linked with the compiled object code of the main C program using the Microsoft linker (LINK).

Certain conventions must be observed in formatting the assembly language source code. All external assembly language routines must begin with the following statements:

```
pgroup          group          prog
prog            segment        byte public 'prog'
                assume         cs:pgroup
```

These statements must be followed by public declarations of all procedures in the assembly language program. All procedures must be declared NEAR.

Individual procedures within the assembly language routine may be called within the C program by specifying the actual name of the procedure as it was written in the assembly language source code. This is accomplished by using the *iret* instruction in the C source code.

Data labels within an assembly language routine can also be referenced by the C program provided that all data referenced is located in the data segment. This is accomplished by using the *extrn* instruction in the C source code. Note that an assembly language routine also can refer to data variables defined in the C source code by means of the extrn instruction.

Calling MS-DOS Functions

Lattice/Microsoft C provides a function which allows you to execute an MS-DOS function call directly within the program. This is accomplished by using the code shown in Listing 11-6.

**Listing 11-6.   Making an MS-DOS Function Call
within a C Program**

```
iret = bdos(fn, dx);
int iret;
int fn;
int dx;
```

The function number is represented by "fn" in Listing 11-6, and the DX register is specified for optional usage. The first two statements in the listing return the result of the function call to the AL register. This method of making a function call, however, doesn't work with those MS-DOS functions that return information in other registers.

For most applications, the capabilities of Lattice/Microsoft C are adequate even without external assembly language routines. However, if assembly language is needed, it can be interfaced very easily to Lattice/Microsoft C with the help of the Microsoft linker (LINK).

Summary

This chapter has shown how the assembly language interfacing features provided by three popular high-level language compilers are used. Although Turbo Pascal, Lattice C, and Microsoft C are simply selected examples of the many high-level languages available for use with MS-DOS, the assembly language interfacing techniques described in this chapter can give you good insight into what to look for when choosing a high-level language for its assembly language interfacing capabilities.

APPENDIXES

Development Tools   Appendix A

Using Batch Files To Automate the Assembly Process
Using Templates To Create .COM and .EXE Programs
Using Library Routines

This appendix describes some "tools" that can simplify and enhance the process of using assembly language to develop application programs. The following text describes automating the assembly process with batch files, creating .EXE and .COM programs with templates, and using library routines.

Using Batch Files To Automate the Assembly Process

The MS-DOS batch processor often is one of the least appreciated facilities in the operating system. This facility can, however, be a very useful tool when you use the MASM macroassembler. Listings A-1 and A-2 provide the sources for two batch files, MASM2EXE.BAT and MASM2COM. BAT. MASM2EXE.BAT is used to automate the process of assembling and linking .EXE programs, and MASM2COM.BAT is a modification of the first file and includes the process of converting a .EXE file to a .COM file. Both files are designed to work with the Microsoft MASM macroassembler version 1.00 only and with up to version 2.00 of the linker LINK.

Modifications to the batch files for later versions of MASM and LINK are provided in the remarks in the listings. Both files require that a second file called AUTOLINK be present. This file contains four carriage return/linefeeds and is used to deal with the problem that LINK (up to version 2.00) has: It cannot accept null parameters on the command line for the listing (.MAP) and library (.LIB) options. AUTOLINK is submitted to LINK by adding the file name on the command line and preceding it with an @ sign. The "@" sign is used for compatibility with MS-DOS versions prior to version 2.00 because these earlier versions don't support command line redirection.

Using the batch files is very simple. Simply enter the name of the batch command followed by the name of the file to be assembled. Do not include the extension, as .ASM is assumed. If you're using MS-DOS version 2.00 or above and the PATH is set correctly, the drives on which any of the related files are stored don't have to be specified.

Listing A-1.   MASM2EXE.BAT

```
echo off
if not exist %1.asm goto NOFILERR
rem
masm %1 %1 nul nul
rem
rem Use the above only with versions of MASM below 2.00
rem Use "masm %1.asm,,;" for MASM version 2.00 and above
rem
link %1 @a:autolink
rem
rem Use the above only with versions of LINK below 2.20
rem Use "link %1.obj,,nul;" for LINK version 2.20 and above
rem
echo Deleting %1.obj
del %1.obj >nul:
echo Done!
dir %1.*
goto END
rem
:NOFILERR
echo The file %1.asm was not found.
:END
```

Listing A-2.   MASM2COM.BAT

```
echo off
if not exist %1.asm goto NOFILERR
rem
masm %1 %1 nul nul
rem
rem Use the above only with versions of MASM below 2.00
rem Use "masm %1.asm,,;" for MASM version 2.00 and above
rem
link %1 @a:autolink
rem
rem Use the above only with versions of LINK below 2.20
rem Use "link %1.obj,,nul;" for LINK version 2.20 and above
rem
echo Deleting %1.obj
del %1.obj >nul:
echo Creating %1.com from %1.exe (and deleting %1.exe)
exe2bin %1.exe %1.com >nul:
del %1.exe >nul:
```

Listing A-2. cont.

```
echo Done!
dir %1.*
goto END
rem
:NOFILERR
echo The file %1.asm was not found.
:END
```

Note that some of the lines in Listings A-1 and A-2 terminate with output redirection parameters. If you're using a version of MS-DOS prior to version 2.00, these parameters should be stripped.

Using Templates To Create .COM and .EXE Programs

Listings A-3, A-4, and A-5 can be useful when you create programs initially. Listing A-3 shows the format for a .EXE program with gaps for you to write your code. Listing A-4 shows the format for a .COM file. Listing A-5 contains some macros that can prove to be useful when writing either .EXE or .COM programs. The macros can either be embedded in your program source file, or they can permanently reside in a separate file which is "included" in your source file during the assembly process (by embedding the MASM INCLUDE directive in the source file).

Listing A-3.   .EXE Program Template

```
        page    60,132                          ; wide listing
FALSE   equ     0                               ; FALSE compare
TRUE    equ     0FFFFh                          ; TRUE compare & mask
stack   segment stack
        db      32 dup ('stack   ')             ; 256 byte stack
stack   ends
data    segment                                 ; data segment
psp     dw      ?                               ; program segment prefix
;
;       < YOUR DATA GOES HERE >
;
data    ends                                    ; end of data segment
code    segment
        assume cs:code,ds:data,es:data,ss:stack
main    proc    far
start:
        mov     ax,data                         ; set up data segment
        mov     ds,ax
        mov     psp,es                          ; save program segment prefix
```

Listing A-3. cont.

```
        mov     es,ax                   ; set up extra segment
;
;       < MAIN ROUTINE GOES HERE >
;
        mov     ax,04C00h           ; terminate program
        int     21h
main    endp
;
;       < THE REST OF YOUR ROUTINES GO HERE >
;
code    ends                        ; end code segment
        end     start
```

Listing A-4.   .COM Program Template

```
        page    60,132              ; wide listing
FALSE   equ     0                   ; FALSE compare
TRUE    equ     0FFFFh              ; TRUE compare & mask
only    segment
        assume cs:only,ds:only,es:only,ss:only
main    proc    far
entry:  org     0100h
        jmp     start
        < INSERT DATA HERE >
start:
        mov     sp,offset top_of_stack   ; set new stack
;
;       < MAIN ROUTINE GOES HERE >
;
        mov     ax,04C00h           ; terminate program
        int     21h
main    endp
;
;       < THE REST OF YOUR ROUTINES GO HERE >
;
; Optional stack. CAUTION! You must use function 4Ch
; to terminate the program if you use a local stack!
        db      32 dup ('stack   ')     ; 256 byte stack
top_of_stack    equ     $
only    ends                        ; end code segment
        end     entry
```

Listing A-5.   Useful Macros

```
        page    60,132              ; full width listing
TRUE    EQU     0FFH                ; TRUE
FALSE   EQU     0                   ; FALSE
;****** ASCII EQUATES ****************************************
bell    equ     07h                 ; bell
cr      equ     0Dh                 ; carriage return
esc     equ     1Bh                 ; escape
home    equ     1Eh                 ; home
lf      equ     0Ah                 ; linefeed
soh     equ     01h                 ; start of header
eot     equ     04h                 ; end of text
ack     equ     06h                 ; acknowledge
nack    equ     15h                 ; negative acknowledgment
cancel  equ     18h                 ; cancel operation
xon     equ     11h                 ; <CONTROL-Q>
xoff    equ     13h                 ; <CONTROL-S>
;****** MACRO DEFINITIONS FOR UTILITIES ************************
        .xlist                      ; suppress listing macro definitions
doscall macro
        int     21h                 ; call MS-DOS function
        endm
;
disk_read macro
        int     25h                 ; read logical sector of a disk
        endm
;
;
disk_write macro
        int     26h                 ; write to logical sector of a disk
        endm
;; Direct I/O Data Available? (nondestructive)
;; --test keyboard & return character & status
;; Z => character available; NZ => no character available
dio$dav macro                       ;; check keyboard status & read
        push    dx                  ; save dx
        mov     dl,0FFh             ; no character to output
        mov     ah,06h              ;
        doscall
        pop     dx                  ; restore dx
        endm
;; ReaD NO ECho
;; Read character from the keyboard w/o echo
rd_noec macro                       ;; read character no echo
        mov     ah,08h              ; read keyboard without echo
        doscall
        endm
;; ReaD BUFfered input from keyboard
rd_buf macro    bufnam              ;; read buffered keyboard input
        mov     dx,offset bufnam
        mov     ah,0Ah
        doscall
        endm
;; DISplay CHaRacter
dis_chr macro character             ;; display a character
```

Listing A-5. cont.

```
        mov     dl,character
        mov     ah,02h
        doscall
        endm
new_line macro                  ;; send a CR/LF
        dis_chr cr              ; display carriage return
        dis_chr lf              ; display linefeed
        endm
;; DISplay STRing from memory
dis_str macro string            ;; display a string
        mov     dx,offset string
        mov     ah,09h
        doscall
        endm
;; .EXE Version of type_s
;; define & display a string in segment "strseg"
;; To use specify "type_s 'string'"
type_s macro    strseg,string   ;; define and display string
        local   a
&strseg segment                 ; change to string segment
a       db      string,'$'      ; define string
&strseg ends                    ; stop data segment
        dis_str a               ; display string
        endm
;; .COM Version of type_s
;; define & display a string
;; To use specify "type_s 'string'"
type_s macro    string          ;; define and display string
        local   a,b
        jmp     short b         ; bypass data definition
a       db      string,'$'      ; define string
&b&:    dis_str a               ; display string
        endm
;; .EXE Version of type_sc
;; define & display a string w/CR-LF in segment "strseg"
type_sc macro strseg,string     ;; define and display string
        local   a
&strseg segment                 ; change to data segment
a       db      string,cr,lf,'$'; define string w/CR-LF
&strseg ends                    ; stop data segment
        dis_str a               ; display string
        endm
;; .COM Version of type_sc
;; define & display a string w/CR-LF
type_sc macro string            ;; define and display string
        local   a,b
        jmp     short b         ; bypass data definition
a       db      string,cr,lf,'$'; define string w/CR-LF
&b&:    dis_str a               ; display string
        endm
;; CASE macro for assembly language
;; **** DON'T FORGET TO ENCLOSE ARGUMENT LISTS IN < >
case    macro   key,case_list,jmp_labels;; CASE
        ??tmp_1 = 0
```

Listing A-5. cont.

```
        irp     match,<&case_list>      ;; sequence through cases
        ??tmp_1 = ??tmp_1 + 1           ;; set index number
        cmp     key,&&match          ; case match?
        ??tmp_2 = 0
        irp     retl,<&jmp_labels>      ;; sequence through jumps
        ??tmp_2 = ??tmp_2 + 1           ;; ... until index matches
        if      (??tmp_1 eq ??tmp_2)
        je      &&&retl              ; yes!
        exitm
        endif
        endm
        endm
        endm
; NOTE: The following macros do not exactly implement the
; iAPX186/188/286 processor instructions PUSHA and POPA.
; PUSHA and POPA do not save and restore the segment registers.
; PUSHA pushes (in order): AX, CX, DX, BX, SP, BP, SI, DI.
; POPA pops reverse order and discards the popped value of SP.
push_all macro                  ; save all registers on the stack
        push    ds
        push    cs
        push    es
        push    ss
        push    ax
        push    bx
        push    cx
        push    dx
        push    bp
        push    di
        push    si
        pushf
        endm
;
pop_all macro                   ; restore all registers off the stack
        popf
        pop     si
        pop     di
        pop     bp
        pop     dx
        pop     cx
        pop     bx
        pop     ax
        pop     ss
        pop     es
        pop     cs
        pop     ds
        endm
;; Change stack
swap_new macro          tos     ;; swap stacks for context switch
        local   bypass
        jmp     bypass          ; skip data area
old_stk_seg     dw      ?       ; space for caller's stack segment
old_stk_ptr     dw      ?       ; space for caller's stack pointer
new_stk_seg     dw      ?       ; space for my stack segment
```

Listing A-5. cont.

```
new_stk_ptr     dw        offset tos ; space for my stack pointer
bypass:
        mov     cs:new_stk_seg,cs  ; set new stack segment
        mov     cs:old_stk_seg,ss  ; save old stack values
        mov     cs:old_stk_ptr,sp
        mov     ss,cs:new_stk_seg  ; get new stack values
        mov     sp,cs:new_stk_ptr
        push_all                    ; save flags and all registers
        endm
;; Change stack back
swap_old macro                      ;; swap stacks for context switch
        pop_all                     ; recover flags and all registers
        mov     ss,cs:old_stk_seg   ; restore old stack values
        mov     sp,cs:old_stk_ptr
        endm
        .list
```

Using Library Routines

If you use a standard set of unmodified routines in all your programs, you may find practical putting these routines in a library file that is always linked with your programs. Using this method simplifies the assembly and linking process and reduces the size of your program source files. A library file is created by assembling the file containing your routines, then processing the .OBJ file with the LIB program included on the MASM disk. The LIB program produces a correctly formatted object code file with the extension .LIB. The external references to the routines should be declared within the source code of the program that is to call these routines. These are written in the format:

```
extrn       routine:distance
```

where EXTRN is the directive that informs MASM that "routine" will be included at link time, either from another object file or a library file. The "distance" parameter is either NEAR or FAR, depending on how the referenced routine was declared. For .COM type programs, "distance" is always NEAR. Once the external routines have been declared, they can be CALLed like any other routine.

Listing A-6 provides the complete source to the library file called BIN2CON.LIB, as discussed in Chapters 6 and 8.

Listing A-6.   Source for BIN2CON.LIB Library File

```
          page 60,132
          public bin2dec          ; LIBRARY ROUTINE
          public bin2hex          ; LIBRARY ROUTINE
;****************************************************************
;
;       I M P L E M E N T A T I O N
;
;; Display a Character Using AX & DX Registers
dis_chr         macro   char
          push    ax                ;; save current registers
          push    dx
          mov     dl,&char          ;; display from DL
          mov     ah,02h            ;; function 2
          int     21h               ;; call MS-DOS
          pop     dx                ;; restore registers
          pop     ax
          endm
code    segment para public 'code'
          assume  cs:code
;****************************************************************
;--------------------------------------------------------------
; BIN2DEC-BINary to DECimal conversion. Displays the contents
; of the AX register on the screen as a signed decimal number.
; Finds the rightmost digit by division. Repeat until all found.
; The CH register contains the minimum # of digits to be
; displayed. AX register is destroyed in this operation.
bin2dec         proc    near
          push    bx
          push    cx
          push    dx
          mov     cl,0    ; clear digit count
          mov     bx,10   ; set divisor = 10
;
; Check for Negative number. If negative, make number positive
;
          or      ax,ax   ; is number positive?
          jnl     more_hex; yes, skip "negate"
          neg     ax      ; make number positive
          push    ax
          dis_chr '-'     ; destroys DL & AH
          pop     ax
;
; Main Division Loop--Get Decimal Digit
; Repeat as long as digits are remaining
;
more_hex:
          xor     dx,dx   ; cleanup
          div     bx      ; divide by 10
          push    dx      ; save remainder
          inc     cl      ; digit counter + 1
          or      ax,ax   ; test quotient
          jnz     more_hex; continue if more
;
; Main Digit Print Loop-Reverse Order
;
```

Listing A-6. cont.

```
        sub     ch,cl   ; min. # dig. reached?
        jle     morechr ; yes, begin display
        xor     dx,dx   ; no, start pushing 0s
morezero:
        push    dx
        inc     cl      ; digit counter + 1
        dec     ch      ; check whether matched yet
        jnz     morezero; no, keep pushing it
morechr:
        pop     dx      ; restore last digit
        add     dl,30h  ; convert to ASCII
        dis_chr dl      ; destroys DL & AH
        dec     cl      ; digits count -1
        jnz     morechr ; continue if more
        pop     dx
        pop     cx
        pop     bx
        ret
bin2dec endp
;****************************************************************
;--------------------------------------------------------------
; BIN2HEX--BINary to HEXadecimal conversion. Displays the
; contents of the AX register on the screen as a hexadecimal
; number. CH register contains count of the number of characters
; to display.
bin2hex         proc    near
        push    bx
        push    cx
        push    dx
        mov     bx,ax   ; use BX as temporary holding
        cmp     ch,0    ; count already set?
        jne     align_left
        mov     ch,4    ; no, set character count
; Align the number on the leftmost side of the AX
; (rotate left by (4-CH) * 4 bit positions
align_left:
        mov     cl,4    ; find number of digits to shift
        sub     cl,ch
        shl     cl,1    ; multiply by 4
        shl     cl,1
        rol     bx,cl   ; align on left side
        mov     cl,4    ; and set minor rotate count
; Main loop--repeat N times ... Print the leftmost digit
more_dec:
        rol     bx,cl   ; left digit to right
        mov     al,bl   ; move to AL
        and     al,0fh  ; right digit only
        add     al,90h  ; sneaky conversion
        daa             ; to ASCII hex characters
        adc     al,40h
        daa
; Print digit
        dis_chr al
        dec     ch      ; digits count-1
```

Listing A-6. cont.

```
        jnz     more_dec; continue if more
        pop     dx
        pop     cx
        pop     bx
        ret
bin2hex endp
;****************************************************************
code    ends
        end
```

As you can see in the listing, both routines must be declared PUB-LIC in the source file in order to make them available to other programs. Any label (which is what a routine's name is) that is to be used in another program must be declared this way.

If the routines are to be included in a .EXE file all that's needed is to use the EXTRN directive, placed *outside the segment definition*. LINK finds the reference in the library and places the referenced routine in its own segment in the final program. However, if the routines are to be included in a .COM type file, both the segment name and "class" name used for the .COM program must match those used in the library routine. To use either the BIN2DEC or BIN2HEX routines, the .COM program must use the segment definition:

```
code    segment para public "code"
```

Note that the segment definition must also be declared PUBLIC. In this case both the segment name (code) and class name ('code') are the same to help in remembering the names. In addition, the EXTRN directives must be placed inside of the segment definition to let MASM know that the external routines are part of the same segment. (PUBLIC and EXTRN labels are given the same segment attributes as the segment that encloses their definitions.)

Additional information about using libraries, PUBLIC, and EXTRN may be found in the Microsoft MASM and LINK reference manuals.

Bibliography

The following are books used by the authors as references. You may wish to consult these texts for further information on specific topics.

Abel, P. *Programming Assembler Language.* 2nd ed. Reston, Va.: Reston Publishing Company, Inc., 1984.

DeMarco, T. *Structured Analysis and System Specification.* New York: Yourdon, 1978.

Disk Operating System. Boca Raton, Fl.: International Business Machines Corp., (for DOS 1.10) 1982, (for DOS 2.00) 1983, (for DOS 2.10) 1983, (for DOS 3.00) 1984, (for DOS 3.10) 1984 and 1985.

Disk Operating System Technical Reference. Boca Raton, Fl.: International Business Machines Corp., (for DOS 2.10) 1983, (for DOS 3.00) 1984, (for DOS 3.10) 1984 and 1985.

IAPX 86/88, 186/188 User's Manual: Programmer's Reference. Santa Clara, Ca.: Intel Corporation, 1983.

Kane, G., D. Hawkins, and L. Leventhal. *68000 Assembly Language Programming.* Berkeley, Ca.: Osborne/McGraw-Hill, 1981.

Kernighan, Brian and Dennis Ritchie. *The C Programming Language.* Englewood Cliffs, N.J.: Prentice-Hall, 1978.

Lafore, R. *Assembly Language Primer for the IBM PC and XT.* New York and Scarborough, Ontario: New American Library, 1984.

Lattice 8086/8088 C Compiler Manual. New York: Lifeboat Associates, 1982.

Microsoft C Compiler: User's Guide. Bellevue, Wa.: Microsoft Corporation, (for C 3.00) 1984 and 1985.

Microsoft C: Run-Time Library Reference. Bellevue, Wa.: Microsoft Corporation, (for C 3.00) 1984 and 1985.

Microsoft Macro Assembler User's Manual. Bellevue, Wa.: Microsoft Corporation, (for MASM 2.00) 1981 and 1983, (for MASM 4.00) 1984 and 1985.

Microsoft MS-DOS Programmer's Reference. Bellevue, Wa.: Microsoft Corporation, (for MS-DOS 2.10) 1981 and 1983.

Morgan, C. L. *Bluebook of Assembly Language Routines for the IBM PC & XT.* New York and Scarborough, Ontario: New American Library, 1984.

Morgan, C. L. and M. Waite. *8086/8088 16-Bit Microprocessor Primer.* Peterborough, N.H.: BYTE/McGraw-Hill, 1982.

Norton, P. *Inside the IBM PC.* Bowie, Md.: Robert J. Brady Co., 1983.

Tausworthe, R. C. *Standardized Development of Computer Software.* Pt. I. Englewood Cliffs, N.J.: Prentice-Hall, 1977.

Turbo Pascal Reference Manual Version 2.0. Scotts Valley, Ca.: Borland International, 1984.

Turbo Pascal Reference Manual Version 3.0. Scotts Valley, Ca.: Borland International, 1983, 1984, and 1985.

Yourdon, E. U. and L. L. Constantine. *Structured Design.* Englewood Cliffs, N.J.: Prentice-Hall, 1977.

Yourdon, E. U. *Techniques of Program Structure and Design.* Englewood Cliffs, N.J.: Prentice-Hall, 1975.

ASCII Cross-Reference and Number Conversions

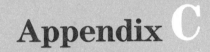

Appendix C

Non-Printable ASCII Character Definitions
Hexadecimal to Decimal Conversion
Decimal to Hexadecimal Conversion

able C-1 cross references terminal keys with their decimal (base 10), hexadecimal (base 16), octal (base 8), and ASCII (American Standard Code for Information Interchange) assignments. The key sequences that consist of < **CONTROL-** > are typed by simultaneously pressing the CONTROL key and the key indicated. These sequences are based on those defined for most standard terminals, such as the Diablo 1640 keyboard and the Televideo series of terminals, and may be defined differently on other keyboards.

Table C-1.   ASCII Cross Reference Table

DEC X10	HEX X16	OCT X8	ASCII	Terminal Key
0	00	00	NUL	CONTROL-1
1	01	01	SOH	CONTROL-A
2	02	02	STX	CONTROL-B
3	03	03	ETX	CONTROL-C
4	04	04	EOT	CONTROL-D
5	05	05	ENQ	CONTROL-E
6	06	06	ACK	CONTROL-F
7	07	07	BEL	CONTROL-G
8	08	10	BS	CONTROL-H, BACKSPACE, LEFT ARROW
9	09	11	HT	CONTROL-I, TAB
10	0A	12	LF	CONTROL-J, LINE FEED, DOWN ARROW
11	0B	13	VT	CONTROL-K, UP ARROW
12	0C	14	FF	CONTROL-L, RIGHT ARROW
13	0D	15	CR	CONTROL-M, RETURN
14	0E	16	SO	CONTROL-N
15	0F	17	SI	CONTROL-O
16	10	20	DLE	CONTROL-P
17	11	21	DC1	CONTROL-Q, XON, No scroll (off)
18	12	22	DC2	CONTROL-R, Tape
19	13	23	DC3	CONTROL-S, XOFF, No scroll (on)
20	14	24	DC4	CONTROL-T, No tape
21	15	25	NAK	CONTROL-U

Table C-1. cont.

DEC X10	HEX X16	OCT X8	ASCII	Terminal Key
22	16	26	SYN	CONTROL-V
23	17	27	ETB	CONTROL-W
24	18	30	CAN	CONTROL-X
25	19	31	EM	CONTROL-Y
26	1A	32	SUB	CONTROL-Z, CLEAR SPACE
27	1B	33	ESC	ESC, ESCAPE
28	1C	34	FS	CONTROL-! (Control/reverse slant)
29	1D	35	GS	CONTROL-` (Control-grave accent)
30	1E	36	RS	CONTROL-= (Control-equal sign), HOME
31	1F	37	US	CONTROL-hyphen), NEW LINE
32	20	40	SP	Space (SPACE BAR)
33	21	41	!	! (Exclamation mark)
34	22	42	"	" (Quotation mark)
35	23	43	#	# (Number sign or octothorpe)
36	24	44	$	$ (Dollar sign)
37	25	45	%	% (Percent)
38	26	46	&	& (Ampersand)
39	27	47	´	´ (Apostrophe or acute accent)
40	28	50	(	((Opening parenthesis)
41	29	51	)	) (Closing parenthesis)
42	2A	52	*	* (Asterisk)
43	2B	53	+	+ (Plus)
44	2C	54	,	, (Comma)
45	2D	55	-	- (Hyphen, dash, or minus)
46	2E	56	.	. (Period)
47	2F	57	/	/ (Forward slant)
48	30	60	0	0
49	31	61	1	1
50	32	62	2	2
51	33	63	3	3
52	34	64	4	4
53	35	65	5	5
54	36	66	6	6
55	37	67	7	7
56	38	70	8	8
57	39	71	9	9
58	3A	72	:	: (Colon)
59	3B	73	;	; (Semicolon)
60	3C	74	<	< (Less than)
61	3D	75	=	= (Equal sign)
62	3E	76	>	> (Greater than)
63	3F	77	?	? (Question mark)
64	40	100	@	@ (Commercial at sign)
65	41	101	A	A
66	42	102	B	B
67	43	103	C	C
68	44	104	D	D
69	45	105	E	E
70	46	106	F	F
71	47	107	G	G
72	48	110	H	H

Table C-1. cont.

DEC X10	HEX X16	OCT X8	ASCII	Terminal Key
73	49	111	I	I
74	4A	112	J	J
75	4B	113	K	K
76	4C	114	L	L
77	4D	115	M	M
78	4E	116	N	N
79	4F	117	O	O
80	50	120	P	P
81	51	121	Q	Q
82	52	122	R	R
83	53	123	S	S
84	54	124	T	T
85	55	125	U	U
86	56	126	V	V
87	57	127	W	W
88	58	130	X	X
89	59	131	Y	Y
90	5A	132	Z	Z
91	5B	133	[	[(Opening bracket)
92	5C	134	\	\ (Reverse slant)
93	5D	135	]	] (Closing bracket)
94	5E	136	^	^ (Carat or circumflex)
95	5F	137	_	_ (Underscore or underline)
96	60	140	`	` (Grave accent)
97	61	141	a	a
98	62	142	b	b
99	63	143	c	c
100	64	144	d	d
101	65	145	e	e
102	66	146	f	f
103	67	147	g	g
104	68	148	h	h
105	69	151	i	i
106	6A	152	j	j
107	6B	153	k	k
108	6C	154	l	l
109	6D	155	m	m
110	6E	156	n	n
111	6F	157	o	o
112	70	160	p	p
113	71	161	q	q
114	72	162	r	r
115	73	163	s	s
116	74	164	t	t
117	75	165	u	u
118	76	166	v	v
119	77	167	w	w
120	78	170	x	x
121	79	171	y	y
122	7A	172	z	z
123	7B	173	{	{ (Opening brace)
124	7C	174	|	| (Vertical line or logical OR)

Table C-1. cont.

DEC X10	HEX X16	OCT X8	ASCII	Terminal Key
125	7D	175	}	} (Closing brace)
126	7E	176	˜	˜(Tilde)
127	7F	177	DEL	DEL, DELETE, RUBOUT

Non-Printable ASCII Character Definitions

ACK (ACKNOWLEDGMENT)—A communication control character that serves as a general yes answer to various queries but also sometimes indicates "I received your last transmission and I'm ready for your next."

BEL (BELL)—A general purpose control character that activates a bell, beeper, or other audible alarm on the device to which it was sent.

BS (BACKSPACE)—A format effector control character that moves the carriage, print head, or cursor back one space or position.

CAN (CANCEL)—A general purpose control character that indicates that the material in the previous transmission is to be disregarded. The amount of material is decided by the user.

CR (CARRIAGE RETURN OR RETURN)—A format effector control character that moves the carriage, print head or cursor on a terminal back to the beginning of the line. On most terminals, the RETURN key causes both a CR and an LF (line feed).

DC1-DC4 (DEVICE CONTROLS)—General purpose control characters that control the user's terminal or similar devices. No standard functions are assigned, except that DC4 frequently means *stop*. The CCITT (Comité Consultatif International Télégraphe et Téléphone [International Telegraph and Telephone Consultative Committee]) suggests a number of possible assignments. In general, CCITT prefers using the first two controls for *on*, and the last two for *off*, and DC2 and DC4 to refer to the more important device. In some systems, these codes are labeled XON, TAPE, XOFF, and NO TAPE, respectively. X means *transmitter*, and TAPE and NO TAPE means *tape on* and *tape off*. These labels are found on the keytops of some terminals.

DEL (DELETE)—A general purpose control character that deletes a character. Called RUBOUT on some terminals DEL is not strictly a control character because it is not grouped with the other ASCII control characters. The DEL function has a binary all-ones bit pattern (1111 1111, base 2). The reason is historic: The only way to erase a bit pattern punched into paper tape was to punch out all the holes so that the resulting pattern was equivalent to a null. ASCII still considers DEL equivalent to a null, although many operating systems use DEL to erase the preceding character.

DLE (DATA LINK ESCAPE)—Communication control character that uses a special type of escape sequence specifically for controlling the data line and transmission facilities.

EM (END OF MEDIUM)—General purpose control character that indicates the end of paper tape (or other storage medium) or is the end of the material on the medium.

ENQ (ENQUIRY)—Communication control character that usually is used for requesting identification or status information. In some systems, this code is WRU (who are you?)

EOT (END OF TRANSMISSION)—Communication control character that marks the end of a transmission after one or more messages.

ESC (ESCAPE)—General purpose character that marks the beginning of an escape sequence. An escape sequence consists of a series of codes, which as a group have a special meaning, usually a control function. On some terminals, ESC is called ALT MODE.

ETB (END OF TRANSMISSION BLOCK)—Communication control character that is used when you want to break up a long message into blocks. ETB marks block boundaries. The blocks usually have nothing to do with the format of the message being transmitted.

ETX (END OF TEXT)—Communication control character that marks the end of a text. See SOH. This code was originally called EOM (end of message) and may be labeled as such on some terminals.

FF (FORM FEED)—Format effector control character that causes the carriage, print wheel, or cursor to advance to the top of the next page.

FS, GS, RS, US (FILE, GROUP, RECORD AND UNIT SEPARATOR)—A set of information separator control characters that delimit portions of information. No standard usage exists, except that FS is expected to refer to the largest division and US to the smallest.

HT (HORIZONTAL TAB)—A format effector control character that tabs the carriage, print wheel, or cursor to the next predetermined stop on the same line. The user usually decides where the horizontal tab stops are positioned.

LF (LINE FEED)—A format effector control character that moves the carriage, print head, or cursor down one line. Most systems combine

CR (carriage return) with LF, and the new line is called NL (new line).

NAK (NEGATIVE ACKNOWLEDGMENT)—A communications control character that indicates *no* in answer to various queries. Sometimes it is defined as "I received your last transmission, but it had errors and I'm waiting for a retransmission."

NUL (NULL)—A general purpose control character that mainly is used as a space filler. See also SYN.

SI (SHIFT IN)—A general purpose control character that is used after a SO code to indicate that codes revert to normal ASCII meaning.

SO (SHIFT OUT)—A general purpose control character that indicates the following bit patterns have meanings outside the standard ASCII set and will continue to do so until SI is entered.

SOH (START OF HEADING)—A communication control character that marks the beginning of a heading when headings are used in messages along with text. Headings usually state the name and location of an addressee. This code was originally called SOM (start of message).

STX (START OF TEXT)—A communication control character that is used as a marker for the beginning of text and end of heading (if used). This code was originally called EOA (end of address).

SUB (SUBSTITUTE)—A general purpose control character that indicates a character which is to take the place of a character known to be wrong.

SYN (SYNCHRONOUS IDLE)—A communication control character used by some high-speed data communications systems that use synchronized clocks at the transmitter and receiver ends. During idle periods, when there are no bit patterns to enable the receiver's clock to track the transmitter's, the receiver may drift out of sync. Every transmission following an idle period therefore is replaced by three or four SYN characters. The SYN code has a bit pattern that enables the receiver not only to lock onto the transmitter's clock but also to determine the beginning and end points of each character. SYN characters may also be used to fill short idle periods to maintain synchronization, hence the name.

VT (VERTICAL TAB)—A format effector control character that tabs the carriage, print head, or cursor to the next predetermined stop (usually a line).

Hexadecimal to Decimal Conversion

Figure C-1 shows how the hexadecimal number 5F9D is converted to its decimal equivalent.

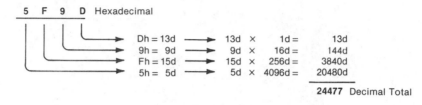

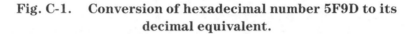

**Fig. C-1.   Conversion of hexadecimal number 5F9D to its
decimal equivalent.**

Each hexadecimal digit is always 16 times greater than the digit immediately to the right.

Decimal to Hexadecimal Conversion

The conversion process is reversed when converting decimal numbers to hexadecimal. Start by selecting the leftmost digit and determine its significance in the number (thousands, hundreds, etc.). The decimal is then divided by the hexadecimal value of the first digit's relative position (if, for example, the first digit is in the thousands position, divide by 4,096 [hexadecimal equivalent of 1,000 decimal]). The result is the first hexadecimal digit. The remainder is divided by the hexadecimal value of the next digit's relative position (that is, divide the hundreds digit by 256, because 256 is the hexadecimal equivalent of 100 decimal). Figure C-2 shows how the decimal number derived in the previous example is converted back to hexadecimal.

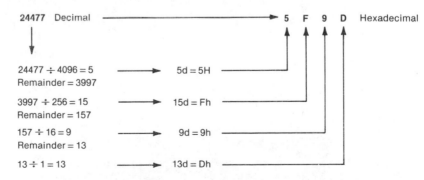

**Fig. C-2.   Decimal number 24477 converted back to its
hexadecimal equivalent.**

Product
Enhancements

Appendix D

Microsoft Macro Assembler (Version 4.00)
Microsoft C Compiler for MS-DOS (Version 3.00)

This appendix describes some of the more important changes made to two products from Microsoft Corporation described in this book: version 4.00 of the Macro Assembler (MASM) and version 3.00 of the C Compiler for MS-DOS. The new versions of these products have revealed more than just the average bug fixes and minor upgrades that normally accompany new releases. Because we were not able to use these new versions of MASM and the C Compiler while this book was being written, this appendix has been included to describe some of the more important enhancements to these products and to indicate how these enhancements affect the information presented in the previous chapters and appendices. Make careful note of the following information if you are using MASM version 4.00 or later or Microsoft C Compiler version 3.00 or later in connection with the information presented in this book.

Microsoft Macro Assembler (Version 4.00)

Microsoft has added several significant new features to version 4.00 of their Macro Assembler (MASM) that are of special interest to the presentations in this book. Enhancements that are general in nature include faster assembly performance (two to three times faster than prior versions) and the ability to assemble larger source files due to the removal of input/output buffers and macro text out of the symbol space. The following paragraphs describe some more of the highlights of MASM version 4.00.

Compatibility with Prior Versions of MASM and Other Microsoft Compilers

If you've been using a version of MASM prior to version 4.00 (or a version of the IBM Macro Assembler prior to version 3.00), you may need to make some adjustments to your source programs before assembling them. The two main compatibility issues are as follows.

1. Some versions of the IBM Macro Assembler prior to version 3.00 wrote segments to object files in alphabetical order. Microsoft MASM 4.00 and IBM MASM 3.00 now write segments to object files in the order encountered in the source file. If you want the segments to be ordered alphabetically when you use these latest of versions of MASM, you must use the "/A" command-line option.

2. Earlier versions of MASM did not have strict type checking. Source code developed with earlier versions of MASM may produce error messages when assembled with Microsoft MASM 4.00 or IBM MASM 3.00. The source code can be made compatible by using the PTR operator.

Microsoft MASM 4.00 and IBM MASM 3.00 is compatible with most Microsoft (and most IBM) high-level language compilers. However, the LINK utility included with the latest versions of MASM must not be used with IBM COBOL version 1.0, IBM FORTRAN version 2.0, or IBM Pascal version 2.0, if programs developed with these compilers use overlays. The linker provided with the compiler must be used instead.

New MASM Options

Several new MASM command-line options have been added. The following paragraphs overview some of the more important options.

The /D*symbol* Option
In Chapter 1, we introduced conditional assembly and presented some examples demonstrating its usefulness. One of the examples showed how to include code for debugging purposes, based on the symbol DEBUG. One of the disadvantages of this approach was that you still had to edit the file in order to change the value of the DEBUG symbol. In version 4.0 of MASM, you can now specify the presence of symbols in a program on the command line with the /D<*symbol*> option. By changing the conditional assembly directive from "IF DEBUG" to "IFDEF DEBUG" and removing the "DEBUG EQU <*value*>" directive from the program you can specify the inclusion of the diagnostics code without editing the file by using "/DDEBUG" on the MASM command line.

The /I*path* Option
Another of the more generally useful command-line options is the new "/I" option, which is used to specify the pathname by which MASM

searches for all files specified in your source file with the INCLUDE directive. Although all "include" files must reside in the same location as specified by the pathname, the use of the option eliminates the need to insert individual pathnames with each "include" file in the source file. Several of the programs described in this book use the INCLUDE directive to include the macros file in Listing A-5 in Appendix A.

The /P Option
The "/P" option has been added to MASM for programs designed to be executed on an 80286 processor. When used, this option checks the source code during the assembly process for "impure" code that causes problems if the assembled program executes on an 80286 processor in protected mode. If any impure code is found during assembly with this option, an error message is generated. The use of this option is strongly suggested if your source file contains the ".286p" directive in your source file along with any 80286 protected instructions.

The /V Option
The "/V" option has been added to MASM to cause the displaying of extra statistical information after a file has been assembled.

The /Z Option
The "/Z" option is used to display source lines containing errors during the assembly process. If the option is omitted, only the error message is shown. (In previous versions of MASM, the source lines containing errors, including the error messages, were always displayed.)

New and Improved Commands

The following describes new commands that have been added to Microsoft MASM 4.00 and enhancements made to existing commands.

The EXEPACK and EXEMOD Commands
Two new commands have been added to the Microsoft MASM version 4.00 package: EXEPACK and EXEMOD. The EXEPACK command is used to pack .EXE files by compressing sequences of identical characters and by optimizing the relocation table. The EXEPACK command can significantly reduce the size of .EXE files and decreases the time required to load them. The EXEMOD command is used to modify fields within the MS-DOS file header in .EXE files.

The LINK Command
The LINK command has two new options added to it. The "/EXEPACK" option performs the same function as the EXEPACK command without

having to enter it separately. The "/HELP" option has also been added to LINK which, when used, causes a list of LINK options to be displayed on the screen.

The SYMDEB Command

The SYMDEB (Microsoft Symbolic Debug) command is a debugging program that provides significant enhancements over MS-DOS's DEBUG command. One of the more important features of SYMDEB is the ability to refer to data and instructions by name rather than by address. SYMDEB can access program locations through addresses, global symbols, or line number references, thereby significantly simplifying the task of locating and debugging specific sections of code. Some new SYMDEB command-line options have been added in Microsoft MASM version 4.00. These are as shown in Table D-1.

Table D-1.   Command Line Options for SYMDEB
Version 4.00.

Option	Meaning
/K	Enables the use of either the SCROLL LOCK or BREAK key as an interactive break-point key.
/N	Enables the use of the non-maskable interrupt (NMI) break in systems that are not compatible with the IBM Personal Computer series.
/S	Enables screen swapping between a SYMDEB screen and another program's screen.
/commands	Enables the execution of commands or parameters to the program being debugged, as specified by commands.

The MAKE Command

The MAKE (Microsoft Program Maintenance Utility) command was originally introduced in Microsoft MASM version 3.00 and is used to automate the process of maintaining assembly and high-level language programs. The MAKE command is a very useful command if you are developing large software projects because it automatically carries out all tasks needed to update a program after one or more of its source files has changed. The MAKE command makes use of a batch-like file, which is customized by you with all the pertinent information about the project. In the Microsoft MASM version 4.00 package, the MAKE command, in addition to several new options, now supports macro definitions and inference rules.

Microsoft C Compiler for MS-DOS (Version 3.00)

There are many C compilers available for MS-DOS systems. Then why single out version 3.00 of the Microsoft C Compiler for special attention? At the very least, because this version is written by the same people who maintain and market MS-DOS itself. In a broader view, because it is one of the most complete and flexible compilers available today for the MS-DOS environment. In Chapter 11, previous versions of the Microsoft C Compiler are described as the "Lattice/Microsoft C Compiler." This is no longer the case with version 3.00 of the Microsoft C Compiler: It has been completely rewritten and is no longer related to the latest version of the Lattice C Compiler.

The very title of the Microsoft C Compiler in its technical manual states that it is specifically intended for the MS-DOS environment. This is a true double-edged sword. Because of Microsoft's great familiarity with MS-DOS, the company is able to produce a compiler that is able to take full advantage of the power of MS-DOS. The price that must be paid is that great effort is required to make the programs developed with this compiler run under foreign operating systems.

Simply put, this is one of the best compilers available for MS-DOS systems, but if your goal is cross-compiling programs for another system, you may be better off to look for another compiler.

This short review is intended only to acquaint you in the most general terms with the capabilities of the Microsoft C Compiler. With this in mind, we have intentionally omitted the actual compiler directives and most of the compiler options. The manual supplied with the compiler should be considered the definitive reference. Quite honestly, we hope that more software developers follow Microsoft's lead in producing *genuine* documentation.

Assembly Language Interfacing

Because this is the *Microsoft* C Compiler, it isn't any surprise that the compiler is fully compatible with the Microsoft Macro Assembler (MASM) and the Microsoft LINK utility. Indeed, the compiler provides an option that is used to produce an assembly listing suitable for input to the MASM assembler.

Segments and Assembly Language
For the advanced programmer, one of the tasks to be accomplished when linking assembly language programs and compiled programs is matching the SEGMENT and GROUP directives. These determine the

segment, class, and *group* names, as well as the *alignment* and *combine* types of the segment. As described in the MASM and LINK manuals, this information is used to order and group the logical segments in a program into physical segments in a load image (.EXE file). This information also determines which code and data references are FAR ("long" addresses consisting of both segment and offset) and which are NEAR ("short" pointers consisting only of an offset). Some example declarations that might be used by the Microsoft C Compiler are:

```
_TEXT      SEGMENT   byte public    'CODE'
for program code, or for data declarations the sequence:
DGROUP     GROUP     NULL, _DATA, CONST, _BSS, STACK
_DATA      SEGMENT   word public    'DATA'
           ASSUME    DS:DGROUP
```

In order to successfully link an assembly language program with a compiled program, both object files must agree as to the segment names, classes, groups, and types. The Microsoft C Compiler manual lists this information for the variety of values that it supports. Note that these values are not the same as those provided by the Lattice/Microsoft C Compiler version 2.03. The programmer has the option of using the appropriate values in the assembly language program or of editing the compiler's assembly language output to make it agree with the assembly language program. When editing the compiler's output the danger always is that the resultant code may not agree with the definitions used in the language library, so the option may not be viable when calling library routines from the C program.

Register Use

Another task that the programmer must attend to when interfacing assembled programs with compiled programs is register use and the preservation of the stack. Microsoft C adheres to the common C convention for passing variables and returning values. The recommended entry and exit sequences for assembly language routines *called* by C programs is as shown below:

```
entry:    push bp        ; always save BP first
          mov  bp,sp     ; BP now used to access passed info
          push di        ; save index registers
          push si
          push cx        ; optional (common in many other C's)
exit:     pop  cx        ; optional (common in many other C's)
          pop  si        ; restore index registers
          pop  di
          pop  bp        ; restore BP
          ret            ; all done
```

Note that PUSHing and POPping the CX register is not required in the Microsoft C implementation. We have shown it because many other C language compilers do require that assembly language routines save the CX register.

The parameters passed to the routine are accessed using the BP register as explained in Chapter 2. Briefly, the first argument for a NEAR routine is addressed by [BP + 4], and the first argument for a FAR routine is found at [BP + 6].

Most values are returned to the calling routine in the AX register. If the value to be returned exceeds 16 bits, the DX register is used to return the high word of the result. If the value to be returned exceeds 32 bits, the programmer must return a *pointer* to the value (that is, the *address* of the value). Segment local addresses are returned in the AX register alone. Long addresses are returned in the DX:AX register pair with the segment address in the DX register.

What about calling a C routine from an assembly language program? The caller need only push the required parameters for the routine, then make the appropriate call. The calling routine is responsible for popping the parameters from the stack after the call.

For C routines calling assembly language routines or vice versa, some conversion may be required to get the returned values into the proper form, using either the CBW (Convert Byte to Word) or CWD (Convert Word to Double) instructions. Note that these instructions assume signed values and load the high byte (or word for CWD) with all ones if the high bit of the returned value is a one. (This process is called *sign extension*.) We've pointed this out because C routines *will* convert values according to the declaration of the routine.

Naming Routines and Variables

Once you have structured your programs so that they use the proper segment declarations and passing techniques, you still have the problem of linking them together. How do the programs know *who* to call? Both the Microsoft C Compiler and the Microsoft Macro Assembler use a similar method for informing the linker about globally accessible labels. In MASM, the pertinent key words are *extrn* and *public*, as shown below:

```
extrn     foo:near
public    start_prog
```

"Extrn" is used to tell MASM and the linker that the referenced labels are external to the current assembly module (file) and whether the reference is NEAR or FAR. In the above example, "foo" is located in another file but in the same segment as the reference. Conversely, "public" informs MASM and the linker that the label may be used by another, separately compiled, program.

In C programs, all labels are public. This means that all routine names and all global data names (variables declared outside of the main routine) are accessible to other C programs and to assembly language programs. Variables declared within a routine (except the routine "main") are dynamic, allocated on the stack when the routine is entered and discarded when the routine exits. External items in C programs are declared using the *extern* keyword (C's "extern" is spelled *with* the second "e"). There are subtleties to using "extern" in C programs that merit reading the compiler manual should you choose to use "extern."

Using the "extrn," "public," and "extern" keywords isn't quite the complete picture. The final piece of information required to interface C routines with assembly language routines is knowing that the Microsoft C Compiler adds an underscore (_) to the front of *all* labels. This is a common practice among C compilers. All that it means is that if a C routine and an assembly language routine wish to exchange labels the assembly language routine must add an underscore to match the C compiler. In the earlier example, if "foo" is declared in a C program that wishes to call a routine called "start_prog," the assembly language declaration should be as follows:

```
extrn      _foo:near
public     _start_prog
```

No modifications are necessary to the labels in the C program.

Compiler Options

The Microsoft C Compiler supports an amazing array of options, of which three deserve special note.

Memory Models
As readers of *The C Programming Language* (the "bible" of C programming) know, *pointers* to items (the *address* of either variables or functions) are NOT integers. Nevertheless, nearly all C language implementations on the 8086 family persist in treating pointers and integers the same. The compilers may complain, but they still use only 16 bits for addresses.

The Microsoft C Compiler *does* make a distinction. One of the options that the compiler supports is the ability to *separately* choose the *size* of pointers used to reference either code or data. The programmer may specify that all pointer references be made using only 16-bit off-sets, assuming the segment value. (This is known as *small model.*) Using the options, all pointer references may be made using 32-bit values, containing both the segment and the offset of the address (known as *large model*). And finally, a mixture of the two may be chosen, using one mode for data and another for code. The result of this flexibility is that multisegment programs may be created. The only restriction is that any individual item of the program may not exceed 64K-bytes.

One other area where the Microsoft C Compiler offers enhanced flexibility is in the selection of segments for storing data and the stack. Most C compilers enforce the restriction that the data segment (DS) and the stack segment (SS) must be the *same segment*. This is to allow arrays that are stored on the stack to be read with the default addressing modes used by the LEA (Load Effective Address) instruction and following indexed addressing. Microsoft allows the programmer to specify separate data and stack segments, allowing new data segments to be specified without corrupting the program chain maintained on the stack.

Structure Packing

Another area where the assembly language programmer can run into problems with compiled programs is in data packing. If you were to declare equivalent structures in both C and assembly language, you might assume that they work synonymously. This is not the case. Ordinarily all byte or character variables in C are word aligned (equivalent to the MASM *even* directive). This would mean that if you use the following two examples to refer to the same data structure, "bigger" and "large" would each be shifted by 1 byte between the two structures. Microsoft C allows the programmer to ignore word boundaries, *packing* the structure into minimum space, and making C structures agree with their assembly counterparts as well.

```
Assembly Structure                  ''C'' Language Structure
example    struc                    struct     example {
small      db    19 dup (?)             char small[19] ;
bigger     dw    ?                      int  bigger ;
large      dd    ?                      long large ;
example    ends                         }
```

Floating Point Support

Not too long ago, you could buy an 8087 or 80287 math coprocessor but be unable to use it because nobody made a compiler that would take advantage of it. This is no longer the case. The Microsoft C Compiler supports *five* different options for floating-point operations. These options allow the use of either an emulator library or a real math coprocessor. If you wish, the decision of which to use can be made at run time, guaranteeing a program that always runs yet still can take advantage of the 8087 or 80287 coprocessor if it is present. Another option allows the programmer to force the use of an emulator library for the purpose of checking how the program behaves without a coprocessor present. Still other options give the programmer the choice of making calls to math routines (which then use either an emulator library or a real 8087 or 80287) or including the functions "inline" for greater speed.

Regardless of which option you select, you can see that the Microsoft C Compiler allows you the flexibility to make the choices that best suit your needs.

Summary of the Microsoft C Compiler

We have only scratched the surface of version 3.00 of the Microsoft C Compiler. Even so, it should be apparent that through the right combination of assembly language and a flexible compiler you can quickly create significant programs to accomplish nearly any goal.

C is a an extremely powerful language in itself, but it must be used with care. The power to create is also the power to destroy. If you feel uncomfortable with the loose syntax and minimal level of control over program structure, you may want to use Pascal instead. If you do decide to use C, the Microsoft C Compiler should be examined, although its price tag may convince you to choose another, less expensive, compiler. Whatever your choice, the features of this compiler should help you decide just what features you would like in the compiler you finally choose.

Index

MORE
FROM
SAMS

☐ **The Best Book of: Lotus™ 1-2-3™**
Alan Simpson
This handy reference manual guides you in building spreadsheets, creating graphs, managing your database, and more. Includes practical examples and an appendix on installing Lotus 1-2-3.
ISBN: 0-672-22307-4, $14.95

☐ **IBM® PC Troubleshooting & Repair Guide**   *Robert C. Brenner*
Repair your IBM PC yourself, simply and inexpensively. Troubleshooting flowcharts help you diagnose and remedy the probable cause of failure. A final chapter on advanced troubleshooting shows the more adventuresome how to perform complex repairs. Some knowledge of electronics required.
ISBN: 0-672-22358-9, $18.95

☐ **The Best Book of: dBASE II®/III®**
Ken Knecht
Written in an enjoyable, conversational style, this book describes how to detect and correct errors, sort files, create new and useful programs, and manipulate data. A time-saving guide for getting the most out of dBASE II and dBASE III and applying these systems to specific business needs.
ISBN: 0-672-22349-X, $19.95

☐ **The Best Book of: Framework™**
Alan Simpson
Practical examples and applications help you get the most from Framework's frames, word processor, spreadsheet, and other features. Learn how to access national information systems; how to interface with WordStar®, dBASE II®/III®, and Lotus™ 1-2-3™; how to use Framework macros; and how to program with FRED™, Framework's programming language.
ISBN: 0-672-22421-6, $15.95

☐ **The Best Book of: Symphony®**
Alan Simpson
Learn to create, edit, and format documents with word processing; figure taxes and amortize loans with the spreadsheet; display graphs and produce slides with graphics; and create a mailing list with the data base manager. Shows how to transfer spreadsheets and programs to other computers and interface with other programs like Lotus™ 1-2-3™ and dBASE II®/III®.
ISBN: 0-672-22420-8, $21.95

☐ **Discovering MS-DOS** ®
Kate O'Day, The Waite Group
A comprehensive study of MS-DOS commands such as DEBUG, LINK, and EDLIN is given the unique Waite touch. The author begins with general information about operating systems, then shows you how to use MS-DOS to produce letters and documents; create, name, and manipulate files; use the keyboard and function keys to perform jobs faster; and direct, sort, and find data quickly.
ISBN: 0-672-22407-0, $15.95

☐ **CP/M® Bible: The Authoritative Reference Guide to CP/M**
Mitchell Waite and John Angermeyer, The Waite Group
Already a classic, this highly detailed reference manual puts CP/M's commands and syntax at your fingertips. Instant one-stop access to all CP/M keywords, commands, utilities, and conventions are found in this easy-to-use format.
ISBN: 0-672-22015-6, $19.95

☐ **Soul of CP/M®: How to Use the Hidden Power of Your CP/M System**
Mitchell Waite and Robert Lafore, The Waite Group
Recommended for those who have read the *CP/M Primer* or who are otherwise familiar with CP/M's outer layer utilities. This companion volume teaches you how to use and modify CP/M's internal features, including how to modify BIOS and use CP/M system calls in your own programs.
ISBN: 0-672-22030-X, $19.95

☐ **Modem Connections Bible**
Carolyn Curtis and Daniel L. Majhor, The Waite Group
Describes modems, how they work, and how to hook 10 well-known modems to 9 name-brand microcomputers. A handy Jump Table shows where to find the connection diagram you need and applies the illustrations to 11 more computers and 7 additional modems. Also features an overview of communications software, a glossary of communications terms, an explanation of the RS-232C interface, and a section on troubleshooting.
ISBN: 0-672-22446-1, $16.95

☐ **The Best Book of: Multiplan™**
Alan Simpson
The Best Book of: Multiplan provides tips, tricks, and secrets which enable you to design more efficient and useful models. Learn to create, format, edit, and print spreadsheets, and much more.
ISBN: 0-672-22336-8, $12.95

More Books from Sams and The Waite Group

PLACE
STAMP
HERE

Howard W. Sams & Co.
Department DM
P.O. Box 7092
Indianapolis, IN 46206